*Transfigured World*

· CAROLYN WILLIAMS ·

# *Transfigured World*

· WALTER PATER'S
  AESTHETIC HISTORICISM ·

Cornell University Press

ITHACA AND LONDON

Copyright © 1989 by Cornell University

All rights reserved. Except for brief quotations in a review, this book, or parts thereof, must not be reproduced in any form without permission in writing from the publisher. For information, address Cornell University Press, 124 Roberts Place, Ithaca, New York 14850.

First published in 1989 by Cornell University Press.

International Standard Book Number 0–8014–2151–9
Library of Congress Catalog Card Number 89–42883
Printed in the United States of America
*Librarians: Library of Congress cataloging information appears on the last page of the book.*

⊛ The paper used in this publication meets the minimum requirements of the American National Standard for Permanence of Paper for Printed Library Materials Z39.48–1984.

ISBN 978-1-5017-0724-7

*For Cecil Lang*

# Contents

Acknowledgments ix
Abbreviations xi
Introduction 1

Part One · Opening Conclusions 11
1. "That Which Is Without" 14
2. "The Inward World of Thought and Feeling" 18
3. Aestheticism 26
4. Answerable Style 37
5. Historicism 46
6. Aesthetic Historicism and "Aesthetic Poetry" 57
7. The Poetics of Revival 68

Part Two · Figural Strategies in *The Renaissance* 79
1. Legend and Historicity 82
2. Myths of History: *The Last Supper* 94
3. The Historicity of Myth 103
4. Myths of History: The Mona Lisa 111
5. Types and Figures 123
6. Low and High Relief: "Luca Della Robbia" 143
7. The Senses of Relief 153

Part Three · Historical Novelty and *Marius the Epicurean*   169

1. The Transparent Hero   172
2. Autobiography of the *Zeitgeist*   184
3. The Transcendental Induction   193
4. Typology as Narrative Form   202
5. Typological Ladders   213
6. Christian Historicism   219
7. Literary History as "Appreciation"   224

Part Four · "Recovery as Reminiscence":
   The *Greek Studies* and *Plato and Platonism*   235

1. Histories of Myth: The *Greek Studies*   238
2. The House Beautiful and Its Interpreter   247
3. The Philosophy of Mythic Form   249
4. The History of Philosophy   258
5. The Anecdote of the Shell   266
6. Dialogue and Dialectic   270
7. Paterian Recollection: The Anagogic Mind   277

Afterword   282
Index   285

# Acknowledgments

Sections 4, 5, and 6 of Part Three appeared under the title "Typology as Narrative Form" in *English Literature in Transition* 27:1 (1984), 11–33. I am grateful to the editor, Robert Langenfeld, for permission to reprint.

Two institutions have materially supported this work. The Mary Ingraham Bunting Institute of Radcliffe College provided a year's fellowship, during which the manuscript was begun, and the community extending from that institution has been lastingly valuable to me. The Humanities Foundation of Boston University then freed me from teaching duties for a semester, when the argument was ready for a final reformulation. I particularly thank William Carroll, who directed the Humanities Foundation and its Society of Fellows toward the model of a truly interdisciplinary conversation. Other colleagues and friends at Boston University sustained the work over the years of its production: Laurence Breiner, Patricia B. Craddock, Albert Gilman, Eugene Goodheart, Misia Landau, John T. Matthews, Katherine O'Connor, and David Wagenknecht. I am grateful to them for their advice, their support, their responses to chapters in progress, and their good company.

My dedication celebrates a long-standing intellectual and personal debt to Cecil Lang. Walter Pater's prose is only one of the many gustatory pleasures I owe to his great generosity. His guidance repaired the work as often as his wit repaired me. Rachel Jacoff's reading of Dante is more present in these pages than their nineteenth-century focus would make evident. I thank her as well for many other gifts of a compendious intelligence, now invisibly at work in this book. Eve Kosofsky Sedgwick strengthened and enabled the work throughout, in part by inspiring a vision of future work to be done—for which I am especially grateful. Nancy Waring, too, contributed important generative questions and continuing help in answering them. Other friends have steadfastly made it possible for me to imagine an audience by being one: Joyce Van Dyke, Barbara Harman, Lin Reicher, and Eleanor Ringel. Rosemarie Bodenheimer, Marjorie Garber, Barbara Johnson, and Mary Poovey have repeatedly aided my thinking and writing. I owe a special debt to the members of the ID 450 Collective, who—both collectively and individually—encouraged the practice of form and voice. Writing has become a different sort of pleasure with Mary B. Campbell, Susan Carlisle, Mary Wilson Carpenter, Anne Janowitz, Nancy Munger, Beth O'Sullivan, Helaine Ross, Eve Sedgwick, Deborah Swedberg, Martha Sweezy, Nancy Waring, and Patricia Yaeger in mind. And Bernhard Kendler of Cornell University Press contributed to the completion of this project in many invaluable ways. I thank him for the acuity of his insight, for deft intervention at crucial moments, and for suggestions of remarkable background reading.

I am grateful to my parents, Mary and James Williams, and my sister, Nancy Williams: their support has been both incalculable and essential. Finally, my deepest thanks go to my husband and colleague, Michael McKeon. I am happy that my debts to him will continue to appreciate as time passes.

CAROLYN WILLIAMS
*Boston, Massachusetts*

# Abbreviations

Quotations from Pater's works, unless otherwise indicated, are taken from the ten-volume Library Edition (London: Macmillan, 1910; reprint, New York: Johnson Reprint, 1973), abbreviated as follows:

| | |
|---|---|
| A | *Appreciations* |
| EG | *Essays from the "Guardian"* |
| GL | *Gaston de Latour* |
| GS | *Greek Studies* |
| IP | *Imaginary Portraits* |
| ME I | *Marius the Epicurean*, volume I |
| ME II | *Marius the Epicurean*, volume II |
| MS | *Miscellaneous Studies* |
| PP | *Plato and Platonism* |
| R | *The Renaissance* |

In addition, I have quoted extensively from "Aesthetic Poetry," which was originally part of "Poems by William Morris" (*Westminster Review*, 1868). The essay is now most conveniently seen in Harold Bloom's edition of Pater, abbreviated here as follows:

| | |
|---|---|
| B | *Selected Writings of Walter Pater*, ed. Harold Bloom (1974; reprint, New York: Columbia University Press, 1982). |

*Transfigured World*

Poetry projects, above the realities of its time, a world in which the forms of things are transfigured. Of that transfigured world this new poetry takes possession, and sublimates beyond it another still fainter and more spectral, which is literally an artificial or "earthly paradise."

—W<small>ALTER</small> P<small>ATER</small>

# Introduction

· I want to begin with a few words about the subtitle of this book: "Walter Pater's Aesthetic Historicism." The problematic and seemingly contradictory usage of the term "historicism" first alerted me to its great formal and conceptual potential. On the one hand, the term is often used to signal an attempt to know an object (a literary work, for example) by placing it within its contemporary historical context, and in this sense historicism seeks to define the specific historicity of the object. But on the other hand, the term often signals skepticism (whether mild or radical) about the possibility of such historical knowledge, and in this sense "historicism" is taken to be the equivalent of "relativism." These two senses represent contradictory but related positions—both of them reductive—and in Part One, section 5, I take the contradiction into account by defining historicism in a more complex and flexible way, as a double dialectic.

Other senses of the term are also relevant to this study. In recent years the "new historicism" has succeeded "new literary history" as the dominant model in a continuing and intensifying effort to place literary and historical study in a fruitful mutual relation. Beginning with a consideration of the problematic involvement of text and context, one might regard the new historicism (in broad terms) as a renewed approach to contextual study which is informed by the analytical finesse of recent psychoanalytic, feminist, and poststructuralist theory. This book instead aims to consider one episode in the literary history of historicism itself. It is an especially interesting episode because Pater's historicism accompanies the aestheticism that has been taken to grant the work of art a supposed "autonomy." However, Pater's notion of aesthetic autonomy is strictly limited, for though he does argue that the work of art should be free from utilitarian appropriation, he does not propose to appreciate it apart from its historical context. The interrelation of aestheticism and historicism in Pater's work is my subject throughout, especially in the theoretical discussions of Part One. "Aesthetic historicism" names that interrelation.

In specifically literary studies, "historicism" often refers to a certain literary form familiar to readers of early-twentieth-century ("high") modernism. The examples of Eliot's *Waste Land*, Pound's *Cantos*, Joyce's *Ulysses*, and Woolf's *Orlando* will serve to indicate the variety within this form of historical or literary-historical pastiche. A critique and revision of these strategies of composition—and the totalizing perspective they establish—is now being conducted under the aegis of the "postmodern," and though they must be distinguished from one another, this critique reminds me of Pater's own, late-nineteenth-century assertion of the re-collective and conservative impulses involved in any modernism. For Pater saliently argues that modernism is a recurrent phenomenon in history. His "appreciation" of composite art forms is one way he recognizes the particular sort of aesthetic value that accrues only through the repetitions and displacements of historical time. The critical voice that we in turn recognize as Paterian is just such a composite re-creation. My reference to Pater's "aesthetic historicism," then, also names his most fundamental literary form.

I have borrowed the phrase "aesthetic historicism" from Erich Auerbach, who used it of Vico.[1] These implied connections, with Vico before him and Auerbach after, immediately place Pater in a tradition of historicist philology. Pater read Vico in 1866, and he seems to have found there a confirmation and historical precedent for his own deeply historical view of cultural forms.[2] Today Vico's *New Science* seems

---

1. Erich Auerbach, "Vico's Aesthetic Historism," in *Scenes from the Drama of European Literature* (New York: Meridian Books, 1959), pp. 183–198. On the comparative nuances of the German-derived "historism" and the Italian-derived "historicism," see Dwight E. Lee and Robert Beck, "The Meaning of 'Historicism,'" *American Historical Review* 59 (April 1954), 568. In his entry "historicism," Wesley Morris uses the phrase "aesthetic historicism" (in a sense related to though different from mine) to name one of his "four major types" of historicism. He refers to an historicism that is "the product of the philosophy of history promoted by Croce and R. G. Collingwood" and that leads to an emphasis on the creative act of the poet "to *make* cultural meanings and values, not merely reflect them." See Alex Preminger, ed., *Princeton Encyclopedia of Poetry and Poetics* (Princeton, N.J.: Princeton University Press, 1965; enlarged ed., 1974), p. 938.

2. Billie Andrew Inman, *Walter Pater's Reading: A Bibliography of His Library Borrowings and Literary References, 1858–1873* (New York: Garland, 1981), pp. 148–57.

uncannily prescient of Hegel and Darwin, who were certainly the more proximate sources for Pater's genetic and evolutionary views of art history. In fact, Pater's assimilation of Hegel and Darwin registers the particularly post-Victorian quality of his vision. His "aesthetic historicism" thus also refers to Pater's Hegelian (and "Darwinian") views of the evolution of art forms in historical time.

I have turned the phrase "aesthetic historicism" to my own uses here. My largest purpose is to argue the deeply interfused relation of Pater's historicism and his aestheticism and to read that relation in specifically literary—as distinguished from philosophical—terms. One of the most important results of the current critical revival in Pater studies has been the growing sense of his pervasive historicism. It has long been recognized as the element that makes his aestheticism special and somehow stronger than any other late-nineteenth-century version of the aesthetic stance. But recently, in the work of Harold Bloom, Peter Allan Dale, Donald L. Hill, Billie Andrew Inman, Wolfgang Iser, and F. C. McGrath, we are beginning to get a clearer idea of exactly how it works. Dale, for example, argues for Pater's "complete historicism" and places it at the apex of a tradition in English criticism which is centrally concerned with the philosophy of history.[3]

My theoretical approach to aestheticism and historicism is developed in Part One. Both aestheticism and historicism are strategies of epistemological self-consciousness and representation, and as such both offer systematic programs for what to look at and how to look. Both begin in skepticism, questioning the very possibility of knowledge, and both turn that epistemological doubt against itself in a dialectical revision of the grounds of knowledge. In this respect, Pater's aesthetic historicism is in the mainstream of the Victorian reaction against romanticism and the consequent attempt to reconstruct a sense of objectivity. But even more than by virtue of its negative reaction, aesthetic historicism is decidedly postromantic by virtue of its positive and thorough absorption of romantic techniques of self-consciousness. In a fierce yet wistful embrace of necessity, Pater acknowledges from the beginning that the simplest act of perception is an aesthetic act. He turns to history—and in particular to the history

3. Harold Bloom, introduction to *Selected Writings of Walter Pater*; Peter Allan Dale, *The Victorian Critic and the Idea of History: Carlyle, Arnold, Pater* (Cambridge, Mass.: Harvard University Press, 1977); Donald L. Hill, textual and explanatory notes to *The Renaissance: Studies in Art and Poetry, The 1893 Text* (Berkeley: University of California Press, 1980); Inman, *Walter Pater's Reading*; Wolfgang Iser, *Walter Pater: The Aesthetic Moment*, trans. David Henry Wilson (Cambridge: Cambridge University Press, 1987), esp. pp. 71–104; and F. C. McGrath, *The Sensible Spirit: Walter Pater and the Modernist Paradigm* (Tampa, Fla.: University of South Florida Press, 1986).

of art—to recover the sense of a world of objects external to the mind, though he realizes at the same time that history itself is in part the result of an aesthetic reconstruction. "Aesthetic historicism," then, names the complex interaction through which Pater's aestheticism and historicism stabilize, support, supplement, and correct each other.

As methods of knowledge or strategies of representation, both aestheticism and historicism begin with strict attention to the unique particularity of each object—the specific, unrepeatable nature of each event—and both finally press beyond that intense concentration in particularity toward an apprehension of form in general. On one end of this methodological spectrum we find Keatsian and Pre-Raphaelite detail, the epiphanic moment, and the Heraclitean flux; on the other end we find mythic repetition, the Yeatsian *Vision*, and a developmental continuity projected to organize and transcend the atomism of epiphanic moments. Once again, then, Pater's aesthetic historicism may be seen as post-Victorian as well as postromantic, for it prefigures the bridge between science and mythopoeia that early-twentieth-century modernism was concerned to construct.

There has been an invidious tendency in Pater studies to treat Pater's historicism separately from—and in many cases as the opposite of or at odds with—his aestheticism. This book argues against that tendency and for the notion that Pater's aestheticism and his historicism represent homologous and absolutely interdependent procedures in a complex and coherent method. Either term is radically incomplete as a description of Pater's critical method without the other, for they are not simply two "themes" in his work, but two sides of the same epistemological and representational coin. This thorough implication of aestheticism and historicism in his work is the precondition for—or the definition of—his own emergent literary modernism.

An extremely rich texture is generated by the mutual implication of aestheticism and historicism in Pater's essays. My readings in Parts Two, Three, and Four are designed to explore this territory. The book's entitling notion of a "transfigured world" comes from the review essay on William Morris, where Pater sets forth many of the strategies of his aesthetic historicism. There he defines the category he calls "aesthetic poetry," by which he means the modern poetry of his contemporary moment, and—as I claim—his own "poetics of revival" as well. I have chosen as my epigraph a passage from that essay. All poetry projects its vision "above the realities of its time," Pater argues, but "aesthetic poetry" seizes upon that already-transfigured world and re-creatively "sublimates beyond it," generating a second-order transfiguration: the transfigured world transfigured again. This formal feature of "aesthetic poetry" is also a symptom of its historicism, for the double movement of transfiguration marks a poetry that specifically incorporates and transforms the poetry of an earlier historical period.

Several implications of my epigraph, each of them discussed much more expansively in the argument to follow, should be noted here: first, that the act of redoubling the distance from the "realities of the time" revives a sense of those realities; second, that aesthetic value is generated in the second of these transfigurative moments; and third, that the word "transfiguration" itself focuses not only on the production of a figure from a previous figure but also on the transferential movement that such figures recall in their forms. The first act of transfiguration moves the figure "across from" or "beyond" or "above" the forms of "realities" or "things" believed to have been directly accessible, original, and present, things irrevocably lost even at the moment they are represented. But the second act of transfiguration establishes a distance not in relation to "realities" or "things" but in relation to other figures. "Aesthetic poetry" is "literally . . . artificial" not only because its form avowedly responds to art of the past, but also because that very form reveals the irreducibly poetic function involved in historical imagination at the same time that it reveals the absolute impossibility of an "actual" return, re-creation, or revival.

Against this background, I have chosen to focus on several central Paterian figures and groups of figures. Each of these figures plays its part in Pater's historical sense of aesthetics as well as in his aesthetic re-creation of history. In my book, a "figure" is first a rhetorical figure. In this sense, I have employed the word along the whole range between its narrowest and broadest constructions to refer to an individual instance of a figure, such as a particular metaphor, and to the general use of a group of figures. I suggest several ways of understanding Pater's fundamental strategies of figuration in this latter, broader sense. For example, Pater's sense of time passing in the flux of present consciousness works both within and against his conservative desire to recontain fragments of time in some imaginary place, and throughout the book I pursue a basic distinction between figures that attempt to represent temporality and figures of spatial enclosure. Another example is Pater's habit of constructing dialectical genealogies in order to represent a sense of time's passage. Aesthetic value is figuratively generated through the self-divisions, doublings, and reunifications that compose these genealogies, and thus they serve to imitate the shape of development as well as to demonstrate Pater's fundamental premise that aesthetic value evolves in historical time.

Yet another example is Pater's elaboration of a number of figures to express the special nature of modern art. One group depends upon the composite assembly of fragments; another depends upon the common structure of figure and ground. In the latter case the figure may take several different forms. A point may be sharply focused within a surrounding field, or (in a variation of the same basic structure) a foregrounded figure or series of figures may be raised against an effaced background in high or low "relief." Pater uses this same figure to describe the production of modern art, the shape of tradition, and the momentary focus provided to the mind by aesthetic experience. Through my exploration of these figures of relief, then, I want to propose a redefinition of Pater's critical "impressionism" that will be based on this model of plastic form. The figures of relief make it clear that Pater's aesthetic impressionism is the correlative of his theory of historical expression.

One of Pater's broadest representational strategies involves figures of a different kind. For a "figure" is also an individual person whose life has been endowed, through the unifying agencies of retrospection, with a shapely form and a representative value. In 1906, slightly more than a decade after Pater's death in 1894, Henry James believed that Pater himself had achieved that stature. In a letter to A. C. Benson, James wrote of

> that strange touching edifying (to me quite thrilling) operation of the whispering of time, through which Pater has already in these few years, little as he seemed marked out for it—become in our literature that very rare + sovereign thing, a *figure*: a figure in the sense in which there are to[o] few![4]

James's own aesthetic historicism here points us back to Pater's practice of retrospectively focusing on a few central and emblematic figures to map out his aesthetic histories. Pater embraced the aesthetic dimension of his retrospective enterprise. He recognized, in other words, that historical figures must always be construed in part as aesthetic re-creations. Like rhetorical figures, but specifically in the realm of historical representation, these personal figures coalesce such a number of confused, opposed, or intractably different forces that they cannot be united except through fictive means.

To construct a tradition using representative figures, a certain per-

---

4. Quoted by Laurel Brake in "Judas and the Widow: Thomas Wright and A. C. Benson as Biographers of Walter Pater: The Widow," *Prose Studies* 4 (May 1981), 51.

sonalization, simplification, and generalization of historical forces must take place. Like rhetorical figures, these historical figures punctuate the now-inaccessible complexity of past time with interpretable form. For though the individual life may be a historical fact, its retrospective *form* is a figure; and as a figure, Pater uses the form of the personal life to project a sense of unity in history. Unlike rhetorical figures, however, historical figures appear to be given (as "data"), not made. Pater is as committed to the historical reality of his figures as to their aesthetic forms, for it is through his faith in a provisional historical objectivity that he can reform and stabilize the flux of present consciousness. Thus, I read Pater's representation of historical persons figuratively, but at the same time I am concerned to show the logic by which he engages their specifically historical value.

On another level, however, that logic is figurative as well, in the sense that the disposition of figures regularly reveals underlying assumptions that are not explicitly argued. My study seeks to follow the unspoken logic of Pater's figures and thus to uncover the assumptions that subtend his aesthetic historicism. I approach these assumptions not as ideas or simple content, but as forms, as habits of organization, as relations through which figures are implicated with one another to compose narratives.

For example, I am concerned throughout this book with Pater's practices of generalization. While a focus on particularity is indispensable to the aesthetic agenda, the historicist's attention ranges from historical particularity to general patterns of development. Thus, Part Two explores Pater's development of "types" from "figures." In *The Renaissance* the Paterian type emerges as a way of relating personal figures to their general culture in both its synchronic and its diachronic dimensions. Like the biological concept of species, Pater's type is the general category without which an evolutionary narrative (in this case of art history) is inconceivable. Part Three begins with an examination of Pater's Diaphaneitè, the transparent character type through whom the forces of history are embodied and expressed. I continue Part Three by reading the vestigial effects of Christian typology in the narrative form of *Marius the Epicurean*. Pater's historical novel secularizes and transfigures this traditional system of historical exegesis, whose types mediate between generality and particularity, identity and difference, continuity and change, repetition and novelty.

Not only Pater's habits of generalization but also his view of the historical development of general categories comes under my analysis. In "The Child in the House" and in the Platonically styled vignette that I have called "The Anecdote of the Shell," Pater describes the process of aesthetic education as the acquisition and use of general categories over time. As the child develops, his "constant substitution of the typical for the actual" signals the imaginative projection of a transcendent "home" where his disparate experiences can be organized and idealized but where their original, hallucinatory intensity has been displaced (MS, 194). In the vignette from *Plato and Platonism*, on the other hand, the story of an individual education clearly stands for the collective development of general culture. There Pater argues that the acquisition of general categories is paradoxically beneficial for the refinement of intense perception, for those categories enable us more and more precisely to grasp the particularity of each object. By shifting the narrative of epistemological development from an individual to a general register, Pater attempts to read the timely increase in general categories as a gain, not a loss.

This shift in registers—from a focus on individual development to a focus on general historical development—is another of my continuous preoccupations in this book. We frequently find in Pater's works the following interpretive movement: a particular historical figure is presented in the vivid concretion of an original historicity; then all the disparate experiences and productions of that figure are summed up and interpreted as representative of the age; and finally both figure and type are read in relation to precedent and subsequent forms as one stage in the diachronic development of something more general still—the "art of Italy," for example, or "the life of humanity." What is initially approached in all its unique particularity soon becomes a vehicle for the abstract forces of History in general, forces that become visible only because they have been embodied or impersonated. Thus the correlative construction of progressively more inclusive wholes makes possible the construction of an overarching developmental narrative.

These linked levels of figuration depend upon a theory of historical expression that is most often associated with Hegel, in which the "spirit" of an individual (already a constructed whole) is taken synchronically to represent a "spirit of the age," and that presumptively unified *Zeitgeist* is then interpreted as one stage in the diachronic development of an overarching *Geist*. Though the Hegelian influence should be appreciated, in the pages that follow I have concentrated my attention on the figural relations within Pater's system of historical expression—rather than on assigning them precise sources in previous philosophy and literature. It is worth pointing out even here at the outset that the fourfold method of Christian exegesis—with its "literal," allegorical, tropological, and anagogical levels of interpretive access—also depends upon systematically linked figures of relative historical concretion and spirituality. The typological description of history features progressive stages of prefiguration and fulfillment, each of which involves the simultaneous negation, conservation, and transcendence of precedent forms; and these transfigurative shifts in register have often been compared to the structure of the Hegelian *Aufhebung*.[5] Both Hegelian and Christian systems operate across the dialectical spectrum with which I have characterized historicism in general, and I have been interested primarily in the secularization-effects that are generated as Pater transfigures elements of each. Pater's assimilation of the Christian system reflects his tenacious hold on the concrete value of the historical figure. But all these historicisms—Christian, Hegelian, Paterian—exert formal pressure toward forms of transhistorical unity above and beyond the things of this world.

The narrative of continuous diachronic development reveals that pressure toward transhistorical unity. Thus, I am concerned throughout this book with the construction of the ground against which Pater's particular figures of history play. In other words, I read the "ground" as a figure as well—a figure for the principle of continuity that underlies all the high points of a constructed tradition, a figure for the amorphous soil out of which new figures "rise." We have perhaps become accustomed by now to noting the frequent recourse of historical narrative to organic figures of growth, but other aspects of these later romantic (or "modern") figures of backgrounds and foregrounds have yet to be sufficiently defamiliarized. Taken together, figure and ground comprise another range of patently "aesthetic," metafigural, second-order, self-reflexive figures that express the aesthetic and historical process of figural formation itself.

Thus when, in the sections on *The Renaissance*, I elaborate Pater's various senses of aesthetic and historical "relief," it is within this larger context that such readings take their place. In the sections on *Marius the Epicurean*, I am interested in Pater's recursive play with notions of figure and ground, for the character of Marius is at once the central figure against the texture of its second-century background and at the same time his consciousness provides the fictive ground upon which the "real" historical figures of the second century are registered. Finally, in

---

5. For explicit and implicit developments of this analogy, see M. H. Abrams, *Natural Supernaturalism: Tradition and Revolution in Romantic Literature* (New York: Norton, 1971), and William Shuter, "History as Palingenesis in Pater and Hegel," *PMLA* 86 (May 1971), 411–21. For the Derridean critique of the *Aufhebung*, see "Violence and Metaphysics: An Essay on the Thought of Emmanuel Levinas," esp. pp. 111–17, and "From Restricted to General Economy: A Hegelianism without Reserve," pp. 251–77, and the translator's notes to that essay, esp. pp. 335–36, in Jacques Derrida, *Writing and Difference*, trans. Alan Bass (Chicago: University of Chicago Press, 1978).

the sections on *Greek Studies* and *Plato and Platonism*, I analyze Pater's figurative approach to the inarticulate ground of his culture. He describes the beginning of history in aesthetic terms, as differentiation emerging from the prehistoric manifold of mythic character, and he treats the emergence of written culture from orality through a meditation on the "two-sided" figure of Socrates/Plato.

Narratives of continuous development testify to the pressure toward transhistorical unity, but in their modern, secularized forms such narratives are apt to displace teleology and defer or subvert the sense of closure. Thus the full vision of transhistorical unity resides in the comprehensive function of retrospection itself. I am concerned throughout this book with the figurative construction of retrospection—as the point at the end of the line, the place beyond time, the structure that organizes temporality. These spatial figures express the aesthetic desire that historical differences might be rationalized finally as parts of the same complex whole. As personal memory provides an overarching structure for the vagrant and evanescent moments of consciousness, organizing them as parts of an identity and casting them into the form of a development, so historical retrospection creates the form of "comprehension," in which understanding is represented as the synthetic activity of grasping disparate and discontinuous parts within a compendious and familiarizing relation.

This structural analogy between personal memory and historical retrospection reaches to the very heart of Pater's aesthetic historicism. For the place of transhistorical unity is most often embodied as the personal figure of an infinitely capacious mind. In *The Renaissance* this place of transhistorical unity is represented by the interiority of Mona Lisa, in *Marius the Epicurean* by the nineteenth-century narrative voice, and in *Plato and Platonism* by the synthetic capacities alike of Plato and of his late-nineteenth-century Interpreter. In *Plato and Platonism* (as well as elsewhere in his work) Pater transfigures and secularizes Bunyan's "House Beautiful" as his own favorite image of the transhistorical place where all the luminous figures of the past reside together, at "home" at last in a kind of aesthetic afterlife. Thus the very assumption of the retrospective position paradoxically—and figuratively—places the aesthetic critic beyond historical time, even as he bends his attention to the absolute particularity of things in time. And indeed, the Paterian persona depends upon occupying this position. The mind of the aesthetic historicist in any present moment represents that spacious repository where the world of temporal differences may be figuratively re-collected in one place.

## P·A·R·T · O·N·E

# Opening Conclusions

· My choice to begin with the "Conclusion" is not an empty gesture, though it is a familiar and almost traditional opening gesture in discussions of Pater's work. My reason has little to do with the fact that the "Conclusion" to the 1873 first edition of *Studies in the History of the Renaissance* was, and is, Pater's most controversial piece, that it inaugurated the career of public notoriety which he both invited and evaded, and that it established him as the inspiration of an elite counterculture whose further elaborations often shocked him, precipitating his lifelong recoil into less and less vivid restatements of his original positions. The "Conclusion" might have been more readily understood (or at least less radically misunderstood) if it had been positioned as an introduction or invocation to the volume, and therefore I want to begin by exposing the several senses in which the essay serves more properly as an introduction than as a conclusion to the volume.

Of course, the "Conclusion" was never written to conclude *Studies in the History of the Renaissance*—it was written originally to conclude another work altogether. It first appeared in 1868 as the last few paragraphs of Pater's review essay "Poems by William Morris" and was therefore written before all but one of the other essays in the Renaissance volume.[1] But the "Conclusion" should be read as an

---

1. For dating of the essays, see Samuel Wright, *A Bibliography of the Writings of Walter H. Pater* (New York: Garland, 1975). "Winckelmann" was published in 1867 and therefore antedates "Poems by William Morris." Inman has forcefully argued that Pater originally intended to conclude the volume of Renaissance studies with his essay on Wordsworth. See Billie Andrew Inman, *Walter Pater's Reading: A Bibliography of His Library Borrowings and Literary References, 1858–1873* (New York: Garland, 1981), pp. 264–66.

introduction to Pater's work for reasons more profound than its priority in the chronology of his publication record. Though Pater strategically positions it at the end of his first published volume, and though its title claims the rhetorical function of conveying in summary fashion what has been logically or experientially derived from the volume as a whole, its conclusions instead prefigure and enable all of Pater's "aesthetic criticism," including the Renaissance studies.

It was necessary for Pater to arrive at these conclusions before even beginning the series of "studies" whose fundamental value depends on circumventing certain philosophical problems that threaten to make any study of history virtually impossible. Before approaching a consideration of history, in other words, Pater had to answer several questions raised in his mind by modern physical science and epistemological philosophy. His particular version of aestheticism is then formulated in the "Conclusion" as Pater's answer to the problems posed by what he there calls "modern thought." The volume of Renaissance studies, and the inaugural moment of Pater's literary career, are founded on the theoretical position taken in the "Conclusion": that the problems of modern thought could be solved only by fully acknowledging them, confronting them, and regulating their effects.

Pater's "Conclusion" is still regarded as the major theoretical statement in English of nineteenth-century aestheticism, and yet it is still frequently misunderstood.[2] The stock literary-historical view of Pater's career has always taken his "Conclusion" as if it represented in its entirety Pater's own conclusions, and perhaps this is as good a reason as any for us to begin there. The popular misreading still takes the essay to be Pater's impassioned statement of his belief in relativism, subjectivism, nihilism, and hedonism—when it is nothing of the kind. Instead, in the "Conclusion" Pater briefly but painstakingly outlines the material and epistemological conclusions drawn by "modern thought," and then he devotes the full force of his rhetorical, figurative, and philosophical energies to proposing an alternative stance. His formulation of aestheticism is that alternative stance.

It is an irony of literary history that Pater has been repeatedly accused of propounding the very philosophies he meant to expose and combat, but it is an irony with its own interpretable significance. Pater had so thoroughly assimilated the most dangerous "modern thought" of his day that his vigorous and subtle defenses against it,

2. For a recent example, see Perry Meisel, *The Absent Father: Virginia Woolf and Walter Pater* (New Haven, Conn.: Yale University Press, 1980), pp. 114–15, and Inman's response to Meisel in "The Intellectual Context of Walter Pater's 'Conclusion,' " *Prose Studies* 4 (May 1981), 13.

as well as his profound desire to assimilate it *to* the traditional past of his culture (and therefore to domesticate it), were often missed. In Pater we find a quintessentially "transitional" figure who holds together in an unstable equilibrium ideologies from both sides of what will later come to be seen—and to a great extent was seen even at the time—as a historical divide. Pater is a deeply conservative writer whose conservatism nevertheless had a radical effect, in part because it engaged so closely with its dialectical counterpart. His aestheticism can be fully understood only if we see it in its role as a dialectical response, operating both within and against the forces he outlines in paragraphs one and two of the "Conclusion."

In these initial paragraphs, Pater distills and generalizes two strands of argument within "modern thought," embodies them in lushly figurative language, and takes the implications of each to its extreme limits, to the point where the argument dissolves at the boundaries of the articulate. Pater stages in these paragraphs the "passage and dissolution" of mind, body, soul, self, and text. But the rhetorical position he takes toward these paragraphs is neither straightforward nor even simply ironic, but oblique in another way, for he is engaged in conveying the full entangling force of these "modern" arguments while remaining at a distance from them—representing and at the same time disowning the train of thought represented. As Richard Wollheim has correctly suggested, the first two paragraphs of the "Conclusion" should be read as if they were enclosed in quotation marks.[3] But whom, then, is Pater quoting, or pretending to quote, and to what end? Why is he engaged in this form of ventriloquism, and what do the projected voices say?

The opening paragraphs of the "Conclusion" are known to more readers, perhaps, than any other passage from Pater's work. In the following two sections I pursue a close reading of these paragraphs in order to recall some already-established territory in Pater studies as well as to introduce a few of the central concepts and strategies of reading that will guide this book.

---

3. Richard Wollheim, "Walter Pater as a Critic of the Arts," *On Art and the Mind* (Cambridge, Mass.: Harvard University Press, 1974), pp. 161–64: "Without in any way being seduced by the theory, we are made to feel its seductiveness; and we are made to feel it not the less but the more so for our comparative detachment or distancing. Initially we might take the passage . . . as though it asserted the very theory it was about: but, as we read on, the passage puts itself into inverted commas for us. . . . [W]e do right to take the passage obliquely and not literally. It does not address us, we overhear what it says." See Graham Hough's partial recognition in *The Last Romantics* (1947; reprint, London: Methuen, 1961), p. 140: "But Pater does not really mean it."

# 1 · "That Which Is Without"

Λέγει που Ἡράκλειτος ὅτι πάντα χωρεῖ καὶ οὐδὲν μένει

To regard all things and principles of things as inconstant modes or fashions has more and more become the tendency of modern thought. Let us begin with that which is without—our physical life. Fix upon it in one of its more exquisite intervals, the moment, for instance, of delicious recoil from the flood of water in summer heat. What is the whole physical life in that moment but a combination of natural elements to which science gives their names? But these elements, phosphorus and lime and delicate fibers, are present not in the human body alone: we detect them in places most remote from it. Our physical life is a perpetual motion of them—the passage of the blood, the wasting and repairing of the lenses of the eye, the modification of the tissues of the brain under every ray of light and sound—processes which science reduces to simpler and more elementary forces. Like the elements of which we are composed, the action of these forces extends beyond us: it rusts iron and ripens corn. Far out on every side of us those elements are broadcast, driven in many currents; and birth and gesture and death and the springing of violets from the grave are but a few out of ten thousand resultant combinations. That clear, perpetual outline of face and limb is but an image of ours, under which we group them—a design in a web, the actual threads of which pass out beyond it. This at least of flamelike our life has, that it is but the concurrence, renewed from moment to moment, of forces parting sooner or later on their ways. (R, 233–34)

Although it serves generally to frame the essay in its place at the end of the volume, Pater's epigraph, from the *Cratylus*, must be understood more particularly in relation to what it immediately precedes. Plato characteristically represents the words of Socrates, but in this case Socrates's words themselves quote a fragment of Heraclitus: "Heraclitus somewhere says that all things are moving along and that nothing stands still." Pater gives the epigraph in its original Greek, inviting translation by the initiated and implying at the same time that he himself is chief among them, for the first two paragraphs of the "Conclusion" in effect "translate" these words of Heraclitus into their nineteenth-century English equivalent. The dense and explicit intertextuality of the epigraph condenses a whole history of voices: Heraclitus and Socrates subsumed, contextualized, and voiced by Plato, whose words in turn are given by Pater as a prefiguration of his own. In this small prefatory gesture, opening with an ancient fragment in order to interpret "modern" thought, Pater almost ostentatiously displays his command of the entire history of Western philosophy, positioning himself at one and the same time at the latest and at the earliest verge of his tradition's written record.

But even more important than Pater's tacit claim to mastery of the tradition is the hint that "modern" thought is not so thoroughly new, but is in many ways only a "modernization" of the classical tradition. The epigraph quietly shows, to those who read Greek, that Pater believes the threat of "modern" thought to be an ancient, a persistent, even a traditional threat. For the present study, this epigraph will serve as a brief introduction to Pater's habit of finding "mythic" recapitulations in the history of thought, since here the latest findings of science and philosophy suggest to him an analogue in Heraclitus.[1] The epigraph enacts, moreover, one characteristic Paterian strategy of quotation, although the first two paragraphs of the "Conclusion" make use (as we will see) of another, more subtle and pervasive intertextual strategy.

After the first sentence of paragraph one—which briefly and simply announces the subject under scrutiny—Pater begins to explore the extremes of this "tendency of modern thought" by presenting summary arguments meant to characterize entire intellectual disciplines. In the first paragraph, he represents the extreme conclusions of modern physical science, as in the second he will represent the extremes of epistemological philosophy. Here in the first paragraph, life is shown reduced to its "physical basis."[2] Within the terms of this discourse, the complexities of life become mere biological "processes which science reduces to simpler and more elementary forces." Here Pater highlights the relation between the methods of a discourse and its effects: the analytical practices of "science" both mimic and describe the perpetual fragmentation of bodies into their constituent "elements." That sense of perpetual reduction and fragmentation is ac-

---

1. *Cratylus* 402a. I have used the unidentified translation given by Gerald Monsman in *Pater's Portraits: Mythic Patterns in the Fiction of Walter Pater* (Baltimore, Md.: Johns Hopkins University Press, 1967), p. 4. On Pater's similar response to the *Thaetetus*, see Inman, "The Intellectual Context of Pater's 'Conclusion,' " p. 19. For the figurative comparison of "mythic" recapitulation in the history of thought to "translation," see Herbert N. Schneidau, *Sacred Discontent: The Bible and Western Tradition* (Baton Rouge: Louisiana State University Press, 1976).

2. Huxley's famous essay "On the Physical Basis of Life" was not published until 1869 in the *Fortnightly Review*, but for the sources of Pater's vision of modern science, see Inman, "The Intellectual Context of Pater's 'Conclusion,' " pp. 13–16; Inman, *Pater's Reading*, pp. 182–92; and Donald Hill's textual and explanatory notes to Pater's *The Renaissance: Studies in Art and Poetry, The 1893 Text*, ed. Donald L. Hill (Berkeley: University of California Press, 1980), pp. 451–54 (hereafter, Hill's notes). Inman points out that this scientific vision entailed a redefined understanding of identity.

companied by an equally pervasive sense of instability, of constant movement, the Heraclitean "flux" of phenomena in time. The particular form of "perpetual motion" set forth in this first paragraph is the never-ending process of physical bodies "wasting and repairing."

This paragraph represents the discourse of "objectivity." To view "life" as purely physical or material—to view "life" as an object of scientific study—depends upon establishing a certain distance between the viewing subject and the object of observation, a figurative "distance" that expresses in spatial terms the disciplinary practices necessary to establish "factual" or "scientific" knowledge. But here this analytical distance is extended by the "long view" of late Victorian, post-Darwinian science. That extremely distant perspective regards change over such vast periods of time that the solidity of physical objects seems only an illusion of our limited, transitory, and human perspective. Transformations taking a lifetime or more may be imagined as happening incrementally at every moment. Within this view there is no small oasis of stability; each moment rushes by, full of decay. In this particular configuration of space and time, distance and speed, we can perhaps see the clash of classical physics and chemistry with evolutionary geology and biology, each with a different view of the constitution of the object of study, the latter involved in a profound contemporary redefinition of historical change.

From the perspective of Pater's immediate literary tradition, it is as if Wordsworth's visionary image of monumental permanence in continuity, the "woods decaying, never to be decayed," from Book 6 of *The Prelude*, were represented not as a stable visual image but in an accelerated, time-lapsed moving picture, with each momentary frame implicated in the dissolving process of the whole. Looking back at paragraph one from paragraph two, Pater does seem to see the Wordsworthian illusion of permanence preserved within the discourse of objectivity: "the water flows down indeed, though in apparent rest" (R, 234). But here in the midst of paragraph one, Wordsworth's vision is revealed as wishful thinking, the illusion of permanence shattered by a discourse in which physical appearances are not allowed their common deception. Despite "apparent" rest, the truth is "perpetual motion"; all is wastage and dispersal, decomposition and reformation. The elements, forces, "threads" of which each of us is composed, "extend beyond us," for human life is but a "flamelike" and momentary "concurrence" of forces soon to be dispersed. Despite the allusive literary memorialization granted past life by "the springing of violets from the grave,"[3] all of human "gesture" is reduced to the one word

---

3. *Hamlet*, 5.1.

lodged between "birth" and "death." Human life occupies a very small space within this view of things; after all, only "a few out of ten thousand combinations" ever result in human form.

The only concept of continuity preserved in the vision of paragraph one lies in the regeneration implicit in nature's constant recycling of elements, but that concept of regeneration makes any particular physical body only an arbitrary and passing combination. The stoic faith—that dead bodies, dispersed into their constituent elements, constantly recombine to form new wholes—can operate as comfort only from a cosmic or a scientific perspective. But from the perspective of Christian humanism—against which this post-Darwinian view contends here—a new body can be no comfort unless it is the *same* body, for reformation implies as well a change or loss of content, and in the realm of incarnational poetics the "content" of a human body is its soul. Like a scientific version of mythic recurrence, this reincarnational vision of continuity involves so much transformation that it undermines the value of individual identity. In this discourse, any notion of the "self" disappears as irrelevant. This discourse, then, represents a crucial destabilization of the incarnational view, for visible bodies are themselves so unstable that they cannot be confidently seen to "contain" selves or souls.

In other words, the scientifically objective view of physical bodies in time has both epistemological and aesthetic consequences, for it implies that visible form can no longer be trusted to mark stable content. The "outline" of an object marks only our mental effort to believe in permanent form, to "group" elements together momentarily while nevertheless "far out on every side of us those elements are broadcast," to "fix" the play of forces in some fictive combination we can recognize, "an image of ours," a figure in the carpet whose "actual threads . . . pass out beyond it." These metaphors attempt to implicate two incompatible forms of incoherence: atomism and inextricable interrelation, one as old as Lucretius, the other a characteristic formulation of late Victorian aesthetics and social analysis.[4] Whether every element or particle is separate from every other, or whether every fiber or thread is woven into an inextricable texture

---

4. On atomism, see Harold Bloom, introduction to *Selected Writings of Walter Pater*, ed. Harold Bloom (New York: Columbia University Press, 1982), p. xv: "Pater's strange achievement is to have assimilated Wordsworth to Lucretius, to have compounded an idealistic naturalism with a corrective materialism." On the Victorian concept of inextricable interrelation, see Josephine Miles, *Poetry and Change* (Berkeley: University of California Press, 1974), p. 126; and John Holloway, "Thought, Style, and the Idea of Co-Variance in Some Mid-Nineteenth-Century Prose," *Studies in the Literary Imagination* 8 (Fall 1975), 1–14.

with every other—within the logic, that is, of either metaphor—discrete form is understood to have been imposed by the eye, not to be inherent in the object. Together the metaphors suggest that what the eye can see is the merest mask for the unseen truth: that the chief activity of the world is its speedy decomposition.

With an eye to behold it, the world becomes a text to be read and deciphered, but a text understood to have been written in the very act of reading, composed by the will to envision design. Within the terms of paragraph one, the perception of form has been relegated to the status of personal wish or aesthetic illusion, a myth that modern science dispels with its brutal truth.

## 2 · "The Inward World of Thought and Feeling"

In the objective framework of paragraph one, then, subjectivity is cast in the role of irrelevant illusion, but in paragraph two the tables are turned. There the experience of the individual perceiving self is taken as primary, but the consequences are the same: the object again loses its definition, and the notion of a stable, unified self dissolves as well. Taken together, these opposite and interlocking discourses seem to suggest that "modern thought" in general—regardless of the specific mental processes or the particular disciplinary methods enforced—tends to dissolve subject and object in relation to one another, correlatively. Pater himself made this destructive correlation vividly clear, in a passage that originally followed paragraph two and thus framed his discussion of "modern thought":

> Such thoughts seem desolate at first; at times all the bitterness of life seems concentrated in them. They bring the image of one washed out beyond the bar in a sea at ebb, losing even his personality, as the elements of which he is composed pass into new combinations. Struggling, as he must, to save himself, it is himself that he loses at every moment.[1]

But the correlative relation of the two paragraphs should be clear even at the beginning of the second paragraph, where a rhetorical turn signals that a different position will be taken toward "modern thought" and

---

1. Hill's notes, p. 273.

"The Inward World" · 19 ·

prefigures Pater's demonstration that another modern discourse leads to essentially the same conclusions. The blatant parallelism opening each paragraph—"Let us begin . . . Or if we begin . . ."—seems unmistakable, yet it has often been missed, along with its important implication that the two opposed discourses present parallel and interlocking hypothetical cases of "passage and dissolution."

> Or if we begin with the inward world of thought and feeling, the whirlpool is still more rapid, the flame more eager and devouring. There it is no longer the gradual darkening of the eye, and fading of color from the wall—the movement of the shoreside, where the water flows down indeed, though in apparent rest—but the race of the midstream, a drift of momentary acts of sight and passion and thought. At first sight experience seems to bury us under a flood of external objects, pressing upon us with a sharp and importunate reality, calling us out of ourselves in a thousand forms of action. But when reflection begins to play upon those objects they are dissipated under its influence; the cohesive force seems suspended like a trick of magic; each object is loosed into a group of impressions—color, odor, texture—in the mind of the observer. And if we continue to dwell in thought on this world, not of objects in the solidity with which language invests them, but of impressions, unstable, flickering, inconsistent, which burn and are extinguished with our consciousness of them, it contracts still further: the whole scope of observation is dwarfed to the narrow chamber of the individual mind. Experience, already reduced to a swarm of impressions, is ringed round for each one of us by that thick wall of personality through which no real voice has ever pierced on its way to us, or from us to that which we can only conjecture to be without. Every one of those impressions is the impression of the individual in his isolation, each mind keeping as a solitary prisoner its own dream of a world. Analysis goes a step farther still, and assures us that those impressions of the individual mind to which, for each one of us, experience dwindles down, are in perpetual flight; that each of them is limited by time, and that as time is infinitely divisible, each of them is infinitely divisible also; all that is actual in it being a single moment, gone while we try to apprehend it, of which it may ever be more truly said that it has ceased to be than that it is. To such a tremulous wisp constantly reforming itself on the stream, to a single sharp impression, with a sense in it, a relic more or less fleeting of such moments gone by, what is real in our life fines itself down. It is with this movement, with the passage and dissolution of impressions, images, sensations, that analysis leaves off—that continual vanishing away, that strange, perpetual weaving and unweaving of ourselves. (R, 234–36)

To move us "inward" at the beginning of paragraph two, Pater first stages a loss of distance in relation to physical objects. As distance is lost, the definitive marks of the object's "objectivity"—its externality and its wholeness—are perforce lost as well. Without distance between observer and object, there can be no perceivable definition, no "outline"; nor can there be the sense of a "sharp" and "importunate" external reality "outside," ready to "[call] us out of ourselves." This is the discourse of the "inside," of extreme subjectivity. If paragraph one took the extreme long view, paragraph two takes the extreme close view, in which subject and object are one, as the mind becomes the object of its own self-reflexive regard.

With his usual keen attention to etymological nuance, Pater reminds us of the literal significance of "analysis" and of a certain sense in which the scrutiny of mental operations must always tend to "break up" or "loosen" the coherence of the mind and its objects. When "reflection begins to play upon those objects," they are "loosened" into their separate sensory attributes; their coherence seems to be "suspended like a trick of magic." Again, as in paragraph one, but here even more explicitly, language "invests" objects with a solidity and coherence they would otherwise lack; names counteract "analysis" by creating the illusion of an overarching wholeness even where none can be directly experienced.

Reflection's "trick of magic" is also a trick of time. As in paragraph one, tropes of fragmentation, reduction, and acceleration express the connection Pater draws between the distance taken on an object and the resulting sense of time. In this case the crux of the equation is the notion of "impressions," the middle term between mind and object. United in the notion of the impression are the effects of fragmentation and speed, for like the "elements" of paragraph one, the "impressions" of paragraph two represent parts of objects in the perpetual motion of dissolving and "reforming." And this is a temporal, not spatial, phenomenon: "each of them is limited by time, and . . . as time is infinitely divisible, each of them is infinitely divisible also." Impressions are problematic, in other words, not only because they are mental phenomena rather than physical objects, and not only because they are representatives of parts rather than wholes, but also because they pass so quickly they cannot be grasped. Faster than the "currents" of paragraph one, their passage here is "still more rapid," the "race of the midstream."

Behind the words of this paragraph lie the empiricist epistemologies of Locke and Hume, but also and more immediately the critiques of Berkeley and Kant.[2] Pater seems to grapple here with the difficult

---

2. And many others. In addition to Locke, Hume, Berkeley, and Kant, Inman mentions Fichte, Bacon, Hegel, and Plato (*Walter Pater's Reading*, pp. 182–92); see also Hill's notes, pp. 454–55.

notion that the long tradition of empiricist epistemology has undergone a dialectical reversal: a discourse instituted to counteract the classical form of idealism by relying on the evidence of the senses seems to have circled back to enunciate another, subjectivist form of it. And again the clue to this doubleness is the particular notion of the "impression" found in paragraph two. The empiricist sense-impression has been replaced by a subjectivist, idealist "impression" that has only a "relic" of "a sense" left in it, a distant reminder of the sensory experience that stimulated it in the first place. The difference between the empiricist "impression" and the subjectivist "impression" has to do with the one's relative attention to the object and the other's relative absorption in the mind's own processes. Another way to draw this distinction would be to characterize the traditional empiricist project as an attempt to balance the claims of object and mind through the mediating agency of the "sense-impression." But here Pater portrays a notion of "impressions" very far from their stimuli in the world of objects. It is true that elsewhere in Pater the notion of the "impression" retains a greater degree of fidelity to the evidence of the senses. In other words, in Pater's explicit unfolding of his own theory of impressionism, the impression retains its empiricist role as the crucial mechanism of internalization from a real outside.[3] But here in paragraph two, where Pater's goal is to portray the extremes of subjectivism, the impression has accordingly lost touch with its objective source.

This second paragraph presents Pater's famous late romantic restatement of the anxious agonies of solipsism. In attempting to provide another response to this problem, the "Conclusion" falls squarely in the philosophical and literary tradition of Johnson kicking a rock to prove Berkeley wrong, of Wordsworth grasping for dear life at the wall.[4] Once again Pater places his words at the end of a modern tradition (which itself recapitulates a classical tradition, as his epigraph vigilantly insists). As Wordsworth is more anxious than Johnson, Pater is more anxious than Wordsworth, and at the same time Pater is more familiar with the anxieties of self-consciousness, which are by now a traditional part of his late romantic literary culture. He pushes the literary tradition of romantic epistemology further toward its limits by figuratively expressing the danger as even more acute, reflexive, and involuted.

  3. For my reading of Pater's impressionism, see below, Part One, sec. 3; and Part One, sec.7.
  4. For a recent treatment of these anecdotes and of the romantic responses to the anxieties of solipsism, see Charles Rzepka, *The Self as Mind* (Cambridge, Mass.: Harvard University Press, 1985).

In Pater's representation of "modern thought," the mind can no longer resort to a physical, bodily, or common-sense solution: in the first paragraph the "physical basis of life" provided no solid ground, and here in the second no solid object can even be imagined for long. The Wordsworthian wall cannot be reached for its steadying influence, for it is no longer figured "outside," at the objective distance that makes it available to be grasped. Instead, in the famous Paterian figure, the wall is represented as constitutive of subjectivity, and "personality" has consequently become a figurative prison. The passage in which Pater gives us "the thick wall of personality" behind which each mind keeps "as a solitary prisoner its own dream of a world" probably characterizes the extreme subjectivist position as vividly as any in English literature. But it is therefore crucial to recognize that if Pater uses this paragraph to enact his profound understanding of—perhaps even his temptation toward—the position of epistemological nihilism, he holds that position at a hypothetical distance from his own.

What are the consequences of figuring the "wall" as constitutive of subjectivity? Once the wall is figuratively located inside, its effect is to articulate another inside and outside, both figuratively contained within the internal territory of the mind. In the words of the figure, each individual mind is a walled-off, isolated "narrow chamber," and then inside each already-isolated mind is the solitary figure of a prisoner, a figure for the mind's dream of a world outside. The figure, in other words, is metafigural in structure and content: it depicts multiple and recapitulatory layers of containment, and it represents in spatial form, as a place or "scene," the essentially figural, aesthetic act through which the mind recreates the world. If the usual account of literary figuration represents the metaphorical figure as having an inside and an outside, a meaning conveyed by a linguistic vehicle or contained in a covering layer, Pater's figure (of the chamber) has another figure (of the prisoner) "inside" it, and that inner figure is a figure for the act of figuration (the mind's "dream of a world"). In bringing the Wordsworthian wall "inside," making it constitutive of subjectivity instead of a sign of the stabilizing world of external objects, Pater makes a figure for the mind in the act of constructing itself and the world together: both inside and outside have been recontained, both are now understood to be inside. Mind and object in relation to one another—the mind together with its object—is now the object of the mind's representations. Subject and object together have become the revised content or object of consciousness. This important Paterian figure, in other words, represents the tradition of romantic epistemology as metafigural discourse.

This move of metafiguration—in which the mind figuratively steps outside itself in one further self-reflexive gesture, to represent itself in the act of representing itself and the world—provides Pater with a way to slip out of the "prison" of solipsism. On the level of meaning, the gesture is tantamount to the bracketing admission that every perception as well as every utterance is already an aesthetic creation, and on this level the metafigural figure has frequently been associated with literary modernism. Both paragraphs include this modernist avowal that the perception of form is generated in the eye of the beholder, or by language itself. But the figure of the prisoner is metafigural in a particularly spatial way, a figure of what I will be calling "recontainment." And it will be possible to see why this strategy of recontainment might be appealing when we note that the alternative model of mental activity at work in this paragraph—consciousness figured as "stream"—presents, in several senses, a much graver danger.

Of course, the metaphor of the "stream" of consciousness is the quintessential figure for the temporality of mental experience. As Pater's evocation of Heraclitus reminds us, you cannot step into the same stream twice. But paragraph two of the "Conclusion" gives us the passage of temporal experience in a vastly accelerated version, the "race of the midstream," moments of experience "in perpetual flight." By the end of the paragraph, all of experience has been reduced to "a single moment, gone while we try to apprehend it, of which it may ever be more truly said that it has ceased to be than that it is." Throughout these first two paragraphs, Pater uses the word "passage" to characterize the Heraclitean "flux," the perpetual motion of physical and mental phenomena in time, but when the "passage of the blood" succeeds to the "passage and dissolution of impressions" here in paragraph two, the double and triple implications of the word begin to resonate. Here the word calls attention to the inability of the mind to grasp its own experience as that experience passes into the past.

In a certain sense, the problem is the very opposite of solipsism. When the mind turns to reflect upon itself, all it can observe are these "passages" of impressions, until the mind itself seems nothing more than the site of their passage. What, then, is the mind? Can it exert any control over this "drift"? Or is it capable only of registering the impressions as they pass? Is it a site at all, a location, a place? Are there depths below the surface of the "stream," where invisible things are stored away from the drift? As these questions indicate, this model too has potentially spatial implications as well as temporal ones. Pater described the Kantian issue of the "substantial reality of mind" this way:

> What remained of our actual experience was but a stream of impressions over the ⟨supposed but⟩ wholly unknown mental substratum which no act of intuition or reflexion could ever really detect.[5]

"Substantial" and "substratum" suggest the attempt to rationalize a metaphorics of depth to describe mental process, but those implications are more or less refused in paragraph two of the "Conclusion," where the "relic" of sensory experience floats on the surface of the current as "a tremulous wisp . . . reforming itself on the stream." What is really at issue here is the mind's questionable ability to "grasp" or "apprehend," to "hold" or "contain" anything at all.

Given the problems implied in the figure of the stream in its passage, it may be possible now to see how the figure of the prisoner might be relatively appealing to Pater. Even though that figure represents the "outside" as conjectural, unreal, and dreamlike, still the metafigural logic of the metaphor permits the faith that there *is* an outside into which the dreamer might wake, the prisoner be freed. The discourse of the "outside" in paragraph one admits of no such more objective realm, whereas the alternative metaphor of the stream in paragraph two questions the ability of the mind to hold or to grasp anything at all. By contrast, the figure of the prisoner depicts the mind in the act of holding on to the faith or "dream" of another world, an outside, objective world.[6] If it portrays the mind completely isolated and cut off from the world, it also portrays the mind keeping its dream or faith securely inside, as content.

Of course, the figure of impressions in their passage on the stream of consciousness has its own version of this doubleness: if it portrays the mind with no control over what passes through it, it also portrays the mind free, unrestrained, and mobile—the very opposite of solipsistic, immobilized, and imprisoned. The two metaphorical systems are in many ways incommensurate. As in paragraph one, where we found contradictory figures for the incoherence of the material world—atomism and inextricable interrelation—paragraph two reveals contradictory figures for the impossibility of knowing: solipsism and mania, radical containment and radical noncontainment, the metaphorics of

---

5. Hill's notes, p. 455.
6. For variations on the figure of imprisonment and the desire for a "sense of escape" or a "sense of freedom," see, e.g., "Aesthetic Poetry" (B, 190, 193) and "Winckelmann" (R, 231).

the "prisoner" and those of the "passage." The problem that nothing stays in the mind for very long seems to be the opposite of the problem that nothing can get out, and their juxtaposition and doubleness indicate a confusion about the relation of these models. On the other hand, the ability of each to articulate, at one and the same time, both impediment and capacity suggests the sense in which they may overlap or dialectically interact (on the question of depth, for example). Each model has its aesthetic consequences, but in the largest sense they may be made to work together, each correcting the other in a model of mental activity that escapes the perils of "modern thought." In the next section of this book, I shall show how Pater constructs this alternative model in elaborating his own discourse of aestheticism.

Finally, it must be noted that Pater stresses the inextricable interdefinition of subject and object not only in the figures for self-consciousness that dominate paragraph two, but also in the relationship that obtains between the two paragraphs. There *are* two discourses represented here, but together they form one argument, the parts of which interlock logically as well as rhetorically.[7] By relating every subject to its uneasy grounding in "the physical basis of life," and every object to its uneasy grounding in an isolated and ephemeral subject, Pater presents scientific objectivity and romantic epistemology as two opposing but correlative modes of deriving the radically relativist position at the extremes of "modern thought." The inevitability of material annihilation makes the self irrelevant; epistemological nihilism makes the world of objects—and finally the mind itself—unknowable. Without at least a provisional outside, there is no inside; without solid objects, there can be no subject; without a provisional other, there is no certainty of "our own elusive inscrutable mistakable self."[8] Pater's simultaneously late romantic, late Victorian, and early modern position in the English literary tradition may be seen in this intensified awareness that the problem of "objective" knowledge and the problem of "subjectivity" are intractably one and the same problem.

7. Inman sees here two separate discourses and a "central inconsistency" between them (Inman, "The Intellectual Context of Pater's 'Conclusion,' " p. 13), but Meisel notes their crucial interrelation, though he misses the obliquity of the two paragraphs (Perry Meisel, *The Absent Father* [New Haven: Yale University Press, 1980], pp. 114–15).

8. Pater's formulation, in Hill's notes, p. 455.

# 3 · Aestheticism

Many years later, in writing *Marius the Epicurean*, Pater attempted to explain more fully the thoughts suggested by his "Conclusion."[1] At that point he wrote into Marius's character the "peculiar strength" of having "apprehended," from the very beginning of his career, the possible consequences of "what is termed 'the subjectivity of knowledge' ":

> That is a consideration, indeed, which lies as an element of weakness, like some admitted fault or flaw, at the very foundation of every philosophical account of the universe; which confronts all philosophies at their starting, but with which none have really dealt conclusively, some perhaps not quite sincerely; which those who are not philosophers dissipate by "common," but unphilosophical, sense, or by religious faith. The peculiar strength of Marius was, to have apprehended this weakness on the threshold of human knowledge, in the whole range of its consequences. (ME I, 137–38)

Certainly Pater understood Marius's "peculiar strength" to be his own. In this section of my argument I want to ask how Pater's aestheticism functions as an "apprehension"—both as grasp, or understanding, and as arrest or halting—of this "weakness" and how it responds to this "weakness" with its own "peculiar strength." If the problem of "objective" knowledge and the problem of the "subjectivity" of knowledge are, for Pater, correlative problems, then they must be solved correlatively. That is exactly what his theory of aestheticism attempts to do. And the solution depends upon reconstituting, upon new grounds, a provisional objectivity.

Aestheticism, as the suffix implies, proposes itself as a systematic attitude of self-consciousness, a coherent stance or perspective on things, a method of attention. Whether the word accurately refers to a coherent "movement" or not,[2] a coherent account of the method

---

1. He makes this clear in the famous footnote restoring the "Conclusion" to the third edition of *The Renaissance*, after its suppression in the second. For the wording of that footnote, see below, Part Three, sec. 2.

2. For the ongoing argument about whether aestheticism should be understood as a "movement," see Ruth Z. Temple, "Truth in Labelling: Pre-Raphaelitism, Aestheticism, Decadence, Fin-de-Siècle," in *English Literature in Transition* 17, no. 4 (1974), 201–22; and Ian Fletcher, "Some Aspects of Aestheticism," in *Twilight of Dawn: Studies in English Literature in Transition* (Tucson: University of Arizona Press, 1987), pp. 1–31. Germain d'Hangest assigns Pater "the decisive role" in the aesthetic movement in "La Place de Walter Pater dans le mouvement esthétique," *Études anglaises* 27 (April–June 1974), 158–71.

was propounded in English both by Pater and by Wilde. I want to describe here, as succinctly as possible, how I see the method working. I continue to focus on the "Conclusion," but I shall also begin to range freely among the other essays in which Pater specifically addresses himself to articulating theoretically the function and operation of "aesthetic criticism."

The "Conclusion" presents an extraordinary texture of metaphorical doubleness and transformation. All the dominant figures of paragraphs one and two are reworked and transvalued in paragraphs three through five. This is one way the discourse of aestheticism answers modern thought in its own terms—figuratively—and the instability of figures here is evidence both of the problem and, dialectically, of its solution. In the "Conclusion," the systematic transvaluation of figures enacts on the level of form what has been clearly announced on the level of theme: Pater's commitment to engage with and assimilate "modern thought" and then to turn it against itself under the auspices of aestheticism. In his original introduction to the paragraphs that eventually became the "Conclusion," Pater made it quite clear that the essay would discuss the response provided by "the desire of beauty" to the destructive tendencies of modern philosophy. The "desire of beauty," Pater wrote, in another of his graphic characterizations of modern thought, is "quickened by the sense of death."[3] That phrase resonates with his description at the end of the "Conclusion" of the goal and end of the aesthetic attitude: a "quickened, multiplied consciousness." The essay was framed, then, by phrases describing the aesthetic attitude as "quickened," which Pater uses to mean both

3. This passage is rarely seen, having never been reprinted after its 1868 publication in the *Westminster Review*, n.s. 34 [October 1868], 300–312, until Hill's 1980 edition of the 1893 *Renaissance*. Following these words, the first two paragraphs of the "Conclusion" appear quite clearly as an exercise in the ironic ventriloquism of "modern thought": "One characteristic of the pagan spirit these new poems have which is on their surface—the continual suggestion, pensive or passionate, of the shortness of life; this is contrasted with the bloom of the world and gives new seduction to it; the sense of death and the desire of beauty; the desire of beauty quickened by the sense of death. 'Arriéré!' you say, 'here in a tangible form we have the defect of all poetry like this. The modern world is in possession of truths; what but a passing smile can it have for a kind of poetry which, assuming artistic beauty of form to be an end in itself, passes by those truths and the living interests which are connected with them, to spend a thousand cares in telling once more these pagan fables as if it had but to choose between a more and a less beautiful shadow?' It is a strange transition from the earthly paradise to the sad-coloured world of abstract philosophy. But let us accept the challenge; let us see what modern philosophy, when it is sincere, really does say about human life and the truth we can attain in it, and the relation of this to the desire of beauty" (Hill's notes, p. 272). David DeLaura explained this setting of the "Conclusion" in *Hebrew and Hellene in Victorian England: Newman, Arnold, and Pater* (Austin: University of Texas Press, 1969), pp. 224–25.

"enlivened" and "accelerated." And indeed, quickness (as mental mobility) is closely associated with the sense of "life" promised by aestheticism, just as the rapidity of dissolution was associated in the first two paragraphs with "the sense of death." If we follow a few of these doubling, transformative turns for a moment, we will be able to find out what Pater imagines in a "quickened" and "multiplied" consciousness.

The "moment," for example, which in paragraphs one and two signified only impermanence, temporal fragmentation, and the vertiginous speed of decay, is transformed in paragraph three into the culmination of a temporal sequence in which beauty and, above all, form is finally achieved:

> Every moment some form grows perfect in hand or face; some tone on the hills or the sea is choicer than the rest; some mood of passion or insight or intellectual excitement is irresistibly real and attractive to us,—for that moment only. (R, 236)

Here form is taken at its face value, not dismissed as illusion; it may be accurately perceived, but it is alive and changing every moment, so it must be pursued actively. In the terms of modern thought, experience was portrayed as drastically ephemeral, "all that is actual in it being a single moment, gone while we try to apprehend it"; but Pater's aestheticism proposes that we may in fact "apprehend" that moment if we will only speed up and "fasten" our attention:

> How shall we pass most swiftly from point to point, and be present always at the focus where the greatest number of vital forces unite in their purest energy? (R, 236)

Recommended here is a mental "quickening" that would enable us to keep up with moments in their passage by "passing" along with them, so that our attention could coincide with their brief points of focus. But in addition to the rush to "be present"—in spatial and in temporal terms, to be "there" and to be in the present moment—Pater's aestheticism also promises an active, prehensile and formative capacity to grasp and focus those moments as they pass:

> While all melts under our feet, we may well grasp at any exquisite passion or any contribution to knowledge that seems by a lifted horizon to set the spirit free for a moment. (R, 237)

Pater's exhortation here means not only that "we may as well" grasp but also that we may do it well—that is, skillfully—though through the years most readers have heard Pater resignedly making the best of a bad situation and have missed the overtone promising skill and strength. This active, prehensile attention, which "may well grasp" and "fix on" moments before they pass, is one answer to the "passage and dissolution" of modern thought.

This notion of mental attachment in the moment allows for tropes of reduction and contraction to be revalued as concentration and stillness—the answering opposite of the rapid mental dissolution of paragraph two. The famous injunction "to burn always with that hard, gemlike flame" may be seen, then, as the culminating moment in Pater's transvaluation of "modern thought." This figure portrays mental life as intense, concentrated, and pointedly organized, not as fragmentary, chaotic, and dissolute. Because the discourse of modern science in paragraph one had represented the passage of our physical life as "flamelike," and the discourse of modern philosophy in paragraph two had described impressions that "burn and are extinguished with our consciousness of them," this well-known Paterian figure might literally be said to fight fire with fire. Gerald Monsman, wittily recognizing Pater's gesture of responsiveness here, has remarked that the "hard, gemlike flame" evokes "the spirit of the Bunsen burner" no less than "the spirit of the waxen candle in a holy place."[4]

On the other hand, the aesthetic stance promises not only concentration in the "moment" but also—paradoxically— expansion as well. As a response to the brevity of life, "our one chance lies in expanding that interval"; in that attempt "we may well grasp" at anything "that seems by a lifted horizon to set the spirit free for a moment." In this apparent contradiction, we may once again recognize Pater's attempt to imagine a response to the seemingly opposite problems of modern thought: fragmentation and solipsism. Tropes of contraction and intensity respond to the speed of the "stream" in its "passage," while tropes of expansion "set the spirit free" from its figurative imprisonment. The paradoxical joining of contraction and expansion is resolvable only in temporal terms, not in spatial terms, as experience— or as literature—not as philosophical systematics. The key here is mobility or movement, shifts in attention that temporalize what was before, invidiously, conceivable only as the spatial figure of the prison. The mind in the act of passing "swiftly from point to point" constantly moves "outside" or "beyond" its former frame of awareness. There is

---

4. Monsman, *Pater's Portraits*, p. xvi.

a sense of freedom in this constant activation of a self-consciousness that is now no longer fixated, immobilized, and spatially "contained," but is constantly moving outside itself, away from one point in time and toward another moment and another point of view.

Pater is proposing a dynamic of attention in which mobility or "quickening" plays off against fixation, "grasp," or "apprehension." What we find here, in the terms of our earlier discussion, amounts to a transvaluation of the "passage" as an activity of the shaping mind, interrupted by moments that have themselves been redefined as moments of active focus. As a description of an epistemological strategy, we can begin now to hear in the word "passage" both its musical and its textual senses, for this mental strategy involves a regulated articulation of time's passage in which extended phrases of play are punctuated by moments of "apprehension" or fixity. Responding to the mental chaos engendered by "modern thought," Pater has created an order by distinguishing the "moments" from their correlative, ongoing, overarching "passages." This model has the double advantage of marking out brief points of stillness and yet also liberating those moments of focus from any sense of permanent immobilization because they are constantly taken up in an overarching mobility. Both "moment" and "passage" are endowed, in this model, with the conscious shaping power of aesthetic formation.[5] And this transvaluation of "moments" and their "passages" (each in itself and in relation to the other) has consequences also for the figure of the "prisoner," as we have just seen. For now the spatial metaphorics of solipsism can be transformed in successive moments of ecstasy, as consciousness evades entrapment by continually moving outside or beyond its former point of view.

"To burn always with this hard, gemlike flame, to maintain this ecstasy, is success in life." The aesthetic "ecstasy" recommended here—in its literal sense of "standing apart from (oneself)"—is as important to "maintain" as the intensity and concentration of the "hard, gemlike flame." We may note in passing that this figure of ecstasy also involves an important metaphorical transvaluation of

---

5. The articulation of this systematic relation marks Pater's revision of the Wordsworthian "spots of time." As all revisions are, his revision was both an advance (toward Joyce's "epiphanies" and Woolf's "moments of being") and a return (for this systematic relation is embodied throughout *The Prelude*). For a short history of the epiphanic moment, which unaccountably slights Pater's pivotal role, see M. H. Abrams, "Varieties of the Modern Moment," in his *Natural Supernaturalism* (New York: Norton, 1971), pp. 418–27; and Bloom, introduction to Pater's *Selected Writings*, pp. x–xv. Bloom argues that Pater "de-idealizes" the epiphany by effecting a return to Wordsworth after Ruskin's critique of the pathetic fallacy.

Aestheticism · 31 ·

"modern thought": the essential self as "prisoner" has been succeeded and joined by an overseeing self, standing outside itself. Thus this passage is important because it offers us a way to see what Pater imagined as the "multiplied" consciousness. In one sense I am simply pointing to Pater's embrace of the figure of self-division familiar from romantic epistemology and poetics, but Pater turns it into an active, operating principle with new consequences. Not only does it represent to him a stance that can be actively chosen, taken and retaken moment by moment, rather than suffered, however passionately, but it also creates a space of difference, a figurative gap within consciousness across which an object may be perceivable again. This attempt to recreate a sense of objectivity places Pater directly in the mainstream of Victorian poetics, but his temporalizing of the ecstatic stance represents one of his crucial shifts toward the "modern."

What is at stake here is recreation of the sense of distance—a figurative and internal distance, to be sure, but one that will serve to reconstitute the grounds of a provisional objectivity. In his description of the aesthetically mobile, experimental state of mind, Pater describes a rhythm of identification and detachment that is, in effect, the mobilization of this internal distance. He cautions, for example, against any "interest into which we cannot enter, or some abstract theory we have not identified with ourselves." But he also warns against static fixation on any one object: "what we have to do is to be forever curiously testing new opinions and courting new impressions"; we must "gather up what might otherwise pass unregarded," and then we must pass on, detaching from one object in order to be receptive to another. At first the object, in its state of "identification" with the self, is practically invisible. But through a process of discrimination it can be distinguished from the perceiving consciousness, and it is through these oscillations in internal distance, these successive acts of identification and detachment, that the object is "objectively" perceivable again. Thus aesthetic experience permits a revised form of knowledge.[6]

6. This internal distance is related to but different from what is commonly called "aesthetic distance," which is usually taken to mean the adoption of an "aesthetic attitude" toward an object or event that might under most circumstances seem to demand a more practical response. See Edward Bullough's 1912 essay, "'Psychical Distance' as a Factor in Art and an Aesthetic Principle," in Marvin Levich, ed., *Aesthetics and the Philosophy of Criticism* (New York: Random House, 1963), pp. 233–54. Though Bullough mentions the dynamics of internal "distance" or self-division, the essay concentrates on the "outward" consequences of that assumed distance, in the turning away from utilitarian or practical considerations. The initial example given (which incidentally recalls the aesthetics of Ruskin, Turner, and Whistler) involves appreciating a fog at sea for its beauty rather than exerting oneself actively in the pursuit of safety.

We may see in this procedure the embrace of further self-consciousness as a dialectical "remedy" for the ills of self-consciousness itself, and in this sense it is a typically romantic gesture—here especially interesting in its historical sequence after one strain of romantic (Carlylean) and Victorian (Arnoldian) anti-self-consciousness.[7] But a better way to specify the literary-historical moment of this strategy would be to take Pater's own cues from the "Conclusion," where aesthetic "ecstasy" appears as an internalization of "objective" distance. Aestheticism, then, appears as an ironic transvaluation of the stance of scientific objectivity. Not only does the distance established by self-division serve, epistemologically speaking, to reconstitute any object as an "aesthetic object," but also historically speaking, Pater has blatantly presented his solution after a summary representation of the specifically contemporary ills it was designed to cure. In other words, he marks this particular "solution" explicitly as a return to rethink romantic self-consciousness and the role of art "after"—meaning "later in time," as well as "in imitation of" and "against or in reaction to"—the specific developments of contemporary science and philosophy.[8] We can see the sense in which his version of "aesthetic distance" is offered as a figurative simulacrum structured on the model of scientific or "objective" distance, and his aesthetic method of representing knowledge of an object is modeled as a cross between the methods offered by skeptical scientific empiricism and epistemological philosophy.

This provisionally objective stance enables an object to be perceived once more, but the object has now been relativized, reconstituted in relation to the subject. According to this model, the "aesthetic object" is "aesthetic" largely because it is admittedly recreated within the perceiving consciousness. This explains the curious circularity of one tenet of aestheticism: that any object can become an "aesthetic object" when regarded in the "aesthetic attitude."[9] We can see all this

---

7. The *locus classicus* is Geoffrey Hartman's essay "Romanticism and 'Anti-Self-Consciousness,' " revised and expanded in Harold Bloom, ed., *Romanticism and Consciousness: Essays in Criticism* (New York: Norton, 1970), pp. 46–56. For an excellent critique of this romantic self-characterization, see Jerome J. McGann, *The Romantic Ideology* (Chicago: University of Chicago Press, 1983), pp. 40–41.

8. D'Hangest also argues that Pater's aestheticism was "based . . . directly on the contemporary disenchantment; he derived it from that very disenchantment and presented it as a remedy, the only one possible, for the confusion in which scientific progress had plunged Victorian spirits" (quoted in Hill's notes, p. 451).

9. On this circularity and the general dilemma of the "aesthetic attitude" in relation to the constitution of an "aesthetic object," see Monroe C. Beardsley, "Aesthetic Objects" and "Postscript 1980," in *Aesthetics: Problems in the Philosophy of Criticism* (1958; rpt. Indianapolis, Ind.: Hackett, 1981), pp. xvii–74.

Aestheticism · 33 ·

clearly in the following passage from the "Preface," where Pater's revision of Arnold figures prominently:

> "To see the object as in itself it really is," has been justly said to be the aim of all true criticism whatever; and in aesthetic criticism the first step toward seeing one's object as it really is, is to know one's own impression as it really is, to discriminate it, to realize it distinctly. The objects with which aesthetic criticism deals, music, poetry, artistic and accomplished forms of human life, are indeed receptacles of so many powers or forces; they possess, like natural elements, so many virtues or qualities. What is this song or picture, this engaging personality presented in life or in a book, to *me*? What effect does it really produce on me? . . . How is my nature modified by its presence, and under its influence? The answers to these questions are the original facts with which the aesthetic critic has to do; and, as in the study of light, of morals, of number, one must realize such primary data for oneself, or not at all. . . . The aesthetic critic, then, regards all the objects with which he has to do, all works of art, and the fairer forms of nature and human life, as powers or forces producing pleasurable sensations, each of a more or less peculiar and unique kind. This influence he feels, and wishes to explain, analyzing it, and reducing it to its elements. (R, viii–ix)

The sly subversion of Arnold here has frequently, and "justly," been noted as the very linchpin of Pater's revisionary, aesthetic procedure.[10] However, his introductory claim to be following Arnold's dictum is not a simple pretense but a complex and dialectical gesture. For one thing, it is in ways like this that Pater signals his awareness of his own particular historical moment, the proximate source or immediate precursor of his position, and his own critical difference from that precursor. In turning away from the "aim" of objectivity, he does not turn away entirely, and he puts in its place not the subjectivism with which he is continually—and wrongly—associated, but a regulated

10. On the complex relation of Pater to Arnold, see David DeLaura, *Hebrew and Hellene in Victorian England*. On Pater in relation to Arnold's "object," see Richard Ellmann, *The Critic as Artist: Critical Writings of Oscar Wilde* (New York: Vintage, 1968), pp. xi–xii. "There are not two but three critical phases in the late nineteenth century, with Pater transitional between Arnold and Wilde. . . . In 1864 . . . Arnold declared . . . that the 'aim of criticism is to see the object as in itself it really is.' . . . Nine years later Walter Pater [pretended] . . . to agree with Arnold's definition. . . . But Pater's corollary subtly altered the original proposition; it shifted the center of attention from the rock of the object to the winds of the perceiver's sensations. . . . [E]ighteen years later . . . Wilde rounded on Arnold by asserting that the aim of criticism is to see the object as it really is not." Bloom (introduction to Pater's *Selected Writings*, p. viii) repeats this formulation in 1974 and adds: "Between Arnold's self-deception and Wilde's wit comes Pater's hesitant and skeptical emphasis upon a peculiar kind of vision."

process, a method of recreating a provisional objectivity through a dynamic of internalization and discrimination within.

To answer the famous question "What is this . . . to *me*?" is not Pater's final "aim," after all, but only the "first step" in a dialectical model of self-consciousness, whose aim is finally to discriminate the object again by analyzing its "influence" within the aesthetic critic:

> The function of the aesthetic critic is to distinguish, analyze, and separate from its adjuncts, the virtue by which a picture, a landscape, a fair personality in life or in a book, produces this special impression of beauty or pleasure, to indicate what the source of that impression is, and under what conditions it is experienced. His end is reached when he has disengaged that virtue, and noted it, as a chemist notes some natural element. (R, ix–x)

Those "adjuncts" are partly in the object and partly in its context, which is, in this frame of reference, the mind of the observer. The "disengagement" of the object's "power" or "virtue" is a second-order process: first the aesthetic object must be distinguished from its context in the self—through its "impression" and the way that pressing force shifts the internal shape of things—and only then can one quality of the object be distinguished from another. And if the experiences of its effects on the subject are the "original facts" or "primary data," then the knowledge of the object would be a "secondary" result of this analysis. This process of "disengagement" is modeled here on the process of chemical analysis, and that explicit analogy tacitly assigns to the aesthetic critic the function of answering the "analysis" of one science with a scientific analysis of his own.

This line of thought suggests that Pater's particular "impressionism" should be more rigorously identified as a late romantic model of the correlation of poetic imagination, science, and philosophy. Above all, his impressionism must be understood in the plastic sense of "impression," for it represents a mode of renewed belief in the possibility of internalizing the experience of real objects from a real outside.[11] (One result of this reconstituted and aesthetic "objectivity" may be

---

11. The best discussion of critical impressionism in its Swinburnean sense may be found in Jerome J. McGann, *Swinburne: An Experiment in Criticism* (Chicago: University of Chicago Press, 1972), pp. 14–23. Pater's style is deeply influenced by Swinburne throughout, and he does of course engage in famous passages of this sort of impressionism—for example, in his reading of the Mona Lisa. But as Wellek pointed out, these passages are rare in Pater and are not representative of his method (René Wellek, *The History of Modern Criticism: 1750–1950*, vol. 4: *The Later Nineteenth Century* [New Haven, Conn.: Yale University Press, 1965], p. 382).

seen in a related shift in the notion of "content." Though objects are still called "receptacles," they contain not "content" but the "powers or forces" of "influence."[12] Impressed with an object from the outside, the critical consciousness then scrutinizes itself for the "influence" of the object on its own "modified" configurations. Pater will use a wide range of figures for this relation, especially figures of backgrounding and foregrounding, in which the object is figuratively cast into "relief" against the background of an experiencing or observant subject.

Aesthetic "objectivity" remains provisional. It is always to be regarded as figurative, not "given" by the object as data but "made" from the object's effect on the subject, not absolute but relative, and continually in the process of being reconstituted through this dialectic of identification and detachment. By asking the crucial question—"what does it mean to *me*?"—an aesthetic, analytical, observant aspect of the subject differentiates itself from the receptive, vulnerable, "impressed" aspect of the subject laboring in the toils of experience. At any given moment, in other words, the aesthetic stance of self-division stops the uncontrolled "flux" with a sense of fixated attention. And, as we have seen, this very activity also seems to reduce the experience of time to fragments, isolated moments "with no before and after," as T. S. Eliot would later complain. However, when this same stance is mobilized in time, figured in temporal terms, it gains an operational value of another kind, for the aesthetic method is not only a method of positioning attention in such a way as to recreate the object. In Pater the romantic "ecstasy" of self-division also establishes an instrumental position from which an organized and totalized sense of the experiencing consciousness may be restored. The aesthetic, "critical" division within the subject is mobilized in time so that it may precipitate the sense of continuous identity, the sense of "self."

How does this work? With each self-conscious move "outside" or "beyond" itself, the subject establishes a still point, a present moment from which the "passage" of experience will then be regarded in the past. In other words, the gap constructed between one part of the self and another is refigured as the space of difference between present and past. By the time it is discriminated from the subject and perceivable as an object again, the object has already been reconceived, reconstituted, remembered. Analogously, that aspect of the subject which had been "impressed" has now been reformed; the "impression" records a for-

---

12. Crinkley points out that the notion of the object in "eternal outline" gives way to the notion of the object as "receptacle." See Richmond Crinkley, *Walter Pater: Humanist* (Lexington: University of Kentucky Press, 1970), p. 9.

mer state of being, now remembered. Mobilized in time, as one moment of self-division succeeds another, the aesthetic position becomes the federating power of memory. In the mobility of these recreative self-divisions, both object and self are correlatively reconstituted as distinct and whole—but in the past and *as* the past.

The interrelated dynamics of attention I have been discussing as the method of Pater's aestheticism—both the dynamic of mobility and fixation (figured as the passage punctuated by moments of focus) and the dynamic of romantic self-division (figured as "impression" followed by detachment or "ecstasy")—reconstitute the self in relation to its objects as a function of retrospection. It should be possible now to see the conservative force of Pater's aestheticism—and to begin an approach to his historicism. When cast in temporal terms, these dynamics of attention project the "passages" of experience into an ideal, overarching continuity of attention, a personal identity in time. Put another way, Pater uses the language of temporality to recontain the self as a whole. Perhaps it is clear that these operations yield not the "substratum" Pater wanted to intuit from Kant, but rather a decentered, "outer" layer of awareness always in the process of reforming. Describing Goethe as the type of his aesthetic attitude, Pater wrote that "such natures rejoice to be away from and past their former selves" (R, 229). That "former" self is also the "formed" self, from whom the reforming self, in its continually reconstructed present moment, continually flees away.

Nevertheless, though Pater theorizes this decentering flight into an absolute present, he does so from within the traditional commitment to a central self. In fact, he finally does so in order to conserve its centrality and wholeness in a sense of history or continuity.[13] Surely this is one reason that Pater should be reexamined in our current critical moment. In an effort to preserve its wholeness, this aesthetically or critically divided self is continually in the process of projecting a transcendent identity to oversee its own passages of experience. That the metaphysical implications of this projection are undergoing a rigorous critique today should make Pater more, not less, interesting to us.[14] Pater is explicitly aware of his aesthetic projection of identity—

---

13. For a discussion of the conflict between modernity and the concept of history, see Paul de Man, "Literary History and Literary Modernity," in his *Blindness and Insight: Essays in the Rhetoric of Contemporary Criticism* (1971; reprint, Minneapolis: University of Minnesota Press, 1983), pp. 142–65.

14. The names Foucault and Derrida will suffice to indicate the broad outlines of that critique, but I mean specifically to call attention here to their stress on the correlative projections of the unitary subject and of an overarching history. Thus Foucault, in *The Archaeology of Knowledge*, trans. A. M. Sheridan Smith (New York:

Aestheticism · 37 ·

as I shall show in discussing *Marius the Epicurean*—and aware also that the projection of an overarching history is its necessary corollary. Throughout his work, Pater employs a transformed, secularized version of Bunyan's "House Beautiful" as an image of the transcendent place where disparate moments of individual and cultural time are gathered together and restored. Of course, this end point, the result of Pater's aesthetic dialectic, is Hegelian and sublationary—as is so much of Pater, including all the formal techniques explored in this brief section: his dialectical transvaluation of metaphor, the subsumption of distinct moments in their "passage," the notion of memory as the overarching re-collection of successive moments of self-division.

Pater's attempt to reread the figurative "distance" of self-consciousness as a difference between present and past should remind us that in the nineteenth century the notion of scientific objectivity was often conceived as historical distance. It is within the historical realm that the already-made thing, the work of art, becomes the exemplary instance of Pater's aesthetic solution. As the quintessential relic from the past, the work of art is effective *because* it is definitively and already "different" from the self in the present. Before turning to the historical dimension of Pater's method, however, I want to conclude the discussion of his aestheticism by asking how these strategies of self-consciousness are registered on the level of his style.

## 4 · Answerable Style

How does Pater's aestheticism present itself as an ironic, synthetic, and revisionary discourse? If his aestheticism was meant as a response to modern thought, how might the "style" of the prose (that is, its

---

Pantheon, 1972), p. 12: "Continuous history is the indispensable correlative of the founding function of the subject: the guarantee that everything that has eluded him may be restored to him; the certainty that time will disperse nothing without restoring it in a reconstituted unity; the promise that one day the subject—in the form of historical consciousness—will once again be able to appropriate, to bring back under his sway, all those things that are kept at a distance by difference, and find in them what might be called his abode. Making historical analysis the discourse of the continuous and making human consciousness the original subject of all historical development and all action are the two sides of the same system of thought." Derrida makes a similar argument toward the end of his "Structure, Sign, and Play in the Discourse of the Human Sciences," in *Writing and Difference*, trans. Alan Bass (Chicago: University of Chicago Press, 1978), p. 291: "It could be shown that the concept of *epistēmē* has always called forth that of *historia*, if history is always the unity of a becoming, as the tradition of truth or the development of science or knowledge oriented toward the appropriation of truth in presence and self-presence, toward knowledge in consciousness-of-self."

particular rhetorical strategies) be seen as an "answerable style"? Several features of the Paterian text display the formal strategies of self-consciousness—the rhythms of "impression" and "disengagement," mobility and fixation, experience and retrospection—that we have just been examining. In fact, Pater ends his representation of "modern thought," and turns to begin his own conclusions, with the wistful image of the self as text:

> It is with this movement, with the passage and dissolution of impressions, images, sensations, that analysis leaves off—that continual vanishing away, that strange, perpetual weaving and unweaving of ourselves. (R, 236)

Still a part of Pater's representation of "modern thought," the "passage" here refers to the stream of impressions passing uncontrolled through the mind and to the self dying and passing away, but the image of "that strange, perpetual weaving and unweaving of ourselves" hints too at the correlative, creative power which, as we have seen, is the key to Pater's theory of aestheticism. The problematized notion of a stable, unified self will be replaced not by dissolution but by a rhythm of dispersal and gathering, and Pater's analogy between self and text here suggests his powerful redefinition of the "passage" as a model of that rhythm, represented in the passages of language itself.

When, at the end of paragraph two, we read that "analysis leaves off," those words remind us of Pater's rhetorical strategy: not "Walter Pater" *in propria persona*, but the hypostatized, just-barely-personified figure of "analysis" had been conducting that train of thought. Pater "disengages" after having "identified" himself with "the tendency of modern thought," and then, at the beginning of paragraph three, he turns toward his theory of aestheticism in an unusual way. He quotes, in German, a passage from Novalis, and then loosely translates it:

> *Philosophiren,* says Novalis, *ist dephlegmatisiren vivificiren.* The service of philosophy, of speculative culture, toward the human spirit is to rouse, to startle it into sharp and eager observation. Every moment some form grows perfect in hand or face; some tone on the hills or the sea is choicer than the rest; some mood of passion or insight or intellectual excitement is irresistibly real and attractive for us,—for that moment only. Not the fruit of experience, but experience itself, is the end. (R, 236)

By the end of this passage we are securely within the representation of Pater's own discourse, but it is worth remarking just how we got there. Even before the explicit contextualizing tag ("says Novalis"), the italicized opacity of the word *Philosophiren* establishes a new position. It is recognizable, cognate in English, but still defamiliarized, projected into another voice, language, and national culture—in fact, a language and culture that is particularly associated with modern philosophy. As Pater translates the motto from Novalis into English, he also subtly interprets it, translating it closer to "himself," appropriating it to his own particular rhetorical context even as he moves closer and closer toward the representation of his own voice.

The quoted words of Novalis operate as a hinge, a pivot-point around which the essay turns in a new direction. The implicit sense of this turn around Novalis would go something like this: "But we should not use philosophy to analyze, annihilate, and 'unweave' the self. On the contrary, as Novalis says, philosophy has a function or 'service,' to rouse the human spirit, to startle and bring it to life." But this is not exactly what "Novalis says." Pater has generalized and extended his words quite a bit, as well as taken them out of context.[1] "To rouse" is a good translation of *dephlegmatisiren*, as if philosophy could stir the phlegmatic spirit into mobility, energy, a livelier mood. But *Philosophiren ist dephlegmatisiren vivificiren* might be more literally rendered as "To philosophize is to unclog, to enliven." Pater seems to associate the clogged or phlegmatic spirit with philosophical abstraction, and I hear in his use of Novalis a prophetic hint of the "quickened, multiplied consciousness" that is the end of this essay on aesthetic method. Indeed, a phlegmatic, "clogged" homogeneity is soon to be broken apart and reformed in the mobile discourse of aestheticism. Certainly in the simplest thematic sense, Pater "quickens" and enlivens the essay by turning it away from modern forms of death and moving it in a new direction.

As it turns in a new direction, the essay also takes a retrospective stance toward what has gone before. Just as "analysis leaves off" and the answering discourse of aestheticism begins, the quotation from Novalis serves as a fixed point from which the essay looks both before and after. Retrospectively understood, this rhetorical turn involves the revision of a discipline of thought: what we thought was philosophy turns out not to be "true" philosophy after all. Highlighted in

---

1. Inman shows that Pater takes both the quote from Novalis and the later quote from Hugo out of context ("The Intellectual Context of Walter Pater's 'Conclusion,'" pp. 21, 25–26; see also Inman, *Walter Pater's Reading*, pp. 184–86).

German for a moment at the verge of the new paragraph, and framed by the two words in English ("says Novalis"), the word *Philosophiren* conjures an abstract, totalized, and semipersonified "Philosophy." The rhetorical turn taken here uses that generalized force not to repudiate but to redefine "Philosophy," as Pater disowns what had been called "analysis" and identifies with another, specifically aesthetic characterization. The new position taken toward philosophy has been "translated" through Novalis. His words have served somehow as an intermediate point between "modern thought" and Pater's own.

Pater now adopts a functional definition of philosophy, deciding how it should "serve" the human spirit, not what "truths" it might feel itself to "possess."[2] Philosophy should yield "instruments of criticism" or "points of view":

> What we have to do is to be forever curiously testing new opinions and courting new impressions, never acquiescing in a facile orthodoxy of Comte, or of Hegel, or of our own. Philosophical theories or ideas, as points of view, instruments of criticism, may help us to gather up what might otherwise pass unregarded by us. (R, 237)

Here the resistance to Comte or Hegel recapitulates in small the larger movement of the "Conclusion" as it turns away from extremes both of positivism and subjectivism. But it is significant that Pater resists resting in any "facile orthodoxy" even "of our own," for the goal of primary importance is to keep the spirit moving. No view, no opinion, no idea should be conceived as a thing to "have" or "hold" for long. General theories can serve as nets to catch and gather what otherwise might slip through our grasp as it passes, but the "end" of their use is their yield in terms of concrete, particular experience, not their content in and of itself. As instruments specifically of "criticism" (from the Greek "to separate"), theories or ideas will serve as tools to differentiate between one thing and another:

> In a sense it might even be said that our failure is to form habits: for . . . it is only the roughness of the eye that makes any two persons, things, situations, seem alike. (R, 236–37)

---

2. Pater's biting challenge to "philosophy" for thinking it could "possess" truth occurs in the excised paragraph that originally introduced the "Conclusion" (Hill's notes, p. 272). See above, Part One, sec. 3, n. 3, for the passage.

A philosophical theory, then, may be used as an instrumental principle of difference or, in the case of Novalis's little motto about philosophy, as a performative aid to disengagement, like a lever that opens up a "critical" distance and literally turns the essay around.

To understand more about the way Pater uses bits of philosophy as "instruments of criticism," I want to emphasize, in addition to the argumentative value of their content, the material, textual effect of quoted words from another writer and another language. The words perform a disengagement as well as signifying one; they mark a dividing-place, a transition as a translation across to a new position, in this case outside or beyond the claustrophobic discourse of modern thought. They visibly establish a new position and also a new *kind* of position, for the very notion of a "position" has been redefined in aestheticism as a stance rather than a stand. The sense of held beliefs has yielded to the sense of places strategically taken in order to get a critical distance or perspective. Likewise, the notion of "views" as opinions or ideas has yielded to a perspectival sense of viewpoints, or points of vantage.

This shift to regard theories or ideas functionally or instrumentally reflects again the crisis I mentioned in the notion of "content," which is no longer something "held" in the mind but something that passes through it. Pater's early essays are full of petulant, witty endorsements of what one might call an anti-idealist theory of ideas.[3] This difficult and often contradictory reworking of the notion of content is perhaps the most refined—or even rarefied—instance of the aesthetic turn away from the utilitarian, practical evaluation of experience. (And we would want to note here the revisionary imitation of the utilitarian, as a part of that turn away: since, according to the aesthetic point of view, nothing should be valued because of its practical use, this functional approach to ideas appears as a subtle revision of the notion of utility itself.[4]) The polemical rallying cry to "art for art's sake" highlights this aesthetic goal of divesting the aesthetic of its duties toward society, religion, or practical utility.[5] And though it may be

---

3. "Plato, as we remember him, a true humanist, holds his theories lightly, glances with a somewhat blithe and naive inconsequence from one view to another, not anticipating the burden of importance 'views' will one day have for men" (A, 69–70). "There is a violence, an impossibility about men who have ideas, which makes one suspect they could never be the type of any widespread life" (MS, 254).

4. In his excellent study, McGrath discusses Pater's "functionalism" in a chapter instructively titled "Pragmatic Idealism." See F. C. McGrath, *The Sensible Spirit: Walter Pater and the Modernist Paradigm* (Tampa: University of South Florida Press, 1986), pp. 140–63.

5. On this signal phrase, see L. M. Findlay, "The Introduction of the Phrase 'Art for Art's Sake' into English," *Notes and Queries*, n.s. 20 (July 1973), 248; and Hill's

difficult, it is not impossible to imagine what it would mean for art also "to get rid of its responsibilities to its subject," to become a matter of pure form (R, 138). When Pater writes in his essay on Giorgione that "*all art constantly aspires towards the condition of music*," one thing he has in mind is this perfect assimilation of content into form (R, 135).

But musical form—or the "play" of light or water, analogous examples also from "The School of Giorgione"—is crucially defined not as objective structure or even rudimentary reference, but as sheer movement or passage in time. In terms of experience, or "life in the spirit of art," the adjustment of form to content is somewhat more difficult. Here art itself is instrumental in lending "the highest quality to your moments as they pass, and simply for those moments' sake." Here again, content—and similarly, belief—is refused in favor of aesthetic "passage"; the "end" of experience is further experience, not a certain content that can be internalized as a possession. In attempting to find a place for ideas in aestheticism, Pater shifts them away from being valued as content and toward being valued as part of temporal form. No conclusions should be conclusive; no conclusions should be held for long, not even "our own."

It is evident that Pater's recharacterization of philosophy at the beginning of paragraph three is related to the transvaluation of scientific objectivity we have already observed in Pater's "Preface." In both cases, Pater translates a whole modern discourse into a new context, an ironic, self-differentiated whole that then seems "higher" or "larger" by virtue of the inclusion and revision of subordinated parts. With a technique like the "anti-metaphysical metaphysic" that he later writes into Marius's character, Pater turns both philosophy and science against themselves, not to obliterate them but to subsume them within another discourse, the ironic, synthetic, and self-consciously revisionary discourse of aestheticism.[6]

To call attention to Pater's frequent practice of characterizing disciplines of thought as generalized wholes, I have consistently been using the word "discourse" to refer to Pater's representations of modern science and philosophy. This is a representational technique and should be appreciated as such.[7] Several important studies show that

---

notes, pp. 457–58. Pater was variously influenced in the doctrine of "art for art's sake" by Gautier and Swinburne (above all), Baudelaire, Goethe, and Hegel.

6. ME I, 142.

7. One early critic to have recognized this was Helen Hawthorne Young, in *The Writings of Walter Pater: A Reflection of British Philosophical Opinion from 1860 to 1890* (Lancaster, Pa.: Lancaster Press, 1933), p. 45.

the discourses of science and philosophy from the beginning of the "Conclusion" are both carefully constructed composites.[8] But Pater himself tacitly insists on the constructed nature of both, as we have seen. "Let us begin . . . fix upon it . . . or if we begin"—these rhetorical directions announce the procedures of scientific demonstration and at the same time underscore the hypothetical nature of the argument. The doubled, relativist argument of "modern thought" is of course not "given" but made, itself an aesthetic reconstruction. In hypostatizing, totalizing, composing, and reifying each disciplinary discourse to serve a function within an overarching textual strategy, Pater also historicizes them; by summing them up and subsuming them within the discourse of aestheticism, he also figuratively casts them into the past. His practice of "aesthetic criticism" first identifies with, then differentiates itself from these disciplinary discourses to constitute a synthetic discourse made up of mobile parts.[9] And here, in writing of his "discourse" of aestheticism, I mean again to use the word carefully, for even though the theory of aestheticism is represented as his "own," it is still ostentatiously a "made" thing, a new discourse represented as such.

But the variety of textual strategies I have been examining in this section persistently reminds us not only that Pater's aestheticism is a "made" thing, but also that its novelty is in part a function of its composite form. Aestheticism is a new discourse made up of not-so-new parts, but its construction by means of the ironic sublation of other modern "discourses" is only one of a number of related strategies. The epigraph from Plato represents another, and the direct quotation from Novalis yet another.[10] Pater's critical voice emerges in the texture of these other voices. I am *not* arguing here that Pater's voice is merely a pastiche of other voices; certainly to the extent that I do imply it, I mean to transvalue the notion of "pastiche" so that it may be seen as a positive strategy with its own comprehensive rationale. To avoid confusion, however, I generally use the word "composite" to refer to this set of related techniques. But Pater's critical voice is not only a composite of others. In Pater, intertextuality is highlighted rather than absorbed, and it takes its place as part of his systematic

---

8. See esp. Inman, "The Intellectual Context of Walter Pater's 'Conclusion,' " pp. 12–30; and Hill's notes, pp. 451–56.

9. I respond here to the initial question raised by Ian Small in "Pater's Criticism: Some Distinctions," *Prose Studies* 4 (May 1981), 31–38. Pater derives a large part of his critical power from his own realization that "criticism" cannot be seen as a totalized, unified practice, but must consist of dialectically mobilized parts.

10. And perhaps even misquotation is another. See Christopher Ricks, "Pater, Arnold, and Misquotation," *Times Literary Supplement*, 25 November 1977, p. 1384.

preoccupation with the aesthetics of reception and transmission. I shall say more about this in relation to *Marius the Epicurean*. For now, it is important to see Pater's intertextual strategies always as part of a dynamic, in which a representation of his "own" voice periodically gives way to form the effaced but generative background within and against which these other voices rise and fall.

Pater frequently uses overt quotations from individual, historically identifiable sources to turn his essay away from an abstract passage of argument. Even when he does not name his source—as later in the "Conclusion" the epigrammatic idea from Hugo that "philosophy is the microscope of thought" is offered in quotation marks but without attribution—the effect of the quotation marks remains to separate one represented voice from the overarching passage. By fixing an idea momentarily in the register of a personal voice, he enacts a return from discursive generalization to a more concrete form of argumentation. For a moment, then, Pater's discourse relinquishes itself to the words of another, and when he resumes in his own voice, those other words appear transitional. Through them his essay has been translated into a new position. As in Montaigne, the quotation acts both as a fixed point around which to turn and as a hypothesis in an experimental genre like the "essay," in which judgment may be "suspended" rather than "concluded."[11] And like Montaigne, Pater gestures in these quoted passages toward a notion of received authority which is primarily useful in generating further turns of his own reflective experience. Unlike Montaigne, however, he places the greater emphasis on the process of reception itself; his relation to the authority of the past is tellingly different, though the formal technique is much the same.

The rhetoric of Pater's essay does not remain disengaged long enough for it to be called "factual" or "historical" in style, and yet it is encrusted with data, report, and quotation. Neither does it remain in the "subjective" register long enough to be accurately called a "personal" style, and the use of the first-person "I" is rare indeed. Other essayists whose voices seem particularly "personal" or "subjective" *own* (or own up to) the personal "I,"[12] whereas Pater conveys the sense of personality instead through these fluctuations of identifica-

---

11. "Suspended Judgment" is the title of Pater's chapter on Montaigne in *Gaston de Latour*, pp. 91–115.

12. I am thinking of Montaigne and Lamb, among the critical essayists Pater mentions often. Monsman aptly regards Marius as an "Elian figure" who both reveals and conceals the author, but the case is more difficult in the essays that present no fictional persona. See Gerald Monsman, "On Reading Pater," *Prose Studies* 4 (May 1981), 2.

tion and disengagement. His prose feels haunted, as if the spirits of the dead come out when no one else is home. The sense of a person behind the scenes is often conveyed primarily by the sense of aesthetic choices constantly being made about what the text will take in, represent, and then turn away from. In other words, the sense of a person behind the scenes of his prose is generated in large part as a textual effect.

Like the discourse of aestheticism which asserts itself as "new" by passionately identifying with and then standing back at a critical distance from a collection of relatively old parts, Pater's "voice" as a representation of personal identity is also the result of a sublationary construction. It is useful to see that "strange, perpetual weaving and unweaving of ourselves" as one of Pater's recreative textual effects. As another facet of his answerable style (answering "modern thought" in its own terms), he surrenders to the dissolution of "unweaving" before restoring the structure of compositional "weaving." Here—in the self-effacement of his "own" voice, in the textual dissolution he admits before reasserting structure—he is at his most radical and modern. His gestures of "recontainment" stabilize the prose momentarily, taking a retrospective position toward what has gone before and asserting the sense of an overarching personal identity, but strategies of stability always yield again to mobility, displacement, and the effect of temporality.

In another sense, however, Pater's strategies of voice are quintessentially romantic and lyrical. Like Shelley's passion of inspired instrumentality in the service of a higher power ("not I but the wind that blows through me!") or Wordsworth's genial sense of an internal, "correspondent breeze," Pater opens his prose to the forces of the other. But Pater makes himself the Aeolian lyre not of the "naked and sleeping beauty" of transcendent forms, nor of the conjugal reciprocity between the mind and nature, but of the historical past of his own culture. In fact, his strategy of quotation should be seen in part as a lyric dynamic of apostrophe and prosopopoeia, calling upon and taking on the voice of the other, as a way of reflexively generating the power of poetically original voice for one's own work.[13]

In this sense, Pater's pivotal use of Novalis amounts to a subdued lyric cry: "O Novalis, lend me your power for a moment, that I might

---

13. See Paul de Man, "Autobiography as De-facement," *Modern Language Notes* 94 (1979), 919–30; and Jonathan Culler, "Apostrophe," in *The Pursuit of Signs* (Ithaca, N.Y.: Cornell University Press, 1981), pp. 135–54.

renew philosophy!" And it may be seen in part as a fundamentally dramatic strategy, like the negative capability of Keats's Shakespeare. Perhaps Pater's prose technique can best be specified as late romantic and post-Victorian by placing it between Browning's dramatic monologues and Wilde's critical dialogues: the one represents the lyric "I" completely inhabited by the voice of a fictive persona, usually from another age and culture; the other represents the "I" divided among different "views" or opinions, each of which is represented by a different personal voice and all of which are reunified only on the level of the work as a whole. Pater's style and strategies of voice arise from his determination to recover a sense of unity that can still be expressed in personal form. And in order to do this, he makes himself a medium to the voices of the dead, a lyre to the winds of change. Pater's prose stages the achievement of modern voice as the medium of historical re-collection.

## 5 · Historicism

The scandal provoked by Pater's manifesto of aestheticism has been well rehearsed.[1] His suppression of the offending "Conclusion" in the second edition, and his eventual reinstatement of it in the third after he had "dealt more fully in *Marius the Epicurean* with the thoughts suggested by it," seem to testify to Pater's deep concern at the charges against his work. As we shall see, the strategy he develops in *Marius* to "deal more fully" with the issues raised by the "Conclusion" is one of painstaking historical inclusiveness. Yet one of the best of the post-"Conclusion" anecdotes suggests that Pater had already achieved that careful sense of self-possession through summing up the entire history of his culture in an individualized yet representative critical voice. That is the story of his scrupulously peevish remark to Edmund Gosse: "I wish they wouldn't call me 'a hedonist'; it produces such a bad effect on the minds of people who don't know Greek."[2]

But when *Studies in the History of the Renaissance* was published in 1873, it was attacked on grounds other than the supposed hedonism

---

1. Excellent discussions may be found in Hill's notes, pp. 443–51; in the introduction to the *Letters of Walter Pater*, ed. Lawrence Evans (Oxford: Clarendon Press, 1970); and in Michael Levey, *The Case of Walter Pater* (Plymouth: Thames and Hudson, 1978), pp. 141–44.
2. Edmund Gosse, *Critical Kit-Kats* (London, 1896), p. 258.

and immorality of its aesthetic "Conclusion." Mrs. Mark Pattison famously charged the volume with not being sufficiently "historical"; in fact, she complained in the *Westminster Review* that Pater's "title is misleading.... The historical element is precisely that which is wanting."[3] Intimidated by this criticism, and perhaps in retrospective agreement with it, Pater changed the title of his study in the second edition. He no longer called the volume *Studies in the History of the Renaissance* but, taking care to deemphasize his claim to be writing history, he retitled it *The Renaissance: Studies in Art and Poetry*. From our point of view in the present, it seems clear that Mrs. Pattison was right, though it is possible to understand Pater's treatment of historical material as a coherent treatment even so. Pater's volume is *not* exactly historical. It is historicist.

In fact, it is precisely Pater's historicism that distinguishes his aestheticism from other versions of aestheticism in English.[4] Peter Allan Dale recently broke new ground in this area by placing Pater in a tradition of English critics concerned with the philosophy of history. Following Carlyle and Arnold, in Dale's study, Pater's work demonstrates what Dale calls his "complete historicism," or historicism "as *Weltanschauung*."[5] My aim in this book is to join the ongoing discussion of Pater's historicism by demonstrating the homology and interdependence of aestheticism and historicism in Pater's formulation—and then to explore the consequences of that relation in several of his major works. We shall then be able to see the extent to which Pater's literary strategies for representing a historical aestheticism—and an aesthetic historicism—in turn have shaped the tradition within which Pater places himself.

---

3. *Westminster Review*, n.s. 43 (April 1873). Mrs. Pattison's remark may be found in Hill's notes, p. 285.
4. This is a widely accepted view. See, e.g., R. V. Johnson, *Aestheticism* (London: Methuen, 1969), pp. 74–75; Wellek, *The Later Nineteenth Century*, esp. pp. 396–99; Bloom, introduction to Pater's *Selected Writings*, pp. xv–xxi; and Inman, *Pater's Reading*, pp. xi, 94–95, 148–57. Johnson asserts that "Pater's historicism distinguishes him from other, more extreme exponents of aestheticism"; Inman finds its source in Renan, who "helped him relax into historicism"; Bloom alludes to Pater's "historicisms" in the plural, mentioning Renaissance, romantic, Christian, and Darwinian variants; Wellek deplores Pater's historicism as "Alexandrian eclecticism" and "historical masquerade" and claims that it "had to be transcended" by Eliot and Malraux.
5. Peter Allan Dale, *The Victorian Critic and the Idea of History* (Cambridge, Mass.: Harvard University Press, 1977), pp. 171–255. Dale prefigures this aspect of my book by suggesting (p. 205) that "the attitude adopted by the complete historicist ... is essentially an *aesthetic* attitude." He suggests "a special kind of conjunction in intellectual history—a conjunction which may also be observed to an extent not only in Dilthey, but in Meinecke, Croce, and Collingwood—between, on the one hand, the tendency toward a complete historicism ... and on the other, the rise of a predominantly

The distinction between "historical" and "historicist" turns on a variant of the figurative "distance" of objectivity we have been contemplating so far. As I have been insisting, the aesthetic strategy of recreating a provisional objectivity crucially depends upon establishing a retrospective stance, even if that stance must be reconstructed moment by moment. To put my point another way: the characteristic stance of romantic self-consciousness serves to divide both the self from itself and the present from a past that can then be regarded at a provisionally objective distance. In the terms of this familiar romantic epistemological strategy, we can begin to see how historical distance comes into play as a form of "scientific" objectivity. Anything regarded in the past can be regarded in the aesthetic attitude as "given," different, and already formed. And as a sort of corollary, works of art acquire a special appeal in part because they seem to represent a hybrid of aesthetic creation and scientific or historical "data"; their obvious status as aesthetically "made" joins with a sense that their historical difference is securely "given." But at the same time, the "given" status of the work of art can be endangered when questions are raised about the ability of the mind in the present to cross the given distance between present and past.

Aestheticism's characteristic rhythm of identification and disengagement becomes especially complicated, and especially effective, when the object under consideration is a historical object. Separating the historical object from its "adjuncts" (as the "Preface" to *The Renaissance* recommends) eventually involves discriminating the particular characteristics of the object from other objects in its own time and place, but the "first step" as usual involves disengaging or differentiating the object from the sensibility of the observer in the present moment. Only after this dialectic of perception and detachment does the observer become an "aesthetic critic."

In all of his works, Pater attempts to represent historical objects and developments while simultaneously reflecting on the principles and difficulties of historical representation. Though he is known primarily for the closeness of his view, it is actually the intricate shifts between identification and disengagement that characterize the special power of his "imaginative sense of fact."⁶ His distinction in the

---

aesthetic interpretation of life, which stands at the threshold of and points toward distinctly modernist concerns."

6. The phrase is Pater's, from his 1888 essay "Style" (A, 8). In discussing "certain qualities of all literature as fine art," Pater strategically sets aside the distinctions between poetry and prose and between the "literature of fact" and the "literature of the imaginative sense of fact." Recently the latter phrase was chosen as the title of a special issue of *Prose Studies* devoted to Pater (ed. Philip Dodd, vol. 4, May 1981).

English critical tradition owes a great deal to this mobility, to the sheer variety of his poised positions and slippages along a double spectrum of possible identifications and disengagements in relation to an object, both within the context of his own present moment and across the space of historical difference. And it is this strategically historical self-consciousness that keeps his criticism from becoming a simple subjectivism, much less the solipsism he ironically portrays in the "Conclusion."

Pater was concerned with the difficulties of historical knowledge and representation from the very beginning of his career. For example, in a discussion which begins his first published essay (on Coleridge, in 1866), Pater draws a sharp distinction between modern thought and ancient:

> Modern thought is distinguished from ancient by its cultivation of the "relative" spirit in place of the "absolute." Ancient philosophy sought to arrest every object in an eternal outline, to fix thought . . . in a classification by "kinds," or *genera*. To the modern spirit nothing is, or can be rightly known, except relatively and under conditions. (A, 66)

We have already examined one of Pater's many efforts to characterize modern thought, and we should note that here the effort to distinguish modern from another, different and "ancient" mode of thought is a more particularly historical strategy than that adopted in the "Conclusion." Pater continues in a familiar vein. This philosophical conception of the "relative," he goes on to say, has developed in the modern age under the influence of the sciences of observation:

> Those sciences reveal types of life evanescing into each other by inexpressible refinements of change. Things pass into their opposites by accumulation of undefinable quantities . . . . The faculty for truth is recognised as a power of distinguishing and fixing delicate and fugitive detail. The moral world is ever in contact with the physical, and the relative spirit has invaded moral philosophy from the ground of the inductive sciences. (A, 66–67)

I have already remarked the difficult and ingeniously ironic absorption of scientific method by Pater's aestheticism; here we can begin to see the other dimension of his late romanticism—his historicism—responding to modern science and philosophy as well. But here Pater alludes to the science of biology, which is metaphorically as available to the discussion of history as chemistry is, in the "Preface," to the discussion of "elements" and their aesthetically fused "combinations."

As a discipline, evolutionary biology joins the consideration of the individual organism and its history with a consideration of generalized "types" of organisms and their histories. In the passage above, Pater concentrates on the enormous difficulty of distinguishing one object from another when this distinction must be made diachronically as well as synchronically. How is it possible to discriminate the object, when each "type" is constantly "evanescing" into another? And how is it possible to know what is related to what in time, when those relations follow "inexpressible" and "undefinable" routes? These changes in time seem invisible and "inexpressible" while they are happening, apparent only *after* they have been accomplished. In other words, historical change can be perceived only after the fact, and then it might easily be misread.

Pater's tacitly romantic equation of a historical culture with a living organism will produce some interesting results when he attempts to construct models of cultural history. But for now let us simply formulate the difficulty of the double relativity Pater is describing here. Diachronically, any object is related to the past through "undefinable" connections; synchronically the object is inextricable from its own historical context. Here is Pater's discussion of these related problems:

> Man's physical organism is played upon not only by the physical conditions about it, but by remote laws of inheritance, the vibration of long-past acts reaching him in the midst of the new order of things in which he lives. When we have estimated these conditions he is still not yet simple and isolated; for the mind of the race, the character of the age, sway him this way or that through the medium of language and current ideas. It seems as if the most opposite statements about him were alike true: he is so receptive, all the influences of nature and of society ceaselessly playing upon him, so that every hour in his life is unique, changed altogether by a stray word, or glance, or touch. It is the truth of these relations that experience gives us, not the truth of eternal outlines ascertained once for all, but a world of fine gradations and subtly linked conditions, shifting intricately as we ourselves change—and bids us, by a constant clearing of the organs of observation and perfecting of analysis, to make what we can of these. (A, 67–68)

The difficulty of distinguishing a "simple and isolated" object seems even greater here than in the "Preface," for here the object must be separated from "adjuncts" both in its present and in its past. By the end of the passage, "he" has blended into "we," with both object and subject in constant motion—not parallel but correlative motion, for "we ourselves change" as a result of the "influence" of objects. Because "external conditions," too, are "shifting intricately as we ourselves change," motion is perpetuated on several levels at once.

But Pater's modernist motto from the essay on Coleridge—"To the modern spirit nothing is, or can be rightly known, except relatively and under conditions"—does not mean that nothing can be rightly known. Rather, it expresses the recognition that a new "faculty for truth" must be employed if it is to operate within a field of relations so fluid and almost inconceivably complex. Otherwise, the very sensitivity to these "inexpressible refinements of change" could prevent the perception of form altogether. But Pater's motto also expresses the faith that a newer canon of "truth" than the scientific or verifiable truth of positive knowledge will emerge. If every hour these relations shift and must be "estimated" anew, the new "faculty for truth" is distinctly an aesthetic faculty. The new "truth . . . that experience gives us" is decidedly not the truth of the absolute or the "given," but the relative truth of the "made" thing. The "ancient" object had definitive "outlines" that separated it from its surroundings with unproblematic clarity, but in this essay (as in the "Conclusion") the modern object has been redefined as object and subject together, and the demarcating "outlines" must be redrawn internally, provisionally, figuratively. Here again, objective truth is for Pater succeeded not by radical subjectivism but by the painstakingly constructed "truth of relations."[7]

At the very beginning of the same theoretical "Preface" in which he explains the aesthetic dynamic of identification and disengagement by revising Arnold's famous desire to see the object "as in itself it really is," Pater also differentiates himself from his other major precursor. He tacitly revises Ruskin by insisting on fundamentally historicist principles of aesthetic evaluation:

> Beauty, like all other qualities presented to human experience, is relative; and the definition of it becomes unmeaning and useless in proportion to its abstractness. To define beauty, not in the most abstract, but in the most concrete terms possible, to find not its universal formula, but the formula which expresses most adequately this or that special manifestation of it, is the aim of the true student of aesthetics. (R, vii–viii)

---

7. Pater seems to have been influenced in his developing idea of the "truth of relations" by John Stuart Mill's 1865 discussion of relativity in *An Examination of Sir William Hamilton's Philosophy*. See Dale's discussion in *The Victorian Critic and the Idea of History*, pp. 174–79.

At first this seems to be a polemic in favor of the concrete particular as against philosophical abstraction, another of Pater's arguments for aestheticism as an antiphilosophical philosophy.[8] But his polemic here must be appreciated as a plea for a particular kind of particularity—for a sense of historicity, a heightened sense of historical difference and concreteness.

Later in the "Preface" he makes this quite clear, and it is important to see the later statement as another thread in Pater's reweaving of Ruskin. Because all periods produce different forms of beauty, he argues, the important thing for the aesthetic critic to convey is the historical particularity of each form:

> He will remember always that beauty exists in many forms. To him all periods, types, schools of taste, are in themselves equal. In all ages there have been some excellent workmen, and some excellent work done. The question he asks is always:—In whom did the stir, the genius, the sentiment of the period find itself? where was the receptacle of its refinement, its elevation, its taste? (R, x)

This passage also highlights one of Pater's prime strategies for generating a sense of historical particularity. He "characterizes" an age by personalizing it, literally choosing a character whom he invests with representative value. He then makes that individual—who is often but not always an artist—represent the general culture of his age. As in this passage, the ultimate point of such a strategy is to discover the irreducible individuality of the historical period, with its "spirit," but the means toward this spiritual end must be the visible and concrete evidence of the documents, legends, and works of art from the period.

The idea that the work or the life history of an individual artist or writer could represent the spirit of an age has all the force of a grand tautology, and it is historicizable itself as a particularly nineteenth-century representational strategy related to literary realism. This strategy uses one historical individual to stand for another, invisible, collective—but still historically particular—individual, the "spirit of the age," or *Zeitgeist*. In this mode of representation, the generalization of a particular case is meant to convey the particularity of a general case.

---

8. Hill points out (Hill's notes, p. 294) that while this opening gesture would be recognized by most contemporary readers as a response to Ruskin, Pater was also responding to the abstraction of German aesthetic philosophy. His response was double, because he speaks against their abstraction in the same passage in which he reveals his understanding of their historicism. In addition to Hegel, Inman mentions Sainte-Beuve in this respect (*Pater's Reading*, p. 274).

If the "truth of relations" is doubly problematic—both because of the object's relation to the subject and because of its relation to other objects in its historical context—then Pater addresses the first of these problems by revising Arnold, and the second by revising Ruskin. In other words, Pater's aesthetic historicism is established through the act of historicizing his own chief influences. Pater makes his own place in the English critical tradition by taking a perspective on Ruskin and Arnold. By assuming this critical distance with respect to his own most powerful contemporary influences, he figuratively casts them further into the past. By subsuming their positions in his own and differentiating himself from them, he establishes his voice as more comprehensive, diversified, and therefore modern. He asserts his own critical identity, then, by opening a space of difference that is at once aesthetic and historicist.

Pater's aestheticism and his historicism deal with the same tangle of relations in an attempt to establish the modern "truth of relations." His aestheticism acknowledges the mind's shaping activity in even the simplest perception of "isolated" form, but his consistent historicism adds another dimension to the difficulty—and to the possibility—of telling the "truth of relations." Each method is involved in two strategic efforts: the effort to separate the present moment from the past, and the effort to separate the object of perception from its context in the present viewer. Whether the object of regard is understood to be in the present or in the past, the same dual effort is needed, to distinguish it from other contemporary and past objects and from its ground of knowledge in the present.

Historicism, then, like aestheticism (as the suffix again implies) is a systematic attitude of self-consciousness, a point of view or perspective proposing itself as a consistent, coherent method. This particular "ism" takes a reflective stance toward the constitution of historical knowledge. It names a mode, or stage, of historical consciousness in which one inquires about a thing in the past and at the same time questions the procedures of that inquiry and the meaning of its results.[9] Pater's modernist motto from the essay on Coleridge offers us

---

9. The word gained widespread use in the twentieth century, but it dates from the mid- to late-nineteenth century. Dale gives an 1895 use in which Lord Acton argues before a Cambridge audience that all things are subjected to "that influence for which the depressing names historicism and historical mindedness have been devised" (*The Victorian Critic and the Idea of History*, p. 3). See also Raymond Williams, "History," in *Keywords: A Vocabulary of Culture and Society*, rev. 2d ed. (New York: Oxford University Press, 1983), pp. 146–48; and Hayden White, "Romanticism, Historicism, and Realism: Toward a Period Concept for Early Nineteenth-Century Intellectual History," in White, ed., *The Uses of History* (Detroit, Mich.: Wayne State University Press, 1968), pp. 45–58.

a way into the subject both of historicism in general and of Pater's own version of it. For when Pater's "modern spirit" enters the field of historical inquiry, that spirit becomes the spirit of historicism, searching out the way historical phenomena may be "rightly known"—that is, "relatively, and under conditions."

To "know" an object historically involves in the first place the effort to conceptualize it within the conditions of its own milieu in the past, to learn the circumstances of its growth or production in order to understand what it meant in its original time and place. This strategy of mentally replacing an object under the conditions of its own time and place is the foundation of historicist thinking. And initially, the strategy yields a sharper sense of historicity, an intensified awareness of the object's particular reality, a feel for historical difference. Allied to empirical observation in any other scientific field, contextual researches of this sort express one aim of history-as-science.

But the other aim of a science of history is to achieve in its way the standard of repeatability, to discover, by generalizing from its data, the laws that govern historical development.[10] When such efforts to find "covering laws" attempt to test their results, they may seem to be involved in an attempt to predict the future, and Popper's critique of the "poverty of historicism" especially focuses on this particular extension of the method.[11] Moreover, if the historicist attempt to formulate covering laws also aims to interpret the meaning of those laws and the patterns of historical development they generate, the science of history modulates into a philosophy of history. In this zone of disciplinary interfiliation, scientific repeatability hovers close to mythic repetition. But the important point for us here is that "historicism" comprehends this entire range or spectrum of attitudes toward historical knowledge. The objects of knowledge range from factual data to generalized laws, from the particular reality of a time and place to the patterns of historical change over time and across space. In this full range of its senses, "historicism" is close in meaning to "history" as such, but with an intensified consciousness of its aims and operations.

On the other hand, if "historicism" is a mode of knowing historically, it also is a mode of not knowing; for the term also refers to a

---

10. The classic statement is by Carl G. Hempel, "The Function of General Laws in History," *Journal of Philosophy* 39 (January 1942), 35–48. On the virtues and problems of historical thinking in terms of covering laws, see Maurice Mandelbaum, "The Problem of 'Covering Laws,' " in Patrick Gardiner, ed., *The Philosophy of History* (Oxford: Oxford University Press, 1974), pp. 51–65.

11. Karl Popper, *The Poverty of Historicism* (Boston and London: Beacon Press, 1957).

range of skeptical attitudes toward the very possibility of historical knowledge itself. Like his aestheticism, which is proposed against the radical threats enacted in the second paragraph of the "Conclusion," Pater's historicism acknowledges a subjectivist skepticism about the very possibility of historical knowledge, and then goes on to resist that radical skepticism with a more moderate and regulated one.

The principle of placing each object under the "conditions" of its particular age begins as a strategy for knowing each thing "as in itself it really was"—"*wie es eigentlich gewesen*," in Ranke's famous phrase.[12] But that same principle tends uncannily to displace the very object of its research. The more one knows of its context, the more detail one accumulates, the less the object itself stands out; it begins to seem inseparable from the conditions of its age, contextually entangled and difficult to tease out. At first so positive an undertaking, the attempt to know a thing "relatively, and under conditions" seems finally to yield only a highly conditional sort of knowledge.

And there is a further problem. If the object in its own time can seem to disappear into its context, seen from an explicitly acknowledged perspective in the present it may likewise seem to disappear into the knowing subject. In historical inquiry, the "conditions" under which a thing must be seen in order to be "rightly known" are conditions both of the thing and of the knower: conditions of the object in the past, but also conditions of the individual perceiving mind in a particular culture at a particular time in the present. When we turn to the historical context in which the subject is entangled, we find the epistemological problem of subjectivity writ large. Analogous to solipsism but projected on the collective level, the threat of cultural relativism puts the very possibility of historical knowledge in question. To what extent are we limited in our efforts to understand another time or place by the assumptions of our own culture? To what extent do we project our historically specific categories onto the past, thus effacing its difference? Does the attempt to formulate generalizations inevitably lead to this violation? If the difference between cultures cannot be bridged somehow, the difference that makes for "history" in the first place may also make knowledge of it inaccessible.

Can we know the past? "Historicism" has been employed on opposite sides of this question, and each side of the question offers a complex

---

12. According to Inman (*Walter Pater's Reading*, p. 228), Pater read some Ranke, but my point here has to do not with Pater's knowledge of Ranke but with the similarity of Ranke's position to Arnold's. In response to positions like Arnold's and Ranke's, Mill's *Examination of Hamilton's Philosophy* argued very clearly—in an empiricist rather than an idealist context—that an object cannot be known "in itself."

range of positions. The word has been used alike to express "the exaggerated belief that the study of history can recreate actuality or the opposite view that historical knowledge is impossible."[13] Today, using the word to indicate either of those extreme positions is a reductive move, a failure to appreciate the complexity of the concept. The unthinking equation of historicism with radical relativism has prevented a proper appreciation of the method in our day, as surely as Popper's critique of historicism did in its day. Throughout the history of its use, "historicism" has always been a "struggle-concept,"[14] and its contradictory implications are a fundamental part of its full definition.

In other words, the contradiction between belief in, and skepticism toward, the possibility of historical knowledge lies at the very heart of historicism. In effect, it spans that contradiction, recasting it as a dialectical doubleness. The supple mobility of historicism as a method depends on the fact that it does not answer the problems of historical knowledge with an either/or response. Its method is rather to link opposite perspectives and to move between them, allowing each a continual modification of the other. The double dialectic I have been describing might usefully be represented in schematic form, as in Figure 1.

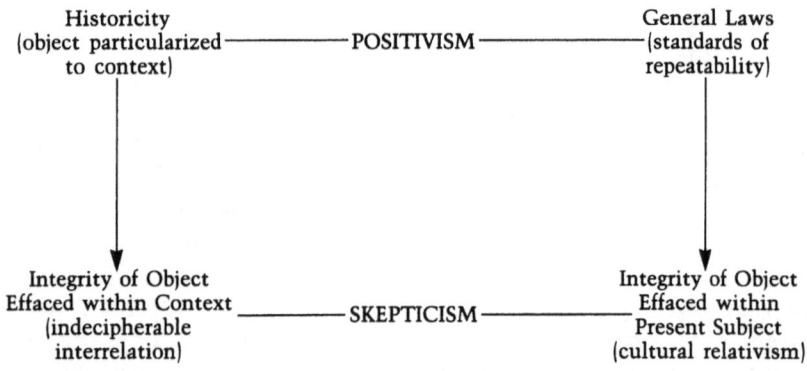

Figure 1. Historicism as a double dialectic

13. Walther Hofer, in Dwight E. Lee and Robert Beck, "The Meaning of 'Historicism,' " *American Historical Review* 59 (April 1954), 570. For other definitions, see Wesley Morris, "Historicism," in Alex Preminger, ed., *Princeton Encyclopedia of Poetry and Poetics*, enlarged ed. (Princeton, N.J.: Princeton University Press, 1974), pp. 937–40; Maurice Mandelbaum, "Historicism," in *Encyclopedia of Philosophy* (New York: The Free Press, 1967), 4: 22–25; Wesley Morris, "Toward a Discrimination of Historicisms," in *Toward a New Historicism* (Princeton, N.J.: Princeton University Press, 1972), pp. 3–13; and Hayden White, "Historicism, History, and the Figurative Imagination," in *Tropics of Discourse* (Baltimore, Md.: Johns Hopkins University Press, 1978), pp. 101–20.

14. Hofer, in Lee and Beck, "The Meaning of 'Historicism,' " p. 570.

As a feature of Pater's method, "historicism" will refer to this complex of possible strategies for overcoming, bypassing, or resolving (for working or for playing out) the epistemological difficulties of historical inquiry. A proper appreciation of the method recognizes its potential for playing across the entire range of attitudes and strategies *between* the extremes of naive positivism and epistemological nihilism, recognizing the pull of each extreme, refusing them equally. In this sense, Pater's historicism may, like his aestheticism, be seen as a systematic, mobile, skeptical, and finally reconstructive epistemology.[15]

Pater does consider the possibility "that nothing man has projected from himself is really intelligible except at its own date" (PP, 10), but he turns away from these nihilistic extremes of skepticism on the cultural level as he did on the individual level in the "Conclusion." Early in his career—as a matter of fact, in the same essay from which the "Conclusion" was taken—he shows that he has questioned the procedures of historical knowledge and has incorporated those questions as part of his perspective. But there, as always in Pater, the subject of interest is not history as such, but aesthetic history. Let us turn now to that essay, "Aesthetic Poetry," to read the conjunction of aestheticism and historicism at work.

## 6 · Aesthetic Historicism and "Aesthetic Poetry"

When Pater's historicism and his aestheticism intersect, a complex matrix of possible identifications and differences comes into play because the range of relations between the present and the past is articulated against the mobile relation between the self and itself. Pater deals with these complex relations in the same 1868 essay whose last paragraphs eventually became the "Conclusion," the essay now

---

15. This homology I am working out is meant to be a historical category, which belongs to a particular historical moment and which must itself be historicized, not an absolute. This late romantic, early modern moment—for which I am invoking Pater as the figure—falls between the rise of the social sciences and (crucially) before World War I. For histories of historicism, see Friedrich Meinecke, *Historism: The Rise of a New Historical Outlook*, trans. J. Anderson (London: Routledge and Kegan Paul, 1972); Friedrich Engel-Janosi, *The Growth of German Historicism* (Baltimore, Md.: Johns Hopkins University Press, 1944); and Hayden White, "On History and Historicisms," translator's introduction to Carlo Antoni, *From History to Sociology: The Transition in German Historical Thinking* (Detroit, Mich.: Wayne State University Press, 1959). Most of this work deals with postwar views of historicism. The earlier (nineteenth-century) history of historicism has not been sufficiently explored.

called "Aesthetic Poetry." There he takes the occasion of reviewing the poems of William Morris to consider the principles, problems, and possibilities of historical representation.

Pater opens with a crucial distinction between "aesthetic poetry" and all other forms of poetry, and he bases that distinction on the formal historicism of aesthetic poetry. The very quality that makes it "aesthetic," he claims, is its poetic involvement in the question of whether (and how) a past age can be represented in the present. Pater argues that aesthetic poetry imitates a former age and poetic style, not with the mimetic aim of reproducing the former age, but with the antithetical aim of differentiating it *from*, and the synthetic aim of comprehending it *within*, the present. Through this strategy of representation, the poetry of the present defines itself as modern, different or distant from the past, older, wiser, and more "refined."

That refinement is the result of a two-stage historical process. All poetry refines upon the primary material of life, nature, or sentiment, Pater argues,[1] but "aesthetic" poetry refines specifically upon earlier poetry:

> The "aesthetic" poetry is neither a mere reproduction of Greek or mediaeval poetry, nor only an idealisation of modern life and sentiment. The atmosphere on which its effect depends belongs to no simple form of poetry, no actual form of life. Greek poetry, mediaeval or modern poetry, projects, above the realities of its time, a world in which the forms of things are transfigured. Of that transfigured world this new poetry takes possession, and sublimates beyond it another still fainter and more spectral, which is literally an artificial or "earthly paradise." It is a finer ideal, extracted from what in relation to any actual world is already an ideal. Like some strange second flowering after date, it renews on a more delicate type the poetry of a past age, but must not be confounded with it. The secret of the enjoyment of it is that inversion of homesickness known to some, that incurable thirst for the sense of escape, which no actual form of life satisfies, no poetry even, if it be merely simple and spontaneous. (B, 190)

Aesthetic poetry redoubles the distance from the immediate, the direct, simple, or real—what Pater calls here the "actual." It "projects above," "sublimates beyond," or "extract[s] from" an already-idealized representation to represent a further ideal. And its specifically "aesthetic" value results from the second stage of this representational process. Pater's language strains to convey the several levels of intensification, transcendence, and repetition necessary to establish the re-

---

1. See passages in "The School of Giorgione" (R, 133 and 141).

fractory concept of re-refinement, the representation of a representation, the further transfiguration of an already-transfigured world. Here, as elsewhere in his work, he is keenly alert to the reduplicative or reflexive structures of representation in which the secondary or displaced position is also valued as "higher" or "deeper."[2] According to this theory, the "aesthetic" is the inverse of the immediate, and aesthetic poetry achieves the "sense of escape" through these shifts in the representational register, fictive shifts away from the "actual."

But the most important thing to stress here is the fact that Pater characterizes this second stage of aesthetic refinement as taking place later in historical time than the first stage.[3] In Pater, the "aesthetic" is generated as a distinctly historical phenomenon. The specific historicity of "aesthetic poetry," as well as its sense of historical difference, must be maintained; it must not be "confounded" with the earlier poetry to which it strategically alludes. By the same token, its sense of history is generated as an aesthetic phenomenon, through strategies of self-division, displacement, and sublation. In other words, the "aesthetic" and the "historicist" are mutually implicated, generated as correlative functions, and represented in the same set of figures.

Characterizing Morris's poetry now as a "strange second flowering after date," Pater makes a sweepingly recognitive gesture that involves simultaneously recollecting and establishing distance from an original, "primary" growth. When he calls aesthetic poetry an "afterthought" of the "romantic school," he explicitly historicizes aestheticism as a late romanticism, and in the process of doing so he constructs a peculiarly "aesthetic" literary history. The account of the literary history of romanticism that follows his definition of aesthetic poetry is certainly highly shaped—"aesthetic" in the sense of displaying its own artifice. But I mean also that his account of literary history is marked repeatedly by divisions and bifurcations, fulfilling the definition Pater has just offered of the "aesthetic" as the secondary, the intensified, and the refined, all by virtue of its self-conscious position later in historical time.

2. Compare the German mystic's idea of the second rose in "White-Nights" (ME I, 13) and the chapter in Part the Third entitled "Second Thoughts" (ME II, 14–28).
3. Possibly an obvious point. But note the fundamental difference between aesthetic historicism and simple aestheticism. The systematic epistemological strategies I characterized as "aestheticism" may be described using the rhetoric of temporality; moreover, the negative "moment" of the aesthetic dialectic, the moment of detachment, re-creates its object in and as the past. Here, however, Pater projects the same structure as a function of historical, not phenomenological, time. Compare the distinction Paul de Man draws between the structures of irony and allegory in "The Rhetoric of Temporality," *Blindness and Insight*, pp. 187–228.

Pater begins by dividing the "romantic school" into two currents of historical revivalism: one a "return to true Hellenism," the other a "sudden preoccupation with things medieval." Having thus characterized the "romantic school" by reference to its basic, doubly-preoccupied historicism, Pater subdivides each of these two currents into earlier and later stages, and he argues that greater intensification or profundity corresponds in each case to a later chronological stage. The earlier stages of each revival were "superficial," the later "stricter" and closer to the "genuine" or the "true." At this point he replaces Morris's poetry within the backwardly ramifying romantic family tree he has just sketched. He argues that Morris's earlier poems are already "a refinement upon this later, profounder medievalism" but that his later poems excel the earlier by representing the refinement of *both* the medievalizing and the Hellenizing strains of romantic revival. In Pater's theory, then, Morris's poetry too is divided into earlier and later stages, and the later poetry reunifies romanticism itself by joining the second and more intense phases of *both* its revival movements. If Pater defines "the 'romantic school' " as historicist to begin with, then aestheticism, as a refined and compendious "afterthought," would be doubly so.

But my point has little to do with the accuracy of Pater's history of romanticism—though his placing of Morris hardly seems dated even today—and much to do with its form, which is as late romantic as its argumentative content. Pater's history is thoroughly dialectical and genealogical. He divides romanticism into parts synchronically (two always simultaneous strands of revival: medieval and Greek) and diachronically (each strand consisting of chronological stages), and when put in motion that very strategy of division establishes the notion of a putative "whole," the overarching "growth" of romanticism. In other words, he describes a diachronic process as successive self-divisions within the "same" thing, departures from a source that are also returns to and recreations of it. With all the stately balance of a grand tautology, Pater's argument creates a contextual background for Morris's poetry, a background of divided and rewoven strands that imply a primary, first growth in order to rationalize the status of the "second flowering."

The dialectical structure of this account, as well as the genealogical structure, is further and most remarkably underscored when Pater goes on to sexualize the story of literary history he has just set in motion. In order to understand the atmosphere of Morris's medievalizing early poetry, he turns first to the history of the Arthurian legends and is at pains to show that—like Morris's aesthetic poetry itself—

they were most poignant when removed from their original historical context: "In truth these legends, in their origin prior to Christianity, yield all their sweetness only in a Christian atmosphere" (B, 191). That full "sweetness" turns out to be none other than the historical strife between two rival forms of worship, religious and "imaginative," described here as "a deliberate choice between Christ and a rival lover." Pater turns then to characterize Provençal courtly love poetry, which emerged against the background of the Christian Middle Age, as "a rival religion with a new rival *cultus* . . . the rejection of one worship for another." And the "jealousy of that other lover"—Christ—"for whom these words and images and refined ways of sentiment were first devised, is the secret here of a borrowed, perhaps factitious colour and heat" (B, 191). Both these genres of literature gain their heightened aesthetic effects against the contextual background of Christianity.

Pater's pretext for this account is Morris's title poem, "The Defence of Guenevere," which he calls "a thing tormented and awry with passion like the body of Guenevere defending herself from the charge of adultery" (B, 191). But his subtext is the shape of modern history itself. Guenevere's body, and her adulterous self-division, are implicitly allegorized to refer (on one level) to the historical development of courtly love and (on a further level of abstraction) to the secularization that accompanied the rise of Renaissance humanism. In other words, the "spiritual" meanings of Pater's allegorical vignette are at once aesthetic and historical. The rival cult of "imaginative" worship supersedes the cult of Christ, who becomes in this story a lover turned away and spurned. In courtly love, then, the inaccessible object of sexual desire substitutes for the "absent or veiled" object of cult devotion, and the "aesthetic" poetry of that era (Arthurian romance and Provençal poetry, which Morris's poetry then "sublimates beyond") springs from that substitution.

> Of religion it learns the art of directing towards an unseen object sentiments whose natural direction is towards objects of sense. Hence a love defined by the absence of the beloved, choosing to be without hope, protesting against all lower uses of love, barren, extravagant, antinomian. (B, 192)

The sexual energy of courtly love and the "borrowed, perhaps factitious, colour and heat" of its poetry are "imaginative" both because they are directed toward an absent object and because they are generated through a strategic displacement from a religious context to a more secularized context.

Like the body of Guenevere or Morris's poetry, then, the surprising (and suppressed) narrative of Christ and his rival lover is the vehicle of an allegory whose burden is aesthetic—in this case literary—and historical. Pater's sexualization of Christ turns out to be his strategy for representing the process of secularization.[4] The element of sexuality finally serves to underline the graphically antithetical and dialectical structure of the modern literary history he is constructing. Interpreting courtly love poetry as "the mood of the cloister taking a new direction" and gaining thereby "a later space of life it never anticipated," Pater creates a spatial metaphor for a turn or trope in his aesthetically reconstructed vision of historical time. Provençal poetry turns the course of history away from the cloister, while at the same time the cloister clears "a later space of life" for itself within its ostensible opposite. In the most profound sense, however, that opposition is only apparent, because it does not mask the synthetic and relative truth that the language, mood, and strategies of courtly love poetry derive from the very background against which they emerge. Thus, in relation to Christianity, courtly love is portrayed as an antithetical, later development of the same, self-divided thing.

At this point we can see that Pater's theory of secularization itself serves as a model of how aesthetic effects and aesthetic value emerge in history. His chief example, Provençal poetry, derives its very "romance" from the background in Christianity within and against which it "rises." Pater argues that much of its "colour and heat" is "borrowed" and "perhaps factitious," because it was devised originally for "that other lover," Christ, whose "jealousy" now stimulates the antinomian, rebellious posture of the later, "imaginative" lovers. The "imaginative" then enfolds a triple implication—romantic, aesthetic, and also secularized—for it is precisely this shift from an "original" context to a "secondary" context that creates aesthetic value.

Pater's theory of secularization can be approached in other useful ways. We can attend, for example, to the revision of Ruskin entailed in Pater's decisive preference for Renaissance art over the Christian "Gothic" and to the anti-Christian stance that revision seemed, at the time, to imply.[5] But from our perspective it is most important to recognize that Pater was "anti-Christian" only as a result of his charac-

---

4. Crinkley (*Walter Pater: Humanist*, p. 37) notes that Pater turns a discussion of religion into a discussion of physical love.

5. On Pater's "emptying" of Ruskin's "moral aesthetic," see Bloom, introduction to Pater's *Selected Writings*, pp. x–xviii.

teristic strategy of internalization, disengagement, and ironic sublation of Christianity, not through overt opposition to it. His antithetical stance was elegantly modulated, subtle, "refined," not "outlined" or harshly contrastive. The language, tone, and strategies of Christian aesthetics and Christian historicism weave through his passages—never rejected, but themselves exquisitely ironic, aestheticized, and historicized. Of course, to some this transformation seemed more dangerous to Christianity as a system of belief than any overt opposition could have been, and the most powerful reason for that reaction, I think, is the aesthetic effect of Pater's calm and distant "long view," reading secularization not as a nineteenth-century issue of controversy but as a persistent, centuries-long, modern tradition. He places the rivalry between Christ and "imagination" far in the past, where it seems to be a beautiful but remotely inaccessible issue—beautiful *because* remote and unchanging—now thoroughly transfigured and self-consciously historicized.

But my larger point here is about "borrowed" effects in general, of which the secularization and persistence of Christian effects is only a supremely pertinent example in Pater's work and in his nineteenth-century context. Pater also considers, in both *Marius the Epicurean* and *Plato and Platonism*, the "secularization" of classical, pagan culture as it is absorbed into the Christian era. In all such cases, a shift out of the original historical and formal context not only adds a certain *frisson* of irony as a signal of aesthetic effect, but also creates that effect *as aesthetic* in the first place. The shift in context frees content or belief into form, detaches it from its original contextual function, and frees it to "play" rather than to work in the service of some disciplinary system, and the shift leaves behind an aura or residue of the formerly "sacred" (or "scientific" or "utilitarian" or "philosophical") function that has now been displaced as the "aesthetic." The "secularization-effects" I shall repeatedly analyze in the following pages are, then, like all "aesthetic" effects, secondary, derivative, and transferential. Their origins were fictively elsewhere, and they "speak of something that is gone." But that loss or distance can be translated; at least, the category of "the aesthetic" is generated in the first place as an expression of a conservative impulse, a strategy of believing that the losses incurred in historical self-consciousness may be redeemed. The "aesthetic" is meant to answer the transfiguration of loss with another, recreative transfiguration.

Pater describes this recreative transfiguration on several levels in his essay "Aesthetic Poetry." His overall strategy is analogical and allegorical, aiming to make the stages of development in Morris's poetry stand for the overall development in aesthetic history at large. I have shown how he uses Morris's early poetry to represent the moment when Arthurian romance and courtly love take over from the cloister, but the crucial turn of the argument involves what Pater sees as a stylistic shift in Morris's later poetry, after the medievalizing lyrics of *The Defence of Guenevere*. Pater calls this "change in manner . . . characteristic of aesthetic poetry" and praises it as a "simplification," an imaginative revival of an earlier, more immediate art. Yet it might at first appear to be a complication rather than a simplification, for the lyrics in *The Defence of Guenevere*, which were related to one another only thematically and tonally, were followed in *The Earthly Paradise* by a volume whose overall structure was dialectical, synthetic, spacious, and extraordinarily complex. In any case, on the level of its form, it is easy to see how Pater's response to *The Earthly Paradise* could generate his definition of "aesthetic poetry," for the work embodies the two-stage process of refinement and recollection we have come to recognize in more abstract terms.

*The Earthly Paradise* is a compendious frame tale, in part modeled on *The Canterbury Tales*, but with an additional historicizing level in the frame structure, to which Pater particularly responds. The situation given in the poem is this: A band of Norse wanderers, despairing of their search for the "earthly paradise," settles in a "nameless city" whose Elders are descended from the ancient Greeks. Each month, over the course of the year, they exchange stories with those city Elders. The wanderers tell a story from medieval sources, and their hosts in turn tell one from classical sources, both stories cast in an imitation of the style of their fictive present time in the Middle Ages. The whole cycle is reframed by lyrics marking and introducing each month's narratives, and the voice of those intercalated lyrics is implicitly the poet's own, speaking in the present time in which this past scene of tale-telling and all its diverse tales are re-collected. Thus the double-frame form of the work represents a two-stage revival of the past: the stories of classical antiquity are retold in the late Middle Ages, and then both medieval and classical stories are retold in the late nineteenth century. This formal scene of recollection across historical distance creates "literally an artificial or 'earthly paradise,' " the only earthly paradise it is possible to achieve in the modern world (B, 190).

According to Pater, Morris achieves his own "simplification" by recalling an earlier scene of revival and simplification. But on a more general level, Pater also makes Morris's later poetry representative of a "simplifying" historical development. He reads the change in

Morris's literary form as an embodiment of "a transition which . . . is one law of the life of the human spirit, and of which what we call the Renaissance is only a supreme example." In Part Two of this book I explore Pater's representation of the Renaissance more fully, but as we can see here, even the Renaissance, though "a supreme example," is "*only*" an example of "one law of the life of the human spirit."

If specific, unrepeatable historicity, on the one hand, and general laws of repeatability, on the other hand, mark the positive range of historicist representation, then this "law" is the "covering law" of Pater's aesthetic historicism, for it describes the repeating patterns he half creates and half perceives across the history of his culture. Pater does not attempt an explicit explanation of historical causation in this essay. Somehow "complex and subtle interests . . . sooner or later . . . come back with a sharp rebound to the simple elementary passions" (B, 195). But his explanatory model for historical revival is implicitly an aesthetic model: as the Renaissance revival resulted from the recovery of classical art and culture, so a modern, "aesthetic" revival comes about when or because the earlier revival has been strategically represented.

I emphasize the Shelleyan, prophetic strain in Pater's romanticism, attenuated though it may be, for it is very important to recognize that his aesthetic historicism is a productive program. By representing the formal mechanisms of revival, Pater hopes to bring about a revival in his own time.[6] And he identifies with Morris's achievement of "literally an artificial or 'earthly paradise,' " because, to Pater, Morris represents not only the Renaissance but also the "aesthetic" recollection of both strains of late romanticism, and thus a renewed renaissance in his own contemporary art. If representing the Renaissance retrieval of classical art against the background of the Middle Ages can recreate the feeling of that Renaissance, then Pater in all his work is hoping to do the same. To emphasize that program, in "Aesthetic Poetry" Pater portrays the medieval situation in terms that are strikingly similar to his portrait of modern solipsism in the "Conclusion." He projects a threefold analogy between the Christian, the courtly lover, and "the medieval mind," all desiring an object out of their reach: Christ; the inaccessible beloved; and an "objective" sense of the real world of nature, a "real escape to the world without us" (B, 193). In a single essay,

---

6. A. Dwight Culler, *The Victorian Mirror of History* (New Haven, Conn.: Yale University Press, 1985), pp. 241–78.

then, Pater has characterized "modern thought" and the "medieval mind" as suffering from the same problem and needing the same "sense of escape" that aesthetic poetry provides.[7]

This sense of escape is bound up with the sense of revival, which Pater represents—in Morris's poetry as well as in "the life of the human spirit"—as a change in the natural light, the rising dawn a figure for a revival of imaginative earliness. On the one hand, he extends the logic of this romantic, mythic figure by equating morning with childhood. But Pater is divided in his representation of this change in the light, for on the other hand he refigures morning as convalescence, the experience of waking from a fevered dream or delirium, which brings "relief . . . with the first white film in the sky" (B, 194).[8] If childhood is irretrievable, "recovery" is still possible also for the late, the old, and the sick or insane, and thus "recovery" in Pater carries the full sense of the pun: both recovery from illness, and imaginative or historical retrieval of loss. This doubleness emphasizes again the importance of the dark background against which the figure of renewed life emerges: because of the dreadful night that has gone before, "the sensible world comes to one with a reinforced brilliancy and relief" (B, 193).

Along with the change in the light, the song changes. The aubade decisively supplants the nocturne as the favored genre for commemorating "mixed lights," times of transition between night and day, here used to represent times of aesthetic and historical transition. The "medieval mind" had been shut away from "the sensible world," too preoccupied with soul to remember the body of nature. But now the "absent or veiled" object is fictively re-presented or made to seem present again, and access to the world of nature, the world outside the self or soul, is again imaginably direct. With the rise of the Renais-

---

7. The place he assigns to Wordsworth in this scheme is interesting from the point of view of Pater's attempt to recapitulate the Renaissance revival in the nineteenth century. In order to praise Morris, he denigrates Wordsworth, whose simplicity he judges to be forced by comparison, or "sought out," not a "desire . . . towards the body of nature for its own sake" but "because a soul is divined through it" (B, 195). Wordsworth's earlier romanticism, then, is put in the position of the "medieval mind," so that Morris (and Pater) may again be affirmed in the later, Renaissance position.

8. As Paul de Man points out, the human figures that epitomize modernity are defined by such experiences as childhood and convalescence, by "a freshness of perception that results from a slate wiped clear, . . . the absence of a past that has not yet had time to tarnish the immediacy of perception" ("Literary History and Literary Modernity," in *Blindness and Insight*, p. 157). For a different interpretation of this figure, see Monsman, *Pater's Portraits*. Dealing mainly with the imaginary portraits, Monsman interprets the movement from clarity to delirium to imaginative rebirth as a mythic cycle based on the Apollonian-Dionysian opposition.

sance, the balance tips toward morning, and the world awakens once more to the sense of recovered originality, Adamic language, the "simple" and "direct" grasp of its objects, and the "primary" passions of an organic whole, composed once again of both body and soul.

Pater himself scrupulously underscores his awareness that this revival happens not in "actuality" but in stylistic or formal terms. "The song sung always *claims* to be sung for the first time," Pater argues, the word "claims" acknowledging the figurative and aesthetic nature of this awakening (B, 195; emphasis added). Morris's "simplification" of romanticism, as well as the historical simplification represented by the Renaissance, has been achieved aesthetically, or antithetically, through the negation of a negation. The first stage of refinement moves away from nature, denaturing art and the "human spirit," but the second stage brings a renaturalized return to the fiction of direct access, now understood *as* a fiction. The "aesthetic," then, represents not only the inverse of immediacy but also its simulacrum.

This process of simplification through complication is Pater's revised version of the familiar three-term, two-stage romantic itinerary—innocence, experience, and "higher" innocence; origin, exile, and return; unity, self-division, and the reunified incorporation of diversity—here projected in simultaneously historical and aesthetic terms.[9] Pater's late romantic, aesthetic genealogies are constructed on the same dialectical model as his epistemological reconstructions; the dynamic of identity, self-division, and recollection describes them both. Both presuppose a unity that is divided against itself and articulated into its parts, which then are re-collected once again as an overarching identity. Pater generates figure after figure for this dialectical struggle away from undifferentiated unity, and the aesthetic reconstruction of a complex, revised, and antithetical representation. And in a certain sense these figures crucially presuppose that the aesthetic critic occupies a position at the end of time, because the effect or sense of "escape" can be generated only as a function of retrospection. By repeatedly constructing transvalued versions of the familiar romantic dialectic, Pater thereby continuously reinscribes his position at the end of the line.

---

9. For the most compendious treatment of this aspect of romanticism, see Abrams, *Natural Supernaturalism*. Abrams traces this strategy rather thematically than otherwise, and he is interested primarily in the secularization of the Christian paradigm, but he does securely establish the derivation of this narrative strategy from both Christian historiography and German romantic philosophy.

# 7 · The Poetics of Revival

The representational dynamic of identity, self-division, and recollection that characterizes Pater's historical reconstructions is a generalized version of the aesthetic or epistemological dynamic of identification, disengagement, and retrospection. My reading of Pater's "aesthetic historicism," then, emphasizes this homology between the dialectic of self-consciousness and his strategies for representing history. A sense of objectivity may be aesthetically reconstituted in the past, *as* the past, and correlatively, the past may be reconstructed through strategies of "impression" and distance within. It is to this last dimension of Pater's aesthetic historicism that I now turn.

I have been exploring one system of figures in Pater's work, figures that depict lines of development. His critical recreation in "Aesthetic Poetry" of a romantic genealogy with himself at the end of the line has provided a good example of that group of figures. The group portrays revival as the periodic refreshment of "the human spirit" in historical time. But another complex figure portrays the periodic "relief" of the human spirit as a recreative relation of the mind in the present to the historical past. These figures allude in their forms to questions of historical knowledge. In representing not so much *what* is known of the past but *how* it is known and how it is represented, these figures are implicitly or explicitly metafigural, for they represent a figure of aesthetic history at the same time that they represent the mind in the act of making the figure. Like the second level of the frame structure in Morris's *Earthly Paradise*, these figures depict revival as the process of representation itself, the process of bringing the past back to life in the mind of the present.

Both figural systems represent the recollected unity of aesthetic history, with its dialectically differentiated parts, but they do so in different ways and from different perspectives. One figure is linear, the other a figure of enclosure or containment. One represents aesthetic history as already shaped, the other represents the mind in the act of shaping it. One figure portrays aesthetic history leading up to the mind in the present—and thus it effaces the aesthetic act of retrospection that inevitably constitutes it—while the other portrays the mind in the present looking back and encompassing the past. In Pater's "poetics of revival" the two are related to each other in a number of ways, many of which I examine in the chapters to come. For now I will concentrate briefly on the figure of relief, which may be understood as Pater's master trope of revival.

In "Aesthetic Poetry," the figure of relief bridges between the two systems I have just outlined, to represent both the shape of historical development and the mind in the present making that shape. We are already familiar with the first sense of the figure: at certain times when aesthetic history takes a "new direction," the division of one period from another creates a sense of "relief." Pater allegorized that relief as dawn succeeding the dark, or as clarity and sanity finally recovered after fevered delirium. The emotional valence of "relief" at the removal of oppression suggests the presence of a subject to whom "the sensible world comes . . . with a reinforced brilliancy and relief" or to whom "there comes something of relief from physical pain with the first white film in the sky" (B, 193–94). But when Pater comments more directly on Morris's representational procedures, the emotional value of relief is joined to an aesthetic and historical dimension: Morris's "medievalisms . . . coming in a poem of Greek subject, bring into this white dawn thoughts of the delirious night just over and make one's sense of relief deeper" (B, 197). And when Pater stands even further back to characterize the structure of Morris's double revival, the figure of relief achieves its full sense of plasticity: Morris's poetry provides "precisely this effect, the grace of Hellenism relieved against the sorrow of the Middle Ages" (B, 197).

Like "recovery" or "revival," the word "relief" has an actively double meaning in Pater. On the one hand, "relief" signifies the removal or lightening of an oppressive force, the means of breaking monotony or boredom, the ability to enliven ("*dephlegmatisiren vivificiren*"), which is the "true service of philosophy" in the "Conclusion." On the other hand, "relief" refers to a range of plastic, spatial forms in which figures rise against a plane surface with relative degrees of heightened effect. Relief is an art form that expresses the relation between levels of focus and distance as foreground to background, or figure to ground. And in both the emotional and the plastic senses, "relief" is Pater's figure for aesthetic history. The emotional value of relief primarily expresses the achieved sense of historical difference. In imagining the forward movement of time, any age seen against the background of the previous age creates this feeling of "relief"; or conversely, through retrospection, the past projected against the background of the mind in the present also creates the sense of "relief" or the "sense of escape" from what otherwise would be an oppressive, solipsistic imprisonment.

The full range of the figure is felt when the emotional and the plastic senses join, as they do in a stunning passage toward the end of "Aesthetic Poetry," quite near the paragraphs that now form the

"Conclusion." There Pater raises in explicit terms the questions of historical relativism and romantic self-consciousness, historical knowledge, and representation. What follows in the remaining pages of Part One is a close reading of that passage:

> In handling a subject of Greek legend, anything in the way of an actual revival must always be impossible. Such vain antiquarianism is a waste of the poet's power. The composite experience of all the ages is part of each one of us; to deduct from that experience, to obliterate any part of it, to come face to face with the people of a past age, as if the Middle Age, the Renaissance, the eighteenth century had not been, is as impossible as to become a little child, or enter again into the womb and be born. But though it is not possible to repress a single phase of that humanity, which, because we live and move and have our being in the life of humanity, makes us what we are, it is possible to isolate such a phase, to throw it into relief, to be divided against ourselves in zeal for it; as we may hark back to some choice space of our own individual life. We cannot truly conceive the age: we can conceive the element it has contributed to our culture: we can treat the subjects of the age bringing that into relief. Such an attitude towards Greece, aspiring to but never actually reaching its way of conceiving life, is what is possible for art. (B, 196)

It is immediately apparent that this model incorporates the problem of historical knowledge as its first premise. There is no pretense made of direct access to the past: "we cannot truly conceive the age." Any hope for an "actual" revival is dismissed as "impossible" and disparaged as "vain antiquarianism," an aspersion that Pater casts elsewhere to differentiate his own method from a factual, distant style of historical report.[1] What *can* be achieved is an aesthetic revival or a figurative representation of present access to a past age. In Pater's words, "we can conceive the element it has contributed to our culture." In "Aesthetic Poetry," Pater praises Morris for the "charming anachronisms" that result from that poet's balance between distance and closeness in observation: "while he handles an ancient subject, [he] never becomes an antiquarian, but animates his subject by keeping it always close to himself" (B, 195). Just as in the "Preface" (where the aesthetic critic first asks, "What does this object mean to *me*"?), here, too, Pater is concerned with the particular kind of validity possible when the object is known first subjectively and only then disengaged or set at a distance—in this case, the distance of historical difference.

---

1. See his remarks on Carlo Amoretti in "Leonardo" and on the "new Vasari" (Crowe and Cavalcaselle) in "The School of Giorgione" (R, 99–100, 143–47).

In Pater's present inquiry, the "object" is a chosen time in the past. The "zeal" involved in choosing the object precipitates a division within the self, as well as an act of "isolating" one age from the rest of historical time. "It is possible to isolate such a phase, to throw it into relief" against the rest of historical culture and against the mind in the present. One way to highlight the results of this particular figure would be to point out that the consciousness of the subject in the present is portrayed at once as the active force that "isolates" and "throws" a past age into relief and as the receptive background against which the past age is thrown. The "isolation" achieved this way is of course only relative, provisional, or partial, for the past age is still located "within" as well as projected "against" its background or context in the present self. As Pater's essay on Coleridge made clear, no sharp, absolute "outlines" may be drawn around the modern object of knowledge; in its plastic sense, this figure spatially portrays the object within its "conditions."

The figure of relief is therefore a model of "relative truth" or contextual knowledge. To "know" an object, it is necessary to establish a distance, and this figure of self-division generates the sense of relative distance by "relieving" the object so that it emerges into clear visibility against its background without detaching it fully from that background. Here "distance" within the self represents historical difference, as "distance" within time can be figured within the self.[2] As a model of relative knowledge, then, the figure of relief imagines historical difference within the self at the same time that it projects romantic self-division as historical periodization.

The crucial assumption that makes the logic of this figure possible is Pater's belief in a certain homologous and reciprocally expressive relation between the individual and general historical culture. In the present passage the relation is expressed as a structure of mutual containment in which the culture of all the ages lives "within" each individual at the same time that each individual lives "within" it. As Pater puts it, "the composite experience of all the ages is part of each one of us," and reciprocally, "because we live and move and have our being in the life of humanity, [it] makes us what we are." It is a striking fact that unlike the other representational relations we have been examining, Pater does not acknowledge this relation as a figurative strategy, but identifies with it totally as an unquestioned article of faith. As such it has a crucial importance, for it underwrites his aesthetic historicism.

2. Again, see Paul de Man, "The Rhetoric of Temporality," in *Blindness and Insight*, pp. 187–228.

If the individual person and the "life of humanity" are mutually internalized, they participate in the same "spirit"; they have the same "character." This is a familiar idea in the period, but it is important at the outset to discriminate three interlocking levels of conceptualization operating in Pater's version of this period concept: that of the individual, historical person; that of the immediately surrounding historical context, the *Zeitgeist* or "spirit of the age"; and that of the overarching "world-spirit," or *Geist*, a transhistorical category generated from and projected beyond any "actual" historical phenomenon. McGrath is right to argue that Pater rejected the notion of absolute spirit,[3] but his understanding of *Zeitgeist* reaches in that direction. On the synchronic side, Pater's *Zeitgeist* is the "spirit of the age," but on the diachronic side, *Zeitgeist* is the "time-spirit," an overarching spirit evolving from age to age. It is in this latter sense that Pater's use of *Zeitgeist* often reaches toward *Geist*, and in this latter sense Pater usually calls it the "life of the human spirit," the "life of humanity," or the "mind of man."

In the passage under discussion here, Pater brackets the "spirit of the age" and considers the relation between the individual person and the "life of humanity" over all the ages. However, already we have frequently seen him hypostatize a *Zeitgeist*—as, for example, in "Aesthetic Poetry" he speaks of the "medieval mind," or in the "Conclusion" he speaks of "modern thought." The hypostasis involved in generating the concept of the "spirit of the age" is characteristically achieved as a dialectical sublation in Pater —for example, when he posits the "medieval mind" as an enveloping category to resolve the opposition between Christianity and courtly love, thus establishing a "higher" unity over the space of supposed historical difference. Likewise, on the largest level, the transhistorical *Geist* is projected in order to unify without annihilating historically different ages in one overarching development. These totalizing moves on the level of historical representation should seem familiar, for they recapitulate what we have seen on the individual level, where the sense of continuous identity is achieved as a result of the dialectical subsumption of impression and disengagement in retrospection.

The pervasive debt to Hegel in Pater's thinking about history may be seen most clearly here, as my use of the terms *Zeitgeist* and *Geist* suggest.[4] Pater's knowledge of Hegel has been well documented. Early

---

3. McGrath, *The Sensible Spirit*, pp. 122–23.
4. As well as my use of the verb "to sublate," which is the usual English translation of *aufheben*: to negate or cancel, but also to preserve by elevating as a part of a dialectical synthesis.

in his career Pater read the *Phenomenology*, the *Logic*, the *History of Philosophy*, and the *Philosophy of Fine Art*—most, and perhaps all, in the original German. His interest in Hegel was well-known to his contemporaries, and it was said that he owed his Brasenose Fellowship to his knowledge of German philosophy, especially Schelling and Hegel.[5] Indeed, his interest in Hegel was part of a recognized movement, for during the decades of his greatest productivity Pater was friendly with several of the leading Oxford Hegelians.[6] And of course by Pater's day there is a long native literary tradition of attention to German idealist philosophy and aesthetics, whose most important early-nineteenth-century figures are Coleridge and Carlyle. Even philosophers whose projects lay in entirely different directions had absorbed elements of this influence, as Mill's famous 1827 essay on the "spirit of the age" makes clear. There Mill identifies the very belief in a "spirit" of the age as the chief defining characteristic of the spirit of his own particular age.

Several scholars—notably Anthony Ward, William Shuter, Peter Allan Dale, Donald L. Hill, Billie Andrew Inman, F. C. McGrath, and Wolfgang Iser—have traced the Hegelian influence in Pater's conceptual framework and to some extent in his literary form.[7] Ward points out the particular appeal for Pater in Hegel's description of historical change, which fully takes account of the "flux" and yet provides stability in the concept of the overarching *Geist*.[8] Up to this point, I have been most interested in the systematic homology that Pater draws between phenomenological experience and historical change, which is reflected in the interlocking aspects of his method: his aestheticism and his historicism. In general, this homology may be seen

---

5. Inman, *Pater's Reading*, pp. 9, 32–35, 38–41, 49–58.
6. Beginning during his undergraduate days with his election to the "Old Mortality" society whose members included T. H. Green, E. Caird, and William Wallace. On Hegel's growing popularity in England during the second half of the nineteenth century, see Anthony Ward, *Walter Pater: The Idea in Nature* (Worcester and London: Macgibbon and Kee, 1966), pp. 43–45, 52. For more on the "Old Mortality," see Gerald Monsman, "Pater's Aesthetic Hero," *University of Toronto Quarterly* 40 (Winter 1971), 136–51.
7. Ward, *Walter Pater*, pp. 53–77; William Shuter, "History as Palingenesis in Pater and Hegel," *PMLA* 86 (May 1971), 411–21; Hill's notes; McGrath, "Historical Idealism: Hegel," in *The Sensible Spirit*, pp. 118–39; and "Hegelian Schematism" and "Historicity," in Wolfgang Iser, *Walter Pater: The Aesthetic Moment* (1960; Eng. trans., Cambridge, Mass.: Harvard University Press, 1987), pp. 71–81 (see also p. 173, n. 46). Though Dale and especially Inman discuss Pater's exposure to Hegel, they both believe that the *Philosophy of Fine Art* was the only work of Hegel's to have an important or lasting effect. See Inman, *Walter Pater's Reading*, p. 49; and Dale, *The Victorian Critic and the Idea of History*, pp. 179, 189, 209.
8. Ward, *Walter Pater*, pp. 46, 68.

as a forceful reminder of Pater's pervasive Hegelianism, but in the chapters to come, I concentrate also on the effects of this system of interlocking levels of generalization, under whose auspices the spirit of the individual person, the spirit of the age, and the overarching spirit of humanity become reciprocally expressive.

We must constantly remind ourselves that these are figures, each one unifying disparate phenomena under the aegis of a personal spirit. I am not so much interested in demythologizing this Hegelian system of historical representation, though that worthy project has been undertaken by others, in Pater's age and in our own. Instead, I am primarily interested in how it works, in relation to other elements of structure and texture in Pater, as literary form. In synchronic terms, the relation between the individual and the *Zeitgeist* or "spirit of the age" is usually figured as a relation of microcosm to macrocosm, emphasizing their analogous content or homologous structure. But in addition to the synchronic relation, Hegel's model takes into account the diachronically homologous relation between the individual life and the "life of the human spirit" unfolding in time. In other words, the homology is figured both spatially, as a structure of containment, and temporally, as a process of development.

The biological concept that ontogeny recapitulates phylogeny offers us a scientific version of this latter conception of the relation between individual and type over time.[9] Pater works again and again with this notion that the development of the individual person recapitulates the development of the culture at large. Because the late-nineteenth-century conception of the relation between individual and surrounding culture was conceived as both "spiritual" and "organic," it is easily identifiable also as romantic, and perhaps it could be specifically distinguished as late romantic by saying that the "spirit" in question is that of history not nature. It is important to recognize that both the "spirit of the age" and the "life of the human spirit" are projected on the ontogenetic model, as both organic and personal, even though they are explicitly understood to be collective or transpersonal. The

---

9. Stephen Jay Gould, *Ontogeny and Phylogeny* (Cambridge, Mass.: Belknap Press, 1977). Gould argues that the biological concept of phylogeny may have been originally derived from categories of cultural analysis. For this, and for discussion of confusions between cultural and biological applications of the concept of the ontogenetic / phylogenetic relation, see ibid., pp. 115–66. Gould discusses the literary "survival" of this notion long after its scientific validity had been shaken; he notes the aesthetic analogy often drawn between earlier, "primitive" cultures and individual childhood; and he traces the influence of recapitulationist theories on Freudian psychoanalysis. For another literary discussion of this concept, see W. J. Harvey, "Idea and Image in George Eliot," in Barbara Hardy, ed., *Critical Essays on George Eliot* (London: Routledge, 1970).

passage under immediate consideration itself displays one such result of conceiving the aesthetic history of Western culture as an individual person's life. Personal memory and historical retrieval are conflated, with the allegorical result that classical Greece becomes the "childhood" of the Western world, the mythic, pastoral past we cannot "actually" recapture.[10]

This entanglement of the spiritual, the historical, and the biological becomes richly suggestive in Pater, for the relation drawn in Pater between the individual and the surrounding or overarching historical culture (which I have related now to a German and English tradition of historical transcendentalism and to the biological and early anthropological conceptions of ontogeny and phylogeny) is also clearly recognizable as a secularization of Christianity. The *Geist* is a romantic and secularized conception in the sense that "spirit" is an ideal, overarching, and transcendent projection of phenomenological process. We could say that the concept of the *Geist* marks a stage in what Pater calls the "secular process" (PP, 10), a stage in which the transcendent is no longer understood as wholly other but is introjected, on the one hand, to establish the romantic self, and projected outward, on the other hand, to establish this overarching, ideal vision of history. In the passage under discussion, the spirit of history replaces the God of Acts 17:28, the God in whom "we live and move and have our being." And, since the experience of historical "relief" is possible because "the composite experience of all the ages is part of each one of us," history is figured as the new muse, filling us full of its spirit, divinely inspiring each one of us as if from "outside."

This biblical allusion is an instructive case in point, for Pater's intertextual strategy offers a good example of the sort of shift in context that produces an aesthetic effect. The force of this particular allusion asserts the divinity of the *Geist* by appropriating the Pauline description of the Christian God to describe "the life of humanity." In a doubleness that is characteristic of secularization-effects, the Christian text is secularized and converted into a support for Paterian-Hegelian historicism, even as that historicism remains partially Christianized. In this respect, Pater's biblical language is particularly poignant and ironic, for he expresses an "aspiration" toward the impossible but nonetheless ardently desired retrieval of classical Greece in the very terms of what—historically and imaginatively speaking—

---

10. The notion that the "childhood" of the Western world was spent in ancient Greece is a commonplace of German Idealism, occurring in Winckelmann, Herder, Goethe, Hegel, and even Marx. On Marx's famous lapse into this romantic myth, see Maynard Solomon, ed., *Marxism and Art* (New York: Vintage, 1974), p. 423.

stands between him and the realization of that desire: the historical fact of Christianity.

The other biblical intertext in this passage, from the story of Jesus and Nicodemus in John 3:4–21, elaborates Pater's view of the historical fact that Christianity intervened between the classical Greeks and his own late romantic, late nineteenth century. In doing so, it reminds us of the Christian answer to the question of personal revival. Pater transposes the skepticism of Nicodemus into the aesthetic and historical register: "to come face to face with the people of a past age . . . is as impossible as to become a little child, or enter again into the womb and be born." Of course, in its original context, Nicodemus's question is answered with Jesus' explanation that one *can* return, can be born again, spiritually. Again the trope of secularization reveals its characteristic ironic doubleness. On the one hand, this intertextual reference supports Pater's stoic admission that an "actual revival [is] impossible," for it demonstrates the sense in which allusion strategically confuses historical difference; in this case, the traditional force of the gospel story has been turned to a secular use. But on the other hand, it forcefully argues that a spiritual or "imaginative" revival *is* possible by enlisting the Christian belief in spiritual "rebirth" or conversion on behalf of his belief in an imaginative, aesthetic, and historical revival. In this exchange, Pater commands the power of spiritual return for his own poetics of revival.

Finally, Pater's treatment of the relation between historical culture and the individual permits us to see here the beginnings of a theory of the unconscious. The theory is figured as a sort of collective unconscious, because "the composite experience of all the ages is part of each one of us" and no age can be "obliterated" or "deducted" or "repressed" totally. Pater's fervent tone, as well as the allusion to Christian rebirth, seems to express a wish that repression could be more effective, as if then he could "actually" come "face to face" with the people of classical Greece. In the spirit of Pater's rhetoric and logic of containment or internalization, it is as if the epistemological dilemmas of historical relativism and romantic self-consciousness are figured here as physical obstructions, as if historical experience were dense, occluding matter "filling up" the space of difference between present and past. If only that matter could be "deducted" or "obliterated" or "repressed"—Pater's wish seems to be—then we could see across the space of historical difference as if it were empty, transparent, and clear as air. But the matter needing to be "repressed" is the historical fact of Christianity itself! If we correlate the terms of Pater's three-stage historical narrative (classical Greece, medieval Christianity, the modern age) with the Christian rhetoric of rebirth or conversion (as Pater does in this passage), Christianity itself assumes the surprising role of the former life of "sin" he would turn away from or "obliterate." Pater's wish to see, not through a glass darkly but "face to face," implicitly and ironically denigrates Christianity as that which blocks his view of the Greeks, as that which, in historical, personal (and latently sexual) terms, is the too, too solid body of adulthood.

Using the plastic figure of relief, however, the intervening ages can be imagined as "relatively" repressed, to form the effaced or indefinite background against which the chosen age is consciously "thrown" into relatively higher "relief." Thus classical Greece, for example, can be thrown into relief against—and can grant relief to—a nineteenth-century consciousness whose strategy is to repress the intervening ages in its favor. In linked individual and historical terms, the "poetics of revival" describes a dynamic of strategic remembering and forgetting. The same plastic figure portrays the unconscious as well as consciousness, strategic forgetting as well as aesthetically controlled recollection. What we know and remember is surrounded by and emerges from what we do not know, do not remember. What we know, in this model, is not the past itself, but its configuration within our own culture, the shadow it casts, the shape it has impressed upon the background of our present consciousness. That plastic "impression" within "each one of us" may be externalized, "thrown" or projected away from the self again, and thereby recovered, revived, and represented as "relief."

P·A·R·T · T·W·O

# Figural Strategies in *The Renaissance*

· Pater's volume of Renaissance essays was his first major experiment in the "poetics of revival." In that volume he attempts to stage a revival of the historical period preeminently known for its own revival. Pater's choice of period was easily recognized (even at the time) as a subtle but sweeping polemic against Ruskin's "Gothic."[1] Pater chose instead to "throw into relief" the age when classical art seemed to bring "the mind of man" back to its senses after the dark night of Christian asceticism. The perspective of *The Renaissance*—Pater's volume, like his imagination of the period—asserts a disengagement from the "medieval mind," but it also identifies *with* the Middle Ages (though here again, against Ruskin) by recognizing in it another period of romantic inwardness, like his, yearning for the "sense of escape."

As every critic of Pater has pointed out, Pater's definition of the Renaissance extends finally to include both the Middle Ages and the nineteenth century. His definitive period is famously and flagrantly inclusive, finally co-extensive with Western history in general. Abstracting the shape of time described in the Renaissance volume yields as usual a three-term sequence, as well as the additional level of a framing perspective in the late nineteenth century which is implicitly identified with each of the three past ages. Thus, from Pater's perspective, aesthetic history takes the familiar romantic form of unity-in-

---

1. See e.g., the remarks of William Dean Howells (Donald Hill's textual and explanatory notes to Pater's *The Renaissance: Studies in Art and Poetry, The 1893 Text*, ed. Donald L. Hill (Berkeley: University of California Press, 1980), p. 300 (hereafter, Hill's notes).

diversity, achieved this time specifically as partial, historical "periods" together forming an overarching, "composite" whole.[2] The modernity of Pater's volume depends on this vision of history, which I examine in more detail in the pages to come. Like Morris's "aesthetic poetry," a "strange second flowering after date," Pater's *Renaissance* attempts to represent not just a revival but a revival of a revival.

Because the issue of difference between classical and Christian traditions was raised so graphically, the Renaissance is characterized in part by an intensified consciousness of history.[3] For Pater, Renaissance art reveals "the mind of man" first faced with the problems of historical representation: the difficulty of drawing a relation between a past age and the present, the aesthetic choice of representative figures, the delineation of difference, and the projection of continuity. Certainly Pater recognizes in the Renaissance the beginning of his own modernity, with its sense of difference not from one past but from two or more. Renaissance art presents Pater with an ideal occasion to consider a fundamental question: how can art formally represent the sense of historical context? In the Renaissance, Pater recognizes the emergent recognition that art must be understood historically, but in his own late nineteenth century he saw the need for an additional level of reflexivity. For art to be understood historically, history itself must be regarded aesthetically.

His contemporaries were not accustomed to such reflexivity. Pater's treatment of the "historical element" was attacked on many grounds and in many voices.[4] As we have seen, Pater responded to these charges by changing the title in the second edition, from *Studies in the History of the Renaissance* to *The Renaissance: Studies in Art and Poetry*. But this change did not amount to a recantation any more than did his temporary removal of the "Conclusion." Just as some of Marius's "sensations and ideas" deal "more fully with the thoughts suggested" by the "Conclusion," so the form of *Marius the Epicurean* deals more fully with problems of historical representation raised in *The Renais-*

---

2. Again, see Jerome J. McGann, *The Romantic Ideology* (Chicago: University of Chicago Press, 1983), for a trenchant critique of such romantic self-representations as "unity-in-diversity." McGann's doubly historical argument also explores the persistence of these self-representations in the criticism of the romantics. Perhaps it is clear that in my view Pater's work falls squarely within the "Romantic ideology" as McGann has defined it.

3. See George Huppert, "The Renaissance Background of Historicism," *History and Theory* 5 (1966), 48–60.

4. Mrs. Pattison's review appeared in *Westminster Review*, n.s. 43 (April 1873), 639–41. See Robert M. Seiler, ed., *Walter Pater: The Critical Heritage* (London: Routledge & Kegan Paul, 1980), pp. 71–73, 97–98. For other contemporary reactions, see Hill's notes, pp. 284–89.

*sance*. In each of his works, Pater continues to consider these same problems and to generate responsive literary forms.

Pater's first volume displays his characteristic play between historical and "imaginative" styles of discourse.[5] He bluntly juxtaposes passages of documented cultural history or biographical detail against passages of interpretive analysis, legend, and symbolic reverie. These stylistic shifts seemed more objectionable in *The Renaissance* than in his later works, I believe, largely because this first volume is less clearly rationalized as a genre than the "imaginary portraits," the "Greek studies," the historical novels, and the lectures on Plato and Platonism that succeeded it. Those later works also mix levels of representation in striking ways, but they do so within ingenious and to some extent original literary forms that more overtly and more thoroughly organize or encode their relative claims both to factuality and to aesthetic recreation. But in *The Renaissance*, Pater's shifts from fact to fiction do not seem as fully integrated in a comprehensive discursive or literary plan. Did he mean his essays to be read as "studies" of "history" or of "art and poetry"? Pater's change of title in the second edition (from *Studies in the History of the Renaissance* to *The Renaissance: Studies in Art and Poetry*) may be taken to signal his consideration of a more integrative approach to genre, and his works after this first volume certainly announce more clearly what they take themselves to be.

Pater's extraordinarily mobile critical stance, though it made *The Renaissance* vulnerable to attack from the historical point of view, is an indispensable feature of his "poetics of revival." Each of the representational styles along the spectrum between fact and fiction marks a certain distance taken by the aesthetic critic in relation to his object, as he undergoes the passionate identification and dispassionate separation that enables aesthetic recognition. Pater's constant repositioning represents an effort literally to "revive" or "animate" his subject "by keeping it always close to himself" and at the same time to indicate historical distance by throwing the past age "into relief." In *The Renaissance*, as in his other works, Pater takes up documented facts and converts them into strategies of perception, making knowledge a mobile and relative matter, letting facts as well as ideas fall away as soon as their "service" of startling the mind to "constant and eager observation" has been performed.

---

5. The recent reclamation of Pater has been based on a defense of his "imaginative sense of fact." See, e.g., Gerald Monsman, "Criticism as Creation," in *Walter Pater's Art of Autobiography* (New Haven, Conn.: Yale University Press, 1980), pp. 9–36.

## · 82 · Figural Strategies in *The Renaissance*

*The Renaissance* is one of those Victorian works which "appear to be histories, but in fact create historical myths."[6] In this case, the historical myth created is at once a myth of "actual" history, a myth recollecting other historically specific myths, and a myth of History in the abstract and "spiritual" sense of that word. The volume, then, is both mythological (in the sense that it recounts and reinterprets myths from the past) and mythopoeic (in the sense that it generates a new myth out of the old ones). In Pater's work, the sense of a unifying power inherent in the external world, a sense absolutely necessary for mythopoeic art, is grounded not in nature but in his sense of history.[7] Indeed, as I have argued, the conception of history restores his very sense of objectivity or externality in the first place, as well as his belief in a power of imaginative reunification. The work of aesthetic historicism mobilizes creative consciousness and history to stabilize and nourish each other. In the final analysis, but *only* in the final analysis, the mythopoeic element predominates over the historical, but it is generated in the first place *by* the historical sense, which must not be overlooked in an interpretive plunge toward the mythopoeic element. To take that interpretive plunge too precipitously would be to elide the very value of the work as neither myth nor history, but precisely as literature.

## 1 · Legend and Historicity

Like Botticelli, Pater was a "visionary" who "lived in a generation of naturalists." He is quite clearly characterizing his own method when he describes Botticelli's:

> The genius of which Botticelli is the type usurps the data before it as the exponent of ideas, moods, visions of its own; in this interest it plays fast and loose with those data, rejecting some and isolating others, and always combining them anew. (R, 53–54)

---

6. Carol T. Christ, *The Finer Optic: The Aesthetic of Particularity in Victorian Poetry* (New Haven, Conn.: Yale University Press, 1975), p. 90. In this regard, Christ also mentions Ruskin's *Stones of Venice* and *Modern Painters* and Carlyle's *Past and Present* and *The French Revolution*.

7. I have relied for these distinctions on David G. Riede, *Swinburne: A Study of Romantic Mythmaking* (Charlottesville: University Press of Virginia, 1978), pp. 1–3.

In Pater's work, "data" are used to advocate, to interpret, or to raise to a higher power the idea or vision of which they are "the exponent." Every critic must come to terms with this aspect of Pater's work: not only his habit of playing "fast and loose" with the data, but also his habit of characterizing his own method, style, or vision when he ostensibly refers to another artist.[1] These features are not best understood in terms of Pater's "subjectivism," but are parts of the more complex set of strategies I have been calling his aesthetic historicism. Thanks to the wonderful edition of the 1893 text by Donald L. Hill and to the work of Billie Andrew Inman, we now know more than ever where Pater is faithful, and where he is unfaithful, to the historical record.[2] Now more than ever, we are in a position to evaluate his identifications with and disengagements from the "data" as part of a coherent method.

Pater begins his essay on Leonardo with an explanation of his own critical procedures toward fact and fiction. He refers to Leonardo's "*legend*, as the French say," "one of the most brilliant chapters of Vasari," comprised of all those "anecdotes which everyone remembers" (R, 99). Later writers simply copied Vasari's account, Pater goes on to explain, until Carlo Amoretti in 1804 "applied to it a criticism which left hardly a date fixed, and not one of those anecdotes untouched." What is interesting here is Pater's perception that Amoretti's corrections have "unfixed" (rather than accurately "fixing") the securely received data, as if the "scientific" attempt to correct the historical record were merely irreverent tampering, admitting a dangerous principle of indeterminacy to that record. As he would later attack the "new Vasari" (Crowe and Cavalcaselle) for their narrowly construed attributions to Giorgione, he here attacks Carlo Amoretti for his scientific procedures of attribution, which strictly separate "by technical criticism . . . what in his reputed works is really his, from what is only half his, or the work of his pupils" (R, 100).[3] Here too he complains against Amoretti's iconoclastic "mere antiquarianism," which reduces rather than enhances the received story of Leonardo's life. Pater objects, in other words, to a scientific criticism that reduces

---

1. Most critics deduce a simple "autobiographical" relation. For my critique of this position, see (in addition to this section) Part One, sec. 4, and Part Three, sec. 2.
2. From these two works we learn a great deal more than that; both offer illuminating commentary and cultural history, as well as fundamental research. See Pater, *The Renaissance: Studies in Art and Poetry, The 1893 Text*, ed. Donald L. Hill (Berkeley: University of California Press, 1980), and Billie Andrew Inman, *Walter Pater's Reading: A Bibliography of His Library Borrowings and Literary References, 1858–1873* (New York: Garland, 1981).
3. See R, 143–47.

the body of Leonardo's work and the story of his life instead of construing both as broadly and generously as possible. He receives traditional stories as "data," whether scientific method would support him in this or not, and yet nonetheless he achieves a sense of objectivity in his prose.

In the essays on Leonardo and Giorgione, Pater fights against the practice of restricting the historical "data" to the historical "facts." He accepts "legends" as "data" for sound historical reasons. As stories that come down from the past, legends may be regarded as historical evidence even though they are not scientifically verifiable. They have a documentary historical life of their own, and they comprise a part of the history of criticism, whether or not they are true in fact. Pater believed that past responses to a life and work offer a legitimate "first step" in the approach toward an object of research "as in itself it really is." On the theory that direct access is impossible and that past responses represent the ages standing between Pater and his object, he uses legends to mediate his more extreme distance from the object of his interpretation. Here we find Pater working with an early version of reception-aesthetics, in which he accepts and analyzes "received" views, implicitly defining them as "data" simply because they are historically "given." Within the logic of aesthetic historicism, in other words, tradition is the source of "data." The scrupulous aesthetic historian's attempt to deduce historical context through several layers of response is not hindered by the possibility that each response is more properly "aesthetic" than factual. Even the legend has objective value as a documented, historically specific response.

Pater explains his interpretive procedures in relation to the legends about Leonardo:

> A lover of strange souls may still analyse for himself the impression made on him by those works, and try to reach through it a definition of the chief elements of Leonardo's genius. The *legend*, as corrected and enlarged by its critics, may now and then intervene to support the results of this analysis. (R, 100)

This essay provides a good example of the critical practice that Pater's "Preface" rationalizes in theory. Pater's "first step" is to analyze "the impression made on him"; then, through critical disengagement from that impression, he will be able to discriminate the "formula" for Leonardo's genius. But the role of the legend in this procedure is curious. Surely "the impression made on him" was formed in large part *by* these received legends, but he claims the legends instead, after the fact, as corroborations of a vision supposedly arrived at through an unmediated encounter with his object. The circularity of the method's logic as usual serves the purpose of creating a provisional sense of objectivity: because it is "given" from without, the legend itself functions as an object, endowing Pater with a sense of access to past reality which he then uses to support his present impression. That sense of objectivity comes from the legend's status as a historical document, not from its factual accuracy. Through Pater's aesthetic revision of the principle of historical documentation, the legend itself becomes an "inter-preter." It "intervenes"—the process of history has put it—between Leonardo and Pater. When the interpreter in the present can have his impression confirmed by another interpreter closer in historical time to the object under analysis, the sense of historical distance is mediated by that agreement.

Despite his grudging acceptance of "antiquarian" criticism here, Pater more often incorporates an "enlarged" legend than a "corrected" legend in his own essays. But fact is pivotal to his method, too, even though a reader will be hard-pressed to find in *The Renaissance* more than a sentence or two in sequence of "fact" unblended with interpretive intervention. Facts literally establish pivot-points around which the prose turns. "The year 1483 is fixed," Pater writes, with a tone of vindicated recovery after the remarkable paragraph on Leonardo's love of alchemy, divination, clairvoyance, and occult knowledge.

> The year 1483—the year of the birth of Raphael and the thirty-first of Leonardo's life—is fixed as the date of his visit to Milan by the letter in which he recommends himself to Ludovico Sforza, and offers to tell him, for a price, strange secrets in the art of war. (R, 108)

It is entirely characteristic of Pater to mark a date by crossing the lives of two artists in this way. But it is interesting also to note that he has used the antiquarian Amoretti here to "fix" this date, for the letter to Sforza was first published there, as Hill pointed out.[4]

Interesting, too, is the word "fixed," which occurs frequently throughout Pater's work. We encountered it in the "Conclusion," for example, where he urges his readers to "fix on" a particular moment as the quintessentially aesthetic strategy for stilling the Heraclitean flux. If we read the present passage against the "Conclusion," the anxiety aroused in Pater by Amoretti's having "left hardly a date fixed" becomes clearer. The notion of flux in the historical record

---

4. Hill's notes, p. 367.

threatens Pater's extremely hard-won epistemological stability. He needs the sense of a stable, external historical reality to ground the fluctuations of present consciousness, yet, unlike most of his contemporaries, he also knows that the reception of the historical record is itself a creation, an aesthetic act. Like the aesthetic "moment," a date can serve as a formative, fixed point amid the amorphous unknown of past time. As a register of this service in his prose, a date interrupts present interpretation with a return to its presumptively "objective" ground.

In *The Renaissance*, facts are used to close off long passages of interpretation by enacting a return to the historical record. Like punctuation, they mark the place where one train of thought ends and another begins. Like ballast, they bring Pater's prose back down to earth. They anchor passages of symbolic animation to the historical basis of that animism, the spirit of the age, and they provide a new ground from which another flight will take off in turn. In the midst of his discussion of Du Bellay's *Deffense*, for example, after a passage on the "music and dignity of languages," he uses fact to take the essay in a new direction: "Du Bellay was born in the disastrous year 1525, the year of the battle of Pavia, and the captivity of Francis the First" (R, 164). Or later in the same essay, to turn from his discussion of a trivializing tendency in the work of The Pléiade, he begins again: "Ronsard became deaf at sixteen" (R, 170). These pivotal facts typically occur at the beginning of the paragraph, and they function more clearly than any other stylistic device to establish the essay in a new position. In the sense that it "turns" the prose, this gesture is in all its forms a trope on factuality.

A supposed fact can serve this pivotal function when it is not adequate to the truth Pater wants to tell, or even when it turns out not to be true at all. In these cases, Pater's dialectical troping on fact becomes quite clear. For example, in his effort to unravel the sources of Leonardo's image of the Mona Lisa, Pater admits: "but for express historical testimony, we might fancy that this was but his ideal lady, embodied and beheld at last" (R, 124). Here Pater seems at first resentful of the historical fact for arguing against or standing in the way of an idealistic interpretation. But the Mona Lisa soon turns out to embody the end of a particularly Victorian quest for the "true ideal in the actual," or the concrete universal, here realized in the specifically historical and personal terms most congenial to Pater.[5] And so the fact

---

5. See William Wimsatt, "The Structure of the 'Concrete Universal' in Literature," *PMLA* 62 (March 1947), 262–80; and René Wellek, "The Concept of Realism in Literary Scholarship," in *Concepts of Criticism* (New Haven, Conn.: Yale University Press, 1963), pp. 222–55.

of Lisa's historically documented existence grounds Pater's symbolic interpretation of her portrait in the actual; he cannot "raise" her "to the seventh heaven of symbolic expression" without a ground to raise her above, without a ground to raise her *against*. Her historical factuality is not adequate to the higher reality he wants to reach, but the particular sort of symbolism Pater specializes in depends upon just such a secure historical foundation.

Another example may serve to show what happens when a "fact" turns out not to be true. At one point in "Joachim Du Bellay," Pater quotes two stanzas of "Avril" to show how Ronsard transforms the French *chanson de geste* into a Pindaric ode, only to admit immediately after the quotation: "That is not by Ronsard, but by Remy Belleau, for Ronsard soon came to have a school" (R, 159). Caught within the temporality of the reading process, one has no choice but to recognize each of these positions in turn as fact.[6] This passage is set up, then, like a problem in historical research. First the poem is accepted as Ronsard's, then one learns the facts. And the fact is that these poetic styles were so closely identified with one another in their original historical time and place that together (along with others) they form a "school," a constellation of figures called "The Pléiade." On the one hand, the words of "Avril" are offered as completely concrete and historically specific, but on the other hand, they represent a more generalized and abstract, though still historically specific, force, the spirit of the age. Pater's use of fact here mediates between the linked levels of specification and generalization characteristic of the Hegelian element of his aesthetic historicism.

Legend is often employed in the same dialectical way, first presented as factual history and then revealed as traditional story. It, too, serves a pivotal function, as Pater frequently interrupts a passage of historical information with an illustrative fable that advances the historical argument figuratively. The difference in discursive registers is especially felt when he explicitly announces (as he often does) that the story is in fact a fable or legend, thus setting it off against the background of a less formally differentiated passage by delicate but definitive signals. Sometimes he admits this only after the fact, so to speak, allowing us to imagine that we are reading a factual account, only to be disabused in the end. For example, Pater tells a long story of Verrocchio's stunned disappointment when he sees an angel's face painted by the young Leonardo and realizes for the first time that he

---

6. Compare Stanley Fish's related description of the "self-subverting" process of reading Pater in "Literature in the Reader: Affective Stylistics," reprinted in *Is There a Text in This Class?* (Cambridge, Mass.: Harvard University Press, 1980), pp. 30–37.

has been surpassed; Pater concludes by saying, "But the legend is true only in sentiment" (R, 102).⁷ Sometimes Pater prepares his reader ahead of time. When he alludes to the anecdote in Vasari about Leonardo frightening his father with a decorated shield covered with pictures of lizards and snakes, he offers a disclaimer before detailing the story itself: this "story of an earlier Medusa . . . is perhaps an invention; and yet, properly told, has more of the air of truth about it than anything else in the whole legend" (R, 105–6).

This particular maneuver displays Pater's self-conscious awareness of the reconstructive effort involved in the historical record itself. At the same time, it shows him playing with the ambiguity generated by such an awareness, as he closes the space between fact and interpretation momentarily, only to open it again with his brash disclaimers. He likes to establish a foundation in the factual and then to let the facts recede or fall away in the service of another "higher" or "deeper" truth. In this sense, historical legend provides a paradigm for the aesthetic historicist, for it represents the effect of interpretive intervention that has *already* taken place, shaping the received views of future ages with the force of the given "data."

Pater frequently achieves the "sense of objectivity" in his prose by highlighting a historical legend and by effacing his own powers of interpretation in the present. The resulting sense of objectivity is an aesthetic creation in at least two senses. As the locution "sense of" should always remind us, Pater renounces the belief in direct access and aspires instead to a recreated, dialectical simulacrum of the object.⁸ But more important, this sense of objectivity in his prose is aesthetic because it depends completely on regarding the objects "with which it has to do" as objects of art. A legend may be regarded in this light—as an expression of the spirit of the age—just as much as a poem may be regarded as the expression of a particular individual spirit. This sense of objectivity, then, comes not from scientifically verifiable truth or factuality, but from the historical integrity of objects. Here again Pater depends on the historical difference or distinction of art objects for his very concept of a modern, relative form of knowledge, and what most makes it possible to regard something in the spirit of art is to apprehend it in all its unique historicity.

---

7. Though Mrs. Pattison attacked Pater for using this story on the grounds that it was historically inaccurate, and though Pater himself offers this characteristic disclaimer, he has in the twentieth century been vindicated. The "legend" turns out to be true, according to the latest scientific findings. See Hill's notes, p. 365.

8. As in "sense of escape," "sense of freedom," "imaginative sense of fact" (B, 190; R, 231; A, 9–10).

Interpolated quotations function this way, as pivotal, as historically specific, and as "objective." This function is served—this effect is produced—whether or not they are quoted accurately [9] and whether or not they are attributed properly. In the example given above, in which we read a poem supposedly by Ronsard only to find out that it is really by Belleau, the quoted stanzas still appear before us as concrete and objective, despite the shifting attribution. Pater uses this object, these stanzas, as a fulcrum for an operation in historicist aesthetics. He shifts the historical register up one level in generalization, making the stanzas of "Avril" evidence of a period style, not of a personal style, evidence not of an author but of the "spirit of the age." Of course, this concrete, objective effect of quotation is felt even more strongly when the attribution turns out to be correct, but even then the "sense of fact" inherent in a quotation derives from its physical, material presence in a passage and from the effect it gives of momentarily effacing Pater's individual perspective, not from its accuracy.

Interpretation will always intervene to gloss the significance of the quotation, but meanwhile Pater's impulse to push beyond the concrete toward a "spiritual" meaning is arrested momentarily by the objective reality of the words on the page. This is especially the case when, as so often in Pater, the passage is partially or wholly given in a language other than English. As I argued in Part One, section 4, Pater's use of the pivotal quotation from Novalis in the "Conclusion" depends upon the German words appearing momentarily defamiliarized, before Pater's very loose translation turns the essay away from its initial representation of "modern thought" and toward a closer identification with Pater's own views. The "objectivity" of the German words is functional, contextual, and relative; the perspective of the essay shifts around them in order to take a retrospective stance toward "modern thought." Soon they become thoroughly absorbed or "translated" into Pater's own perspective, but for a moment they seem to come from elsewhere. And like objects of art, these quoted words come already endowed with a sense of historicity, uniqueness, and difference. Concrete words from the past, then, like paintings or sculptures, have their own plastic value in aesthetic prose.

Pater's profound sense of the absolute historicity of every aesthetic object grounds his work, even at its most abstract or visionary. The concept of historicity is finally much more useful for an understanding

---

9. I respond here to Christopher Ricks, "Pater, Arnold, and Misquotation," *Times Literary Supplement*, 25 November 1977, p. 1384. See also Monsman's reply to Ricks in *Walter Pater's Art of Autobiography* (New Haven, Conn.: Yale University Press, 1980), pp. 15–17.

of Pater's critical method than the discussion of fact and departure from fact can ever be. His attention to the value of historicity emphasizes once more that Pater's aestheticism has first to do with the empirical values of concretion and particularity, and only then with aesthetic form in a more general sense.[10] Like historicism, aestheticism works along the spectrum from the most particularized points of representation toward the most generalized points. The ideal is reached only through the actual, the visionary through the historical, and even when Pater's vision pushes insistently beyond the concrete it remains grounded there.

Pater's attention to historicity is more profound and complex than the simple (though potent) recognition of the unique, objective features of any work. He frequently attends to the history of a given historicity. He reads through the visible characteristics of an object for signs of its story: details of its original context, its relation to kindred objects, and curiously, its fortunes in the world *after* its creation. All its accidental transformations over time contribute to its particular formal features in the present. To Pater, for example, the Venus of Melos no longer looks incomplete—or rather, its incompleteness has interpretable significance as a feature of a present, reintegrated, objective reality. Its "frayed" surface and "softened" lines speak to Pater of its burial for centuries under the furrows of that "little Melian farm" and of its exhumation early in the nineteenth century (R, 67–8). But aside from its burial and fragmentation, the sculpture exemplifies the historically composite form that Pater loves, for its head derives from one era, its nudity from another, and its posture from yet another.[11] Pater's sense of its present historicity incorporates the historical life summed up in its form, as well as the ways in which it changed after its creation. For Pater the Venus of Melos surprisingly demonstrates the aesthetic power of a geological and evolutionary form built up over centuries of modification.

Furthermore, Pater recognizes the incompleteness of the Venus as a historically specific form of incompleteness, pointedly different from the "studied incompleteness" of Michelangelo's slaves. Though the present form of the Venus results from the accidents of history rather than the purposive shaping of an individual artist, it has no less aesthetic value for that reason, and perhaps in some senses it has more.

10. Bloom (introduction to *Selected Writings of Walter Pater*, ed. Harold Bloom [New York: Columbia University Press, 1982], p. viii) reminds us that "Pater meant us always to remember what mostly we have forgotten, that 'aesthete' is from the Greek *aisthetes*, 'one who perceives.' "
11. Hill's notes, p. 341.

It redoubles the concretion of historicity, of historical "difference": like all aesthetic objects, its form is different from every other form and is the result of a unique history, but the Venus of Melos also records in its form the signs of historical difference as composite parts of its present objective wholeness. Pater characteristically generalizes the significance of this composite form as evidence of the historically evolving spirit of art. To him the fragmentary form of the Venus produces the sense of "some spirit in the thing . . . on the point of breaking out, as though in it classical sculpture had advanced already one step into the mystical Christian age" (R, 67–68). Pater interprets the unique object as an embodiment of a more general movement, the recovery of classical art in the Middle Ages, a movement that is significantly replicated in the nineteenth-century archaeological discovery of the object. Pater grounds his interpretation in the particular, then translates the objective sense of historicity into a more generalized, spiritual register.

This tendency to concentrate on the history of an object reflects Pater's desire to see all aesthetic form—whether particular or in general, whether object or genre—as historical form, expressive of and formed in history. But he often goes further and animates the history of an object by figuratively giving it a life history, as if it were a person. The story of "Aucassin et Nicolette," Pater writes, "has come to have . . . a sort of personal history, almost as full of risk and adventure as that of its own heroes" (R, 16–17). The "risk and adventure" to which he alludes turn out to be the historical, accretive formation of a composite and transitional genre called the *cantefable*, a tale told in prose with interpolated songs. Pater describes this aesthetic form as a double structure of two intertwined historical developments, for the prose framework coalesces around the songs during the history of their transmission, while the songs themselves evolve, promising "a novel art . . . arising, the music of rhymed poetry" (R, 17). In three linked levels of increasingly generalized historical representation, Pater makes "Aucassin et Nicolette" stand for a new art form, and that new art form stand for the spirit of the age. If biographical legend can be regarded as a historical object, an object can also have a personal history.

The concrete historicity of an object is most vividly apprehended in stylistic terms. For Pater, style is the mark of *personal* expression, and here again we can see why biographical legend figures so prominently in his work.[12] As he would later explain in *Plato and Platonism*:

---

12. Monsman discusses the "tendency to portraiture" that was already evident in the critical method of *The Renaissance*; see Gerald Monsman, *Pater's Portraits: Mythic*

If in reading Plato, for instance, the philosophic student has to re-construct for himself, as far as possible, the general character of an *age*, he must also, so far as he may, reproduce the portrait of a *person*. (PP, 125)

"Style" as *stilus* registers the impression the artist (and the age) makes on every one of its products. Pater's aesthetic historicism grants the "spirit of the age" an aesthetic agency like that of any individual artist, to inscribe its characters on the plastic shape of time. Pater does sometimes use the Goethean-Carlylean figures of the "seed-bed" or the "loom" of time, but his vehicles for the shaping force of the *Zeitgeist* are more often plastic, stylistic or inscriptive, and biographical. He studies the "characters" of time, written in the lives and works of aesthetic history.

Style in Pater is the quintessential register of the historical existence of art. In Pater's work, to speak of style is immediately to speak historically; to describe a style is to represent the unique historicity of an artist or a period. In "Joachim Du Bellay," for example, he writes of the period style of The Pléiade:

There is *style* there; one temper has shaped the whole; and everything that has style, that has been done as no other man or age could have done it, as it could never, for all our trying, be done again, has its true value and interest. (R, 167)

Pater's sense of the uniqueness of style here comes directly from his poignant sense of the absolutely different and unrepeatable past. The fact that "for all our trying" it can "never . . . be done again" is exactly what gives style its aesthetic value. "We feel a pensive pleasure," he writes of Ronsard, "observing how a group of actual men and women pleased themselves long ago" (R, 166). Pater's effort to interpret past styles is an attempt to revive within the present what must also be appreciated as irrevocably past.

In this effort, the related strategies of totalizing the "temper" of a whole age and of projecting that putative wholeness as an individual person serve to create a sense of reunification and recovery. Pater's concept of style is grounded in the (biographical) specificity of each individual artist's "genius," but it depends equally upon projecting that model on a more general level. Thus, his interpretation of art history is based on these systematically linked levels of historical

---

*Pattern in the Fiction of Walter Pater* (Baltimore, Md.: Johns Hopkins University Press, 1967), pp. 36–37.

specificity and generalization: aesthetic object, person, "school," *Zeitgeist*, and overarching *Geist*. The *Zeitgeist*, though spiritual, disembodied, and therefore not "objective," is figuratively given "objective" wholeness and spiritual "life" by being analogically projected on the model of the individual person. A personal life history is absolutely specific and concrete. With the implicit belief that all the disparate events and products of a life add up to some sort of unity in the end, Pater sets out to discover or reconstruct that unity; he then generalizes its form and makes it representative of the age.[13] The stakes are high. The story of an individual life, interpreted in this manner, yields Pater a stage in the overarching curve of "the life of humanity," a phase of the *Zeitgeist* represented in an individual, concrete body.

In this system of historical aesthetics, an artist's life story is the ultimate evidence, for it links the history of an individual person with the spirit of his age, on the one hand, and with the objects that survive into the present, on the other. Pater finds a precedent for this view in the early humanist terms of Pico della Mirandola, who wrote that the individual person is *"nodus et vinculum mundi"*—the "bond or copula of the world," in Pater's translation (R, 40). Pico meant to stress the place of humanity between heaven and earth. But in Pater the individual person is the *"nodus et vinculum"* that links the *Zeitgeist* to its enduring material evidence in objects of art. In Pater's version of a later and decisively more secular humanism, the *Zeitgeist* has replaced "heaven" as the spiritual referent, but "earthly" forms still refer to their spiritual ideal. Thus, Pater's aesthetic historicism regards each aesthetic object and each person as fully concrete, loved "for its own sake" alone, yet at the same time historical phenomena must be exegetically read as evidence of things not seen. The historicity of style, according to this view, is both intensely "objective" and intensely "spiritual," based on the transfigured logic of an older metaphysical system whose very transformation into aesthetic terms is Pater's devotion.

If the life story of an artist is legendary rather than factual, it only serves to heighten the sense in Pater's work that aesthetic reconstruction is a necessary and unavoidable part of all retrospective knowledge. Pater's interpretation is all the more true to his poetics of revival

---

13. Here, too, Carlyle is the important precursor: his concept of heroic "types" in *On Heroes and Hero-Worship*, his essay on biography, his idealist notion in *Sartor Resartus* of the personal body (and institutional "bodies") as "clothes" for the spirit of time. This strain in romanticism may also be illustrated by Emerson's *Representative Men*. Monsman (*Pater's Portraits*) mentions also the historical methods of Burckhardt, Michelet, and the German romantic historians in this regard.

when it thus tacitly acknowledges that it is based already on other interpretive interventions. We cannot "come face to face with the people of a past age," Pater writes in "Aesthetic Poetry." Of a past age we have only "the element it has contributed to our culture; we can treat the subjects of the age bringing that into relief" (B, 196). Basing his own interpretations on the "received" story rather than on scientifically established data, Pater concentrates on that very element, the element a past age has contributed to his own present culture. These are the stories "which every one remembers," whether they are true or not (R, 99).

The facts are obscure, disputed, and indeterminate, and when they are clear they are disappointingly meager, bare bones where flesh and breath are wanted. Pater registers the difficulties of historical knowledge in his recognition that all we have of the past are relics that have somehow survived. He appreciates the composite forms that testify to those accidents of transmission. The received story perhaps is adulterated, perhaps entirely illegitimate, but a legend's questionable status reinforces its interpretive value because it marks the effects of the time that has intervened between Pater and the object of his research. A legend is fact transfigured in time. Thus, a legend is all the more true to the fact that the past is seen in retrospect from a distant present, for a legend registers in its own questionable shape the ineffable space of historical difference.

## 2 · Myths of History: *The Last Supper*

The word "legend" derives from the Latin *legere*, "to gather," and behind the Latin lies the Greek *legein*, "to gather" or "to say," a variant of *logos*, "speech" or "reason." That its ultimate derivation from the *logos* has been transformed over the years into "legend"—the name in English of a traditional story whose factual basis is assumed though it has been transfigured during the course of its transmission—is curiously appropriate to Pater's use of the word, for he nostalgically but stoically lays to rest the belief in immediate, direct access to knowledge and concentrates instead on gathering up whatever can be received through historical mediation. In his modern, historical age, to gather is not "to say" but to recollect what has been written. A legend embodies, in Pater's words, what "every one remembers," that part of the past which has survived in the present, in stories that are appreciated half historically, half aesthetically (R, 99).

But Pater begins his discussion of Leonardo's legend by invoking the *"legend,* as the French say." Referring to the French opens another range of nuance, for the French say *légende* is an inscription on an object, or a descriptive caption under an image, or an explanatory key to a symbolic system. Indeed, a legend often underwrites Pater's interpretation of a work of art, and that interpretation usually refers ultimately to the working of history in general. With legendary fragments of the artist's life as an explanatory key, works of art supply Pater with a vast symbolic system through which he reads the signs of History itself. In order to see Pater's method at work over the course of an entire essay, I will concentrate in sections 2 and 4 on "Leonardo Da Vinci" but in section 3 I will make a detour to examine Pater's own critical distinctions between history, allegory, myth, and symbol.

Pater introduces the essay by naming Leonardo as the painter "who has fixed the outward type of Christ for succeeding centuries." This he presents as a historical fact, which came about despite the irony of Leonardo's reputation for "holding lightly by other men's beliefs, setting philosophy above Christianity" (R, 98). Later Pater will build on this tension between Leonardo's enormously influential representation of Christ and his legendary skepticism toward Christianity as belief, to characterize the doubleness of aesthetic history in general. But to posit it as a tension in the first place is to begin already having interpreted, and this particular interpretation is based on legend, as Pater easily and immediately acknowledges: "Words of his, trenchant enough to justify this impression, are not recorded, and would have been out of keeping with a genius of which one characteristic is the tendency to lose itself in a refined and graceful mystery." Here the very remoteness of Leonardo's life, the very absence of historical evidence, ostensibly supports Pater's point. In order to find the suggestion of Leonardo's apostasy, Pater returns to the first edition of Vasari, for in the second edition (he points out), "the image [of Leonardo] was changed into something fainter and more conventional" (R, 98). The founding moment of this essay, in other words, is based on a search backward through the legendary sources, the acknowledged choice of one legend over another, and the preference for a story more vivid and antithetical over one more conventional and "faint." The chosen story, too, is "closer" in time to its historical original. Pater reaches back toward the actuality of Leonardo's life through a mediator less distanced than he in time, and he reaches past Vasari's conventionalized revisions to the earlier, more colorful version of the legend.

Almost the entire first half of the essay is devoted to setting up a complicated interpretive framework based on the legends of Leonardo's life. Leonardo's illegitimate birth, his apprenticeship to Verrocchio, his interest in the occult, his lifelong preoccupation with smiling women, his homosexuality—all contribute to Pater's portrait of Leonardo as the possessor of secret wisdom. The epigraph Pater adds in the third edition, *"homo minister et interpres naturae,"* only encapsulates as a literal legend the portrait that is quite palpable throughout: Leonardo "living in a world of which he alone possessed the key" (R, 107). A lover of "remote beauty," Leonardo "weighted" Italian art with the deeper, richer humanity "of a later age" (R, 105, 110, 103), for the "nature" Leonardo interprets is also quintessentially the nature of human personality, which he "embodied with a reality which almost amounts to illusion" (R, 111). He had learned "the art of going deep" and was

> no longer the cheerful, objective painter, through whose soul, as through clear glass, the bright figures of Florentine life, only made a little mellower and more pensive by the transit, passed on to the white wall. (R, 104)

Pater hypothesizes here a mythically transparent, "cheerful, objective painter," in order for Leonardo to mark the historical difference from that clarity. As usual, aesthetic value is produced as historical effect: later, deeper, and more difficult of access. Sometimes, as Pater says, Leonardo goes too deep, "too far below that outside of things in which art begins and ends" (R, 112).

This conflict is expressed in Pater's "formula" for Leonardo ("curiosity and the desire of beauty") which establishes the idea of a dialectical struggle between knowledge and art. Leonardo's problem was the "transmutation of ideas into images" (R, 112). In that respect, the science of his age was not entirely antithetical to art, for unlike "our exact modern formulas" it was itself devoted to clairvoyance, divination, and alchemical transmutation, "seeking in an instant of vision to concentrate a thousand experiences" (R, 106). Though Pater detects in Leonardo's genius a "German element" that, "as Goethe said, had 'thought itself weary'—*müde sich gedacht,"* yet in the moment of *"bien-être"* Leonardo's inspired execution enables him to embody the idea in the image and thus to refine a "cloudy mysticism" into "a subdued and graceful mystery" (R, 113–14). (Meanwhile, the German and French tags insistently remind us of Pater's own synthetic transmission.[1])

Like Leonardo's vision of nature, Pater's vision of Leonardo's life and work reveals a system of correspondences between things, "through which, to eyes opened, they interpret each other" (R, 103). He uses the legend of Leonardo's life as the key to unlock an interpretation of his work, and his interpretation of the work becomes the key to a significance even "more remote." Pater purports to see *through* Leonardo's legend to the mysteries of historical process. The famous passage on the Mona Lisa will seem less obtrusive and at the same time more profoundly important if we see it in its context, near the end of an essay that generates it as an emblematic recollection.

Not until the second half of the essay does Pater pause over individual works at any length, and then, too, biographical legend forms the chief support of his interpretations. When he turns to Leonardo's *Last Supper*, for example, he does not at first write of the visual appearance of the painting itself. He first approaches it through the legends that have grown up about its execution, its subsequent decay, and the many attempts to restore the painting. "A whole literature has risen up," he writes, and he singles out the comments of Goethe as perhaps the best. No matter how apocryphal, legendary, or interpretively variant the contents of the record may be, it is a historical fact that a tradition of commentary has "risen up," and Pater accordingly treats the legends and commentary as received historical "data." For example, he reports that a "hundred anecdotes" have been told about Leonardo's painstaking, hesitant, inspired execution of the painting. For Pater, the tradition of belief in Leonardo's careful execution is beyond dispute, whether or not he was actually as fastidious as the anecdotes claim, whether or not he actually refused to work except at the moments of *"bien-être."* Like Leonardo's "fix[ing] the outward type of Christ," these anecdotes fix in the minds of succeeding generations a portrait of Leonardo. Pater identifies himself with the received view of Leonardo's method, accepting the legend as that part of the past which has survived to become a part of his own present culture.

According to the anecdotes, Leonardo scorned the idea of art by "industry and rule" and worked only in the "moment" of intensity, yet at the same time he pursued a new method of execution because it "allowed of so many afterthoughts, so refined a working out of

---

1. I have been developing certain effects of the German influence. For the French influence, see John J. Conlon, *Walter Pater and the French Tradition* (Lewisburg, Pa.: Bucknell University Press, 1982).

perfection" (R, 120). Passionate and careful, inspired and self-possessed by turns, both an artist and a scientist, Leonardo exemplifies in another age and medium Pater's understanding of aesthetic practice. Yet Pater's interpretation of Leonardo's legend turns on a significant fact from the technical history of painting. It turns out that Leonardo's new method—painting in oil on a plastered wall—though admirable in its refinement, was less durable even than fresco. The painting has faded terribly over the course of time. In other words, from a perspective in the late nineteenth century, Leonardo's image of "the outward type of Christ" is less fixed in any present, objective sense than it is through the tradition of copies taken from its original. Like Pater's image of Leonardo, it is impossible to grasp directly; it must be seen in large part through the mediation of others. Pater goes on to make the painting a vehicle first for the difficulties of historical revival and finally for the attenuation of Christian faith since the Renaissance.

First he comments on the secularization involved in Leonardo's image of Christ:

> Here was another effort to lift a given subject out of the range of its traditional associations. Strange, after all the mystic developments of the middle age, was the effort to see the Eucharist, not as the pale Host of the altar, but as one taking leave of his friends. (R, 120)

Seeing in Leonardo's painting the portrait of Christ's humanity, Pater sides with Clément and Goethe against Rio, for Rio had argued against Goethe that the figure embodies a meditation on Christ's divinity.[2] This interpretive choice also tacitly identifies in Leonardo an earlier stage of the "higher" or historical criticism of Pater's own modern moment. His quiet pun on "Host" (as the one who receives guests, as the Communion he offers them) is quintessentially Paterian. And in another characteristically Paterian shift toward a higher level of historical generalization, he interprets Leonardo's portrait of a human Christ as evidence of the Renaissance return to sensuality after the "mystic" representations of the Middle Age.

Pater then suggests that the painting has been etherealized by the fadings of time, that it owes "part of its effect to a mellowing decay" (R, 120). He concentrates on the passage of time as it is registered in the visible, formal features of the painting, which to his eyes gains in

---

2. Hill's notes, pp. 376–77. Pater in general follows Clément and Michelet in his general view of the Renaissance as a representational return to the human body, the senses, and the natural world. See also Inman, *Walter Pater's Reading*, pp. 197–201, 206–7.

aesthetic value from its evidences of great age and the accidental effects of change. To Pater, those accidents of history have an interpretable historical significance of their own. In an amazingly unconventional interpretation, he reads the very head of Christ to signify the waning of belief in Christianity over the centuries.

> The head of Jesus does but consummate the sentiment of the whole company—ghosts through which you see the wall, faint as the shadows of the leaves upon the wall on autumn afternoons. This figure is but the faintest, the most spectral of them all. It is the image of what the history it symbolises has been more and more ever since, paler and paler as it recedes into the distance. Criticism came with its appeal from mystical unrealities to originals, and restored no life-like reality but these transparent shadows—spirits which have not flesh and bones. (R, 120–21)[3]

Unlike the method of the "cheerful, objective painter," through whose transparent soul the "figures of life . . . passed on to the white wall," Leonardo's dialectic of interiority—moments of inspiration followed by painstaking afterthoughts—produces translucent, fading figures, through which the wall soon begins to show. Pater's metonymic passage through the painting to the wall enacts, in more than one respect, a metaphorical displacement. On the simplest level, the figures of the disciples become first ghosts and then the shadows of leaves, a double transformation through which Pater first rids the wall of the images of human life and then dispenses even with the ghostly copies of human form. The autumnal leaves that remain to shadow the wall duplicate that loss of life, because life is leaving them too: they are dying at the year's end, and they are being displaced by their shadows. But more important, Pater makes our ability to see through these fading figures to the wall beneath them a figure for the demystifying process of secularization. As the images of belief fade in time, more and more we can see the blank wall they formerly concealed.

In this remarkable passage, Christianity itself appears to have been an aesthetic construct whose method of representation has not been equal to the forces of time. The painting fades in vividness despite all efforts to preserve it, and its fading reveals the blank ground against which an image of belief has been raised by the effort of human hands. Pater's figure, in other words, is a composite figure, composed of

---

3. The last sentences (from "It is the image" to the end of this passage) do not appear in the 1893 edition but do appear in all other editions. The phrase "as it recedes into the distance" appears in the 1888 and 1900 editions; all others, including the *Fortnightly*, read "as it recedes from us." See Hill's notes, p. 233.

Leonardo's figures of Christ and the disciples, taken together with their background; and Pater's figure metafigurally records both the aesthetic act of projecting the image of Christ upon the wall, as well as the subsequent historical fact of its decay. Leonardo's "faint" and "spectral" figure "symbolises" to Pater the Renaissance attempt to return to the historical, physical, and "natural" reality of Christ, a reality now "paler and paler as it recedes into the distance." But Pater's figure, which consists of Leonardo's figures against their ground, symbolizes not just the historical process of secularization, but even more radically, the aesthetic act necessary to cover the blank wall with sacred images in the first place. This is a figure of historical "relief," in other words, here employed to express not the act of historical knowledge, but its opposite, the brevity of life in historical time, the fading of historical memory.

There is a cutting irony in the doubleness engendered by Pater's aesthetic historicism here. In retrospect, even the Renaissance attempt to renaturalize religious imagery seems to have reinscribed instead the "mystical unrealities" of the Middle Ages. The modern attempt to bring Christ closer by imagining his humanity rather than his spirituality has had the unexpectedly opposite effect of bleeding the image of its spiritual color and making his historical reality seem even further away. Pater shows that Leonardo "fixes" the "outward type of Christ" as human, he paradoxically "fixes" the moment when Christian belief begins to come unfixed, to fade into the "humanism" of modern representation. As Leonardo's fixation literally comes unfixed, it signifies to Pater not its original but the necessity for later copies. In this submerged allegory of the remorseless irony of secularization, the loss of spirituality has been figured as the loss of aesthetic form, which paradoxically creates the sense of greater spirituality—but this time as an aesthetic and historical effect. Images of human "nature" and aesthetic color avail only partially to represent spirituality, and always ironically; this particular Renaissance attempt to return Christian imagery to a more natural and sensual reality has produced instead the denatured effect of ghosts, specters, shadows, and transparencies. This attempt of "criticism" to return to "originals" has succeeded only in marking the distance from them.[4]

4. Monsman illuminates Pater's interest in copies and lost originals with a Derridean light; see, e.g., *Pater's Art of Autobiography*, pp. 22, 26, 58. I agree with Monsman (and Hillis Miller, "Pater: A Partial Portrait," *Daedalus* 105 [Winter 1976], 97–113) that Pater was acutely conscious of the infinite regress involved in a search for origins. Perhaps for that very reason I believe that, while it is important to pursue the poststructuralist critique of Pater, it is equally important not to equate Pater's own strategies of reading with poststructuralist strategies.

Another way to grasp this irony would be to examine the complexities of Pater's vertiginously shifting perspective here. On the one hand, the "humanism" of Leonardo's portrait of Christ identifies the Renaissance with the nineteenth century, and in this light the Renaissance represents a true difference from the Christian Middle Ages. The very term "Middle Ages" is a sign of this difference, which, from the point of view of Pater's modern synthesis, redefines the Christian era as the "middle" term in a three-term history, the "antithesis," in other words, of the classical age. But on the other hand, from Pater's late-nineteenth-century perspective of difference from both, the Renaissance difference from the Middle Ages collapses into likeness, all one continuously developing attenuation of Christian imagery. It seems, too, that the denaturing of the Christian tradition and Pater's heightened rhetoric are in an inverse and dynamic relation to one another, history and symbolism rising as belief fades. And characteristically, after this passage of densely compressed and heightened rhetoric, Pater re-anchors his discourse with a pivotal recourse to the historical facts. The next paragraph begins with the matter-of-fact, contextualizing statement that "the *Last Supper* was finished in 1497; in 1498 the French entered Milan . . ." (R, 121).

Pater's treatment of Leonardo's *Last Supper* represents one characteristic movement in *The Renaissance*. From the various legends of an artist's life, Pater moves toward the stability and objectivity of the surviving work. He concentrates intently on a particular object, appreciating the historicity of its appearance, the legends of its special creation, its history since then, and the effects of that history on its objective form. Together with his focus on the particular object, he begins to weave the sense of a deep correlation between the legendary life and the work. Both present Pater with aesthetically objective forms; both refer to the same period of original, specific historicity; and both have histories of their own, which show visibly in their forms. As Pater's correlation between the recreated legend and the survivng work attains a certain level of coherence, it generates a shift to a higher level of generalization. The special history of the life and work are then projected as a model for historical process in general. Finally the object with its special history exists in Pater's prose within a penumbra of symbolic, allegorical, and mythic associations.

When Pater writes that the image of Christ in the *Last Supper* "symbolises" a certain history, he uses that term to pretend that the meaning he has assigned somehow inheres in the object itself. In the sense that Leonardo's image of Christ "symbolises" the historical existence of a human Christ because it is painted in a more realistic, less stylized manner than previous images of Christ, the term is accurate, but in the sense that the faded image is made to stand for the modern process of secularization, "allegory" would be a more accurate term. In other words, Pater's interpretation of the painting is *both* symbolic and allegorical. In fact, in the course of the passage, Pater shifts the rhetorical register from symbol toward allegory. This is an extremely important point, for the conjunction of symbol and allegory indicates Pater's subjective identification with the object of his regard and at the same time indicates his disengagement. He circumvents the problems of solipsism through the assertion of symbolism, the assertion that the meaning actually inheres in the object. Then, refreshed by this belief in the objectivity of the symbol, he goes on to develop allegorical narratives of historical process, in which the "spiritual" significance is "more remote" from its vehicle, that vehicle is no longer an object but the history of an object, and the interpreter has clearly intervened to institute this allegorical remoteness between object and meaning.[5]

But Pater's is a peculiar form of allegory in which the spiritual meaning is a generalized and temporalized extension of signs that may be perceived in the object itself. The allegorical significance takes us far beyond the object to the workings of historical time, but that level of spirituality as well as narrative extension has been unfolded from an objective point, through a symbolic interpretation of the object's unique historicity. And to the extent that the interaction of symbol and allegory generates an interpretation of History in general, Pater has also produced a myth. Here again it is a peculiar form of myth, not only because it is a myth of History (a common form in the nineteenth century), but also because the narrative or temporal form of the myth is unfolded through the symbolic interpretation of an object. These interpretive practices reach their apotheosis in Pater's reading of the Mona Lisa, but before we turn to that passage, it would be helpful to have in mind Pater's understanding of history, allegory, and myth.

5. I am indebted to de Man's discussion of the distinctive structures of symbol, allegory, and irony in "The Rhetoric of Temporality," in Paul de Man, *Blindness and Insight* (1971; reprint, Minneapolis: University of Minnesota Press, 1983), pp. 187–208.

## 3 · The Historicity of Myth

In "Pico Della Mirandola," Pater draws a fundamental distinction between the historical method and the allegorical method. The Renaissance of the fifteenth century was a great age, he says, in part because of what it attempted instead of what it actually achieved. He goes on to argue that much of what it aspired to do was accomplished only in the eighteenth century, "or in our own generation." The particular aspiration Pater has in mind is the "reconciliation of the religion of antiquity with the religion of Christ." He evaluates the difference between history and allegory specifically in relation to that synthetic aspiration. And, as usual, the distinction he draws between the two methods leads him both to differentiate his modern, historical age *from* the allegorical Renaissance and to identify his age *with* the Renaissance as an earlier stage in the overarching attempt to forge the modern synthesis.

> A modern scholar occupied by this problem might observe that all religions may be regarded as natural products, that, at least in their origin, their growth, and decay, they have common laws, and are not to be isolated from the other movements of the human mind in the periods in which they respectively prevailed; that they arise spontaneously out of the human mind, as expressions of the varying phases of its sentiment concerning the unseen world; that every intellectual product must be judged from the point of view of the age and the people in which it was produced. He might go on to observe that each has contributed something to the development of the religious sense, and ranging them as so many stages in the gradual education of the human mind, justify the existence of each. The basis of the reconciliation of the religions of the world would thus be the inexhaustible activity and creativeness of the human mind itself, in which all religions alike have their root, and in which all alike are reconciled; just as the fancies of childhood and the thoughts of old age meet and are laid to rest, in the experience of the individual.
> Far different was the method followed by the scholars of the fifteenth century. They lacked the very rudiments of the historic sense, which, by an imaginative act, throws itself back into a world unlike one's own, and estimates every intellectual creation in its connexion with the age from which it proceeded. They had no idea of development, of the differences of ages, of the process by which our race has been "educated." In their attempts to reconcile the religions of the world, they were thus thrown back upon the quicksand of allegorical interpretation. The religions of the world were to be reconciled, not as successive stages in a regular development of the religious sense, but as subsisting side by side, and

substantially in agreement with one another. And here the first necessity was to misrepresent the language, the conceptions, the sentiments, it was proposed to compare and reconcile. Plato and Homer must be made to speak agreeably to Moses. Set side by side, the mere surfaces could never unite in any harmony of design. Therefore one must go below the surface, and bring up the supposed secondary, or still more remote meaning,—that diviner signification held in reserve, *in recessu divinius aliquid,* latent in some stray touch of Homer, or figure of speech in the books of Moses.

And yet as a curiosity of the human mind, . . . the allegorical interpretation of the fifteenth century has its interest. With its strange web of imagery, its quaint conceits, its unexpected combinations and subtle moralising, it is an element in the local colour of a great age. It illustrates also the faith of that age in all oracles, its desire to hear all voices, its generous belief that nothing which had ever interested the human mind could wholly lose its vitality. (R, 33–35)

In this passage there are also many "element[s] in the local colour of a great age," Pater's own late nineteenth century. In addition to the thoroughly historicist assumption that "every intellectual product" must be evaluated in relation to the age and culture in which it was produced, we can see Pater's characteristic hypostases of "the religious sense" and "the human mind itself" as overarching, totalizing categories. Religions are "natural products," which have their "root" in the soil of the *Geist* and which exhibit life histories of "growth and decay." But in this passage the underlying horticultural organicism is entirely supplanted by the metaphor of the transhistorical, inexhaustible "human mind" as an individual person. One familiar consequence of this metaphor, as usual, is to equate historical retrospection with personal memory in old age, when the overall diversity of an entire life span may be most comprehensively "reconciled."

Here Pater explicitly reworks the Wordsworthian dynamics of compensatory retrospection, this time on the general historical level. He obliquely acknowledges this transfiguration of Wordsworth later in the same essay. Arguing that Pico's life perfectly reflected his philosophical attempt to reconcile the pagan and Christian religions, Pater describes Pico in old age as if he were one of Heine's gods in exile, lying down in his Dominican habit, "reconciled" at last to Christianity but remembering his "comely" pagan earlier life. Pointedly misquoting Wordsworth at this point, Pater commends Pico's desire "literally to 'bind the ages each to each by natural piety' " (R, 44). Apparently the shift in emphasis from a person's "days" to the historical "ages" was common in the period, and Pater may have borrowed it from Jowett.¹ This particular piety is anything but "natural," though the invocation of Wordsworth clearly shows Pater's desire to see it as so.

Here the basic personal metaphor for historical growth and retrospection is joined to the notion of "education," with the additional consequence that earlier religions are related to later ones as childhood "fancies" are related to mature understanding.² When *Bildung* is thus projected on the level of the *Geist*, the potential for nationalistic and totalitarian extremes in historicist thinking comes clearly to the foreground. In this passage, Pater's concern for the process through which "our race" has been "educated" affords us a hint of the conclusions that can follow upon this particular constellation of assumptions in the world of practical activity. Indeed, Pater's "aesthetic" historicism may be seen as the dialectical counterpart of contemporary Social Darwinist, imperialist, and racist historicisms.³ This particular myth of history, in other words, has its own historicity, and we are still partially in its shadow.

But the main focus of the passage is Pater's graphic contrast between the historical method and the allegorical method. He draws this contrast as the difference between temporal and spatial modes of "reconciliation." The fundamental representational strategy of "the historic sense" involves "ranging" things in a series, "as so many . . . successive stages in a regular development." Allegory, on the other hand, "reconciles" by first placing things "side by side" and then going "below the surface" to "bring up the supposed secondary, or . . . more remote meaning." The developmental series imitates the sense of change over time, whereas allegorical juxtaposition imitates "agreement" as coexistence in space. In historical representation, perceived difference on the surface is given priority, whereas in allegory those

---

1. Jowett's essay "On the Interpretation of Scripture" appeared in *Essays and Reviews* (1860). There Jowett likens mankind in its maturity to "the patriarch looking back on the entire past, which he reads anew, perceiving that the events of life had a purpose or result which was not seen at the time; they seem to him bound 'each to each by natural piety' " (quoted in Hill's notes, p. 331).

2. For an excellent discussion of this metaphor, its source in Lessing, and its popularization in English through Frederick Temple's lead essay in *Essays and Reviews*, "The Education of the World," see Hill's notes, pp. 323–24. See also Pater's representation of Pico's "childish dream" of the world as a "painted toy" (R, 41–42).

3. On the abuses of this metaphor, see Stephen Jay Gould, *Ontogeny and Phylogeny* (Cambridge, Mass.: Harvard University Press, 1977), pp. 115–66. A good piece on the relation between the *Geisteswissenschaften* and the rise of the Third Reich is by Simon During, "On Cultural Values and Fascism," *Southern Review* (University of Adelaide, South Australia) 17 (July 1984), 166–81. See also Karl Popper, *The Poverty of Historicism* (Boston and London: Beacon Press, 1957).

surface differences are bypassed in favor of "deeper" agreement "below the surface." In Pater's description, the historical mode aligns itself with the realistic and the symbolic in its attention to the priority of material form, and yet the developmental series does imply its own sort of spiritual "agreement" or unity, and in this it is aligned with allegorical narrative. The material and spiritual terms, though, are very close in historical representation, in the sense that the allegorical signification is merely a generalized version of the material signifier—as, for example, when Pater reads Leonardo's portrait of a human Christ as an embodiment of the spirit of the age attempting to return to nature and human personality. Pater's mode of historical representation temporalizes the concrete universal, which is another way of saying that it is symbolic and allegorical at once. Instead of going "below the surface" to bring up the "diviner signification" of unity, the developmental series projects it "beyond" or "above" the surface, displaying highly visible difference against an invisible assumption of overall continuity. Historical difference is thus transformed into the different stages of the "same" developing thing.

I hope Pater's terms here for the "agreement" achieved through allegorical signification ("secondary" and "more remote" as well as "diviner") will resonate with my discussion of "Aesthetic Poetry" from Part One to suggest once again that Pater's particular strategies of historical representation mix allegorical and symbolic modes in historically significant ways. His description of the allegorical meaning as that "diviner signification held in reserve" seems more reminiscent of Tractarian poetics than of fifteenth-century Neoplatonism, despite the Latin tag from Pico's *Heptaplus*.[4] We shall return to the particular sort of symbolic allegory Pater develops, but we can feel here his attraction to "its strange web of imagery" (a phrase that clearly echoes the famous passage on the Mona Lisa), for it is always on a level either "below" or "above" the surface that the "generous belief" in reconciliation may be fulfilled; on the surface lies the sheer fact of historical difference.

The fifteenth-century "faith . . . in all oracles, [the] desire to hear all voices" is Pater's nineteenth-century faith as well. Though his method of "reconciliation" differs from Pico's, Pater reconciles these historically different methods as earlier and later stages of the same thing, the same overarching desire for "reconciliation" rather than

---

4. On the Tractarian notion of "Reserve," see G. B. Tennyson, *Victorian Devotional Poetry: The Tractarian Mode* (Cambridge, Mass.: Harvard University Press, 1981).

difference. Pater's nineteenth-century version of the "faith in all oracles" holds that his own "true method of effecting a scientific reconciliation" fulfills the promise of Renaissance allegory and that finally "whatsoever things are comely" may be truly reconciled in the present.[5] In this light, Pater sees his own historic method as the development of Renaissance allegory, a "childhood fantasy" of the "human mind," grown to the maturity of a generalized self-reflection.

But my argument that the allegorical method does not remain distinct from the historical method in Pater's critical practice should not blind us to the other important features of this passage. In addition to drawing explicitly the enormously instrumental distinction between temporal and spatial modes of representation, Pater here makes the crucial move of historicizing entire modes of thought and representation. His association of allegory with the fifteenth century exposes another facet of Pater's sensitivity to the absolute historicity of "every intellectual product." Like an object of art, a distinct form of thought has its own aesthetic coherence, and its form reflects a particular time and place. In fact, Pater explicitly makes the connection between works of art and forms of thought, calling Pico's philosophy the "feebler counterpart" of the art of the period, where the spirit of the age is more powerfully, because more concretely, embodied (R, 47). Pater's sense of the absolute historicity of style is a direct result of hypostatizing the "spirit of the age," and his aesthetic understanding of the style of a period's thought is its corollary. Pater finds evidence of historically specific modes of thought in characteristic narrative forms, and he historicizes past modes of thought, embodied in narrative forms, as "mythologies."

A good example occurs in the context of his discussion of Renaissance allegory. Pater has argued that the art of the period was more successful than Pico's philosophy in the attempt to reconcile classical, pagan art with the now-dominant Christian tradition. In this common attempt, Renaissance art produced a new growth, a strange and beautiful hybrid. And Pater offers a little parable to illustrate the successful assimilation of pagan and Christian imagery in Renaissance painting:

> Hence, a new sort of mythology, with a tone and qualities of its own. When the shipload of sacred earth from the soil of Jerusalem was mingled with the common clay in the Campo Santo at Pisa, a new flower grew up from it, unlike any flower men had seen before, the anemone with its

---

5. R, 27. Pater's play on Philippians 4:8 shifts an ethical and theological reference to an aesthetic end.

concentric rings of strangely blended colour, still to be found by those who search long enough for it, in the long grass of the Maremma. Just such a strange flower was that mythology of the Italian Renaissance, which grew up from the mixture of two traditions, two sentiments, the sacred and the profane. (R, 47–48)

Symbolic narrative seems to be one Paterian strategy for concretely representing plastic or pictorial form in aesthetic prose. Here Pater takes the received legend of the sacred soil and adds his own horticultural figure, the anemone "which grew up from the mixture."[6] By calling attention to the special "tone and qualities" of this "new mythology," Pater returns, figuratively, to the subject of Renaissance allegory. His decision to add the anemone focuses the legend of synthesis on another level. In its received version, the legend already suggests the synthesis of sacred and common soil in the Renaissance, but Pater's turn upon it suggests as well the blend of historical and allegorical methods in the late nineteenth century.

On the one hand, the figure of the anemone—an organic, spontaneous growth from a mixture of soil and clay—expresses a nineteenth-century understanding of historical generation from an amorphous, collective ground. That growth is understood dialectically as the result of two variant backgrounds, here literalized as two different types of soil, which generate a new strain—a third, synthetic term. But on the other hand, the figure embodies the Renaissance allegorical method of reconciling pagan and Christian sentiment by finding correspondence "below the surface," here literalized as underground (R, 35). The production of a new type of flower illustrates the modern, historical sense of the evolution of new types, but the particular flower, with "its concentric rings of strangely blended colour," also illustrates the Renaissance practice of spatial, rather than temporal, reconciliation of difference.

Pater uses this organic image of historical "relief" to convey the habits of a precritical age in which classical story was simply accepted and assimilated within the pictorial frame. As an example, he recalls Michelangelo bringing the "sleepy-looking fauns of a Dionysiac revel into the presence of the Madonna" and giving "that Madonna herself much of the uncouth energy of the older and more primitive 'Mighty Mother' " (R, 48). This "picturesque union of contrasts" is exactly that: picturesque. The "reconciliation" effected is pictorial and imagistic rather than temporal, involving "concentric rings" or spatial

---

6. Hill's notes, p. 331.

frames of enclosure. Pater's temporal, narrative "explanation" of this new growth is a hybrid generated from the "strange blend of sentiment" of his own poetics of revival.

Pater is also capable of historicizing the thought of his own present day, as we have already seen several times over. In doing so, he also characterizes a modern form of "mythology," and of course he finds its embodiment in a historically specific aesthetic form—in this case, a narrative form. He wonders, at the end of "Winckelmann," how the human spirit can achieve a "sense of freedom" in spite of the binding forces of modern life,[7] and he answers that the best modern novels provide a model for "regarding . . . life as the modern mind must regard it, yet reflecting upon it blitheness and repose" (R, 231). He interprets novelistic plot as the most effective modern expression of the entangling "network" that inextricably binds the outer and the inner worlds (as we have seen in the "Conclusion"). Pater's historical view of narrative form enables him to see in the modern mode of relating a story a model for the inextricably complex "relations" of "modern thought." In other words, the relations drawn through novelistic plot serve as a model or simulacrum of the modern "truth of relations" (with which we are familiar from the essay on Coleridge):

> The chief factor in the thoughts of the modern mind concerning itself is the intricacy, the universality of natural law, even in the moral order. For us, necessity is not, as of old, a sort of mythological personage without us, with whom we can do warfare; it is a magic web woven through and through us, like that magnetic system of which modern science speaks, penetrating us with a network, subtler than our subtlest nerves, yet bearing in it the central forces of the world. Can art represent men and women in these bewildering toils so as to give the spirit at least an equivalent for the sense of freedom? Certainly, in Goethe's romances, and even more in the romances of Victor Hugo . . . this entanglement, this network of law, becomes the tragic situation, in which certain groups of noble men and women work out for themselves a supreme *Dénouement*. (R, 231–32)

7. The closure of this essay turns on another Paterian revision of Arnold, specifically his rejection of the modern art of consciousness in Arnold's 1853 "Preface" to *Poems*. The cadence of Pater's formulation ("And what does the spirit need in the face of modern life? The sense of freedom") revoices (and revises) Arnold's famous question and its answer: "What are the eternal objects of Poetry, among all nations and at all time? They are actions; human actions." Whereas Arnold attempts to turn away from "the dialogue of the mind with itself," Pater in this essay describes the modern art of "consciousness brooding with delight over itself" (R, 211). For another discussion of Pater's response to Arnold on this matter, see David DeLaura, *Hebrew and Hellene in Victorian England* (Austin: University of Texas Press, 1969), pp. 293, 298.

This modern understanding of "necessity" places it not only "without us" but also deep within. In Pater's analysis here, Goethe and Hugo truly represent the spirit of their age by figuring necessity not as an external "mythological personage" but as "this entanglement, this network of law," not as God but as novelistic plot. Pater calls attention to the historical shift in modes of relation by juxtaposing an older myth with a more modern one, and in doing so he takes a critical distance from both. He confidently speaks "for us" in demythologizing the sacred story of his own culture, but the "mythological personage without us" ambiguously conflates all anthropomorphized gods, secularizing pagan and Christian gods alike and replacing them with a modern determining force no less mythically described, for all its scientific provenance, as the "magic web woven through and through us."

As these examples show, Pater historicizes past and present systems of thought and belief as "mythologies," treating them no longer as forms of knowledge but as aesthetic forms. The comprehensive effect of this distancing and critical treatment is to reinvest skeptically "demythologized" forms of thought with expanded historical and aesthetic value. In this frame of reference, we can see clearly what Pater means when he says that certain stories "properly told" acquire the "air of truth" (R, 105–6). "Properly told," a story can simulate in its form the "relations" that characterize the spirit of a person's life or of an age. In this view, the form of narrative—like any other aesthetic form—represents the inaccessible past by imitating this spirit in a model or structure. That model makes no claim to revive the past directly, but as an aesthetic and historical object it bestows a provisional "objectivity," or as Pater might say, a deeper, more remote *sense* of objectivity. Its form of truth—the truth of form—depends not on objects "in themselves" but on their internal relations. The "air" of truth, then, is its spirit, the representation of those invisible relations that Pater believes obtain alike in lives and works, both participating in a *Zeitgeist* that etches "every intellectual product" with its "style." An interpreter is necessary to unlock the symbolic form with a legendary key and to unfold its significance in narrative, historical terms. This process of generating the "spiritual" level of historical significance produces what from our point of retrospection may be seen as Pater's own modern myth of history.

## 4 · Myths of History: The Mona Lisa

"Properly told," Pater writes, the story of an "earlier Medusa" has more of the "air of truth" than anything else in the entire legend. This story tells of the young Leonardo painting a wooden shield with a grotesque amalgamation of lizards, snakes, bats, and glowworms, all rendered so true to life that they frightened his father. In calling this the story of the "earlier Medusa," Pater draws a connection between this legendary childhood prank and the adult Leonardo's "fascination with corruption," which Pater finds embodied in the corpselike *Medusa* of the Uffizi.[1] And within the structure of Pater's essay, both early and later Medusas prefigure Leonardo's portrait of *La Gioconda* (the Mona Lisa).

When Pater draws this relation between earlier and later versions of the supposedly "same" image, he tacitly attributes to Leonardo a certain psychological coherence, and that internal coherence is understood to be reflected in his works over time, as long as they too are read in developmental terms. The arc of continuity projected beyond or above the local invention of each different "phase" is the contribution of the interpreter, who unifies all phases by "ranging them in a series." The embedded, implicit narrative in Pater's essay on Leonardo creates this sense of an essential coherence that develops over time, the retrospective, aesthetic sense of a story "properly told," a story that breathes the "air of truth" because the revelation of a last Medusa fulfills the developmental promise of the earlier ones in the series. So too Pater's interpretation of her image lends the "air of truth" to his previously expressed "formula" for Leonardo's genius. Like the presence that rose so strangely beside the waters, Pater's passage on the Mona Lisa rises against the elaborate groundwork of the essay as a whole to show that Leonardo's inherent fascination with "the smiling of women and the motion of great waters" emerges at last in that portrait. In other words, both Leonardo's masterpiece and Pater's famous modern poem appear more visibly "heightened" when seen against their backgrounds, for they gather and sum up Leonardo's artistic development, the processes of history, and the movements of Pater's essay in one emblematic recollection.

---

1. In his edition of *The Renaissance*, Kenneth Clark notes that the Medusa of the Uffizi is a seventeenth-century painting after Caravaggio but that it may be based on a lost original by Leonardo (quoted in Hill's notes, p. 366). See also Monsman, *Pater's Art of Autobiography*, who reads the Medusa as an allegory of the relation of the author to his text (pp. 59–62).

The essay begins its approach toward the Mona Lisa through a thicket of brief glances at other works by Leonardo (at first chiefly drawings) and these pages are characterized by nervous energy, wandering attention, and erratic passion (R, 114–18). The theme of sexual indeterminacy weaves into Pater's consideration of the mysteries of influence just at the point in the essay when the short passage on Leonardo's "clairvoyants" begins moving explicitly toward the Mona Lisa. A brief consideration of Leonardo's "feeling for maternity" leads Pater to his passionate remarks about the drawing (after Leonardo) of a "face of doubtful sex." Pater loved this drawing and used it in an engraved vignette on the title page of his Renaissance volume. This face leads him to consider another, "which might pass for the same face in childhood, with parched and feverish lips." And the "thread of suggestion" generated by these two versions, early and late, of the supposedly "same" beautiful face "of doubtful sex" leads Pater, by means of a significant displacement, to a brief consideration of "Leonardo's type of womanly beauty."

Pater's tone shifts to the vatic and sinister when he considers the clairvoyants, but the notion of their "chain of secret influences" soon returns him to a consideration of Leonardo's favorite young men, and there the tone shifts again. At this point in the essay, the "chain of secret influences" shimmers in a multivalent haze of signification, linking female figures of both benign maternity and sinister clairvoyance, fantasies and biographical legends of male homosexuality, and the dissemination of Leonardo's painterly style through copies. His "lost originals" have been historically transmitted through copies made by devoted pupils and servants, who were "ready to efface their own individuality" in return for initiation into Leonardo's occult knowledge. The "chain of secret influences" refers explicitly, then, to the historical transmission of Leonardo's images, which has been implicitly linked here to the erotics of heterosexual generation, on the one hand, and to homosexual, aesthetic transmission, on the other. After another glance at mother and child, Pater turns to the naked and womanly picture of John the Baptist with his "treacherous smile." He considers both its likeness to the Bacchus hanging nearby in the Louvre and the gradual disappearance (over the history of its transmission in copies) of the cross from the Baptist's hand. Through this image, in other words, Pater associates a theory of secularization with his sexualized theory of historical transmission.

Much commentary precedes Pater's on this famous androgyne Baptist, and he bows in passing to Gautier and Heine. These influences (especially Gautier and the unacknowledged but essential Swinburne) are behind Pater's text both at this point and later, in his discussion of the Mona Lisa.[2] The complex and shifting relations here—between homosexuality, maternal sexuality, sexual indeterminacy, intertextuality, and the notion of aesthetic "generation," dissemination, and influence—need and deserve much more critical attention. But my immediate purpose in sketching these movements so briefly is to establish the sexually charged atmosphere gathered around Pater's consideration of the *Last Supper* and the Mona Lisa. These nervous, electric pages appear to sublimate their energy in and through Pater's symbolic treatment of the Mona Lisa. Certainly the energy of these pages must be remembered when Pater admits that the "given person or subject . . . is often merely the pretext for a kind of work which carries one quite out of the range of its conventional associations" (R, 119).

Leonardo's problem, according to Pater, was the "transmutation of ideas into images," and that is Pater's problem as well. He describes the painting's effect of "subdued and graceful mystery," in the very same phrase he used to describe the moment of *bien-être*, when the alchemy is complete and an idea is successfully "stricken into colour and imagery" (R, 114, 123). He stresses again the legendary controversy about Leonardo's method: Was the painting done in a fevered burst of inspiration, "as by a stroke of magic," or was it done over years and years of painstaking labor, never really to be finished at all? He calls Leonardo's painting the "revealing instance of his mode of thought and work," but he leaves the exact nature of the revelation uncertain, double, mysterious. Pater, like Leonardo, uses *La Gioconda* as a "vent for his thoughts." He seizes on Leonardo's images of the Last Supper and of Lisa in the same way that Leonardo finds his pretexts as easily in the "incidents of the sacred legend" as in the faces of the "living women of Florence." Pater takes Lisa's image "as a symbolical language for fancies all his own . . . and rais[es] her, as Leda or Pomona, Modesty or Vanity, to the seventh heaven of symbolical expression" (R, 123).[3]

As in his treatment of the *Last Supper*, Pater approaches the Mona Lisa more closely through the legends of its execution. Unlike Leonardo's paintings of the "sacred legend," this portrait was done from life. Pater stresses that fact, although he wonders at the relation between the "real" source and its "ideal" resonances, between the element of "mere portraiture" and what Pater soon will call "imaginary portraiture."

---

2. Pater's remark about the *Last Supper* applies with even greater justice to the Mona Lisa: "a whole literature has risen up" around it (R, 119). Others include Clément and Taine. For remarks of Gautier and Heine, see Hill's notes, pp. 374–75.

3. The 1893 edition of *The Renaissance* reads "cryptic language for fancies all his own"; all other editions read "symbolical language" (Hill's notes, p. 234).

Were it not for "express historical testimony," Pater argues, we might believe that this lady was Leonardo's "ideal," realized at last in an image. But it is important to Pater's argument that her physiognomy was a recorded, historical fact. He uses the "express historical testimony" dialectically, proposing it and immediately turning it against itself, bringing it forward only to protest its inadequacy as an explanation of the image. He goes on to propose a range of alternative "sources" for the image, generating a rich sense of the "secret influences" behind the "express historical testimony." But then, in the midst of this meditation on the mysteries of influence, Pater brusquely returns to anchor his argument in the fact that the picture was copied from nature: "Besides, the picture is a portrait" (R, 124).

Pater's argument here has to do with the mysterious concatenation of outer and inner forces that link an individual artist's soul with the spirit of his age. The highest concentration of pure invention seems often to go hand in hand, Pater argues, with an element "given to, not invented by, the master" (R, 123). Pater's concept of this "given" element joins historical "data," the world of nature, a secularized notion of grace in the moment of *bien-être*, and the mysteries of aesthetic "influence" in a complex interplay of forces from outside, a modern and revised notion of inspiration. "Express historical testimony" first anchors the source of the image in the world outside the self. And yet Lisa's smile reminds Pater of Leonardo's earlier drawings, indicating a coherent development, over time, of an essentially inward fixation. That development, in turn, might indicate an even "earlier" source in obsessional fantasy, a dream persisting unaccountably from childhood, or it might indicate Leonardo's deepest psychic structure, an entelechy, an ontogenetic coding that Pater usually calls "temperament," the irreducible element of individuality neither "influenced" nor even "accidental," but simply "given." On the other hand, the smile seems to predate Leonardo himself, for it reminds Pater also of Verrocchio's personal style. Perhaps the smile was internalized and transfigured through Leonardo's own devoted apprenticeship, his self-effaced copying of his earlier master's work. In this aspect as "given," as "present from the first," the Mona Lisa becomes a symbol to Pater of all the "lost originals" gathered up and finally recovered in one image.

> The presence that rose thus so strangely beside the waters, is expressive of what in the ways of a thousand years men had come to desire. Hers is the head upon which all "the ends of the world are come," and the eyelids are a little weary. It is a beauty wrought out from within upon the flesh, the deposit, little cell by cell, of strange thoughts and fantastic reveries and

exquisite passions. Set it for a moment beside one of those white Greek goddesses or beautiful women of antiquity, and how would they be troubled by this beauty, into which the soul with all its maladies has passed! All the thoughts and experience of the world have etched and moulded there, in that which they have of power to refine and make expressive the outward form, the animalism of Greece, the lust of Rome, the mysticism of the middle age with its spiritual ambition and imaginative loves, the return of the Pagan world, the sins of the Borgias. She is older than the rocks among which she sits; like the vampire, she has been dead many times, and learned the secrets of the grave; and has been a diver in deep seas, and keeps their fallen day about her; and trafficked for strange webs with Eastern merchants: and, as Leda, was the mother of Helen of Troy, and, as Saint Anne, the mother of Mary; and all this has been to her but as the sound of lyres and flutes, and lives only in the delicacy with which it has moulded the changing lineaments, and tinged the eyelids and the hands. The fancy of a perpetual life, sweeping together ten thousand experiences, is an old one; and modern philosophy has conceived the idea of humanity as wrought upon by, and summing up in itself, all modes of thought and life. Certainly Lady Lisa might stand as the embodiment of the old fancy, the symbol of the modern idea. (R, 124–26)

Pater reads the famously enigmatic expression as the sign of a deep, modern interiority. In this he follows a tradition that begins with Renaissance humanism, for Dante and Castiglione named the smile as the distinguishing human feature. This "presence" rises as the present, the culminating moment of all past history, and her monumental figure is represented at a great distance from the natural world exterior to the self.[4] "Older than the rocks among which she sits," she transcends nature in priority, as if the human figure were represented against a natural landscape only hypothetically or by convention. Pater's reading highlights the notion that consciousness is represented allegorically "against nature," in the purely oppositional sense as well as in the dialectical and pictorial senses. Her image has been so vertiginously foregrounded as to render the natural background inaccessibly remote and mysterious. This is Pater's image of modern "consciousness brooding with delight over itself," a characterization of interiority very different from Arnold's "dialogue of the mind with itself" (R, 231). Here there is no dialogue, for the lips are shut in a mystic smile; and "the eyelids are

---

4. Both Bloom and Monsman reflexively link Pater's vision of the Mona Lisa to his own critical method. Bloom discusses this passage in connection with Pater's "deidealizing" of the epiphany and his embodiment of Renaissance and romantic historicisms; see Bloom's introduction to Pater's *Selected Writings*, pp. xv–xxi. Monsman (*Pater's Art of Autobiography*, pp. 24–25) makes the point that Lisa represents the aesthetic, present "moment," which contains both past and future.

a little weary," not only because they are closing on the memory of all past history but also because they are expressive of a gaze turned inward, a mystic half-shutting of the eyes.[5]

Even more than the Mona Lisa's visible signs of interiority, her summation of all history makes her "modern" in a particularly Paterian sense. Of course, interiority and recollection are inextricably linked through Pater's theory of historical expression. If the idea of "expressive" form depends on a relation between an inside and an outside, then Pater's vision of the portrait derives its extraordinary power from his strategic conflations and recursive inversions of outer and inner worlds. Lisa's beauty is "wrought out from within upon the flesh," at the same time that she represents "humanity as wrought upon by . . . all modes of thought and life." Her form, in other words, is "wrought" both from within and from without. Pater's plastic and inscriptive sense of form is evident here. The *stilus* of the world spirit has "etched and moulded" the "changing lineaments" of her outward form, making it purely "expressive" of all she has experienced and internalized. At the same time, her outward form embodies that internalized spirit, making it visible and holding it within, as content.

This view of "expression" is the precise counterpart of the Paterian "impression." It justifies a reading of outward form as signifying an inward, spiritual reality, through the assumption that the interior has first been impressed with the character of the outward world, then turned inside out to display on the surface what has been "etched and moulded" within. Pater's systematically linked levels of historical representation are at work here too in all their wit and economy: the expression on Lisa's individual face stands for the development of an expressively "humanistic" period style and for the dynamics of historical expression in general. The "life of humanity" is given a body and soul, an outside and an inside, by being "embodied" in her image. Pater's Mona Lisa represents a profound historical paradox, a specifically embodied "figure" of the transhistorical *Geist*, the overarching unity-of-development beyond figuration, the point of view from which all specific figures are merely "phases" of the "same" expression. The *Geist* is here figured as a person, and correlatively the modern person encompasses the present state of consummate development in the *Geist*.

The modernity of this "expression"—both Lisa's facial expression

---

5. I am here playing on Pater's etymological discussion of the word "mystic" in "Pico Della Mirandola," in which he locates its source in the Greek "to shut" and then meditates on whether the lips or the eyes were to be shut (R, 37).

and Pater's interpretation of her face as an expression of the "modern spirit"—must be carefully understood on all its levels of specificity and generalization. In the first place, Pater distinguishes modern from ancient, but he does so in a surprising way, by posing a small hypothetical exercise: "Set it for a moment beside one of those white Greek goddesses or beautiful women of antiquity, and how would they be troubled by this beauty, into which the soul with all its maladies has passed!" Given his description of allegory in the essay on Pico, Pater's directive here—to "set it beside" an oppositional figure—has vaguely allegorical overtones, in a passage devoted (as this one is) to historical "reconciliation." But Pater also distinguishes modern from medieval, focusing on the "rise" of the modern spirit in the Renaissance. Much of the introductory groundwork of "Leonardo Da Vinci" is devoted to the premise that Leonardo's work represents Italian art becoming definitively "humanistic." In other words, the "presence that rose . . . so strangely" is a specifically *human* figure, as "rising" against a background is a specifically historical metaphor. At the other end of the particular line originating in Leonardo, Pater's acute consciousness of the human figure as "figure" might well be described as "aesthetic humanism."

For Pater, Leonardo's work embodies the return to nature as *human* nature, but this supposed return is fraught with the signs of departure. Leonardo's love of depth and remoteness marks the distance between nature and the human spirit, whether the human spirit is foregrounded against a natural landscape or hidden within an exotic, *recherché* landscape (R, 110).[6] Leonardo must represent both the return to nature and the turn "against nature" in order to be dialectically significant in Pater's aesthetics of history.

Pater's view of the Renaissance in general (for which Leonardo and his masterpiece are both made to stand) is similarly doubled and dialectical. In one sense, Pater locates the development of romantic inwardness in the Renaissance. However, the word he uses to characterize the formation of the Mona Lisa's deep interiority is "soul," and in this sense the modern spirit stems not from the Renaissance but from the Christian Middle Ages. As we know from his "Aesthetic Poetry" and "Conclusion," Pater associates the "maladies" of the medieval "soul" with his own late romantic consciousness. But again, Lisa is also pagan and pre-Christian, for "the return of the Pagan

---

6. Bloom persuasively uses the historical psychoanalysis of J. H. Van den Berg to argue this point about the relation between the subject and the landscape. See Bloom's introduction to Pater's *Selected Writings*, pp. xx–xxi, as well as "The Internalization of Quest Romance," in Harold Bloom, ed., *Romanticism and Consciousness* (New York: Norton, 1970), pp. 4–7.

world" within the Christian setting is a necessary part of the modern spirit. There is no conflict or contradiction here; Pater's modern spirit is most profoundly characterized as "development," always rising within and against its background, produced recollectively out of everything that came before, oppositionally against what came most immediately before.

In Pater's myth of modernity, the historical and dialectical succession of the Renaissance upon the Christian age is best described as a process through which the "soul" is first generated and then "embodied." Those Greek goddesses have no "soul" to trouble them; their beauty is of the body alone, unselfconscious, innocent, "white" and not yet "wrought upon" by the characters of history. In the Christian age, the "soul" is formed, but the medieval soul has no body; it is unhoused, faded, vagrant. According to this myth, the "spirit of humanity" returns to its senses in the Renaissance, and the soul is clothed in a body again. This "embodiment" creates a space of enclosure within and differentiates inner from outer in a figure.

That these are the familiar terms of literary figuration since Augustine, as well as the terms of Pater's aesthetic historicism in particular, should not be surprising, for Pater's myth of history involves a dialectic of generation through which body and soul come together in the Renaissance and are expressed in certain types of aesthetic objects. Within this system, a literary figure, an aesthetic "embodiment" or work of art, a human life, and the "life of humanity" all display the same basic structure, and they depend on each other for representation. The same relative series describes the moment of fusion in which a work of art is formed, the moment in which a figure is aesthetically revived against a new background, the moment when modern humanism is generated, or the moment when a dialectical view of spiritual history becomes the "given" mode of representation. In other words (to return to the more concrete level of this argument), Pater figures the dialectical synthesis of classical and Christian as human embodiment, emblematically presented here and literalized in the image of a human figure.

This modernist dialectic can be seen only in retrospect, from a post-Renaissance point of view. The strategies of Pater's historical retrospection determine that modernity is defined by lateness and inclusiveness in point of view. His interpretation of the Mona Lisa has Lisa representing this viewpoint, the moment in present consciousness which enfolds all the disparate moments of the past. When this retrospective, ecstatic position is taken, Pater's other figure of historical representation, the series, collapses into one point. As all time is conflated in the aesthetic, epiphanic moment, all narrative, all history, is enfolded in this aesthetic object. A temporal series of successive stages is recast as an image or spatial figure.

Pater's myth of modernism holds that body and soul are completely united, that Mona Lisa lives in the "seventh heaven of symbolical expression"; and in the sense that she unifies all time in one point, the sheer density of conflation represented in her figure must indeed be called symbolic. But on the other hand, the figure suggests the distance between levels of signification more typical of allegory, in the sense that every different past has been placed side by side and united beneath the bodily surface in her deep interiority. Perhaps the "strange webs" she has "trafficked in" are the "strange webs" of fifteenth-century allegory which Pater described in the essay on Pico; those "webs" too revealed "unexpected combinations and subtle moralising" below the surface (R, 35).

Pater's interpretation of *La Gioconda* suggests a modernist revision of allegory, an allegory precisely of History, of one way the passage of time may be imagined in a figure. The metaphor of the person—the figure of the human figure—engineers this conflation of the historical, the allegorical, and the symbolic. Change over time is impersonated in a placed, stable body; the outer form both contains and displays the evidence of a soul. Perhaps of all the secularizations involved in Pater's notion of the rise of modernism in the Renaissance, this is the most fundamental: that the "medieval," Christian soul is reinterpreted as personal memory joined with a sense of history.[7] This fundamental secularization has enormous repercussions as the basis of Pater's physiognomic metaphors and biographical fantasies.[8]

Pater's Mona Lisa is figured both as origin and as end point of a temporality that has collapsed into interior space. Like Pater's retrospective point of view from the present, she represents the end of the line. The biblical allusion ("hers is the head upon which 'the ends of the world are come' ") recalls the Pauline sense of prophetic fulfillment in the present moment, for which the past was understood typologically as an admonitory, prefigurative example (1 Corinthians 10:11). But here the Christian sense of prophetic fulfillment has been

---

[7]. Monsman points out that the difference between Lisa and the goddesses of antiquity is her knowledge of history (*Pater's Art of Autobiography*, p. 45).

[8]. And it may be usefully seen as a feature of the period as well. On the tenacious hold of physiognomy on the nineteenth-century imagination, see Neil Hertz, "Medusa's Head: Male Hysteria under Political Pressure," *Representations* 4 (Fall, 1983), 27–54. Among other things, Hertz discusses the belief in seeing history as the features of a face, "lineaments" and "features" of physiognomy as the chief metaphors for historical interpretation in Hugo and Tocqueville, and Hegel's critique of Lavater on this point in the *Phenomenology*. For Pater's interest in Lavater, see R, 185–86.

secularized as a historical vision of development in which the entire past contributes to the definitive fullness of the present moment. "As Leda" and "as Saint Anne" she originates both classical and Christian traditions, in a figure that again makes sexual generation a metaphor for historical dialectic. Pater reaches back behind the history of each tradition to find a mythic, personal figure for the generative source within which it was still enfolded.[9] Again, Pater allegorically sets two female figures "side by side" in order to make a point about historical "reconciliation." Leda and Saint Anne figuratively represent the two historical traditions that together make up the modern spirit. In Pater's understanding, the modern spirit is generated from these two traditions dialectically and over historical time, but here both traditions are de-temporalized, collapsed into their origins and enfolded within figuratively originary names, as if within the body of the mother.

Because Mona Lisa represents both the modern spirit and the primal mothers of the modern spirit, she could only have given birth to herself, in a figurative equation of parthenogenesis and palingenesis.[10] As both origin and end, she rises from her own conception, consciousness giving birth to itself. Pater's visionary figure, in other words, both strains to represent and at the same time negates his theory of history, for Mona Lisa expresses dialectical generation in time even as she collapses all time into one interiorized point. In this sense she embodies the pull of Hegelian historicism away from the body and toward the spirit, but these allegorical, maternal figures for tradition and dialectic may suggest as well that Pater's image of the "consciousness brooding with delight over itself" has nurturant, incubational, and generative connotations, as well as the moodily solipsistic connotations so frightening to Arnold.[11]

This vision of what Yeats would later call Unity of Being is seductive for many obvious reasons.[12] Mona Lisa is "expressive of what in the

   9. This line of argument is indebted to Monsman's discussion of the Magna Mater in *Pater's Portraits*, pp. xiv, 19–20, 27, 106–7, 115, 126, 137–8, 167–9, 183.
   10. See William Shuter, "History as Palingenesis in Pater and Hegel," *PMLA* 86 (May 1971), 411–21.
   11. See the valences of "brooding" which Hopkins evokes in "God's Grandeur":

   And for all this, nature is never spent;
   There lives the dearest freshness deep down things;
   . . .
   Because the Holy Ghost over the bent
   World broods with warm breast and with ah! bright wings.

   12. Bloom (in introduction to Pater's *Selected Writings*, p. xvi) points out Pater's prefiguration of Yeats's Unity of Being. Paul Barolsky expands upon this argument in chapter 2 of his *Walter Pater's Renaissance* (University Park: Pennsylvania State University Press, 1987), pp. 29–39.

ways of a thousand years men had come to desire." What they had come to desire (at the moment in historical time during which Pater wrote of *La Gioconda*) was the belief that they could recapture, restore, and incorporate the past. If each person can spiritually contain all of history, and if History can be embodied in a personal form, then nothing must ever be estranged, lost, or uncomprehended. Whatever has been locked away may be reopened with the right mediating key or "legend." Pater's historical retrospection, grounded in Christian historicism and aesthetics, as well as in the romantic aesthetics of interiority and personal memory, could recover the lost world, could stabilize, recontain, and unify past time. This is Pater's vision, a vision of the immense powers of interpretation.

But this vision has its dark side as well. Lisa's portrayal as a fatal female with connections both to Muse and to Medusa indicates her danger and power simultaneously, for if she contains the entire past in a present moment of silent, expressive fulfillment, she also embodies a vision of its inaccessible, absolute anteriority.[13] One cannot look at her face through the lens of Pater's prose without becoming, like her, immobilized in the collapse of temporality. Her enigmatic expression is full of significance precisely *because* its meaning is remote and uncertain; like any divinity, her expression demands interpretation, but the more it is interpreted the more remote it seems. "Sweeping together ten thousand experiences," she produces a vertigo of retrospection in which all historical distinctions spin together. There is no difference, no "relief," within the metafigural figure of transfiguration itself. Like Tennyson's Tithonus, one learns through Pater's vision of Lisa the horror of immortality without eternal youth. To have a sense of rebirth or revival as "relief," a sense of death must first make the critical separation. "Like the vampire, she has been dead many times," but her face betrays the frightening paradox of death-in-life as well as the hope of renewed life after death.

Pater extricates himself from this terrible vision by taking a retrospective position *toward it* in the passages of his own prose. The last two sentences turn away from her "presence" to comment on its significance. "The fancy of a perpetual life . . . is an old one," he placidly states, pulling out of an identification that would threaten to destroy the subtle balancing act that makes his aesthetic historicism possible. He assumes a stance toward his vision of Mona Lisa which imitates the stance he has imagined her taking toward everything

---

13. Bloom, introduction to Pater's *Selected Writings*, pp. xix–xx: "Lady Lisa perpetually carries the seal of a terrible priority."

prior to herself. He subsumes her, relativizing, historicizing, and recontaining her as an "earlier" phase of his own "modern philosophy." The disengagement here shows Pater's aesthetic historicism at its strongest and most ambivalent point. He implicitly historicizes his own vision of *La Gioconda* as a past mythology with its own style of expression, like a work of art. And, characteristically, he detaches himself from his impression with an allusion to scientific discourse, the realm within which what will later be seen as "myth" may for the moment, and for that moment only, be read as fact.

From our point of view, then, it is possible to historicize Pater's stunning use of the "modern philosophy" of evolution. Nowhere is it more clear that Pater both deeply understood and deeply feared Darwin's theory than here, when he tries to neutralize its difference by figuring it merely as a modern version of an ancient belief in the transmigration of souls. This is the same strategy he used in the "Conclusion," finding comfort in an ancient version of "modern thought" from the *Cratylus*. Pater may also be seen to mark a particular moment in the late-nineteenth-century development of a popularized Social Darwinism. His critical fallacy here lies in the tacit equation of cultural "humanity" with a biological species, as if historical development and biological evolution were easily assimilable. In one sense, Pater bases his faith that the past may be recaptured in the notion that each individual's cultural growth recapitulates and therefore contains in personal memory the development of the culture at large, a belief that ontogeny recapituates phylogeny in the realm of cultural history. Mona Lisa is Pater's most famous experiment in recapitulationism, but he conducts the same experiment with Marius and with Plato, as we shall see.

Pater's reading of the Mona Lisa is a second-order myth, a myth of myths, and in this it displays its own particular historicity. Within this passage we can see the Platonic myth of recollection transposed into a specifically historical and biological matrix, as earlier in this study we saw Pater grounding his enabling belief that "the composite experience of all the ages is a part of each one of us" in the immediately available contexts of historical and biological science. From our later vantage point, we can historicize Pater's aesthetic, mythic use of the concept of development itself, with its overarching assumption of unity and subsumption of difference, its tendency to see the difference of specific figures as transfigurations of the "same" ongoing spirit.[14]

---

14. This move to historicize certain forms of history-writing is today most associated with the work of Foucault, who exposes many of the perspectives from which "develop-

But we can also historicize Pater's interest in the spirit of the Mona Lisa as a composite form, the quintessential form of historicist aesthetic composition. Gathering former myths into a visionary recollection, Mona Lisa marks the historical moment of early anthropological myth collection, before structuralists systematize the study of myth in general and before literary high modernists make of mythic recollection the dominant literary method. Like the water she rises against, "a network of divided streams," Pater's passage is composite of many pasts, recorded in the words of others, and it generates a divided genealogy of its own (R, 111). At least the reflections of resemblance may be felt in many modernist mythopoeic works: Yeats's *Vision*, Eliot's *Waste Land*, Pound's *Cantos*, the transmigrating soul and shifting sexuality of Woolf's *Orlando*, and Molly Bloom's sleepy question about metempsychosis, not to mention the monumentally recollective modernist structure of Joyce's *Ulysses* itself.

Pater's interpretation of the Mona Lisa forms the climax of "Leonardo Da Vinci." Indeed, coming after it, his closing discussion of *The Battle of the Standard* is in the truest sense anticlimactic, even though there is much to be said for the beauties of anticlimax in this case. The wistful, fading closure of the essay—not in the moment of ecstasy but in the stunned and deliquescent aftermath—provides a point of quiet retrospection from which to feel the reverberating effects of visionary experience. The gradual, closing deflation only serves to emphasize how much weight the vision of the Mona Lisa was meant to bear. As the essay closes, Leonardo looks toward death, the "last curiosity," as if there were nothing left after such vision but to approach that "vague land" (R, 129).[15]

## 5 · Types and Figures

In Pater's reading, then, the Mona Lisa embodies the impossible possibility of gathering all the transformations of historical time together in one place. Pater's vehicle for this poetic figure is an image

---

ment" may be seen as a myth or a system of discursive strategies. For a compressed critique of both "monumental" and Hegelian philosophies of history (the latter most relevant to my own perspective here), see Michel Foucault, "Nietzsche, Genealogy, History," in Donald Bouchard, ed., *Language, Counter-Memory, Practice* (Ithaca, N.Y.: Cornell University Press, 1977), pp. 139–64.

15. On the beautiful closure of this essay, and on Pater's "closure sentences" in general, see David DeLaura, "Some Victorian Experiments in Closure," *Studies in the Literary Imagination* 8 (Fall 1975), 31.

of the human figure, a graphic reminder that his aesthetic is based on the romantic correlation of personal memory and the cultural past. In Pater's scheme of linked levels of generalization in the spiritual history of "the human mind," a personal style is the mirror of the "physiognomy of its age," as surely as a person's face is the mirror of a soul (R, 171). These personal figures, too, are the vehicles of Pater's poetics of revival. As Leonardo paints Lisa, making an aesthetic figure of a particular historical person, Pater performs the second transfiguration, establishing a figure of aesthetic history which is based upon a prior figure: *Pater's* Mona Lisa.

My double use of the word "figure" should be clear by now, in its simultaneous reference to the aesthetic and historical dimensions of Pater's criticism. The double meaning of "figure," both a poetic trope and a representative person, is meant to highlight continually the aesthetic act of figuration involved in retrospection. It is true that the history of a life can be viewed "as a whole" and assigned a significance only retrospectively, that a historical person can be interpreted as a "figure" only after a retrospective act of unification. But how, in Pater's aesthetics of retrospection, are the "figures" related to one another over time? The answer to this question may be found in an analysis of Pater's use of the "type."

In his early essays, Pater develops the type as a category to mediate between absolute specificity and generality in both aspects of historicist speculation. Synchronically, Pater's type is conceptually poised between the unique personal vision and the general "spirit of the age"; diachronically, the type is conceptually poised between absolute historical difference and repetition. As we have seen, the notion of "development" itself serves to mediate absolute difference and similarity over time, utter chaos and immobilized unity, the atomism of the Heraclitean flux, and the visionary but transhistorical order represented by Pater's Mona Lisa, and the type is Pater's fundamental developmental category. The fact that Pater uses it in both synchronic and diachronic critical operations shows how powerful and flexible the type can be as an instrument of historicist thinking. But it is also an aesthetic category, synchronically fixing a figure against its ground, diachronically ranging figures in a rationalized series.

In order to speak of a personal style, one of Pater's favorite strategies is to point out that an artist reiteratively and obsessively wrote about or painted one particular "type" of female beauty. Because this is perhaps Pater's most easily accessible use of the type, it is a good place to begin. Pater writes of Botticelli, for example, that he "has worked out" in his Madonnas "a distinct and peculiar type, definite enough in his own mind, for he has painted it over and over again, sometimes one might think almost mechanically" (R, 56). The originality of Botticelli's vision is further confirmed by the fact that his Madonnas "conformed to no acknowledged . . . type" (R, 50). They reveal a new "type," unique to Botticelli's vision and repeated "over and over again . . . almost mechanically." In this usage, the "type" expresses the artist's obsessive repetition of a "fixed idea." It serves to establish a figural, unified sense of that artist's identity by reducing a series of his images to their common denominator, by collapsing temporality and reading it as structure. The fundamental principle of Pater's expressionist theory holds that the outward image conforms to an inward structure, that expression is the externalized pattern of impression.[1] Thus the expression on the face of the "type" is taken literally to be an expression of the artist's inner configuration, especially if that expression is repeated over and over, no matter who or what the ostensible subject of the representation is.

Two ideas were especially "fixed" in Leonardo,—for example, "the smiling of women and the motion of great waters." Later in the passage, Pater reworks the same idea: the "interfusion of . . . beauty and terror" was "so fixed that for the rest of his life it never left him" (R, 104). Like Botticelli's, Leonardo's fixed "type of beauty" conforms fully to "no acknowledged type"; it is original, unique, so exotic that it must reflect a secret inner world. Pater offers his special "formula" for Leonardo's genius by way of revealing the occult process that results in a typical product: when his curiosity works in union with his desire of beauty, these two "elementary forces" produce "a type of subtle and curious grace" (R, 99, 109).

Both the words—"fixed" as well as "type"—emphasize the essential unity of an artist's temperament and style, with its various and disparate productions stabilized around a fixation; a concentric structure of definition—a fixed point within a more generalized field—enables Pater to insist on unity without literally reducing the variety of the artist's life and work to one image. In other words, casting the generalized aura of the type around this fixed point, Pater emphasizes its representative value while maintaining its absolute specificity.[2] He

1. See R, 54.
2. This use of the "type" is crucial for the theory and practice of literary realism, as Wellek points out in "Concept of Realism in Literary Scholarship," esp. pp. 242–53. He associates the type with the establishment of "objectivity" and begins his discussion of this tradition in English with Coleridge. For a suggestive use of "aura" in the sense I am invoking here, see Walter Benjamin, "The Work of Art in the Age of Mechanical Reproduction," *Illuminations* (New York: Harcourt, Brace and World, 1968), pp. 219–53.

even posits the general type as a foundation for the return to further emphasis upon specificity, for he "names" the type with its "formula," that peculiarly Paterian strategy of describing "scientifically" the unique process of fusion which has resulted in this particular aesthetic object and no other.

All these categories—the fixed idea, the type, the formula—are figurative, of course, produced by the interpreter's will to construct relation. The type, however, is not simply a figure of synchronic unity. It is also the main category in Pater's construction of an aesthetic history. Starting with the notion of Leonardo's fixed idea, for example, and following this "thread of suggestion," Pater muses that "we might . . . construct a sort of series, illustrating . . . Leonardo's type of womanly beauty" (R, 115). The "type" here is derived from (and in turn generates) a series, which reveals Leonardo's essentially fixed identity beneath the surface changes of time. After all, the rhetorical crescendo leading up to the passage on the Mona Lisa depends on Lisa's position as the last and consummate figure woven together from outward, historical reality and "the fabric of his dreams." Pater constructs the series of Leonardo's paintings of smiling women in order that the notion of historical time itself might finally be gathered up and transcended in his vision of the transhistorical ideal; "present from the first," her image is also, figuratively speaking, "present at last" (R, 124). But in other instances as well, the serial expression of a fixed idea works in a similar way, beginning in historical specificity and pressing beyond it. In his essay on Botticelli, for example, Pater uses this strategy:

> The same figure—tradition connects it with Simonetta, the mistress of Giuliano de' Medici—appears again as Judith, returning home across the hill country, when the great deed is over, and the moment of revulsion come, when the olive branch in her hand is becoming a burthen; as *Justice*, sitting on a throne, but with a fixed look of self-hatred which makes the sword in her hand seem that of a suicide; and again as *Veritas*, in the allegorical picture of *Calumnia*, where one may note in passing the suggestiveness of an accident which identifies the image of Truth with the person of Venus. (R, 60)

It is quintessentially Paterian to construct the "identification" of Truth with "the person of Venus" and then to attribute that identification to historical "accident." Her serial embodiments "as Judith . . . as *Justice* . . . as *Veritas*" reinforce the sense of an essential identity beneath (or above) the surface of visible form. When Pater describes these images as a series of representations of the "same figure," he traces a development in time while he preserves the unity of a personal figure. But the series, Pater's poetic figure for the passage of historical time, collapses when each item in the series amounts to the "same" thing.

This is Pater's problem: how to maintain the historical specificity of items in the series while also asserting both their generalized value and their relations to one another over time. He develops his conception of the type as a strategy for doing both at once. On the synchronic level of Pater's aesthetic history, the artist always reflects the spirit of his age, but if an artist's general value outweighs the specific, then that artist survives with only historical, not aesthetic, value:

> But if his work is to have the highest sort of interest, if it is to do something more than satisfy curiosity, if it is to have an aesthetic as distinct from an historical value, it is not enough for a poet to have been the true child of his age, to have conformed to its aesthetic conditions . . . ; it is necessary that there should be perceptible in his work something individual, inventive, unique, the *impress* there of the writer's own temper and personality. (R, 172, emphasis added)

To have both historical and aesthetic value, the artist must "conform" to the "aesthetic conditions" of his age *and* go beyond them with a new, "inventive . . . impress" of his own. We have seen how Pater unifies the notion of the artist's individual "impress" through the notion of the "type." Now let us look briefly at Pater's definition of the artist himself as type, absolutely unique yet also the representative of his age. In other words, before turning to similar problems Pater must face on the diachronic level, let us look more at the synchronic configuration of historical difference and similarity which Pater constructs by means of the type.

Though Pater's use of the "type" registers the unique "impress" of the artist's personality, it also refers to the general spirit of the age. For example, Pater calls attention to the "type of personal beauty" admired by the troubadours, a beloved image historically determined by their time, place, and social rank (R, 20). Or again, Ronsard "loves, or dreams that he loves, a rare and peculiar type of beauty, *la petite pucelle Angevine.*" This is Pater's way of pointing to the absolute historical specificity of Ronsard's style, the work that "has been done as no other man or age could have done it" (R, 167). This use of the type links the artist's unique, personal vision with his historical moment in a way that is not at all surprising, given Pater's theory of style. Each absolutely unique style exists within an absolutely unique surrounding historical milieu;

both levels of this concentric, reflexive figure, in other words, resolutely refer to concrete historical specificity. The sort of general value the Paterian type aims to express is also fully historical; the type is representative in the parliamentary sense, synecdochic rather than metaphorical. But the concentric structure of the figure—spirit of the age surrounding but only visible in a central, representative image—invests its absolutely unique center with a generalized aura.

As *idée fixe*, the type primarily serves to represent and totalize the history of an artist's career as one "impress" or repeated form, but Pater also often refers to the artist himself as a type. In this sense the type is an epitome of its surrounding culture, as in Pater's statement that "Ronsard's poems are a kind of epitome of his age" (R, 166). Here again the type mediates specific to general value in a particularly historical sense. Like Leonardo, who "fixed the outward type of Christ for succeeding centuries," Pater "fixes" Dante as the "central expression and type" of ideal love in the late Middle Ages (R, 98, 23). Leonardo's image of the "outward type of Christ" represents an unrecorded physiognomy from the past, but the unrecorded "physiognomy of an age" is also inaccessible except through representation. Thus a historically typical phenomenon may be represented by its most famous surviving example. Pater makes the historical force of this latter usage very clear. Dante is "*but the expression and type* of experiences known well enough to the initiated, in that passionate age" (R, 23; emphasis added). This figure of typicality takes Dante as the representative of a pervasive contemporary phenomenon, a structure of feeling purportedly shared by many unrecorded, now-invisible persons.[3] The great figure of Dante stands out against this amorphous background, concentrating its significance in one brilliant point.

In "Sandro Botticelli," Pater theorizes the "plaçe" of minor artists in relation to these major types with a variation on the same figure: a few great figures have "absorbed into themselves" the work of "smaller men." Secondary or minor artists like Botticelli are valuable, then, precisely for their "unabsorbed" quality, which helps to fill in the space around the great figures. They give us "a peculiar quality of pleasure which we cannot get elsewhere," communicating a certain charm "just because there is not about them the stress of a great name and authority" (R, 51, 61). Their typicality comes as a result of the sincerity of their very specialness, "the integrity, the truth to its type,

---

3. The concept of "structures of feeling" has been developed by Raymond Williams. See his *Marxism and Literature* (Oxford: Oxford University Press, 1977), pp. 128–35, for a compressed discussion.

of the given force" (R, 185). These types are true to themselves, not to an authoritative model.

Dante is "central," on the other hand, because his figure is visible against a background of "absorbed" historical reality, invisible to us in the present. When Pater defines a figure as type, then, he implies the structure of central point heightened within and against a generalized, amorphous background. As "central expression and type," Dante draws together in one place and concentrates in one name the general experience of a past age. Such a figure—a point at the center of a general field—highlights the particularity of the type and at the same time implies that it represents something "beyond" its "special manifestation" in a particular body. That "something beyond," in the synchronic sense, is the "spirit of the age." It is not too much to say that Pater solves one part of the historicist dilemma by this "faith" that the major figures that have survived from the past truly *are* representative, a faith he enacts by casting the figures of his own aesthetic history as types. The aura of typicality, of historical generality projected around a central figure, in other words, appears in this sense *as* the modern, secularized definition of "spirit."

The synchronic value of Pater's type shows up most clearly when we see it as part of his system of linked levels of specificity and generality in historical representation. We have had occasion to glance already at Pater's frequent argument that the "spirit" of an artist may be read in his followers and copiers. Of Leonardo he writes:

> There is a multitude of other men's pictures through which we undoubtedly see him, and come very near to his genius. . . . At other times the original remains, but has been a mere theme or motive, a type of which the accessories might be modified or changed; and these variations have but brought out the more the purpose, or expression of the original. (R, 118)

This is a sort of "musical" theory of evolutionary art history as theme and variations, motive followed by elaborations. Pater famously develops this metaphor in his later essay "The School of Giorgione," in which the type as "school" takes the role of theme played out in history's variations. Pater's notion of the "school" allows him to speak of a level of generalization that is beyond the individual but more concrete historically than the "spirit" of the age.[4] Sometimes Pater

---

4. For a discussion of the "school" as a term of historical generalization (as opposed to "movement," which T. S. Eliot advances as the correct word for "our time"), see Renato Poggioli, *The Theory of the Avant-Garde* (Cambridge, Mass.: Harvard University Press, 1968), pp. 17–18.

wants to speak of a pervasive period style; the Pléiade for example, though not precisely centralized, are constellated nevertheless, unified and grouped together under one name. But another sort of school, like the type, is structured as a concentric field of similarity, centralized in the works of one major artist.

For this sort of school Pater uses the suffix "-esque," as in "the Michelangelesque" or "the Giorgionesque." "The Poetry of Michelangelo," for example, begins with a Paterian formula for "the true type of the Michelangelesque," a formula that then turns out to be applicable to the Renaissance in general (R, 73). And in his essay "The School of Giorgione," Pater strenuously (and somewhat peevishly) argues that the "aesthetic philosopher" (as opposed to the "antiquarian" scholar) will know that

> over and above the real Giorgione and his authentic extant works, there remains the *Giorgionesque* also—an influence, a spirit or type in art. . . . [A] veritable school, in fact grew together out of all those fascinating works rightly or wrongly attributed to him; out of many copies from, or variations on him, by unknown or uncertain workmen. . . , out of the immediate impression he made on his contemporaries, and with which he continued in men's minds; out of many traditions of subject and treatment, which really descend from him to our own time, and by retracing which we fill out the original image. (R, 148)

The spirit of Giorgione's art ranges "over and above the real Giorgione" both synchronically and diachronically. It extends beyond him during his own time through an "immediate impression" on his contemporaries, which Pater describes by joining an organic metaphor to the metaphor of the typed impression: the school of Giorgione concentrated itself as a general type when copies *"grew* together." And it extends through time into later ages through "many traditions" of theme and variation. In other words, what has frequently been taken as Pater's loose disregard for factual attribution he here defends as part of a theory of influence.

Several levels of typification, then, link the "special manifestation" to the general spirit of the age. As fixed idea, the type concentrates the history of an individual artist around a repeated image; then the artist as type concentrates the spirit of the age around a central figure. Then, too, the spirit of the age itself can be represented as a type, when Pater wants to assert the synchronic unity of a historical period, and in this sense again the period as type proposes one part as a representative of a larger whole. In his "Preface" to *The Renaissance,*

Pater argues that fifteenth-century Italy must be studied "not merely for . . . its concrete works . . . but for its general spirit and character, for the ethical qualities of which it is a consummate type" (R, xiii). He offers in that context a theory of historical periodization. The various forms of culture usually develop in isolation from one another, he argues, though they will "unconsciously" express a "common character." However, in certain "happier" eras that common character is more self-conscious; "the thoughts of men draw nearer together than is their wont, and the many interests of the intellectual world combine in one complete type of general culture." Pater gives the Age of Pericles and the Age of Lorenzo as examples (R, xiii–xiv).

In fact, from one perspective the metaphor of the historical "period" aptly names this concentric figure of invisible forces drawing together to form a central point, and from another perspective it names a well-proportioned rhetorical development of several shapely clauses making up a sentence, with turns of phrase leading to a pointed stop. Here again Pater's expressions of the measurements of time link music and history in a rhetorical figure. Taking the Renaissance as his point of departure, Pater then generalizes from it the whole of modern history, the "particular" whole of which this period is epitome, the central and typical part. This conceptual scheme, involving linked levels of specificity and generality—graduated levels of typification from image to artist to school to historical period—portrays the historical body rising into spirituality. This is the only proper theoretical context for understanding Pater's famous definition of the Renaissance as radically extensive, stretching from the Age of Pericles to the nineteenth century. Pater's notorious liberty in conceiving historical periodicity is a direct function of his theory of historical representation, in which the workings of a "central expression and type" may be taken to stand for the whole.

Though this pressure toward the synchronic is always implicit, *The Renaissance* as a whole (and each essay separately, for that matter) is more explicitly grounded in Pater's attempts to envision the diachronic and to see these unified, synchronic "moments" against the background of time's passage. But on the diachronic level as well, the "type" is Pater's fundamental category. In the above passage on "the Giorgionesque," for example, he associates the type with "an influence." Here again the type is anchored in the historically concrete, factual body of a "real" person, and then its spirit "descends" to connect Giorgione's age with our own. Retrospectively "retracing" this line of descent, "we fill out the original image." Though the language is spatially conceived ("retracing," "filling out"), the process being described is a temporal one. Or rather, the temporal phenomenon of time's passage can be recaptured only in retrospect as a spatial figure. The difference between present and past is conceived as a space—that abyssal figurative distance that permits a provisional "objectivity," but only after threatening the very grounds of knowledge itself. To bridge this gap, Pater imagines a dialectical history of influence. He links the types diachronically—not as levels of rising generalization, but as stages on a continuum. And he understands that continuity as a process of reception and innovation, very much like the aesthetic dialectic of self-consciousness in which an act of division or discrimination follows an experience of absorbed, passionate "impression." This dialectic of reception and innovation over time counteracts the pressure toward synchronic unity inherent in Pater's aesthetic by concentrating on moments of change, division, and movement into the future.

In Pater's scheme, each artist receives as "given" the type of his "last," most immediate predecessor, as well as the other received or "acknowledged" types in his tradition, for the type functions diachronically to focus or "draw together" forces over time; each "type" represents not only the spirit of its age, but also the consummated achievement of a whole tradition, the summary moment and highest point of a genealogical process. Michelangelo, for example, appears in Pater's volume as the "last of the Florentines," whereas Botticelli's minor status leads Pater to judge his art as a representative only of the promise of the "earlier" Renaissance (R, 90, 61–62). Each later artist receives the type of his predecessors; his spirit is "literally" impressed, stamped, imprinted with the "types" most forceful at the time.[5] But he must turn away from these received impressions in order to form a new type of his own. What comes later is always molded within and against an earlier pattern, and that earlier pattern, formerly foregrounded as "highest" and "last," is thus relegated in time to the status of background, against which a new type rises. Each type, therefore, is simultaneously both an end and a beginning, the consummate example of one tradition and the generative background against which another takes form.

Let me illustrate Pater's dialectic of the types with two brief examples: his treatments of Leonardo and Michelangelo. In both cases, the difference between earlier and later is marked by a break from the

---

5. This is my redefinition of Pater's famous doctrine of "receptivity." For the starting-point of all current discussion of this issue, see Gerald Monsman, "Pater's Aesthetic Hero," *University of Texas Quarterly* (Winter 1971), 136–51.

established "type." Pater uses Leonardo as a figure of the two-stage process of true aesthetic creation. The particularly remote type of beauty he captured in his paintings, Pater argues, is

> apprehended only by those . . . who, starting with acknowledged types of beauty, have refined as far upon these, as these refine upon the world of common forms. (R, 105)

The structure of this formulation is strikingly like Pater's description of "aesthetic poetry" in his essay on William Morris. He describes the unfolding of art history, in other words, as another form of "aesthetic poetry."

Taking his cue from Vasari, Pater casts Verrocchio as "the earlier Florentine type" from which Leonardo departs. He reports "a legend true in sentiment only" of Leonardo's father placing him as apprentice in the workshop of Andrea del Verrocchio, where Leonardo was allowed to finish an angel in the left-hand corner of the *Baptism of Christ*. Pater focuses on Verrocchio's reaction when he sees what Leonardo has done:

> The pupil had surpassed the master; and Verrocchio turned away as one stunned, and as if his sweet earlier work must thereafter be distasteful to him, from the bright animated angel of Leonardo's hand. (R, 102)

Pater implicitly allegorizes this narrative of Verrocchio turning away in the distaste bred of his thwarted ambition. The "spiritual" meaning of the allegory is of course a historically general point about the development, through Leonardo, of a fuller, "richer humanity." The confrontation between Verrocchio and Leonardo's angel is reread as "one of those moments in . . . the progress of a great thing—here, that of the art of Italy" (R, 101). With a negative annunciation, this angel announces to Verrocchio that he must step aside. But Verrocchio was not the only one to turn away.

Pater reads Leonardo's entire career as a deeply personal reaction against the "earlier Florentine type":

> And because it was the perfection of that style, it awoke in Leonardo some seed of discontent which lay in the secret places of his nature. For the way to perfection is through a series of disgusts. (R, 103)

The moments of "disgust" which define the turning points on the way to perfection are not only revulsions, dissatisfactions, distastes.

Each moment of distaste is predicated on the perfection of the former type, as if the very surfeit of desire causes the discontent that leads then to further tasting. Pater's attention to etymology here is not merely witty but very subtle, for the word "disgust" also recalls the French *déguster*, to savor, and in turn the Latin *degustare*, to make oneself acquainted with. Thus, the way to perfection is also through a series of tastings, trials, and internalizations, in which the whole successively becomes more and more complex as it includes lesser perfections in its more perfectly differentiated manifold.

The vignette of Leonardo's confrontation with Verrocchio highlights the aspect of Pater's art-historical dialectic which concentrates on moments of reversal, when an earlier perfection of taste is suddenly received with personal "distaste" or "disgust"; these particular turning-points of aesthetic history are reactive, antithetical, distropic. The "progress of a great thing" goes so far in one certain direction until the continuous development is broken. We can see Pater's aesthetic gesture—his creation of historical figures—first in his isolation of such moments against the background of a general development and then in his interpretation of their "legends." And again we should hear "trope" in both senses: the moment of distaste itself, when a historical figure outwardly expresses the tendency of his inward temperament and turns away from an earlier type; and the rhetorical figure that Pater chooses to embody the "spiritual" significance of that radically creative turning-point. (It is worth pointing out in passing that this is yet another of Pater's reflexive, second-order figures, a rhetorical trope expressing a personal and historical tropism, a figure made of a former figure.) The story of Michelangelo, on the other hand, highlights the aspect of Pater's art-historical dialectic which concentrates on the movements of synthesis and division, convergence and bifurcation within the genealogical whole.

Pater sees Michelangelo as a synthetic, consummate type, not as the one who breaks with previous tradition, as Leonardo did. Thus, "if one is to distinguish the peculiar savour of his work, he must be approached, not through his followers, but through his predecessors" (R, 90). By defining him as the culminating moment, Pater can concentrate, through the figure of Michelangelo, on the tradition as a whole, and Pater defines the tradition that Michelangelo consummates in two different ways: as a tradition of dealing with the passions and death of the physical body, and as a tradition of Florentine art. In the former sense, Pater places Michelangelo against the background of Dante and Plato.

In this effort to tranquillise and sweeten life by idealising its vehement sentiments, there were two great traditional types, either of which an Italian of the sixteenth century might have followed. There was Dante, whose little book of the *Vita Nuova* had early become a pattern of imaginative love . . . ; and since Plato had become something more than a name in Italy by the publication of the Latin translation of his works by Marsilio Ficino, there was the Platonic tradition also. (R, 86)

He goes on to argue that Michelangelo synthesizes these two types by displaying elements of both. Thus, in Pater's scheme, Michelangelo becomes a type of the Renaissance itself in the combination of late medieval "strength" and classical "sweetness."

This synthetic tendency is something we did not see in the Leonardo essay, and its effect is to advance a different model of art-historical transmission. Michelangelo is able to reach back *before* (or, in spatial terms, *behind*) the most immediate predecessor type. His work is interpreted, then, not as "disgust" or detachment from an immediate background, but as the retrieval of something lost within that ground. His life story is used allegorically to express the historical process of medieval strength hiding within itself secretly, and finally "secreting" its hidden sweetness. Here again we see Pater telling the familiar three-part romantic history, with the Platonic tradition placed in the role of overarching whole, both earlier (in the absolute chronological sense) and later (in its translated form) than Dante, mediated to the modern world through Ficino's translation and Michelangelo's aesthetic embodiments. In this model, innovation occurs through the recovery of a loss, not the turn away from a present type of perfection, but of course the two models work together to construct the dialectic of historical transmission, from two different angles of vision.

"Sweetness and strength" is the formula Pater invents to describe the "true type of the Michelangelesque," but that code for the synthetic union of opposite qualities also has a temporal formulation, "*ex forti dulcedo*" or, as Pater translates, "*out of* the strong came forth sweetness" (R, 89, emphasis added). As a dichotomous or oxymoronic motto, the formula alludes to Michelangelo's complex unity, but in its temporalized form it alludes to the historical process of "secretion." The formula describes the special instance as if, like an experiment in chemistry, it were repeatable, and indeed this formula is repeated in typical Paterian fashion through all the levels of signification. It is the formula first for Michelangelo, then for "the true type of the Michelangelesque," for the Renaissance as a specific historical period, and finally for the Renaissance as the type of historical process itself. The source of the formula in Samson's riddle to the Philistines (Judges 14:14) poses a riddle of its own. Pater's secularization is forceful in its tacit (and typological) relation of Samson and Michelangelo, with the attendant implication that such secularization-effects are themselves a result of Renaissance humanism. I take this too as a sly allusion to Arnold's discussion (also typological) of the modern Philistine. The force of such an allusion would be double: it would imply Pater's revisionary "disgust" at Arnold's "strength," and at the same time it would self-reflexively promise that sweetness would be secreted later than Arnold, in Pater's own work.

The figure of Michelangelo is "last" in a series that is itself a figure, Pater's model for art-historical tradition. In this case the series traces the development of Florentine art. Michelangelo is "the last of the Florentines, of those on whom the peculiar sentiment of the Florence of Dante and Giotto descended" (R, 90). As he lives on into a great old age, the spirit of the age is diverted into another channel; rising Neo-Catholicism takes the place of the "true" Renaissance. The course of history goes on without him, but "he lingers on; a *revenant*, as the French say, a ghost out of another age, . . . dreaming, in a worn-out society . . . on the morning of the world's history" (R, 90). The "break" in the line of continuous development occurs not through him but after him. The synthesis is shattered as false disciples follow only one "side" of the master's complex unity:

> Up to him the tradition of sentiment is unbroken, the progress towards surer and more mature methods of expressing that sentiment continuous. But his professed disciples did not share his temper; they are in love with his strength only, and seem not to feel his grave and temperate sweetness. (R, 91)

Pater rejects those who "claimed" to be his followers on the grounds that they did not repeat the formula: "that strange interfusion of sweetness and strength." Their illegitimate claim is then cast in the terms of sexual generation, and Pater as aesthetic judge resolves the paternity suit. The line is broken after Michelangelo, but not forever. Pater finds his "true sons" in the nineteenth century.

> William Blake, for instance, and Victor Hugo, who, though not of his school, and unaware, are his true sons, and help us to understand him, as he in turn interprets and justifies them. (R, 97)

Just as Michelangelo recovered the Platonic tradition after a radical break, these "true sons" in the nineteenth century recover the "true type of the Michelangelesque." The "last of the Florentines" is then recast as the first of a new lineage whose creation as an aesthetic figure is due entirely to Pater. The mythic anxiety of paternity (*Pater semper incertus est*, in Freud's modern formulation) is here addressed on the level of aesthetic history.[6] These nineteenth-century artists do not look back consciously to the progenitor of their tradition, for they are "not of his school, and unaware"; the retrospective, aesthetic gesture (in this case, the attribution of paternity) is entirely Pater's own. And of course the creation of a tradition like this is not innocent of self-reflection, for the "sentiment" or spirit of the father "descends," through Blake and Hugo, to Pater himself.

The examples of Leonardo and Michelangelo serve to illustrate two different "moments" in Pater's dialectic of innovation and repetition: the break from an earlier, limited perfection, and the consummate fulfillment of a series. Each of these interrelated moments is conveyed by means of the type, whose value as a diachronic figure can now be clearly seen. Like the privileged, epiphanic moments of experiential time, Pater's art-historical types define fixed points against the flux of past time; they mark, in retrospect, the high points of each progression, the representative points against their background, the points of branching on the genealogical tree.

Furthermore, each may afterward be consulted for the "laws" of aesthetic production:

> The qualities of the great masters in art or literature, . . . are not peculiar to them; but most often typical standards, revealing instances of the laws by which certain aesthetic effects are produced. (R, 96)

This tendency toward the absolute and the normative reaches its apotheosis in the essay "The School of Giorgione," where music is defined as "the typical, or ideally consummate art . . . the true type or measure of perfected art" (R, 134–35, 139).[7] Giorgione, an initiator of

---

6. Sigmund Freud, "Family Romances" (1909), in *Collected Papers*, vol. 5, ed. James Strachey (London: Hogarth Press, 1950), p. 76. Said has argued that the very continuity of narrative depends on the construction of the language of filiation (Edward Said, *Beginnings: Intention and Method* [New York: Basic Books, 1975], p. 146). See also Patricia Drechsel Tobin, *Time and the Novel: The Genealogical Imperative* (Princeton, N.J.: Princeton University Press, 1978).

7. This essay was written last of all the Renaissance essays and included only in the third edition of 1888. For another interpretation of Pater's use of music in relation to its sources in Hegel, see Ruth C. Child, *The Aesthetic of Walter Pater* (New York: Macmillan, 1940), pp. 55–70.

such art, is "typical of that aspiration of all the arts toward music"; correlatively, then, Giorgione represents the aspiration of all art forms toward the condition of the type. We shall hear a new tone resonating in the Paterian dictum that *"All art constantly aspires toward the condition of music"* if we hear it as yet another description of the formation of "aesthetic poetry" within historical time, for in this essay, music only seems to be invoked as a transhistorical ideal, the total identification of form and matter only seems to be projected as a sort of apocalyptic end. A closer reading, however, reveals music to be a generic figure for pure temporality: fleeting moments of "play" and "free passage," "ideal instants . . . on that background of the silence of Venice" (R, 150–52). Ideal art once again is characterized by passages of time marked by epiphanic moments, and this essay, like the "Conclusion," evokes the experience of "moments as they pass" (R, 239). In the moments that the school of Giorgione chooses to depict, "musical intervals in our existence, life itself is conceived as a sort of listening—listening to music, . . . to the sound of water, to time as it flies" (R, 151).

As "standard" or "law," in other words, the Paterian type does not indicate synchronic pressure toward conformity, but rather a diachronic pressure toward the future, an "aspiration" toward the "condition of music," toward further passages of time marked by intervals and further pivotal moments that

> seem to absorb past and future in an intense consciousness of the present . . . exquisite pauses in time, in which, arrested thus, we seem to be spectators of all the fulness of existence, and which are like some consummate extract or quintessence of life. (R, 150)

Each "wholly concrete moment" condenses into itself "all the motives, all the interests and effects of a long history," and after the fixated pause, "appetite" renews itself and is expressed in further "intent" and "listening" faces.

In the diachronic sense, too, the Paterian type expresses concrete historical identity while also expressing something beyond itself. That "something beyond" is the shaping force toward further developments in the future, for though each type in retrospect does become a standard, it is a standard that is not "given" but historically derived. Only in retrospect, from the point of view at the end of the line, can the type be invested with traditional value, only at the point from which it can be seen to have repeated itself in various permutations of similarity and difference. But even though the retrospective vantage point makes it seem as if time stands still, the process after all is understood to be ongoing, as each type that survives into the present forms the template or "impress" of future development. The type possesses not only the power of impression in the present, but also a force toward the future, which is fulfilled alike by those who copy and by those who turn away.

Thus the type may be seen as the central category in Pater's evolutionary art history. In its synchronic dimension, it imitates the modern "species," the realistic, particular object that is invested with general value, an aesthetic and historical construct rather than a Platonic or "essentialist" category, and in its diachronic dimension it exerts a standardizing and productive force toward future types.[8] Pater's use of "type," then, is often very close to "impression" in its plastic sense, or "style" as *stilus*, the mold or shape imposed on receptive matter, the inscriptive force that writes the characters of time. Pater describes the historical figures who leave such lasting impressions as "types," which continue to "impress" or "imprint" their images on the imaginations of later ages. The spirit of the individual artist is just such a malleable or receptive substance, a waxy slate or *tabula rasa*, impressed already with the "acknowledged" types, ready to impress the spirit of the ages with a new style.

In the late nineteenth century this range of connotation owes at least in part to the technologies of printing, in part to the figural tradition of Christian exegesis.[9] Auerbach's magisterial essay on the etymology of "figura" begins by discussing the development of both rhetorical and historical senses of the word from its original meaning as "plastic form"—both the mold and the shape that issues from it. In this sense he compares "figura" to "typos," which not only implies

---

8. Discussing Hopkins, Carol Christ (*The Finer Optic: The Aesthetic of Particularity in Victorian Poetry* [New Haven, Conn.: Yale University Press, 1975], p. 143) invokes the "species specialissima" of Duns Scotus to focus this concept. For a discussion of the historical shift away from essentialism and toward an empirical and historically constructed concept of the species (which Mayr calls "population thinking"), see Ernst Mayr, *The Growth of Biological Thought* (Cambridge, Mass.: Harvard University Press, 1982), pp. 45–47. On the diachronic dimension, see Gerald Bruns, "The Formal Nature of Victorian Thinking," *PMLA* 90 (October 1975), 904–18. Bruns argues that its emphasis on the diachronic characterizes the Victorians, as an emphasis on synchronic and systematic relations characterizes romanticism.

9. Kermode discusses these two traditions behind the "type" in Hawthorne's fiction. See Frank Kermode, *The Classic: Literary Images of Permanence and Change* (1975; reprint, Cambridge, Mass.: Harvard University Press, 1983), pp. 90–114, where Kermode offers in elegant and compressed form a discussion of the interaction of several concepts of the type in the nineteenth century, the changes Darwin's theory enforced on the already-extant traditions of the type, and a detailed example of the literary assimilation of these traditions.

plastic form (specifically that of an impression) but also inclines toward the lawful and the exemplary.[10] Auerbach's citation here of Dante, who uses "figura" to speak of the impression stamped in wax to form a seal (*Purgatorio* 10.45; *Paradiso* 27.52), leads to the Christian sense of the type, an exemplary and reiterative figure in history. Hints of an emergent Christian typology are everywhere apparent in Pater, even in *The Renaissance*, and I discuss his secularization of that powerful Christian historicism in Part Three. But Pater's secularized Christian types are formed against the background of his aesthetic and "scientific" awareness, which predominates in *The Renaissance*.

In all the early essays, Pater's use of the type is more firmly associated with the contemporary sciences of observation, classification, and evolution than with the technology of printing or the Christian types. Pater wrote in his essay on "Style" that one of the necessary tasks for the modern critic is the "naturalisation of the vocabulary of science" (A, 16). His development of the type demonstrates this stylistic aim in several ways. Like the chemical analogies of the "Preface," Pater's use of the type is one of his early strategies for representing aesthetic judgments as answerable to modern science. By using chemistry as his model for the "fusion" that yields a unique aesthetic object, Pater also (and paradoxically) implies the repeatability afforded by a scientifically controlled experiment. Significantly, the aesthetic critic enacts the process of aesthetic creation in reverse, undoing the "fusion" with an aesthetic "analysis" of the compound, and producing a "formula" that describes the identity of the aesthetic object "scientifically."[11] Paterian formulas describe specifics, in other words, but they paradoxically do so in terms that imply generality and repeatability.

Pater's type is answerable not to chemistry but to the nineteenth-century science of evolutionary biology. In "Coleridge," for example, he associates the word with the modern "sciences of observation," which have revealed "types of life evanescing into each other by inexpressible refinements of change" (A, 66). If "types of life" are continuously "evanescing into each other by inexpressible refinements of change," then the representative of the type stands for, and

10. Erich Auerbach, "Figura," in *Scenes from the Drama of European Literature* (New York: Meridian, 1959), pp. 11, 15.
11. The preoccupation with reproduction, both aesthetic and historical, is a central feature of modernism. On the daguerreotype, see Kermode, *The Classic*, pp. 92–94; on the stereotype, see Poggioli, *Theory of the Avant-Garde*, pp. 80–83. Pater's use of the chemical analogy extends a tradition of "romantic chemistry" to the later nineteenth century and turns it in a particularly "Victorian" direction. See Cecil Y. Lang, "Love among the Ruins," *Browning Institute Studies* 15 (1987), 1–22.

thus conceptually stabilizes, a form that is simultaneously understood to be unstable, still in the process of formation, possibly soon to turn into another type altogether. Behind the appearances of present form are inexpressible secret relations stretching toward both past and future. If change is constant, and so gradual as to be almost invisible, then clearly general categories do not mean what they would mean if they were absolute, unchanging, and "given." General categories must be reformulated according to new principles. Pater's vigorous use of the type in the early essays is directly linked to this keen sense of a modern crisis in procedures of classification, brought on in part by, and in part expressing, a contemporary revision of the concept of species.[12]

That a general shift was taking place in the meaning of "type" seems to be indicated by a formalist sense of the word entering the vocabulary at around this time. The *Oxford English Dictionary* gives the first usage of "type" in this modern, formalist sense (the "general form, structure, or character distinguishing a particular kind, group or class") as 1843, from a part of Mill's *Logic* (4.2) that takes up the procedures of classification. Furthermore, the first usage of "type" to mean "kind, class, or order as distinguished by a particular individual" is given as 1854, and the usage of "type" to mean "representative specimen" as 1842.[13] Pater's early usage reflects this tendency to illustrate the class by means of the individual or, conversely, to generalize from the particular instance, as we have seen. With this dialectic he manages to reassert a sense of structure against the atomism of flux, change, and individual difference and at the same time to remain committed to the individual instance. The type helps Pater bridge between two equally extreme reactions to the crisis in classification: the attempt to retain idealist or essentialist modes of categorization, which Pater recognizes in Coleridge as "ancient thought," and the resignation to a form of nominalist skepticism which doubts that general categories express anything but arbitrary and man-made boundaries.[14] Between these two reactions Pater develops a historical and evolutionary concept of the type, and the type enables evolutionary discourse, as the individual instance does not.

12. For a detailed history of the developing concept of species, see "Microtaxonomy, the Science of Species," in Mayr, *Growth of Biological Thought*, pp. 251–97.
13. The *Oxford English Dictionary* offers further examples from natural history dating from the 1840s, and similar technical usages from chemistry dating from 1852.
14. On nominalist thinking about species, see Mayr, *Growth of Biological Thought*, pp. 263–65. Opposition to essentialism began long before Darwin on two fronts: among naturalists and among philosophers. In the latter connection, Mayr quotes Locke.

Pater (in the company of George Eliot, George Meredith, and Thomas Hardy) turns the English critical tradition toward modernism by confronting and assimilating Darwin's epochal vision. There is a strong tradition of evolutionary ideas in English literature before Pater, including Coleridge, Carlyle, Tennyson, Arnold, and Ruskin. Like these writers, Pater is concerned with the spiritual evolution toward "higher things" (*In Memoriam* 1.4),[15] but far deeper than anyone before him, Pater registers both the material forces threatening this vision of spiritual evolution and the conceptual difficulties presented by this new mode of thought. Pater went up to Oxford in 1859, the year *On the Origin of Species* was published, and we know that he read Darwin and discussed the new work with great animation.[16] Unlike many of his contemporaries, Pater accepted the Darwinian challenge, even though he seems to have understood its most difficult implications accurately and profoundly.

There is general critical agreement at this time that the "Darwinian" element in Pater's criticism is strong.[17] Harold Bloom easily states, "*The Renaissance* was already a Darwinian book,"[18] but we still do not know as much as we could about what a "Darwinian book" might look like specifically in its literary form, as opposed to the history of ideas registered in its content. Important contributions to the literary inquiry have been made by Philip Appleman, Dwight Culler, Gillian Beer, and George Levine.[19] In an essay that bears an important relation to the argument of this book, Appleman argues that Pater's "impressionism" and "historicism" mark the two horns

15. See Lionel Stevenson, *Darwin among the Poets* (1932; reprint, New York: Russell and Russell, 1963); Leo Henkin, *Darwinism in the English Novel, 1860–1910* (New York: Corporate Press, 1940).

16. See Inman, *Walter Pater's Reading*, p. 6, and Philip Appleman, "Darwin, Pater, and a Crisis in Criticism," in Philip Appleman, William Madden, and Michael Wolff, eds., *1859: Entering an Age of Crisis* (Bloomington: Indiana University Press, 1959), p. 82.

17. Perhaps we should say the "Darwinistic" element. Peckham has argued that it is not strictly accurate to call a writer "Darwinian" who does not specify the mechanism of evolution to be natural selection, as Pater certainly does not. Several writers have insisted on this distinction, but it does not seem to have caught on. See Morse Peckham, "Darwinism and Darwinisticism," *Victorian Studies* 3 (September 1959), 19–40. I have retained "Darwinian" for ease of reference, but place it in quotation marks to register the metaphorical nature of my claim.

18. Bloom, introduction to Pater's *Selected Writings*, p. xvii.

19. Appleman, "Darwin, Pater, and a Crisis in Criticism," pp. 81–95; Dwight Culler, "The Darwinian Revolution and Literary Form," in George Levine and William Madden, eds., *The Art of Victorian Prose* (London: Oxford University Press, 1968), pp. 224–46; Gillian Beer, *Darwin's Plots: Evolutionary Narrative in Darwin, George Eliot, and Nineteenth-Century Fiction* (London: Routledge and Kegan Paul, 1983); and George Levine, "Darwin and the Problem of Authority," *Raritan* 3 (Winter 1984), 30–61.

of his critical dilemma, that those impulses are "antithetical," and that they are *both* influenced by his awareness of Darwin's work.[20] An understanding of Pater's use of the type is a fundamental step in describing his particular "Darwinism," and in the sections that follow I show how that basic evolutionary category serves to mark the movement of aesthetic time.

## 6 · Low and High Relief: "Luca Della Robbia"

Toward the end of the essay on Winckelmann, Pater shifts his focus to Goethe, moving Goethe's influential predecessor into the background. The "aim of a right criticism," Pater concludes, is "to place Winckelmann in an intellectual perspective of which Goethe is the foreground" (R, 226). Pater's rhetorical strategy accentuates Goethe's relative importance, his "broad" culture as opposed to Winckelmann's intense but narrow gift, and especially his position later in art-historical time, and it echoes Winckelmann's own principles of evolutionary art history. Positioning Goethe in the foreground at the end of *The Renaissance* has the striking effect of pointing self-reflexively toward the further developments of romanticism represented by Pater himself. In these last two sections of Part Two, I want to analyze the particular forms of "intellectual perspective" that are represented by manipulating background and foreground, but before turning to Pater's figures of relief, I shall consider his careful arrangement of the volume as a whole.[1]

In the "Preface," Pater stresses both the chronological form and the spatial form of his volume. He most strenuously emphasizes the chronological, linear, and developmental plot of his story, tracing the

---

20. Though I disagree with Appleman's most basic premise that Pater's historicism and his impressionism are "antithetical" (I am engaged in arguing the case that they are homologously structured and mutually inextricable), I have found the speculative range of this essay most illuminating.

1. In its own day the volume was not credited with careful, or a particularly "historical," arrangement. In a characteristic misunderstanding, Morley claimed that the essays are "grouped in an unsystematic way around a . . . theory of life and its purport" (quoted in Hill's notes, p. 444). DeLaura (*Hebrew and Hellene in Victorian England*, p. 231) correctly refers to the "accretive and random development of *The Renaissance* volume" but does not focus on Pater's aggressive reordering of that randomness.

Renaissance from early to late, beginning with the tentative emergence of humanism within the Middle Ages, and ending with the romantic, revitalized humanism of Goethe. But a spatial form of organization is also readily apparent in his concentric arrangement of essays by nationality: essays on fifteenth-century Italian art are framed by essays on French literature, then half-framed again by German philology and historical aesthetics, then, on the outermost edge, by the English tradition of criticism represented by Pater's voice *in propria persona*.

Pater acknowledges the aesthetic choice involved in this concentric arrangement when he notes in the "Preface" that "Two Early French Stories," which he has positioned as the first essay, does not necessarily provide the best example of the early Renaissance but does complete the French level of his frame. He includes the essay because, as he puts it, "it help[s] the unity of my series" (R, xv). His attempt to correlate this concentric arrangement of national aesthetics with his chronological plan is forced, but significant nonetheless. Pater argues that the "Two Early French Stories" demonstrate the freshness of the early period, "the charm of *ascesis*, of the austere and serious girding of the loins in youth," and that the writings of Joachim du Bellay represent the "subtle and delicate sweetness which belongs to a refined and comely decadence" (R, xii–xiii). Though his rationalization does seem remarkably adventitious in this prefatory context, a related geographical argument for unity makes more sense at the end of the essay on Leonardo, when Pater claims that Leonardo's last days in France open a "prospect" through which art history can view "Italian art [dying] away as a French exotic" (R, 128).[2] Still fanciful in the highest degree as a historical observation, this argument tends to make geographical dislocation a metaphor for the aesthetic itself; everything with aesthetic value is "exotic," for it has been dislocated, exiled, and translated from one context to another.

The form of the volume may be called "spatial," then, not because of its thematic and metaphorical use of geographical location, but because of the concentric arrangement of the essays, which rigidly enforces the "centrality" of the Italian Renaissance at the same time that it calls attention to the present-day, "eccentric" or "exotic" English perspective that ultimately frames the entire vision. Thus the Winckelmann essay plays an oblique and crucial role in mediating the

---

2. Other geographical and mapping devices include the pervasive north-south opposition (e.g., R, 174, 179), the theme of exile and return, especially in relation to Rome (e.g., R, 6–7, 165, 174–75), and the cross-cultural extravaganza staged at the end of "Winckelmann."

central Italian and peripheral French examples to the English reader through a German who grappled with the problem of recovering his senses "in a metaphysical age" and finally "solves the problem in the concrete" by a "happy, unperplexed dexterity, . . . what Goethe called his *Gewahrwerden der greichischen Kunst*, his finding of Greek art" (R, 183–84). According to Pater's theory, Winckelmann establishes a "true" classicism against the background of a "false" and "unhistorical" neoclassicism, and this classical revival enables the full culture of Goethe's romanticism to "blossom."[3] Pater, in other words, also solved the problem Winckelmann solved "in the concrete," though Pater solved it at a second remove, through his "finding" of the Renaissance "finding" of Greek art, his revival of a revival.

The temporal form of the volume is in the end supplanted by the structural force of its spatial form. The concentric layers of enclosure, with Pater's framing perspective overtly positioned on its outer edge, work to imply that an English consciousness in the late nineteenth century is like a spatial location that "contains" the cultures of the past. On the level of the volume's form, Pater's efforts to envision the diachronic seem to fall back into a vision of spatial containment which is the sign of retrospection, the "House Beautiful" where temporality, growth, and development may be peacefully ensconced in memory, rather than experienced as flux. Joseph Frank, in his seminal essay on spatial form, argues that this is the sign of literary modernism: "modern literature has been engaged in transmuting the time world of history into the timeless world of myth."[4] To the extent that Pater's resolutely historicized treatment of the Renaissance is finally gathered

---

3. See the long passage excised after the *Westminster Review* publication of "Winckelmann," in Hill's notes, pp. 268–69: "The first condition of an historical revival is an appreciation of the differences between one age and another. The service of Winckelmann to modern culture lay in the appeal he made from the substituted text to the original. He produces the actual relics of the antique against the false tradition of the era of Louis XIV. A style or manner in art or literature can only be explained or reproduced through those special conditions of society and culture out of which it arose, and with which it forms one group of phenomena. A false classicism, in the unhistorical spirit of the age, had tried to isolate the classical manner from the group of phenomena of which it was a part." He goes on to characterize Winckelmann's historical scholarship as an attempt to reach the "root" of those special conditions in order to understand the "blossom" of the Hellenic manner.

4. "Spatial Form in Modern Literature," in Joseph Frank, *The Widening Gyre: Crisis and Mastery in Modern Literature* (New Brunswick, N.J.: Rutgers University Press, 1963), p. 60. Though Frank's essay has been subjected to rigorous critique (as well as to reassessment by Frank himself), it still provides a provocative address to the notion of literary modernism. For discussion of the Frank thesis in particular and spatial form in general, see Jeffrey Smitten and Ann Daghistany, eds., *Spatial Form in Narrative* (Ithaca, N.Y.: Cornell University Press, 1981).

up into this spatial form, the volume is mythic in this specifically modern sense. In the final analysis, but only in the final analysis, the attempt to represent diachrony falls back into a synchronic, visionary unity. Gerald Monsman is quite right to call it a "visionary text."[5]

Critics have traditionally noted that the figures treated in the volume are strangely assimilable to one another and that together they form an overarching, developing "spirit,"[6] and it is true that the transcendent perspective at the end of time must be assigned to the aesthetic critic himself, as the highest point of development, the most complex position so far evolved. But it is not therefore necessary to equate the trajectory of this overarching spirit with the spirit of Pater himself. It is the formal dynamic of Pater's aesthetic historicism which creates this effect—not his "subjectivism" (as I have shown), nor an autobiographical intention of any conventional kind (as I show in Part Three, section 2).

Implicitly identifying with Goethe at the end of the essay on Winckelmann, Pater begins to seem more palpably foregrounded. Within the terms of his developmental aesthetic, however, identifying with Goethe has the paradoxical effect of simultaneously distinguishing Pater *from* him, pushing Goethe further into the past, where he is decidedly less modern than his later romantic epigone, who stealthily triumphs. The poetics of revival mark out a territory where identification and detachment are not mutually exclusive; retrospection always has the double effect of "fixing" the past more securely in the past, at the very moment of enlivening it with present attention. As I have shown in Part One, Pater quietly completes his move into the foreground at the end of the volume in the "Conclusion," where he gradually emerges in his own voice.

But to feel his emergence at the "Conclusion" only reminds the reader that he has remained, until then, more or less resolutely in the background. That may seem an odd point to stress, especially about a critic reputed to be decidedly "subjective," until we realize that his mind in the present forms the background against which the Renaissance has been "thrown" in "relief." This model will help us understand why his prose seems at once so personal and so oddly impersonal. The "personality" of the aesthetic critic seems to hover everywhere, and yet it is effaced, recessive. Pater's impressionism does not amount to an ungoverned effusion of purple prose or extravagant

---

5. Monsman, *Pater's Art of Autobiography*, p. 37.
6. For a recent example of this argument, see Paul Barolsky, "Walter Pater's Renaissance," *Virginia Quarterly Review* 58 (Spring 1982), 208–20.

feeling; it is a theoretically coherent imitation of this shifting "intellectual perspective," in which the "imaginative intellect" in the present and the projected historical past are alternately merged and thrown into mutual relief.

This form of attention is (literally) complex. Pater's impressionist trick—to recede into the background and to emerge in the end as the foreground—disturbed his Victorian audience, who distinguished between the historical essay and the personal essay according to a strict generic contract that they expected to be straightforwardly fulfilled, not subverted in this complex and subtle way. Thus they misread the "Conclusion" as personal advocacy alone, and of course missed the relevance of Pater's final position to the "intellectual perspective" of the volume as a whole. Readers today may be more appreciative of the aesthetic effects generated by the play of genres. This sort of spatial recursivity—center emerging to frame and contain the outer edges, background becoming foreground, figure and ground changing places—is endlessly challenging, and it is reemerging today in the critical literature as a feature of "postmodernism."[7] But here again it should be more interesting to us as a part of the formal techniques of perspectivism than as a way of bypassing formal analysis by referring everything to a central, personal ground that we call Pater's "sensibility." The truly radical and interesting formal trick here is that the sense of an overarching "person" (or, to change the metaphor, a person "behind the scenes") has been generated by Pater's dynamic of figural evolution.

In addition to collecting essays already published elsewhere, Pater wrote a few pieces especially for the volume of Renaissance studies. These are of particular interest when we consider the form of the published volume as a whole. For example, Pater newly wrote both of the essays that comprise the French level of the frame, and by doing so he more carefully articulated what I have been calling the concentric arrangement of the volume. He wrote the "Preface," which introduces his relativist, historicist definition of beauty against the tacit projection of Ruskinian absolutism. And he wrote "Luca Della Robbia," which in one light seems merely to summarize the argument about classical *Allgemeinheit* and *Heiterkeit* from "Winckelmann." But on the other hand, Pater advances it in a new context, the germ of which may be found in the essay on Michelangelo, published the year before:

---

7. Monsman sees Pater as "impressively bridging the gap between romanticism and postmodernism." He ultimately interprets the recursivity of Pater's texts psychoanalytically, as the "turning of the child back upon the parent" (*Pater's Art of Autobiography*, pp. 4–5 and passim).

> He secures that ideality of expression, which in Greek sculpture depends on a delicate system of abstraction, and in early Italian sculpture on lowness of relief, by an incompleteness, which is surely not always undesigned, and . . . trusts to the spectator to complete the half-emergent form. (R, 76)

In the third edition he adds "As I have already pointed out" before this statement, in order to remind his reader of "Luca Della Robbia." This very repetitiveness should alert us to the importance of the essay, where Pater takes up once again the modern form of representation against a background. It bears, in other words, a great deal of theoretical weight, since it was clearly written to lend greater cohesion to the argument of the volume as a whole.[8]

The essay "Luca Della Robbia" must be read in the context of aesthetic "relief," for in that context it has an enormous importance that has never been granted. The volume is studded with references to relief sculpture: Leonardo from his earliest years "constructed models in relief, of which Vasari mentions some of women smiling"; and as Verrocchio seems now to anticipate Leonardo, so Leonardo always seems to recall the studio of Verrocchio "in the love of beautiful toys . . . and of reliefs, like those cameos which in the *Virgin of the Balances* hang all round the girdle of Saint Michael" (R, 100, 102). The relief work of the early Tuscan sculptors "suggested much of [Michelangelo's] grandest work" and "impressed it with so deep a sweetness" (R, 78–79). Several times Pater mentions the Elgin marbles, and at one point he names the Panathenaic frieze as what he would "perhaps" choose if he could save but one work of Hellenic art "in the wreck of all beside" (R, 218). And of course, in the essay on Luca he takes up the early Tuscan sculpture in low relief, comparing it to freestanding Greek sculpture, on the one hand, and on the other hand to Michelangelo's "half-emergent" figures, left in a suggestive incompleteness by the artist, partially submerged and yet "in strong contrast with the rough-hewn mass" of stone.

The essay graphically displays many typical features of Pater's aesthetic historicism. We should by now be well accustomed to expecting Pater's focus on an art object to have both formal, realistic, and historically concrete value as well as several levels of historically general or

---

8. For the third-edition revision, see Hill's notes, p. 223. For the dating of these essays, see Samuel Wright, *A Bibliography of the Writings of Walter H. Pater* (New York and London: Garland, 1975), pp. xv, 3–9.

"spiritual" value simultaneously. In the essay on Luca, Pater characteristically embodies his general point with recourse to a concrete historical example. And again characteristically, he interprets Luca's work as the visible, surviving representative of an aesthetic practice "common to all the Tuscan sculptors of the fifteenth century," who "worked for the most part in low relief" (R, 64). He chooses Luca quite candidly because enough information has survived to construct a "history of outward changes . . . through his work" (R, 63). And having made Luca's career representative of the general practice of a particular art form, Pater then sees that practice, in turn, as representative of the early Italian Renaissance in general, with its fresh but narrow perfection. Finally, in the most general sense, the art of Luca della Robbia represents the historical emergence of a new form through the familiar dynamic of impression and expression. His work displays "that profound expressiveness, that intimate impress of an indwelling soul," Pater writes, in a phrase that concentrates his aesthetic dynamic of internalization and externalization in its very barrage of intensive and extensive prefixes (R, 63).

Pater's discussion of the sculpture in low relief gathers an ekphrastic value within the volume as a whole, every bit as much as the classical descriptions of the shield of Achilles in *Iliad* 18, the wall murals on the temple of Juno at Carthage in *Aeneid* 1, or the figured pavement on the terrace of pride in *Purgatorio* 12. In fact, Pater is engaged here in a romantic revision of classical ekphrasis. It would certainly be characteristic for him to construct his own modern "equivalent for" the classical qualities of generality, blitheness, and repose as a way to place himself within a "conscious," modern tradition of classical revivalism. If he is engaged in an effort of modern ekphrasis, it would be important that he describe not a particular object but a generic art form. In the first place, the concrete but generic status of "sculpture in low relief" makes it an apt vehicle for representing the spirit of an entire age rather than one artist only. Choosing a generic art form rather than one particular object also ties the Luca essay to Pater's Hegelian theory of an evolution of art forms which represents the gradual emergence of "the human mind" into modern self-consciousness.

But above all, it is important to Pater's argument that he has chosen a plastic form. He quite straightforwardly uses Luca's reliefs to represent the tentative emergence of modern art in the early fifteenth century. But of course he also implies the more general case: the sculpture in low relief ekphrastically represents historical emergence in general, the dialectical process whereby new forms rise and define themselves against a context of precedent and conventionalized types, which then recede into the background. The ekphrastic value of low relief finally refers to the emergence of modern art in history and to the form of modern art as historical emergence. In the most important sense, these two levels of representation are really one. For Pater's greatest importance as a critic and as a precursor of early-twentieth-century modernism lies in his repeated demonstration that it is the conjunction of an aesthetic representation of history and the historical treatment of aesthetics which generates the sense of "modernity."

Despite its relatively thin and graceless composition, the essay "Luca Della Robbia," like "Winckelmann," is devoted to reviewing the fundamentally Hegelian argument that

> as the mind itself has had an historical development, one form of art, by the very limitations of its material, may be more adequate than another for the expression of any one phase of that development. Different attitudes of the imagination have a native affinity with different types of sensuous form. . . . The arts may thus be ranged in a series, which corresponds to a series of developments in the human mind itself. (R, 210)

This time Pater approaches the familiar argument using Renaissance sculpture as his concrete example of modern art, not the modern arts of poetry and painting, as he had done in "Winckelmann." Repeating the same argument about the modern arts of background and foreground, now using a plastic, sculptural form as his exemplary model, seems to be a sign of Pater's more conscious attraction to the aesthetic relief, his attentiveness to it as a historical figure, and his commitment to further interpretation of its aesthetic significance.

All sculpture, Pater argues, attempts to solve the same problem: to get beyond the limitations of its physical medium, its "tendency . . . to a hard realism, a one-sided presentment of mere form" (R, 65). Its hardness is "too fixed" and too unexpressively uniform. Only motion and color could "relieve" it, but because those direct solutions are for all practical purposes impossible, Pater addresses the characteristically revised aesthetic problem of how "to get not colour but the equivalent of colour." Both motion and color are frequently used elsewhere as the index of spirituality, but Pater has also made the typical aesthetic plea—not for the thing itself but for the recreated equivalent, or "sense" of the thing. The "precise value" of sculpture in low relief resides in its exact manner of overcoming the limitations of solid form, "etherealizing, spiritualizing, relieving its stiffness, its heaviness, and death" (R, 65). Like Hegel, Pater places relief sculpture between the classical form of freestanding sculpture and painting, the quintessential modern art form.⁹

After introducing this formal problem, Pater casts the solution to it in evolutionary terms. He sketches a three-term dialectical argument, taking Greek sculpture first, then Michelangelo's sculpture, and then situating Luca's low reliefs as the missing link, "midway between the two systems." Following Winckelmann, Goethe, and "many other German critics," Pater argues that the Greek system seeks "the type in the individual" and by a process of abstraction purges all individuality and accident from the form, leaving only "what is structural, and permanent" (R, 66). This system of course sacrifices personal expression completely. Michelangelo, on the other hand, represents the expressive artist, whose subject matter is the "special history of the special soul" and whose sculptural manner, too, is the result of a fortuitous, personal, and "special" solution to the formal problem. An expressive style "often is, and always seems, the effect of accident" (R, 67), but though it is personal, expressive, and "accidental," Michelangelo's sculpture is also historically representative.

Michelangelo's personal solution is enabled by the spirit of the times, the result of "a genius spiritualized by the reverie of the Middle Ages." Pater's familiar historical dialectic of body and spirit—Greek form without content, medieval Christian soul without bodily form—is at work here, as it was in his fantasy of the Mona Lisa; the Greek body is "penetrated" and filled as a result of medieval Christianity, yielding the Renaissance synthesis of body with soul "indwelling," in the language of Pater's incarnational poetics of historical form and content. The antithetical moment of disgust is present also: because Michelangelo's "genius had been spiritualized by the reverie of the middle age . . . a system which sacrificed so much of what was inward and unseen could not satisfy him" (R, 67). What the ravages of time and burial have done to the Venus of Melos, "fraying its surface and softening its lines, so that some spirit in the thing seems always on the point of breaking out of it," Michelangelo contrives to do consciously, aesthetically, leaving his sculpture in a suggestive and puzzling incompleteness that "trusts to the spectator to complete the half-emergent form" (R, 76). Thus we can see that the art of relief implies an aesthetics of reception. Though it seemed incomplete, it presented "in reality perfect finish," and many have felt that they "would lose something if that half-realized form ever quite emerged from the stone" (R, 68). The result is a freestanding sculpture whose

---

9. See Hill's notes, p. 389.

lines suggest the effect of relief. In this sense, the spirit of humanism, individualism, and expressionism is aptly represented by a freestanding figure, but the figure also refers in a "studied" manner to its difficult birth, its merely partial emergence from its ground.

After producing low reliefs in the high style (using marble) for the *Duomo* and the *Campanile* of Florence, Luca

> became desirous to realize the spirit and manner of that sculpture, in a humbler material, to unite its science, its exquisite and expressive system of low relief, to the homely art of pottery, to introduce those high qualities into common things, to adorn and cultivate daily household life. In this he is profoundly characteristic of the Florence of that century. . . . People had not yet begun to think that what was good art for churches was not so good, or less fitted, for their own houses. (R, 70)

This is a mythic vision of domestic daily life before the separation of sacred and secular generates the modern aesthetic and historical senses, and we return to this sacramental vision in Part Three. In the present context, it is important to point out that the terra-cotta reliefs are plain white at first, but—unlike Michelangelo, who achieved through "studied incompleteness" the "equivalent for colour in sculpture"—Luca eventually uses actual color: blending the exotic, oriental pottery that haunted his imagination with the indigenous Roman pottery of his Tuscan neighborhood. Color provides background, accentuating the relief and creating an "atmosphere," like the sky, the sense of "coolness and repose" in the summertime. The noblest of these reliefs, according to Pater at another point, were the ones colored in blue and white, the colors of the Virgin Mary. "By repressing all such curves as indicate solid form, and throwing the whole into low relief," Luca relieves the hardness of "mere form" and suggests spirituality through the aura of atmosphere or background (R, 69).[10]

Michelangelo's sculpture and Luca's low reliefs share an important formal feature: their incomplete or "repressed" sense of outline. Both sculptural forms incorporate within themselves an expression of figural relativity, for the figures rise out of their ground but remain caught within it. But Pater also distinguishes them as early and later forms of the same development. Thus Michelangelo's value appreciates because his work fulfilled the potential of a precedent form; its aesthetic value is generated in historical time. A formal solution that

---

10. The same terms are used in Pater's discussion of Browning's poetry. See below, Part Three, sec. 1.

in Michelangelo's sculptures is "studied" seems naive or "natural" in these humble Tuscan objects that have hardly separated themselves from the contexts of domestic use or religious ritual to become purely beautiful, "aesthetic" objects. They are not self-conscious yet, but merely emergent in both the aesthetic and the historical senses. Pater's figure of low relief represents a primitive, emergent form of the modern representation of emergence. In "Winckelmann," Pater identified the complex figure composed both of background and of foreground as the quintessential figure of modern art, and here he makes the low reliefs of Luca Della Robbia historically prefigurative of these later, more highly evolved backgrounding and foregrounding strategies, fundamental both to realism and to modernism.[11] His ekphrastic use of this historically concrete genre shows yet another sense in which art history itself can become a form of Pater's aesthetic poetry.

## 7 · The Senses of Relief

If the early Renaissance low relief is used in "Luca Della Robbia" primarily as a figure for the historical emergence of a modern aesthetic, other versions of the figure proliferate throughout the volume as well. The Luca essay serves to concentrate several valences of the figure in one place and to alert us to its profound importance in the overall argument of Pater's *Renaissance*. But in order to understand that importance, we must appreciate its wide range of uses in the volume. The figure works within both dimensions of his aesthetic historicism, for he uses it to imagine both the activity of consciousness in the present and the shape of past time. In fact, the extensive use of this figure is one powerful sign of the coherent relation between Pater's aestheticism and his historicism.

When Pater writes of "throwing" something into "relief," he alludes to the aesthetic construction of an image, a moment, or an object. The figure of relief depicts the result of that aesthetic construction: a "fixed" object displayed within and against its ground. As a figure for modern relativity, the relief portrays the conditional or contextual grounds of knowledge within which any "object" must be recon-

---

11. See Marshall Brown, "The Logic of Realism: A Hegelian Perspective," *PMLA* 96 (March 1981), 224–41.

structed. The modern "truth of relations" will always be construed as an "aesthetic" truth, constructed as a model or simulacrum of the relations between or within things, for it has been conceded that there is only representation, no direct access to "things in themselves." The "conditions" of representation, as we have seen, may be conditions of the subject or conditions of the object; in other words, the object is "thrown into relief" against the flux of consciousness in the present or against its own past historical context. And so, too, may the figure of relief refer either to the problem of the romantic subject or to the specifically historicist elaboration of the same problem: how to know a past object from the distant and different perspective of the present, and how to separate it from the complex network of contextual relations within which it is always entangled.

When the romantic subject forms the ground, the figure of relief expresses the relative repression of the subject while the object is highlighted within and against it. When the historical context is the ground, the object must be "raised" against past conditions simply in order to be visible. Pater characteristically indicates the aesthetic act involved in this selection by using the chosen object as the point from which to induce those general conditions. Thus his prose is characterized by movements of intense focus followed by broad generalization, an alternating rhythm of fixation and expansive dilation. The characteristics of ancient thought ("given" categories, stable, absolute standards) and the characteristics of ancient art (generality and repose) are both indicated in Pater's work by the image of sharp outline, but modern thought and modern art display the "subdued" or "repressed" outline of the low relief—not outline itself, but the "equivalent for" or the "sense of" outline. "Repressed" outlines, which suggest form without sharply defining it, indicate its partial submergence in the experiencing subject (the condition of all historical knowledge) or its partial emergence from an entangling context (the condition of all life in historical time). In both cases, the central object of representation is only provisionally separated from the background within which it must be seen and from which it can never entirely break free. Its independence as a figure is always understood to be relative and fictive; it is only a part of a more complex figure, composed *both* of figure and of ground.

A figure within its ground together form the complex, modern figure of relief. In this sense the figure of relief is quintessentially metafigural, expressing as a part of its complex figural structure the aesthetic activity of "raising" the foregrounded figures against the background. Using the example of Browning's poetry, in which a character is thrown into relief against a "situation," Pater calls attention to "relief" as a self-conscious procedure of modern representation (R, 214).[1] But focusing on an overtly artistic imitation of the modern "truth of relations" only reinforces Pater's fundamental understanding that knowledge is always aesthetically constructed in the modern world. The figure Pater uses for modern art is, in other words, the same figure he uses to portray modern consciousness.

Pater's model of consciousness as relief, the fluid passage of time marked by moments of fixated, "high" intensity, may be seen as a later version of Wordsworth's spots of time rising against the background of a general depression. But their fears are signally different: instead of stultifying depression, Pater fears the manic impulsion of mental process, time's passage in its experienced form. He both recognizes and fears that the moments of relief are actually ungrounded; the aesthetic act of fixing such moments is then accompanied by an equally aesthetic activity of imagining a solid ground. In visualizing this mental dynamic as a plastic form, Pater marks the vast difference between his dialectic of consciousness and Wordsworth's. What Wordsworth felt as an unconscious power "rising from the mind's abyss" Pater has transformed into a model of consciousness in control of time's passages. The spots of time lived on as renovating forces in Wordsworth's memory, but in Pater retrospection is the aesthetic precondition of these moments, which are purchased at the price of their own disappearance into the past. The flux can be stilled only momentarily, and only by looking back upon it. In Pater's aesthetic, the unconscious forces rising from the mind's abyss are forces from the collective, not from the individual past; his personal consciousness is renovated by spots of time stored within the general cultural memory, which is the "spirit" of the ages.

With the figure of aesthetic relief, Pater finds another way of imagining relativity, different from the textual metaphor of the "network" or the "magic web"; thus he defends against the threat that the "clear, perpetual outline of face and limb is but an image of ours, . . . a design in a web, the actual threads of which pass out beyond it" by adjusting the figure. The experience of consciousness, like life in historical time, may only be truly described as the flux of forms continuously emerging, but by "throwing" a form into "relief," the artist (or aesthetic critic) can imitate the modern truth of relative emergence and *at the same time* stabilize it as a static, spatial figure. Though the figure is spatially imagined, it has a temporal as well as spatial refer-

1. Discussed at greater length below, Part Three, sec. 1.

ent—at least it refers not only to the activity of fixation and recontainment within the aesthetic consciousness, but also to the "music" or "play" of temporality against which that stabilization takes place. But the figure of relief imagines temporality from a position after the fact, the retrospective position from which the flux of consciousness or historical time has been reified as a shape, a figure, a plastic form.

As a means of articulating this relation between the individual memory and the cultural past, the figure of relief may be seen also as a visual image of Pater's expressionist-impressionist theory of aesthetic creation and historical development. As we have seen, Pater envisions an individual dynamic of internalization and externalization, through which each artist is impressed by the spirit of his age before he expresses his own special vision, and as we shall see in Part Three, this dynamic holds true not only for artists and the "high" points of concentrated culture they represent, but also for every individual person, however invisible he may be to the eyes of the present. Moreover, the dynamic works on the general cultural level, too, in cycles of memory and repression, burial and renaissance. In other words, individual "impressionism" is echoed on the historical level when forms of cultural life are pressed deeply into (or even buried under) the ground, to be exhumed at a later time.

In other words, with the same figure he uses to describe modern art and modern consciousness, Pater also depicts the shape of historical time. As a synchronic figure, the Paterian type is formed by throwing a particular object or person into relief against a historically general background. When a concrete individual is invested with the aura of general historical value, it is figured in Pater as a fixed point within a surrounding field. The amorphous, indefinite background implies a vast number of similar forms, here grouped together under one "type" and represented by one "name." The aura of generalization around the type signals its value as the bodily representative of a spiritual reality, but the unrealized, amorphous, implied background is important in another respect as well. A texture of substantiating detail has been lost to the present, and here again the difficulties of historical knowledge are implied in a figure. The type as high point in relief against its background expresses a sort of faith that the surviving physical evidence is indeed evidence of things not seen, representative of the lost texture of past historical reality, the flesh that once covered the bones of a deep structure.

Thus the figure of relief expresses the relation between what is remembered and what is forgotten in cultural life at large. But this figure also, and correlatively, theorizes the relation between historical change and permanence. It works across the entire spectrum of historicist thinking, from an absolute commitment to historical difference and particularity all the way to the aesthetic construction of a mythically repetitive series of revivals of the "same" Greek standard:

> Again, individual genius works ever under conditions of time and place: its products are coloured by the varying aspects of nature, and type of human form, and outward manners of life. There is thus an element of change in art; criticism must never forget that "the artist is the child of his time." But besides these conditions of time and place, and independent of them, there is also an element of permanence, a standard of taste, which genius confesses. This standard is maintained in a purely intellectual tradition. . . . The supreme artistic products of succeeding generations thus form a series of elevated points, taking each from each the reflexion of a strange light, the source of which is not in the atmosphere around and above them, but in a stage of society remote from ours. The standard of taste, then, was fixed in Greece, at a definite historical period. (R, 199)

Pater places the "ground" or "origin" of this tradition in Greece during the Age of Pericles, and I have more to say about Pater's fundamental devotion to things Greek in Part Four. Now, still concentrating on the figure of relief, we may note that the permanence Pater envisions beneath the surface of historical change is tacitly understood to be an aesthetic construct, a "conscious tradition" formulated as an image of plastic form. "Constructing a series," as we have seen, is Pater's favorite way to indicate diachronic development, and this "series of elevated points" represents the aesthetic creation of history and the historical development of aesthetics with a familiar model. High points emerge against a background, indicating the "periodic" moments when a Greek standard was consciously revived. But of course the "ground" is as much a part of the figure as the elevated points that rise against it, ranged in a series; without the "fixed" ground, the "elevated points" cannot themselves be fixed. The choice of Greece as ground is the fundamental aesthetic choice that determines where the high points will be and how the "periods" will be marked against the continuum.[2] The sum of an evolutionary or

---

2. These "high points" may be taken as a spatial representation of Arnoldian "touchstones," though Pater's double use of the figure stresses more clearly than Arnold's that the "high points" are to be understood as chosen by the subject in the present as well as "given" by past history as the best that has been thought and said. It is possible also to see Pater's figure as a transfiguration of Arnold's scheme of alternating "epochs of expansion" and "epochs of contraction."

developmental view of history plus an aesthetic practice of "fixing" the high points against the continuous passage of time yields the model of the past as frieze in sculpted relief.

But if the frieze depicts past time literally frozen into tradition by the pressure of aesthetic retrospection, Pater also uses the figure of relief to indicate historical time in process. Leonardo's moment of aesthetic "disgust," for example, represents his detachment from the "former" (earlier and formative) type, which is thereby cast into the background and repressed while the new type rises against it. In this moment of antithetical rebellion, the "relief" expresses an escape from past entanglements, as if the spirit of the ages felt an emotional release at this moment when conventions are broken to make way for a new aesthetic distinction. For the individual spirit in the present, the "relief" is felt as freedom from temporality in moments of fixated stillness; but for the spirit of the ages "relief" is felt as freedom from the binding confinement of prior forms. Thus the figure enables Pater to turn *both* away from and back toward the flux of time. Here we can see how the recursive structure of the historical dialectic—dominant, foregrounded figure repressed as background, new figure rising against that constitutive ground yet never fully freeing itself and eventually becoming, in turn, the background against which yet another new type differentiates itself—provides a plot for Pater's story of historical development. Because his dialectical categories are so deeply identified as concrete historical persons, the plot is enacted by real characters as well, not merely abstract categories.

These moments of dialectical reversal map the "progress of a great thing," a general spirit such as "the art of Italy" or "the human mind itself." In other words, the moments of reversal themselves imply further movement and a larger whole in the process of being formed, of which these recreative turning-points only mark the parts. Thus metafigurality always represents this pressure toward a "higher" and more "complex" unity; it signifies the conscious acts of sublation that characterize Pater's historicism. Of course, it is only too obvious that Pater's historical dialectic exerts a strong metafigural or sublationary pressure toward synthesis.[3] In the historical plot a narrow and "one-sided" type like Winckelmann is always followed by a more "generous" type of "many-sided, complex unity" like Goethe. Or again, Pater sees antinomianism as a very component of the so-called

---

3. For previous discussion of Pater's "synthetic views" in relation to contemporary currents of thought, see Helen Hawthorne Young, *The Writings of Walter Pater: A Reflection of British Philosophical Opinion from 1860 to 1890* (Lancaster, Pa.: Lancaster Press, 1933), pp. 37–62.

The Senses of Relief · 159 ·

"Age of Faith," which will be missed by historians who do not look for the differences covered within such a name. Yet division too, when it becomes "well-recognized," baffles the historian with "rigidly defined opposites" that limit the sympathies and prevent the finer perception of "that more sincere and generous play of the forces of human mind and character" (R, 25–26). Like the "ackowleged" types, these "well-recognized" controversies are too distinctly "classified," "but the painter of the *Last Supper*, with his kindred, lives in a land where controversy has no breathing place. They refuse to be classified" (R, 27).

> The perfection of culture is not rebellion but peace; only when it has realised a deep moral stillness has it really reached its end. But often on the way to that end there is room for a noble antinomianism.

If the maxim from "Leonardo Da Vinci" ("For the way to perfection is through a series of disgusts") expresses the divisive pressure within Pater's dialectic, this maxim ("The perfection of culture is not rebellion but peace") expresses its other, synthetic side (R, 103).[4] Both, however, implicitly promise an end of division as the "end," the goal as well as the conclusion, of the story. The service of antinomian "disgust" is simply to open the way, to enable movement to resume in the direction of an ever higher, more complex synthesis.

Pater's historical dialectic is as much a product of aesthetic retrospection as is his frieze of tradition. Like all historical dialectics, this one indicates change through the interaction of categories, imitating temporality through the recursive alternation of moments of innovating departure and synthetic return, which engage like gears and turn to thrust the plot forward. This dialectic operates in Pater to describe the development both of culture and of self-culture. Here again my larger point is the homologous relation between Pater's dialectic of historical development and his dialectic of self-consciousness, while my more limited focus is the figure of relief:

> *Im Ganzen, Guten, Wahren, resolut zu leben* is Goethe's description of his own higher life; and what is meant by life in the whole—*im Ganzen*? It means the life of one for whom, over and over again, what was once precious has become indifferent. Everyone who aims at the life of culture is met by many forms of it. . . . But the pure instinct of self-culture cares not so much to reap all that these forms of culture can give, as to find in

---

4. The latter maxim was deleted in the third edition. See Hill's notes, p. 213.

them its own strength. The demand of the intellect is to feel itself alive. It must see into the laws, the operation, the intellectual reward of every divided form of culture; but only that it may measure the relation between itself and them. It struggles with those forms till its secret is won from each, and then lets each fall back into its place, in the supreme, artistic view of life. With a kind of passionate coldness, such natures rejoice to be away from and past their former selves. (R, 228–29).

Pater reads Goethean "self-culture," then, as a technique or strategy of consciousness.[5] His "passionate coldness" encapsulates in an oxymoronic formula the temporal dynamic of attachment and detachment. Here the mood is majestic "indifference," not "disgust," but the same process of internal impression and relieving self-division operates. The demand of the intellect "to feel itself alive" is fulfilled by these acts of internalization and discriminating measurement, and the process yields a calm wholeness or "indifference" that is produced synthetically, after many "differences." It also yields an understanding of the general "laws" of historical culture. This is the corollary of Pater's argument, at the end of the Michelangelo essay, that the qualities of the great masters reveal "the laws by which they . . . relieve each other" in historical time (R, 96). As a historicist, Goethe measures the relation between himself and "every divided form of culture," and as an aesthete he accomplishes this differentiation as an internal function. Personal and historical development are mirror images of one another. In this passage, cultural development is experienced against the ground of the romantic self, and the self is formed through the dialectical internalization and discrimination of "external" culture.

Pater's interpretation of Goethean self-culture provides a model for the synthetic wholeness, the "many-sided, complex unity" that is possible from the romantic perspective at the end of the line. From that perspective all aesthetic history may be assimilated within an omnivorous and scrupulously organized consciousness. In this case, the consciousness is understood to be formed on the model of cultural development, but the opposite movement is also apparent in *The Renaissance*, in which cultural development seems to be modeled on the experience of "relief" in an individual consciousness. On this historicist side of the dialectic, Pater discovers a role for unconsciousness which he does not tolerate on the aesthetic side. And here again, the basic figure of aesthetic and historical revival is the relief.

When Pater uses the figure of relief to describe art-historical revival,

---

5. Pater's quote from Goethe here was actually misquoted from Carlyle (see ibid., pp. 439–40).

he literalizes the "ground" to stunning effect. The most common metaphor for historical emergence, "rising," depends of course on the sense of a ground from which that motion could be understood to originate. This metaphor is omnipresent in historical discourse of all persuasions: scientific, popular, philosophical, aesthetic. The metaphor is fundamentally organic, relying on the image of a plant breaking suddenly through the surface of the ground. When Pater argues that the "universal pagan sentiment" is the foundation of human nature and thus of all religions, he uses this organic sense explicitly. Pagan sentiment is

> ineradicable, like some persistent vegetable growth, because its seed is an element of the very soil out of which it springs . . . modified indeed by changes of time and place, but indestructible, because its root is so deep in the earth of man's nature. (R, 201)

The wit of this formulation lies in Pater's use of an organic, horticultural metaphor for the unconscious, "natural" part of human nature. But this organic sense can also express the "human" part of human nature, the conscious "culture" or cultivation of the natural, as in the passage about the new flower, the anemone, which grew when the soil of Jerusalem was mixed with the common clay of Italy (R, 47). Pater is generally suspicious of the organic metaphor as a model for the artist, because it fails to do justice to "the most luminous and self-possessed phase of consciousness" (A, 80), but he does use the metaphor freely for historical "growth."[6]

The archaeological sense of relief is even more forceful in *The Renaissance*, where it is used to portray a collective unconscious periodically disturbed into sudden revelation. Here the figure of relief is imagined from the impressed rather than the detached moment of the dialectic: rather than focusing on the "elevated" points expressed against a depressed background, in other words, the archaeological figure focuses on past forms that have been pressed into and even beneath the ground. Pater's own age was experiencing a second wave of the classical revival, more "scientific" than the Renaissance and provoked by archaeological findings that graphically demonstrated how much of the cultural past lay hidden beneath the surface of the earth. His modern sense of geographical strata hiding the impressions of the past (fossils of organic life pressed into rock, fragments of

---

6. See Robert Nisbet, "Genealogy, Growth, and Other Metaphors," *New Literary History* 1 (Spring 1970), 351–63.

ancient sculpture in repose underground) is evident throughout *The Renaissance*. The delight Pater feels in contemplating the Panathenaic frieze or the Venus of Melos was colored, after all, by the thrill of their recent recovery.[7] The Elgin marbles are quite evidently a part of his aesthetics of relief, but so too is the Venus, which exists in a state of incompleteness both like and unlike Michelangelo's slaves. Her incompleteness bespeaks the aesthetic effects of time rather than the "studied" effects of an artist's intention. Aesthetic value thus appreciates in historical time (to recur to Pater's example of the Venus) and it is signified by the "frayings" of outline that take place after long burial underground (R, 67). When ancient art is "revived" against the context of the present, it comes to life as modern art at the same time that it becomes most truly a "classic."[8]

Pater identifies the particular "ground" out of which antique art first "rose" with the ascetic, Christian "medieval mind." What is most interesting here is the way Pater mobilizes his familiar three-stage development—Greek body, Christian soul, synthetic figure of Renaissance "humanism" composed of a historical body that "contains" a spirit—as a theory of the generation of a collective unconscious. The medieval mind had unconsciously "an aspiration towards that lost antique art, some relics of which Christian art had buried in itself, ready to work wonders when their day came" (R, 225). When that day came, it seemed to the Christian ascetic as if "an ancient plague-pit had been opened." The structure of that figure accords exactly with Pater's view of the Renaissance as an exhumation, though he shifts the value from negative to positive in granting new life to buried forms.

Thus the service of the Middle or "Dark" ages, which Pater romanticizes (as he did in "Aesthetic Poetry") with the image of night, was to provide the time for necessary rest and the latency that enables recognition. Medieval Christianity had caused the "human mind to repose itself, that when day came it might awake, with eyes refreshed, to those ancient, ideal forms" (R, 226). The Christian discipline of introspection both "forgets" the body *and* provides the necessary precondition for remembering it consciously. Thus, from the point of view of the Renaissance, Greek sculpture has a "ground" from which to rise and against which to be seen as historically different. This is a figure for the development of the "historic sense" as well as for

---

7. The Elgin marbles were sold to the nation in 1816; the Venus was discovered in 1820.

8. This paradox is worked out with great subtlety and historical specificity in Kermode's *The Classic*.

The Senses of Relief · 163 ·

the revival of classical antiquity, for the sense of history depends absolutely on this *difference between* parts of a recovered past, signified in the figure of relief.

In this figure the ground marks the difference between unconsciousness and consciousness in collective, historical terms. The surface of the earth serves a diacritical function within the figure, signifying the historical difference that generates aesthetic significance. The time during which antique art was lost and forgotten makes it possible for it to be suddenly recovered; asceticism is the necessary precondition of conscious sensual delight, as loss is the precondition of recovery. The submergence of antique art within "the medieval mind" represents its permanent accessibility as well as its temporary disappearance; its temporary occlusion permits the concept of sudden, though relative, innovation. The "medieval mind" is represented as if it were an individual mind, and change in time is depicted in spatial terms, as classical art rises up from under the ground.⁹ The *Allgemeinheit* and *Heiterkeit* of classical sculpture are thus reconstructed in figural form: submergence beneath the ground provides a modern form of relative repose in unconsciousness, as rising in relief against an aesthetically constituted ground provides a modern form of relative generality.

Pater generalizes this theory of the collective unconscious. The forces of the past have been impressed upon the spirit of each "succeeding age"; they live within the present, beneath the surface, underground:

> The spiritual forces of the past, which have prompted and informed the culture of a succeeding age, live, indeed, within that culture, but with an absorbed, underground life. The Hellenic element alone has not been so absorbed, or content with this underground life; from time to time it has started to the surface; culture has drawn back to its sources to

---

9. The archaeological metaphor was prevalent in late-nineteenth-century and early-twentieth-century discourse in several disciplines. Freud, for example, used archaeological excavation as a figure for probing and reconstructing the psychoanalytic Unconscious: "I had no choice but to follow the example of those discoverers whose good fortune it is to bring to the light of day after their long burial the priceless though mutilated relics of antiquity. I have restored what is missing . . . but like a conscientious archaeologist I have not omitted to mention in each case where the authentic parts end and my construction begins" (*Dora: An Analysis of a Case of Hysteria* [1905; reprint, New York: Macmillan, 1963], p. 27). Of course, my discussion of Pater's concept of the collective unconscious alludes to Jung, and while I do not mean to equate Pater's concept with Jung's, this association will suggest the mythic or archetypal foundation of Pater's model.

be clarified and corrected. Hellenism is not merely an element in our intellectual life; it is a conscious tradition in it. (R, 198–99)

Thus Pater's model of tradition as elevated points grounded in the permanence of the Hellenic spirit is itself based on this dialectic of unconsciousness and consciousness, "absorption" (or impression) and expression. Only from a "superficial view" do periods seem separate and definite, Pater argues; the "deeper view . . . preserves the identity of European culture" by relieving seemingly "definite" periods against an "uninterrupted," "continuous" ground (R, 225–26). Thus the "deeper," more internalized, amorphous, or even "forgotten" position below the surface can (as easily as the high points) be figured in the privileged, secondary, and aesthetic position; in fact, that repressed ground is itself turned inside out and "elevated" at those moments of dialectical reversal when impressed, culturally submerged material is suddenly expressed. This figure brilliantly mediates between permanence and change: the relative definition of the "elevated points" signifies historical concreteness, individuality, and difference, whereas the deep structure is mythic, repetitive, unified, and stable ground. But Pater's commitment to historical difference is not betrayed (or at least it is cleverly maintained) because the grounding "permanence" is repressed, hidden, implicit.

The ground allows for the sense of sudden discovery, even though what is "discovered" is also understood to have been there all along. This sense of sudden revelation is the very opposite of gradual, historical emergence, and in this sense the literalized "ground" serves to create the fiction of a sharp dividing line between absence and presence which Pater himself denies in his other uses of the figure to express gradually emergent historical reality. Pater allows for the sudden creation of form in the aesthetic sense which he denies in the evolutionary, historical sense, and he uses it as a metaphor for sudden recovery in historical time. He takes evident pleasure, for example, in imagining that Michelangelo's vision of the creation of man is decisively nondevelopmental:

For him it is not, as in the story itself, the last and crowning act of a series of developments, but the first and unique act, the creation of life itself in its supreme form, offhand and immediately, in the cold and lifeless stone. With him the beginning of life has all the characteristics of resurrection; it is like the recovery of suspended health or animation, with its gratitude, its effusion, and eloquence. (R, 75)

Here Pater reads the first chapter of Genesis ("the story itself") as if it were arguing for the theory of evolution, and he relishes Michelangelo's *Creation* in the Sistine Chapel because it seems to ignore this canonical story of a gradual "series of developments" and to offer instead a vision of sudden creation.

The aesthetic imitation of divine creation *ex nihilo* is a familiar trope, and here it provides Pater with momentary relief from, and for, his more characteristic evolutionary view. This uncharacteristic "disgust" at the very idea of development nevertheless reinforces Pater's characteristic late "humanist" focus on the human figure. These lifeless stones apparently can live. Renaissance humanism is metaphorically embodied in this passage as resurrection. Of course "humanism" would have to be the result of a rebirth; the "-ism" announces its distance from the unconscious self-sufficiency of the human form in Greek sculpture. Like aestheticism and historicism, it is a modern, systematic, and revisionary form of attention and measurement of effects, a "studied" return to reconsider the "sense of" human form, not a "natural" existence in the senses.

As usual, a profoundly antithetical wit is the effect of Pater's secularization here and of his ironic turn against Ruskin's own earlier secularization. The very historical moment that Ruskin regarded as the Fall, Pater here figures as the Resurrection. Both Ruskin and Pater use the sacred story to ground their interpretation of modern secular and aesthetic history, but Ruskin famously thought this turn into modern history brought error, decadence, and infelicity of form, whereas Pater's oddly transvaluing implication is that the Christian era "really" only begins just at the moment when "the modern mind" distinguishes itself against its Christian background. The dialectical doubleness and wit involve turning Christian doctrine against itself in a powerful way, making the resurrection of the body a figure for the rise of the "humanism" which in turn signifies the attenuation of Christian doctrine. Pater's figure testifies to the resurrection of the secular body, which nevertheless remains within the ground of the sacred story. After all, in Pater's scheme, we could never know what life "in the whole" might be without the punishing asceticism of the early Christian era, which "forgets" the body long enough to impress upon the spirit of the ages its inescapable, romantic interiority.

The figure of relief enables Pater to make a crucial compromise between sudden, "aesthetic" creation and gradual historical emergence. He finds the inspired plastic form of this vision in the sculpture of Michelangelo, which suggests the double sense of "life coming always as relief or recovery, and always in strong contrast with the rough-hewn mass in which it is kindled," "new" life that nevertheless still bears the signs of an archaic, amorphous former life (R, 76). Pater's conception of the Renaissance, then, of which Michelangelo is the consummate type, represents another level of this figurative solution to the problems of historicism. As such it highlights an aesthetically forged compromise between Pater's intellectual commitment to evolutionary gradualism and his nostalgia for special creation, now transferred from the providential to the aesthetic register and transfigured as relief. This is especially evident in his theory of the historical development of the aesthetic, "studied" form of relief.

And on the other hand, the archaeological unconscious provides the historical version of the same compromise: ancient forms suddenly rise up from under the ground *as if* they were new, yet with their "frayed" outlines they display no longer the signs of sudden creation, but signs of gradual, historical emergence and contextuality. Furthermore, this figure works alike (and often simultaneously) on the level of individual consciousness and historical process. Like Pater's Mona Lisa, for example, Winckelmann seems to have a sort of clairvoyance or second sight, a natural or intuitive knowledge of true classical art; "he seems to realize that fancy of the reminiscence of a forgotten knowledge hidden for a time in the mind itself" (R, 194).[10] And here we can see the extent of this figure's dependence on Pater's Hegelian scheme of linked levels in the mind or spirit of the world. Because "the composite experience of all the ages is part of each one of us," what has been hidden "within the mind itself" can be retrieved through Winckelmann's individual spirit.

With the structure of "relief," Pater mobilizes a brilliant complex of figures that operate dialectically or antithetically in order to express both gradual emergence and sudden recreation; contextual entanglement and freestanding form; modern Necessity and the momentary, fictive relief from that Necessity. And in each case, across the spectrum of each antithetical compromise, the figure can represent either individual consciousness or collective historical process, or both at once, for individual modern consciousness is grounded in Pater within a cultural unconscious that provides relief from the sense of time's passages and the devastating losses they entail.

While impressions race past in the present ("while all melts under our feet") Pater finds a sense of deep repose in the ground of the general

10. This passage reworks and recontextualizes a passage from Pater's earliest known essay, "Diaphancitè" (MS, 250). On the relation of this essay to "Winckelmann," see Hill's notes, pp. 424–25, and for my discussion of the earlier essay, see below, Part Three, sec. 1.

culture, a calming faith in resources impressed deep within. Pater's impressionism works in both these senses at once, first grasping the truly radical vision of an ungrounded temporality, and then carefully and painstakingly conserving and reforming that ground.[11] The dynamic interplay of this radical impulse and the patient, conservative return from it has a special beauty of its own. Moments of relief and return succeed one another again and again, as Pater loses and recovers the sense of facility and direct access to the body of the past and its spirit. The ecstatic rhythm of these "subdued" measures is incomparably *moving*, for with each relief the spirit is freed again, momentarily mobilized, unfrozen, and committed again to the passage of time:

> We can hardly imagine how deeply the human mind was moved, when, at the Renaissance, in the midst of a frozen world, the buried fire of ancient art rose up from under the soil. . . . On a sudden the imagination feels itself free. How facile and direct, it seems to say, is this life of the senses and the understanding, when once we have apprehended it! Here, surely, is that more liberal mode of life we have been seeking so long, so near to us all the while. (R, 184)

11. This "reaction" to the threat of ungrounded temporality might be called the nostalgic, "sad," regretful side of modernism, the opposite of the flight away from retrospection that Paul de Man describes in "Literary History and Literary Modernity," *Blindness and Insight*, pp. 142–65. De Man invokes Nietzsche's "ruthless forgetting" as the "authentic spirit of modernity" and goes on to propose and analyze the conflict and interdependence of the concepts "history" and "modernity" in Nietzsche's text. Pater has often been fruitfully compared to Nietzsche—especially because of their similar schemes of Apollonian and Dionysian forces archetypally at work in history—though Pater's version antedates Nietzsche's. (On this relation, see Monsman, *Pater's Portraits*, pp. 18–19; and Patrick Bridgewater, *Nietzsche in Anglosaxony* [Leicester: Leicester University Press, 1972], pp. 21–36.) Pater's ruthful remembering may indeed be seen as the nostalgic opposite of Nietzsche's "ruthless forgetting," and for that reason, among others, it is important to register the dialectical constitution of Pater's particular "modernity."

P·A·R·T · T·H·R·E·E

# Historical Novelty and *Marius the Epicurean*

· During the composition of *Marius the Epicurean*, Pater's letters, usually curt and dry, become somewhat more expansive and revealing as he discusses the plan of his ongoing project. Writing in 1884 to Violet Paget ("Vernon Lee"), he praises the success of her essay "The Portrait Art of the Renaissance," but his attention remains on his own endeavors.[1] "It is not *easy*," he protests (and the plaintive emphasis is his)

> to do what you have done . . .—to make, viz. *intellectual theorems* seem like the life's essence of the concrete, sensuous objects, from which they have been abstracted. I always welcome this evidence of intellectual structure in a poetic or imaginative piece of criticism, as I think it is a very rare thing, and it is also an effect I have myself endeavored after, and so come to know its difficulties.

Though Pater is speaking of his "imaginative criticism" here, he endeavored after the same effect in his historical fiction. He grants priority to concrete, sensuous objects from which "intellectual theorems" are abstracted; the "difficulties" of this sort of composition lie in the effort to reverse the process of abstraction, to reconstruct the object from the idea of the object, or historical novelty from an "intellectual structure."

Pater's emphasis on "intellectual structure" in his fiction is the

---

1. *Letters of Walter Pater*, ed. Lawrence Evans (Oxford: Clarendon Press, 1970), p. 54.

obverse of his attraction to fictional portraiture in the critical essays.[2] In the same letter to Violet Paget, Pater suggests his answer to the compositional "difficulties" he had come to know. Still praising her essay, he explains that he finds in it

> not merely historic learning dominated by ideas, which is certainly a good thing; but ideas gathering themselves a visible presence out of historic fact, which to me, at least, is a far more interesting thing.

Through the "medium" of the transparent hero, whose consciousness filters and transmits the "historic learning" of his day, Pater manages to represent "ideas gathering themselves a visible presence out of historic fact." Here again, for aesthetic historicism, the crucial concept is the representation of historicity, not "fact." Concretion, not factual accuracy, creates the sense of "visible presence."

Just as some of Marius's "sensations and ideas" deal more fully with the thoughts suggested by the "Conclusion," so does the form of *Marius the Epicurean* deal more fully with problems of historical representation raised in *The Renaissance*. In particular, *Marius the Epicurean* works out an interesting compromise between "historical novelty" and mythic repetition. On the one hand, Marius's cultural surroundings are presented in vivid detail and endowed with all the historical specificity of unique, unrepeatable phenomena. The novel carefully offers a "realistic" representation of historicity—one particular consciousness and life history specified to the cultural surroundings of the second century. But on the other hand, the cultural institutions, the other characters, and the literature Marius encounters are portrayed as types, invested with ideal value, and seen to represent second-century instances of forms that are repeated over time. This tendency to find the typical value of past historical phenomena is represented by the retrospective narrator of the novel, who looks back at Marius's age from a vantage point in the late nineteenth century.

Thus, the narrative structure of this novel expresses the tension between "historical novelty" and typicality. The narrator's emphasis on analogy produces the paradoxical effect of simultaneously asserting and denying historical difference. From Marius's point of view, one thing leads to another, and development is made to seem a matter of

---

2. Monsman calls attention to the resemblance and continuity between Pater's aesthetic and philosophical criticism and his imaginary portraits. See Gerald Monsman, "Pater's Aesthetic Hero," *University of Toronto Quarterly* 40 (Winter 1971), 144; and idem, *Pater's Portraits* (Baltimore, Md.: Johns Hopkins University Press, 1967), pp. 31–40.

change as much as continuity. But the narrator's point of view works to familiarize the difference of the second century, to mediate Marius's "sensations and ideas," to conflate past and present through analogical comprehension. Pater's figure for change in time (the developmental series) may here be seen to span the representational potentials of historicism: to read the figure "forward" through its linearity throws the emphasis on the difference between elements in the series, whereas retrospectively to read the figure in its totality throws the emphasis on the unity of development. In the latter sense, each element in the series becomes an instance or manifestation of the "same," overarching thing. The form of *Marius the Epicurean* balances these claims of difference and recognition. Through Marius's life story we read forward along the developmental line, but at the same time the perspective of the narrator gathers all past time into the place of present retrospection, the repository (or place of repose) for the multitudinousness of past forms.

The narrative structure of *Marius the Epicurean* presents another example of Pater's complex figure of relief for our examination. In a sense characteristic of the historical novel, Marius is poised as a central figure against the background of his second-century historical milieu. But because of Pater's emphasis on the dynamics of internalization, the reverse is also true: second-century figures have been placed against the background of Marius's receptive consciousness. Then again, both Marius and his second-century context are staged against the second-order background of the narrator in the late nineteenth century. The position of the narrator, then, becomes that retrospective, metafigural place of recontainment, the position from which the historical figure against its background is transfigured, recontextualized, thrown into relief against another ground, to become the composite figure of aesthetic historicism.

As we have seen, Pater's interpretation of the historicity of myth includes the notion that narrative form represents the past by imitating its spirit in a model or structure. In *Marius* we can see this principle working on several levels at once. The form of the novel presents the historical shift from paganism to the Christian era as a matter of evanescent, extremely gradual change—change so gradual that it is almost invisible at the time. It becomes graphically visible only from the vastly different perspective of the nineteenth-century narrator. Portraying the "secularization" of paganism as it gradually becomes Christianity tends to relativize the late nineteenth-century crisis of secularization by making it too merely one part of an ongoing development. The historicist form of the novel figuratively places the different "spirits" of two different ages side by side, but in the end these turn out to be merely different phases of the same, overarching spirit. The novel begins with the strict premise of historical difference, but in the end pre-Christian, Christian, and even post-Christian seem not so different. In order to focus the ironies of a dialectical reversal whereby Christian principles of historiography are used to explain the process of secularization, I have interpreted the narrative structure of *Marius the Epicurean* on the model of typological exegesis, highlighting Pater's debt to traditional Christian historicism while at the same time showing how that system of interpretation has been transvalued and secularized in its late nineteenth-century form.

In another sense Pater has written the romance of aesthetic historicism. Marius's life story is the story of openness, sensitivity, affinity for "all that is really lifegiving in the established order of things" (MS, 251). Thus Marius's "aesthetic" process of absorption and detachment makes history in several ways. As an exemplary or typical figure, Marius shows how the "time-spirit" comes to life in its concrete representatives—in Marius's transition from paganism to Christianity, for example. But Marius is particularly concerned not only with religious ritual but also with the literature of his day. His reception of that literature forms a major part of the plot, and the form of the novel consequently becomes anthological, composite, and modern. As the fragments of second-century literature are gathered up into a new, comprehensive form—the narrative form of *Marius the Epicurean*—they "appreciate," or gain in aesthetic value, through the staging of their renewed reception later in historical time. *Marius the Epicurean* represents the composite voice of Pater's essays, writ large, as narrative form. Its depiction of historical change and re-collection is his greatest essay in the poetics of revival.

## 1 · The Transparent Hero

In July 1864, Pater read to the Old Mortality the earliest of his essays that now remains to us, the beautiful "Diaphaneitè." He had recently become a Fellow of Brasenose College, and in the next year he would write of the differences between ancient and modern thought in his essay on Coleridge. Three years remained before he published his discussion of the differences between ancient and modern art in

"Winckelmann," and four years before the "Conclusion" first appeared as the last paragraphs of "Poems by William Morris."[1] Yet we can see in "Diaphaneitè" the preoccupations of these more familiar essays taking shape. For the present study, "Diaphaneitè" serves as the "key-signature" of Pater's work, especially because the ideas worked out in that essay are figuratively embodied as a person, as a character, and as a character *type*.[2]

Pater refers in the essay to this character's "clear crystal nature," and following Pater's lead Harold Bloom translates "Diaphaneitè" as "the Crystal Man" (MS, 253).[3] This translation places the emphasis on the several qualities of crystal that metaphorically allude to aesthetic form: its clarity and complex symmetries, the process of pressure and ascesis through which such form is realized (R, xi), and the resulting ethereal suggestion of spirit in material form. Pater twice wrote of Dante (once comparing him to Plato) that in his work "the spiritual attains the definite visibility of a crystal" (A, 212; PP, 135),[4] and it is especially in this latter sense that the "crystal man" functions as a historical representation, embodying Pater's belief that the spirit of time attains visibility in the historical person. This translation highlights the way a life can be lived in the spirit of art. But to translate "Diaphaneitè" as "crystal man" emphasizes the character's solidity of form, his relative visibility rather than his diaphanous or translucent nature, with all its Coleridgean associations.[5] The paradoxical and intermediate state of diaphaneity sets up a complex play of visibility with invisibility, partial permeability with full transparency; and I have chosen loosely to translate "diaphaneitè" as "the transparent hero" in order to throw the emphasis on the character's relative invisibility and permeability and his attainment of a wistful, graceful effacement in the service of historical change.

---

1. Dating of essays from Samuel Wright, *A Bibliography of the Writings of Walter H. Pater* (New York: Garland, 1975), pp. 1–5.
2. Bloom, on the other hand, chooses "The Child in the House" as his "key-signature, the largest clue to his work" (introduction to *Selected Writings of Walter Pater*, ed. Harold Bloom [New York: Columbia University Press, 1982], p. 15, n. 1). His choice emphasizes the "aesthetic" aspect of Pater's dialectic, while mine emphasizes his historicism.
3. "The Crystal Man" is the title of Bloom's introduction to *Selected Writings*, p. vii.
4. Monsman ("Pater's Aesthetic Hero," p. 143) points out that Pater uses the same sentence in these two locations.
5. Ibid. I am indebted to this essay in several ways. Monsman mentions Coleridge's metaphorical use of the crystal. He points out that Pater's "aesthetic hero" is a personification of the forces of history, a dramatic embodiment of "the Coleridgean (or German Idealistic) theory of art, in which the perfect aesthetic object is defined as a balance

In this essay Pater describes a type of figure, a projection of certain personal traits on the general level of historical culture. The aura of generalization projected about this figure is in fact, responsible in part for its formal "transparency," for this type of figure embodies Pater's ideal relations between an individual and his culture at any given time and over time. Pater imagines that it could serve as the "basement" or fundamental type in effecting historical "regeneration" (MS, 254). Thus it is no surprise that it would serve (and this has been noted by other critics of Pater) as the fundamental type in Pater's representations of history. Recognizing in it the kernel of all Pater's "imaginary portraits," Gerald Monsman has called it "a sort of Ur-portrait," and in another context he associates the diaphane with Pater's "aesthetic hero," a character type that Pater will employ again and again in his fiction.[6] In discussing this figure, I want to treat not only its content (that is, the traits that are characteristic of the type) but also its form (its projection as a type, the dynamics of its transparency). For "Diaphaneitè" not only portrays Pater's ideal "aesthetic" character type but also promulgates a theory of characterization for his historical fiction.

As he will later do more fully in the Renaissance volume, Pater works here to articulate a new, "modern" form of generality or typicality. The essay opens with a meditation on the reception or recognition of types. Some "types of character," though they are "unworldly," are nevertheless traditionally recognized by "the world." Pater names the saint, the artist, and the speculative thinker in this regard. The world is predisposed to recognize them; it has "a place made ready for them in its affections." Thus, this sort of type is "given"—individual instances "fill up" the "place" given by preexistent "outlines"—but it is "given" not absolutely but historically, "given" because it has existed many times before. Furthermore, "to constitute one of these categories, or types, a breadth and generality of character is required" (MS, 247). In other words, Pater describes this type of character in terms exactly like those he will use to describe "ancient thought" in the essay on Coleridge and those he will use to describe classical sculpture in the essay on Winckelmann. But "diaphaneitè" is "another type of character" (MS, 247).

---

between noumenal and phenomenal" (pp. 143–44). And throughout the essay he stresses the typicality of Pater's hero.

6. Monsman, *Pater's Portraits*, p. xiv. In that argument, Monsman's search for "mythic pattern" leads him to identify Diaphaneitè with the Apollonian hero (see ibid., pp. xiv, 22, 203, 205, 207). However, in "Pater's Aesthetic Hero," pp. 136–51, Monsman associates Diaphaneitè with the "religious hopefulness," which indicated Pater's "concession to Christianity" in *Marius the Epicurean*. In both cases, Diaphaneitè is taken to be the prefiguration of later figures.

In "Winckelmann," Pater distinguishes between ancient and modern art using the examples of Greek sculpture and the poetry of Robert Browning. Greek sculpture represents "broad" and "general" types in their "broad, central, incisive lines" (R, 213, 216). For this art form, "not the special situation, but the type, the general character of the subject to be delineated, is all-important" (R, 215). Furthermore, these types are "given"; Greek sculpture "has to choose between a select number of types intrinsically interesting—interesting, that is, independently of any special situation into which they may be thrown" (R, 215). "It renounces the power of expression by lower or heightened tones. . . . It has no backgrounds . . . to suggest and interpret a train of feeling. . . . It unveils man in the repose of his unchanging characteristics" (R, 212–13), and it does so through a process of abstraction or purgation, ridding the aesthetic object of all particularity or detail (R, 216). Modern art, on the other hand, is the art of accumulating particularity and specific detail, the art of shading, of "lower or heightened tones," the art of "foregrounds and backgrounds," which represent the relativity of the object within special situations (R, 214–16). Yet like the object of Greek sculpture, the object of Browning's "poetry of situations" also gains general value, but by another route.

The characters of Browning's poetry are not "given" types, for they are themselves unremarkable, of little intrinsic interest. According to Pater, Browning "accepts such a character, throws it into some situation . . . in which for a moment it becomes ideal. In the poem entitled *Le Byron de nos Jours*, in his *Dramatis Personae*, we have a single moment of passion thrown into relief after this exquisite fashion" (R, 214). In other words, Pater uses the figure of relief to describe the means by which the modern object is represented in its unique context, or "relatively, and under conditions." The aura of general value is projected around such a character through the modern technique of "throwing" it "into relief." The process can work in reverse as well, beginning with the general field and concentrating within it; in either case, the result is the complex, modern figure composed of a figure within its contextual ground. The modern poet, according to Pater, attempts "to realise this situation, to define, in a chill and empty atmosphere, the focus where rays, in themselves pale and impotent, unite and begin to burn" (R, 214). This, of course, is the familiar language of the "hard, gemlike flame" from the "Conclusion."

It is the language Pater uses to describe Diaphaneitè as well. The type under discussion in that essay is "fine," not broad. It relates obliquely to the "established order of things," and thus it is unrecognizable by "the world." Its transparency, in other words, is partly expressive of the fact that it is invisible within the world's lexicon of types. In the spatial terms of Pater's figure, it fills up the "blanks" *between* categories, rather than taking "places" the world has already "made ready" in its affections, and thus it invisibly works to "transmit" its influence to "every part" of the moral order:

> It does not take the eye by breadth of colour; rather it is that fine edge of light, where the elements of our moral nature refine themselves to the burning point. It crosses rather than follows the main current of the world's life. The world has no sense fine enough for those evanescent shades, which fill up the blanks between contrasted types of character—delicate provision in the organisation of the moral world for the transmission to every part of it of the life quickened at single points! For this nature there is no place ready in its affections. This colourless, unclassified purity of life it can neither use for its service, nor contemplate as an ideal. (MS, 248)

The fact that it remains "unclassified" testifies to its aesthetic value, for the world cannot "use" it, even for contemplation.[7] The metaphors of focus and refinement make it clear that the diaphane is a "modern" type, formed within but against the background of the world's recognized "organisation." Its spiritual force is registered in its difference from "the world," for it "crosses" the main current, rather than following it, "cutting obliquely" the established "order of things" (MS, 249).[8]

This type is refined and oblique, represented by an "edge" or a "single point," but by virtue of the paradoxes of Pater's characterization it partakes of generality as well. Its "colourless, unclassified

---

7. Monsman ("Pater's Aesthetic Hero," p. 142) points out that this characteristic serves to associate Pater's typical hero with the artists of the Renaissance, who "live in a land where controversy has no breathing-place" and "refuse to be classified" (R, 27). I am pursuing the point that all Pater's types of "modernity" are set off against the "given" types.

8. Possibly Pater remembers here Browning's portrait of Lazarus in "An Epistle . . . of Karshish," who is "at cross purposes" with the world after his return from the realm of pure spirit (l. 158):

> He holds on firmly to some thread of life—
> (It is the life to lead perforcedly)
> Which runs across some vast distracting orb
> Of glory on either side that meagre thread,
> Which, conscious of, he must not enter yet—
> The spiritual life around the earthly life:
> The law of that is known to him as this,
> His heart and brain move there, his feet stay here.
> So is the man perplext with impulses
> Sudden to start off crosswise, not straight on,
> Proclaiming what is right and wrong across,
> And not along, this black thread through the blaze—(ll. 178–89)

purity of life" is the colorlessness of white light, "blank" to "the world" but in reality composed of all colors. As Pater explains, there are two very different ways of being "colourless," which "the world" easily confounds. Most of us are reduced to a "colourless uninteresting existence" by "the play of circumstances," by the "pressing" of "our collective life" upon us. But Diaphaneitè is "neutralised, not by suppression of gifts, but by just equipoise among them" (MS, 252). His "colourlessness" is a sign of inclusiveness and balance: "here there is a moral sexlessness, a kind of impotence, an ineffectual wholeness of nature, yet with a divine beauty and significance of its own" (MS, 253). These very phrases are reproduced in "Winckelmann" to describe the beauty of Greek sculpture, "the colourless unclassified purity of life" to describe its *Allgemeinheit* or generality (R, 221, 218).[9] The transparent hero partakes of the "characterlessness" of Greek sculpture as well as the very particularized character of Browning's modern "poetry of situations."

Pater's modern type, in other words, is synthetic, dialectically constituted, displaying transvalued versions of the very qualities associated with its opposite, the ancient or classical types. This is especially clear from the hindsight of "Coleridge" or "Winckelmann," but it is thematically quite explicit in "Diaphaneitè" as well: "Such a character is like a relic from the classical age, laid open by accident to our alien modern atmosphere. It has something of the clear ring, the eternal outline of the antique" (MS, 251). This "outline," usually Pater's shorthand signal of the ancient, "given" type, is here used to praise the transparent expressiveness of the diaphanous one, whose "simplicity in purpose and act is a kind of determinate expression in dextrous outline of one's personality. Such a simplicity is characteristic of the repose of perfect intellectual culture" (MS, 249). In this way, Pater signals that Diaphaneitè is the successor to the value of Hellenic *Heiterkeit* as well as *Allgemeinheit*, both in their synthetic, modernized, transvalued forms.

The "transparency" or *near*-transparency of this character works in several ways. In the first place, Diaphaneitè is transparent to his own interiority. In this sense, transparency functions as the metaphorical foundation of Pater's romantic theory of individual expression. The "life" of this character is like art in this particular sense: it is a clear translation of what is inward.

---

9. On Pater's repetition of passages from "Diaphaneitè" in the later essay, see Francis X. Roellinger, "Intimations of Winckelmann in Pater's Diaphaneitè," *English Language Notes* 2 (June 1965), 277–82.

> The artist and he who has treated life in the spirit of art desires only to be shown to the world as he really is; as he comes nearer and nearer to perfection the veil of an outer life not simply expressive of the inward becomes thinner and thinner. (MS, 249)

Arnold's exhortation to objectivity here again has been reassimilated to the very romantic project he was attempting to combat. Pater envisions the conventional, inexpressive "outer life" as occluding matter which prevents pure expression; in his ideal type, this material "veil" is becoming "thinner and thinner." "There is an intellectual triumph implied" in this defeat of the "adulterated atmosphere of the world" (MS 249, 253). For "the world" does not manage to impose its conventional categories on this character, and as the "veil" becomes thinner and thinner, this rare type comes closer to being recognized, "shown to the world as he really is."

But what is inward has quite clearly been internalized from what is without. In this sense, transparency functions as the metaphorical foundation of Pater's theory of historical expression. Pater is working here on the dynamics of the reciprocal and analogous relation between the individual and his historical "environment." The diaphane draws together Pater's aestheticism and his historicism in one unified theory of expression.[10] On the one hand, the "order of things" in any given age determines the content of this transparent character; but on the other hand, certain "elements" in his nature magnetically attract certain elements in the age—and not others. His "diaphanous" exterior metaphorically signals a state of almost total permeability to the order of things. But an active force of attraction allows for the character to have an extremely subtle shaping role in what it receives. For this reason, diaphaneity (and not full transparency) is the apt metaphor. In this context Pater spells out what might be called an ethics of internalization:

> Its ethical result is an intellectual guilelessness, or integrity, that instinctively prefers what is direct and clear, lest one's own confusion and intransparency should hinder the transmission from without of light that is not yet inward.... It is just this sort of entire transparency of nature that lets through unconsciously all that is really lifegiving in the established order of things; it detects without difficulty all sorts of affinities between its own elements, and the nobler elements in that order. (MS, 251)

Thus the diaphanous character is formed through an unconsciously regulated receptivity, regulated by his "affinities" with the best that

---

10. On Pater's theory of expression, see F. C. McGrath, *The Sensible Spirit* (Tampa: University of South Florida Press, 1986), pp. 184–214.

has been thought and said in a certain "established order of things." His character is at once an accurate microcosm of the spirit of the age, and yet it has been formed selectively. He has been totally passive to the forces of his environment, and yet he has been "unconsciously" active.

This paradoxical union of sheer passivity with "unconscious" activity is at the heart of this character's role in Pater's scheme of historical representation. For he exerts an aesthetic, shaping force on the "established order of things," transmitting synchronically and diachronically—to his own age, and to future ages—only what is "really lifegiving." And yet he performs this aesthetic function unconsciously, "in the order of grace" (MS, 249). Thus Pater manages simultaneously to imagine an individual power to shape the course of history, while at the same time granting to the movements of the *Zeitgeist* an independent and primary force. Pater's notion of diaphaneity defines the role a cultured but otherwise unremarkable individual might play in the vast movements of historical change. His activity is invisible, for it consists in the internalization (and thus the transmission) of cultural forces surrounding him. Like the "receptacles" of Pater's "Preface" to *The Renaissance*, the transparent hero is the site of forces passing through him, and thus this character type participates in Pater's revision of the notion of "content."

He does not "make history" as the types recognized by "the world"—kings, saints, artists—are conventionally understood to do, but he does "make" history, for he selectively internalizes and transmits what is "really lifegiving" in the "established order of things." Pater is involved in a paradoxical project: bringing into visibility the important shaping function of a character who is by definition—by the world's definition—invisible. His fundamental assumption is that historical change has not taken place exactly in the way "the world" would say. Thus we can see that the play of visibility and invisibility set in motion by the figure of diaphaneity suggests a critique of conventional historical retrospection. Through the character of Diaphaneitè, Pater considers not only the aesthetic shaping of history-in-the-making, but also the retrospectively aesthetic procedures of history-writing. In other words, through the character under discussion, Pater works out a theory of historical fiction.

When he comes to embody Diaphaneitè as Marius the Epicurean, Pater manages to lend that character the full paradoxical blend of visibility and invisibility to the retrospective eye. Pater's Marius is not remembered in received historical records, yet he is personally involved with the figures who *are* memorialized from his age. To this extent he is the typical protagonist of historical fiction, one of whose generic premises is that it makes visible a portion of the past which has become invisible within the scope of present memory.[11] This sort of fiction purports to go "behind the scenes" of received history to show the lives of unremembered characters who nevertheless had an effect on the events of monumental history. But Pater's characterization is particularly interesting in that the very sort of historical efficacy imagined for Marius *depends* upon his near-invisibility from the point of view of traditional history. Transmission of "what is really lifegiving" in the "established order of things" is an activity that by definition (here again, by the world's conventional definition) takes place behind the scenes.

Marius becomes amanuensis to Marcus Aurelius, so he is fictively responsible for the literal transmission of the emperor's words (as he is in a less direct sense responsible for the transmission of the anonymous *Pervigilium Veneris*, fictively attributed to Flavian in the novel). But his more important act of transmission is a more figurative one. In a tour-de-force of passive activity, Marius becomes a Christian at the end of the novel. That closing action is famously more done *to* him than done *by* him. Marius's only real "activity" is to make himself perfectly receptive to the forces of his age. He feels "all sorts of affinities" for the new religion: he is attracted to Cornelius, the Christian knight; and he has chosen to go to the church in Cecilia's house. But at his death, "in the moments of his extreme helplessness," he receives the Host and is made a Christian, not exactly against his will, but crucially without his will having been consulted (ME II, 224). After his death the early Christians count him as a Christian martyr. Let us say, then, that he is swept up in the most important historical change taking place at the time. Thus, at his death Marius represents the vast number of unremembered converts who made up a historical "movement," but more important, he represents the force of the timespirit moving through him into the Christian era. In both senses his invisibility to traditional historical retrospection indicates the "spiritual" nature of fundamental historical change.

In this regard, it is important to Pater's theory that the figure of Marius represents a *type*, for this is one way of suggesting the representative spirit of an age, embodied in concrete but generalized form.

---

11. Lukács makes the important point that the historical novel is characterized by the typicality of its protagonist, as opposed to the "world-historical" figure (in Hegel's sense). See his discussion of characterization in the historical novel and historical drama in Georg Lukács, *The Historical Novel*, trans. Hannah and Stanley Mitchell (London: Merlin Press, 1962), pp. 89–138.

Marius is imagined to be like many others of his age who are no longer remembered, and thus he represents the vast number of cultured individuals who invisibly accomplish the work of historical transmission. Pater's unspoken Hegelian assertion is that the real forces of historical change are not the kings and warriors, or even the artists and writers, but an invisible, spiritual force of which those persons are merely the concrete representatives.[12] In the transparency of this character, and his resultant invisibility to "the world," lies his historical efficacy. His effectuality, in other words, depends precisely upon his ineffectuality in the conventional sense.

The premise that a novel is recording the history of an unremarkable character (or a remarkable character who is nevertheless not recognized by the world for being remarkable) is a familiar technique of literary realism. What is invisible to traditional history is made visible in the novel's ordinary characters and actions. Pater takes this premise of realism to its extreme (as George Eliot does in certain cases) by delineating characters whose rarefied sensitivity indicates that great forces are passing through them but whose very sensitivity at the same time renders them passive.[13] Instead of pretending to actual historicity, realism is based on the principle of analogy or typicality. The realistic novel presents characters who are *like* many others, and so it presumes to give detailed, individualized portraits of general phenomena.[14] Pater alludes in "Diaphaneitè" to the author of *Romola* (MS, 249), and we might usefully compare Pater's representational strategy here with George Eliot's paradoxical claim to write the history of the very sort of character whose history, according to the usual definition of "historical," would always remain unwritten.

The "Finale" to *Middlemarch* tells us that the influence of Dorothea Brooke was "incalculably diffusive" and that "the growing good of the world is partly dependent on unhistoric acts, and . . . half owing to the number who lived faithfully a hidden life, and rest in unvisited

---

12. McGrath discusses the Hegelian underpinnings of Pater's fictional treatment of the concrete universal in *The Sensible Spirit*, pp. 127-29.

13. George Levine makes this comparison between Pater and Eliot during his excellent discussion of the late Victorian and early modern dialectical reversals, or "transformations," of reality (and hence of realism). See part 4 of *The Realistic Imagination: English Fiction from Frankenstein to Lady Chatterley* (Chicago: University of Chicago Press, 1981), esp. pp. 262-74, and "The Hero as Dilettante," pp. 291-316. Elizabeth Deeds Ermarth discusses issues of narratorial effacement and historical transmission in "George Eliot's Invisible Community," in her *Realism and Consensus in the English Novel* (Princeton, N.J.: Princeton University Press, 1983), pp. 222-56.

14. Thus Fielding's narrator in *Joseph Andrews* 3.1: "I describe not men, but manners; not an individual, but a species." See also Marshall Brown, "The Logic of Realism: A Hegelian Perspective," *PMLA* 96 (March 1981), 224-41.

tombs." Dorothea, too, is elaborately constructed as a type in the "Prelude" to that novel. Diachronically she is compared to Saint Theresa, and synchronically to all the other "later-born Theresas" of her own age who were "helped by no coherent social faith and order which could perform the function of knowledge for the ardently willing soul." Like Pater, Eliot is concerned with the modern absence of a "given" order, of received knowledge, of recognized types, and with their replacement by relative ones. As it does in Pater, Eliot's move out of a religious context and into a secular, historical context highlights the aesthetic value of her character's typicality, and in both cases the secularization-effect is in part dependent on the fiction that an invisible, spiritual phenomenon has been made visible. The character of Pater's transparent hero, "like the religious life, . . . is a paradox in the world," for it is precisely in the world, but not of it (MS, 249).

The paradoxical and fictive presumption to represent what "in fact" is invisible has particular implications for these writers' views of historical change. It signals their commitment to a gradualism so extreme that at any present moment change cannot even be perceived. Thus both Eliot and Pater are able to embrace change as a positive value while at the same time maintaining a fundamental conservatism. In "Diaphaneitè," for example, Pater conveys a complex attitude toward historical change. On the one hand, he is wistfully conservative, remarking that "after all progress is a kind of violence" (MS, 252). The type in question may contribute to the regeneration of the world in part because it is "not disquieted by the desire for change" (248). But on the other hand, "its wistfulness and a confidence in perfection . . . makes it love the lords of change" (MS, 251). "Also the type must be one discontented with society as it is" (MS, 254).

The contradiction in these attitudes is resolved in a strategic and paradoxical conception of historical change, made possible by the passive activity of the transparent hero, for "in this nature revolutionism" is transvalued, "softened, harmonised, subdued as by distance" (MS, 252). In Pater's view, change can be regenerative only if it is "softened," if it takes place "without any struggle at all" (MS, 249). When viewed through the present actions of this character, it is evanescent, "inexpressible," at any moment practically invisible. Taken as a matter of faith, historical change does not impose its confusing sense of difference in the present; it is always taking place so gradually that it cannot be seen clearly and graphically except in retrospect. And of course in retrospect it is effectively "subdued as by distance."

The conclusion of Pater's essay looks forward to the future efficacy of this character type, who represents a "natural prophecy of what the next generation will appear": "A majority of such would be the regeneration of the world" (MS, 254). This idea of the future, envisioned precisely as *regeneration*, is another sign of the value of conservation in Pater's view of historical change.[15] It is a prophetic conservatism like Carlyle's, which opens toward the future by passionately transmitting the past. Here again, the notion that the Diaphaneitè is a character *type* becomes important, for its paradoxical blend of unconscious self-consciousness reminds Pater at once of historical revival and Platonic reminiscence:

> It is like the reminiscence of a forgotten culture that once adorned the mind; as if the mind of one Φιλοσοφήσας πότε μέτ'έπωτος fallen into a new cycle, were beginning its spiritual progress over again, but with a certain power of anticipating its stages. (MS, 250)

In other words, it is the type, of Pater's poetics of revival. His clear statement of metaphorical distinction keeps this character from evanescing into the realm of mythic recurrence: it is merely "like" reminiscence, "as if" fallen into an new cycle. But at the same time, this passage reminds us that typicality can become a mode of mythic characterization, within certain conditions. Later in Part Three I argue that Pater manages in his historical fiction to balance historical specificity with spiritual or mythic recurrence. That balance is registered in the dominance of a Christian, historical sense of the type over a Platonic, allegorical sense. For now, however, it is important to see this mythic tendency in the characterization of the hero.[16] In Pater's historical fiction, the central character is more prone to lose the distinction of historical "novelty" than is the background within which he is represented.

"Diaphaneitè" articulates the theory of characterization which Pater practices in *Marius the Epicurean*. The hero of that novel is transparent to his culture, the "medium" through which pass the voices of his age. Invisible though Marius is to conventional history, Pater envisions his central figure as most truly *"nodus et vinculum mundi,*

---

15. See William Shuter, "History as Palingenesis in Pater and Hegel," *PMLA* 86 (May 1971), 411–21.
16. Monsman's first study of Pater's fiction, *Pater's Portraits*, emphasizes this important element of "mythic pattern." Because he ties his notion of "pattern" to the *specific* myths of Apollo and Dionysus, Monsman misses the full abstraction of Pater's tendency in this direction. But my main difference from Monsman in this case is in seeing Pater's attraction to mythic pattern as merely one pole of a dialectic, the other pole of which is historical specificity—what I am calling in this chapter "historical novelty."

the bond or copula of the world" (R, 40). In *Marius,* Pater works out a fictional form in which the central character becomes the pivot-point of an elaborately recursive play with backgrounds and foregrounds.[17] Thus the fictional form of *Marius the Epicurean* is another example of Pater's figure of relief. For in one sense the transparent hero is represented in the foreground, and the reader sees through him into the colorful multiplicity of the second century, but in another sense the consciousness of Marius is the background against which the panorama of the past is displayed. On the one hand, historical specificity is defined in this novel as a matter of background, against which Marius's consciousness is thrown into relief. But on the other hand, Marius's consciousness is the background within which alone the past can be transmitted and thus in retrospect revived or thrown into relief. The elaborate working of this figure of relief on the level of the novel's total form is only one of the important ways in which *Marius the Epicurean* is a magisterial example of Pater's modern art of aesthetic historicism.

## 2 · Autobiography of the *Zeitgeist*

The point has been made many times that the character of Marius the Epicurean is a recognizable mask for Pater's own "epicurean" sensibility. This particular connection of the character of Marius to Pater himself is usually made in order to suggest a palinodic motive for the composition of the novel. In 1877 Pater dropped the "Conclusion" from his second edition of *The Renaissance,* and when he restored it to the third edition in 1888, three years after the publication of *Marius the Epicurean,* he added the following note of explanation:

> This brief "Conclusion" was omitted in the second edition of this book, as I conceived it might possibly mislead some of those young men into whose hands it might fall. On the whole, I have thought it best to reprint it here, with some slight changes which bring it closer to my original

---

17. Monsman makes a similar point and extends it generally to several of Pater's "visionary texts" in his *Walter Pater's Art of Autobiography* (New Haven, Conn.: Yale University Press, 1980). He calls attention to Pater's "multireflexive interplay between inner and outer textual levels" and associates Pater's textual strategy with techniques of postmodernism (pp. 48, 5).

meaning. I have dealt more fully in *Marius the Epicurean* with the thoughts suggested by it. (R, 233)

The pretext of *Marius* was defensive, this argument runs—a defense of *Marius*'s pre-text, Pater's own *Renaissance*. When Lawrence Evans calls *Marius* Pater's *apologia pro vita sua*, it is this specific sense of its "autobiographical" valence to which he alludes.[1]

However, as I began this book by arguing, many of the "thoughts" represented in the "Conclusion" are never owned by Pater in the first place, but are carefully staged as an impersonation of "modern thought." To bring these thoughts "closer to [his] original meaning" is to distance them more definitively. In *Marius the Epicurean*, Pater more decisively detaches himself from those "modern" thoughts by casting them as the thoughts of a fictive, hypothetical persona. When ideas are thus thrown into relief within the mind of a particular character in a particular situation, they are relativized by their context. Like the epigraph from the *Cratylus* prefacing the "Conclusion," Marius's extreme distance in time from Pater's own age works to demonstrate that the disturbingly "modern" thought of the nineteenth century had its analogue in an ancient, venerable, and revered philosophical tradition.

The fictional plot of self-culture works to show what Marius thinks of the thoughts he entertains, how provisionally (though seriously) he regards them, how he "holds his theories lightly," as Pater says of Plato (A, 69). Pater translates the Latin *contextus* as "clothed," and the temperamental coloring of Marius's character does indeed clothe each system of thought he essays (ME II, 59). Marius entertains systems of thought at the distance of speculation, not with the closeness of identification we call belief. In other words, he uses them as "instruments of criticism," as guides along a journey of self-culture more comprehensive than any of its separate, partial phases (R, 237). Like Goethe's, his "proper instinct of self-culture"

> struggles with [every divided form of culture] till its secret is won from each, and then lets each fall back into its place, in the supreme, artistic view of life. With a kind of passionate coldness such natures rejoice to be away from and past their former selves. (R, 229)

Even after his visionary moment of coming to a willed "conclusion," Marius wonders: "Would he be faithful to himself, to his own habits of mind . . . if he did but remain just there?" (ME II, 72). This mobility,

---

1. *Letters of Walter Pater*, p. xxx.

the by now familiar aesthetic dynamic of identification and detachment, is one of Marius's only articles of belief. (The other is that he must "hold by what his eyes really saw.")

But *Marius the Epicurean* is certainly not autobiographical in any conventional sense of the word. The novel focuses so closely on the "sensations and ideas" of its title character that it is almost possible to forget that it is narrated by another "person." A narrator occupies the position of the first person, whereas Marius is described at the figurative distance of the third. We read of "his" sensations and ideas in long passages of free indirect discourse. The narrator is for the most part recessive, an effaced background for Marius's feelings and thoughts in the foreground. Marius's development seems to be seen from the inside out, so to speak, even though the story is told in an objective mode, as if from the outside in.[2] Through its representation of the central character the novel seems introspective, and through its representation of the narrator it seems retrospective, though these two functions of traditional autobiography have been divided between "persons." But how can we accurately speak of autobiography at all when the novel is written in the third person?[3]

The important sense in which *Marius the Epicurean* may be usefully called autobiographical is an effect of its narrative structure. A clue lies in the fact that the narrator is not only distanced from but also explicitly identified with Marius the Epicurean. He narrates this story of second-century Rome from the great distance of a perspective in late-nineteenth-century England, and yet when the narrator assumes the foreground by taking on the personal pronoun "I," that narrator frequently uses the occasion to draw analogies between Marius's age and his own. "Let the reader pardon me if here and there I seem to be passing from Marius to his modern representatives—from Rome to Paris or London," this narrator demurs, after offering the general remark that Marius's "age and our own have much in common—many difficulties and hopes" (ME II, 14).[4] Analogies like these establish similarity across the space of historical difference. They bind the figures of Marius and his narrator together in a relation of mutual reflection, for the narrator interprets Marius's age as not only analogous to but also prefigurative of his own age.

---

2. See Inman's description of "the objective-subjective technique" whereby "he always seemed to be writing about himself, even though he very rarely made a personal reference or even expressed a personal opinion" (Billie Andrew Inman, *Walter Pater's Reading*, [New York: Garland, 1981], p. 58).

3. Philippe Lejeune, "Autobiography in the Third Person," *New Literary History* 9 (Autumn 1977), 27–50.

4. See also, e.g., ME I, 20, 173, 185, 239.

Marius's early experiences are narratively structured to be "formative" of later ones; in other words, his early experiences prefigure his later experiences, establishing structures of thinking and feeling that are recapitulated again and again over the course of his life story. But because the narrator makes analogies between Marius's experiences and his own contemporary conditions, second-century culture in general is made to seem "formative" of later ages. Marius's individual experiences, then, are made to represent structures of cultural experience that are recapitulated again and again over the course of the centuries. The narrator has retrospective access to all ages of Western history. He draws analogies not only between Marius's age and his own, but between any of the "intervening" ages as well. Thus, from the perspective of the narrator all the cultural practices from the pre-Christian survivals of the religion of Numa to the late nineteenth century are knit together in one continuous development. This narrator "binds the ages each to each," using a version of the modern, historic method.

One of Pater's most interesting narrative choices is the construction of this analogous, prefigurative, or evolutionary relation between the central character and the narrator, and this relation is crucial to an understanding of the novel.[5] The narrator mediates the otherness of Marius by showing it to be essentially another, earlier stage of the same overarching development in which he still participates. He looks back, in other words, to an earlier period of his own cultural past. It is as if Marius and the narrator were in relation to one another as past and present phases of the same person, though the "person" in question is not an individual person but an overarching personal figure for Western culture in general.

This narrative presents a wonderful example of what Paul de Man calls "specular structure."[6] In the figure of specularity, two subjects "determine each other by mutual reflexive substitution." De Man argues that this figure occurs to some degree in all texts, but that the "specular structure is interiorized in a text in which the author declares himself the subject of his own understanding," in other words, in a traditional, first-person autobiographical narrative.[7] What we find instead in *Marius the Epicurean* is the interesting example of a text

---

5. For another discussion of this relation, see Avrom Fleishman, *The Historical Novel: Walter Scott to Virginia Woolf* (Baltimore: Johns Hopkins University Press, 1971), pp. 169–77.

6. Paul de Man, "Autobiography as De-facement," *Modern Language Notes* 94 (1979), 919–30.

7. Ibid., p. 921.

in which the figure of self-understanding has been masked by the assumption of difference between "persons." The author has not declared himself the subject of his own understanding in the traditional way, and yet the specular structure of *Marius the Epicurean* operates to generate the effect of self-understanding across the supposed difference between narrator and protagonist.

Theory of autobiography has traditionally drawn this distinction between "narrator" and "protagonist" in order to hypostatize two temporalities of the same "self": the "I" remembering and writing in the present, and the "I" in the past, experiencing the events that led up to and conditioned the present state of retrospection. Subtending this distinction is the fundamental and unspoken assumption of personal development, through which all differences are ultimately united under the figure of the same retrospective "I." James Olney, for example, exploring various types of autobiography, describes the autobiography of memory, in which the "I" controls a double reference: "here and now, there and then, both the perpetual present and the historic past—and it is the tenuous yet tensile thread of memory that joins the two 'I's."[8] Jean Starobinski argues that the "style" of autobiography is characterized by a double "deviation"—of time and of identity—which establishes autobiographical reflection; this double deviation marks the difference between present and past, as well as a change within the "I." That change is obscured by a "personal mark," the "pronomial constancy" of the "I," which covers the difference within and asserts continuity over change. But this "constancy" is an "ambiguous constancy," because the retrospective stance depends precisely on a difference in temporality.[9]

De Man's exposition of specular structure develops further the emphasis found in Starobinski's formulation: an emphasis on defining autobiography not with reference to a "real life" outside the text but through attention to the structure of figuration which produces the illusion of such a reference. This line of argument makes it clear that the distinction drawn between "narrator" and "protagonist" is a working distinction only. The sense of memory is itself an effect of figuration. Whereas the traditional understanding

---

8. James Olney, "Some Versions of Memory / Some Versions of *Bios*: The Ontology of Autobiography," in James Olney, ed., *Autobiography: Essays Theoretical and Critical* (Princeton, N.J.: Princeton University Press, 1980), pp. 236-67; quoted passage on p. 248.

9. Jean Starobinski, "The Style of Autobiography," in ibid., pp. 73-83; quoted phrases from pp. 78-79.

of the autobiographical figure emphasizes the unity of the "I" through memory, the more recent understanding emphasizes the differences within the "I," which are covered by that "personal mark."[10]

Pater's novel graphically displays both the figure of temporal difference which makes for historical retrospection, and the consolidation of temporalities within a figure of personal identity. Instead of emphasizing stability and continuity in the "I," which covers fundamental difference, the novel emphasizes the apparent differences that obscure a fundamental continuity. The figure of self-understanding has been separated into two personae, figuratively reunified in their specular relation. Thus the novel enacts the autobiographical play of similarity and difference within a self-reflexive identity. At first glance, the development represented in the novel does not appear to be *personal* development. And yet through this particular relation of narrator and character, historical development is cast precisely in personal terms.

Rather than the figure of an older, wiser person looking back over the course of a lifetime, to chart his development as the "protagonist" who eventually became the present "narrator"—instead of a narrator who projects a figure of his past self as "other" than his present self, and then in the end recuperates that "other" as "same"—we have a narrator in the present looking back over the course of centuries to chart the growth of a more distantly displaced "other." But the structure of the figure works the same way. Through the framework of analogy, the narrator insists on his developmental relationship with the character Marius; the narrator and Marius are related as later and earlier stages of the same continuing identity. The implication of this relation is of course evolutionary. Young epicureans like Marius are the precursors of their modern representatives, as the second century is the precursor of the nineteenth century. In *Marius the Epicurean* the specular relation between narrator and central character projects transhistorical continuity as a personal figure, "born" in Marius's time, aging and retrospective in Pater's.

In this sense, *Marius the Epicurean* should be read not as an autobiography of Pater himself but as an autobiography of the *Zeitgeist*. The "time-spirit" looks back, in the old age of the nineteenth century, to remember and to "place" an earlier phase of his own life history. Seasoned readers of Pater might think that

10. I am using the figures of Olney, Starobinski, and de Man to sketch the lines of a more complicated debate. Other important figures in this revisionary discussion of autobiographical figuralism include Roland Barthes, Emile Benveniste, Gérard Genette, and Philippe Lejeune.

they recognize both narrator and protagonist as displaced versions of Pater's own habitual persona. The point I am making, however, is a formal one. Even if one had no knowledge of the author of *Marius the Epicurean* or of his other works, one could still recognize the figures of narrator and protagonist as two temporalities of the same figurative identity. But that identity should not be taken to refer to the historical identity of Walter Pater as its autobiographical subject. Let us turn briefly to another example. Pater's first imaginary portrait, "The Child in the House," has also been called autobiographical. It might clarify the point I am making about *Marius* to look at the similar narrative effects generated in that essay-reverie. For again, whether Florian Deleal, the central character of "The Child in the House," can be equated in any way with the historical Pater is less important than the fact that a version of specular structure is set up in the narrative.

In the first paragraph, which tells of Florian Deleal making the decision to note "some things in the story of his spirit," a personalized narrator is not evident. In other words, the narration begins in the position of the third person, at a decisive distance from "Florian": "he" decided to note some things about "his" spirit. The figurative difference between present and past is transfigured as space, as distance, and as reverie: "In the house and garden of his dream he saw a child moving." From his vantage later in time, Florian could "watch" (as if from a distance) the gradual expansion of his soul within "the old house," as if the child were not himself, as if the soul in question were not his own (MS, 173–74). But soon a first-person narrator emerges; by the third paragraph the position of the narrator has been taken by an "I." This transference suggests that the boundaries between "Florian" and the narrator are obscure. The titular "child in the house" seems to refer simultaneously to the young Florian and to an earlier state of the narrator, who describes "the child of whom *I* am writing" (MS, 175; emphasis added). Again, though in a different way from Marius and his narrator, this central character and his narrator are figured both as the same "person" and as different "persons." The slippage from third to first person in this narrative creates the effect of specularity, of gathering both Florian and narrator within the figure of a self-reflexive "I."

The "identity" hypostatized through the specular relation of narrator and character in *Marius the Epicurean* is a personal figure for the historical identity of Western culture. Pater argues in *The Renaissance* against the "superficial view" that divides history into periods, and

Autobiography of the *Zeitgeist* · 191 ·

he reserves his special criticism for the "trenchant and absolute" division conventionally made between Pagan and Christian. That trenchant division between Pagan and Christian is precisely the one that *Marius the Epicurean* works to repair, with its notion of development so gradual as to be evanescent, nearly invisible, diaphanous. Against these "superficial" divisions Pater posits "the deeper view . . . which preserves the identity of European culture" (R, 225). Pater's language here should alert us to the aesthetic status of this "deeper" ground against which separate figures are only apparently or conventionally divided. The specular relation between Marius and his narrator constructs this "deeper view."

Because Marius plays the part of the transparent hero, a sort of specular exchange also takes place between him and the other characters in his second-century cultural milieu. Like Diaphaneitè, Marius's consciousness is the site of the internalization of "all that is really lifegiving in the established order of things" (MS, 251). Thus Marius, like his narrator, sums up and "contains" the important cultural forces of his day. His receptivity is played out in the plot through his relation with supposedly external realities—other characters, cities, books, and cultural institutions—that reflect his state of internal development at any given point in the narrative. Even "world-historical" figures, such as Marcus Aurelius, or documented lesser historical figures, such as Apuleius or Cecilia, are seen chiefly as they relate to Marius's development and are thus rendered as "minor" characters.

These minor characters are ranged in developmental series. Each character reflects a particular stage of Marius's development, and each series reflects the larger arc of historical development he internalizes over the course of his lifetime. The familiar device of the guide-figure, for example, has been multiplied across the text, each guide or companion indicating the issues involved in that particular stage of Marius's life: the young priest of Aesculapius who urges Marius to develop his visual capacity, the pagan poet Flavian, the Stoic Emperor Marcus Aurelius, through whose example of self-consciousness Marius learns to become his own guide, the Christian knight Cornelius, and finally that "divine companion" Marius envisions on the Sabine Hills.[11]

This treatment of minor characters is a familiar feature in first-person narratives, where the shape of everything conveyed is palpably

---

11. I discuss this serial patterning in another, related context and at greater length below. See Part Three, sec. 5.

reflected through the central narrating consciousness. In such narratives, minor characters are often ranged in a series, reflecting the stage-by-stage development of the central character. In *Jane Eyre*, for example, other characters not only are seen retrospectively by and through the autobiographical "I" in the present time of narration but also are somewhat "flattened" (partly because their consciousnesses cannot be fully represented) and reduced to the value they have with respect to Jane's development at each point in the story. The Reed children, Helen Burns, Blanche Ingram, Bertha Mason—even to some extent Edward Fairfax Rochester and St. John Rivers—are in large part represented as foils for Jane Eyre, externalized markers of her current stage of internal development. The pattern they fall into with respect to one another is usually read as a configuration imposed by the adult Jane—that is, the mature retrospective "narrator." The narrative structure thus becomes the sign of her achieved psychological coherence as "protagonist." It is easier, simply because it is habitual, to see this effect when the narration is in the first person, but the same structuring principle is even more pronounced in *Marius the Epicurean*, where all the ostensibly "other" characters seem in a sense to be epiphenomena of the central consciousness of Marius.[12]

The fiction of development is marked in this novel by Marius's internalization of these supposedly external, cultural phenomena. That fiction is maintained by a series of specular relations, as one "external" reflection of Marius's personal development yields to another. With this reflexive relationship established between the individual and his surrounding culture, the borders between exterior and interior are simultaneously asserted and broken down, defended and violated. This continuous exchange between internal and external provides another demonstration of historical *expression*, and the relation between narrator and character personalizes historical retrospection as self-knowledge.

In *Marius the Epicurean*, historical development is imagined as successive stages of internalization and transmission. Thus Marius's consciousness comprehends the cultural developments of his day, and

---

12. My argument here is close to, but pointedly different from, Spengemann's exploration of "poetic autobiography." He too recognizes in modernist texts the peculiar sense that every character is an expression of a central consciousness, but he associates that central consciousness with the author. For example, in his analysis the characters of *The Scarlet Letter* are finally seen to represent aspects of Hawthorne himself. I would argue instead that the "central" consciousness around which all the other characters radiate must be represented as the central figure in the text. See William C. Spengemann, *The Forms of Autobiography: Episodes in the History of a Literary Genre* (New Haven, Conn.: Yale University Press, 1980), pp. 110–65.

the nineteenth-century narrator, from a point much later in historical time, does the same. Both figures occupy the position at the end of the line, for Marius is the last of his pagan "race," and the narrator speaks from the latest moment of development represented in the novel. In other words, both Marius and his narrator, at different points along a continuous line of development, show that "the composite experience of all the ages is part of each one of us" (B, 196).

Thus *Marius the Epicurean* presents a complex example of the interaction of genealogical and metafigural impulses in aesthetic historicism, for the plot of self-culture shows lines of development being absorbed by a mind in the present, and in *Marius* that plot has been doubled. Both Marius and the narrator represent that figurative position at the end of the line, where the retrospective mind in the present preserves all parts of the past in one place. But the narrator, due to his later, more present position, also comprehends Marius as part of his late-nineteenth-century culture. Caught up in "the intoxication of belatedness,"[13] this narrator regards Marius at the distance of speculation and sees an earlier figure of his own developmental type.

## 3 · The Transcendental Induction

The specular structure of *Marius the Epicurean* displays personal identity and historical culture as correlative and interlocking developments. Taken together in their specular relation, narrator and protagonist represent the individual self and its generalized projection, its transcendent "other," the overarching *Zeitgeist*.[1] In examining the specular structure of *Marius*, I have so far concentrated chiefly on the retrospective stance of the narrator, within whose perspective all past ages may be gathered together and preserved. However, the novel also provides an understanding of how that concept of the overarching *Zeitgeist* is constructed, from the perspective of the individual. This section focuses on "The Child in the House" and chapter 19 of *Marius the Epicurean*, "The Will as Vision," both of which are concerned

---

13. The phrase is Harold Bloom's (*Figures of Capable Imagination* [New York: Seabury Press, 1976], p. 18).
1. Monsman notes the coherence of form resulting from "unity of mental development and its reflection of the nineteenth-century *Zeitgeist*" (*Pater's Portraits*, p. 66).

with the process of induction through which the self projects its transcendent other.

Like "Diaphaneitè," "The Child in the House" advances a theory of internalization, but "Diaphaneitè" concentrates on cultural transmission, whereas "The Child in the House" concentrates on individual psychology. It proposes an associationist, inscriptive model for the formation of personality, through which the "accidents" of outward influences "indelibly . . . figure themselves on the white paper, the smooth wax, of our ingenuous souls" (MS, 173, 177, 179). Primitively at first, the soul of the young Florian receives the general influences of beauty and pain; it is in these terms that Pater sets up this particular dialectic of development, and pain is its first term.[2] The Virgilian *lacrimae rerum* have been transfigured in Paterian terms to become a phantasmagoric mechanism of infliction: Florian both recognizes and eventually works himself "that great machine in things, constructed so ingeniously to play pain-fugues on the delicate nerve-work of living creatures" (MS, 184). In this reverie, the "musiclike intervals in our existence" are not only those of clarity, fluidity, play (R, 151). "The Child in the House" is Pater's tone-poem on the shifting vicissitudes of human mood.

Gradually in Florian's experience these two "elementary apprehensions" distinguish themselves further, through narrated incidents in which both beauty and pain make their marks and are "recognized" through particular experiences (MS, 182). The entire theory depends upon the absolute particularity of experience in time. The picture of Marie Antoinette on her way to execution, the white angora with a face like a flower, the treasure of fallen acorns and black crow's feathers, the great red hawthorn in full flower—these things are "impressed" upon Florian's soul in moments of intense reception, and they form ever afterward the stuff of memory.

> I have remarked how, in the process of our brainbuilding, as the house of thought in which we live gets itself together, like some airy bird's-nest of floating thistle-down and chance straws, compact at last, little accidents have their consequence. (MS, 184)

The "house" in which "the child" lives, then, is the most ingenuous and at the same time ingenious figure for the child's soul. Interiority

---

2. Losey stresses the tonal difference between Wordsworth's "spots of time" and Pater's epiphanic moments (Jay B. Losey, "Epiphany in Pater's Portraits," *English Literature in Transition* 29, no. 3 [1986], 304).

## The Transcendental Induction · 195 ·

is represented by the external habitation. The human body that houses the soul, and the house that encloses the body, both represent the spirit that can be expressed in no other way. What is expressed will be what has been impressed there from the outside, and here we have again the familiar, circular epistemology of impressionism, through which figures of interiority and exteriority reflect and replace one another. "The Child in the House" explicitly addresses this paradoxical relation in which "inward and outward [are] woven through and through each other into one inextricable texture" (MS, 173).

In the short passage quoted above, the soul is figured as a bird, making its nest from whatever fragments of the world happen to come its way. In other words, personal identity itself is an example of Pater's favorite composite form. All the "little accidents have their consequences," and eventually a soul "grows" and "expands" within the house. This imaginary portrait highlights the unique formation of each individual identity in historical time. But though it begins with the stress on concrete historicity, "The Child in the House" attends, with equal force and care (though in the second place) to the other side of the dialectic as well. The latter part of the essay moves toward a consideration of ideal typicality.

The development of concepts from sense-impressions is also a feature of life in time, according to this essay. It is, after all, a "house of *thought* in which we live," after the process of "brainbuilding" goes on for a time (emphasis added). "In later years" Florian occupied himself with various philosophies that considered the relation between "the sensuous and the ideal elements in human knowledge" (MS, 186). He chooses to prefer, from among these philosophies, the ones that emphasize the "sensible vehicle or occasion." In other words, searching for a theory that might lend coherence to his experience, Florian chooses the theory that best reflects and generalizes upon that experience. As the narrator puts it: "such metaphysical speculation did but reinforce what was instinctive." And I want to call attention to the specularity of this sort of speculation, for the development described in this retrospective portrait consists of more and more generalized exfoliations of the same, instinctive affinities.

More than the intense receptiveness to sensuous experience, "The Child in the House" explores the successive stages of generalization *from* that experience. Through time, the "accidents" of early, familiar life "in the house" are transfigured, becoming in "later life" and in retrospect "ideal, or typical conception[s]" (MS, 179). A sense of typicality, then, is the result of reflection in time, and the figure of the narrator provides the vantage point from which to see what Florian later made of his early experiences. For example, late in the portrait we find that his "innate sense for the soberer tones in things" was reinforced and at the same time "softened" by a later development of the "religious sentiment." Florian began to love the objects of church ritual "for their own sakes," and from those "actual" experiences he formed ideal conceptions. The linen, the vessels, the holy water—these things became to him "the type of something he desired always to have about him in actual life." An experience from "actual" life, in other words, has been raised to the level of the type: the generalized standard that prefigures later "actual" manifestations. This reflexive exchange between the typical and the actual forms his "way of conceiving religion":

> a sacred history indeed, but still more a sacred ideal, a transcendent version or representation . . . of human life and its familiar or exceptional incidents, birth, death, marriage, youth, age, tears, joy, rest, sleep, waking—a mirror, towards which men might turn away their eyes from vanity and dullness, and see themselves therein as angels, with their daily meat and drink, even, become a kind of sacred transaction—a complementary strain or burden, applied to our every-day existence, whereby the stray snatches of music in it re-set themselves, and fall into the scheme of some higher and more consistent harmony. A place adumbrated itself in his thoughts, wherein those sacred personalities, which are at once the reflex and the pattern of our nobler phases of life, housed themselves. . . . Some ideal, hieratic persons he would always need to occupy it and keep a warmth there. And he could hardly understand those who felt no such need at all, finding themselves quite happy without such heavenly companionship, and sacred double of their life, beside them. (MS, 193–94)

Here we have most prominently displayed a sacramental vision of everyday life. But this passage also expresses an explicitly demythologizing view of religion, through which religion is seen as an elaborate anthropomorphic creation. The "mirror" of religion, in which men might see themselves as angels, has been explicitly envisioned as a projection. This exchange between "actual" life and its idealized, specular double is quite clearly stated. The sacred figures are "at once the reflex and the pattern of our nobler phases of life." The irony should be appreciated: these secularization-effects play so subversively just here, when the thematic content of the passage deals with the supposed sacralization-effects of Florian's habits of thought.

This conception of religion envisions it as "a place" where "sacred personalities . . . housed themselves." We can recognize here another version of Pater's House Beautiful, the place beyond time which gathers up and comprehends idealized recreations of all the effects generated *in* time. Like a "complementary strain or burden" added to the music of everyday existence, this transcendent projection organizes "the stray snatches of music in it"; accidental, random experiences "re-set themselves, and fall into the scheme of some higher and more consistent harmony."[3] Through several levels of generalization and idealized projection, the "actual" childhood house becomes, first, the "house of thought," and finally this house not made with hands.

After this passage on the transcendent "place," a summary statement comes abruptly: "Thus a constant substitution of the typical for the actual took place in his thoughts" (MS, 194). This specular substitution is the basis for Florian's sacramental vision, whereby "all the acts and accidents of daily life borrowed a sacred colour and significance" (MS, 195). The story ends quite quickly after this. Florian moves out of the childhood house. At first the change is eagerly anticipated, but a pet bird is left behind and Florian must return to retrieve it. An agony of homesickness descends upon him as he sees the abandoned, "dead," and empty house. Florian's is the anxiety of the *revenant*, wondering how much of his soul has been left behind. And we can see in the parable of this tale's ending both the "modern" eagerness to move away from the past, and the nostalgic return to memorialize it. Florian was "driven quickly away, far into the rural distance, so fondly speculated on, of that favourite country-road." This departure, of course, is mirrored in the return of the story's beginning, where the figure of specularity is also opened.

Though it points us beyond history, "The Child in the House" presents a historical vision of how ideal types and their transcendent dwelling are generated in time. Pater will work this vision out in *Marius the Epicurean* on the level of cultural development at large, as we shall see in later sections of Part Three. For now, let us turn to the chapter in which Marius the Epicurean projects the same sort of "heavenly companionship, and sacred double of [his] life, beside [him]," for in "The Will as Vision" that transcendent double is understood to be precisely the sense of historical retrospection.

*Marius the Epicurean* meditates upon the process of visionary experience, but the novel never attempts to present it directly in a fictive present, never allows it to open an abyss in Marius's consciousness or to convert Marius's identity, never allows it to break the sequence or

---

3. As Bloom points out, " 'burden' means a bass under-part here," as well as a load under which to "strain." (introduction to *Selected Writings*, p. 16, n. 22).

the retrospective rationality of the narrative surface. The Paterian narrative, in other words, does not represent the Paterian "moment." T. S. Eliot complained that the visionary moment was dangerously discontinuous, "with no before and after." But *Marius the Epicurean* is radically continuous. Mediated by memory—and the nineteenth-century narrative voice ensures that all Marius's "sensations and ideas" are mediated by memory—moments of his "intense consciousness of the present" become strangely rationalized events. Marius's most telling moment of vision is generated in self-consciousness, through a series of logical and psychological projections. It is not an "epiphany" but a "difficult ecstasy" that must be achieved through will.[4]

"The Will as Vision" is carefully placed to mark the end of Part the Third.[5] As the climax of the novel, its placement makes the point that the willed vision achieved here is the necessary precondition for seeing a further vision in "actual" things. But the willed vision has its own precondition in a dream that induces a state of reverie. Like Florian at the beginning of "The Child in the House," Marius has awakened that morning from a particularly refreshing night of sleep. He dreamed that "those he loved best were pronouncing his name most pleasantly" as they passed in a procession before him on the pavement of a city "fairer far than Rome." His serene state of mind, the result of his dream and the precondition of his vision, is only equivocally granted from without. Given *"as if* by favour of an invisible power," it has actually come while Marius's watchful consciousness slept. Pater has retained the idea of an external agent, but his "as if" pushes the notion of external inspiration to the distance of metaphor. Though this chapter extolls the control of self-consciousness, such clarity seems to be the gift of an unconscious. Marius generates his inspiration from deep within, then figures it as coming from without. The successive stages of the transcendental induction to come will elaborately fulfill this initial gesture of self-reflexive "speculation."

The landscape within which this vision takes place is pointedly both picturesque and sublime. The "yellow old temples" and the "shrine of the patronal Sibyl" mark the scene with cultural associations that are in the process of being superseded. But at the same time

---

4. See Robert M. Scotto, " 'Visions' and 'Epiphanies': Fictional Technique in Pater's *Marius* and Joyce's *Portrait*," *James Joyce Quarterly* 11 (Fall 1973), 41–50.

5. William Buckler correctly points out that "the climactic spiritual experience of Marius' life occurs *before* he undergoes the close experience of Christianity" ("*Marius the Epicurean*," in *Walter Pater: The Critic as Artist of Ideas* [New York: New York University Press], p. 263).

the scene is wild and harsh, with floods and precipices, high, rocky crags, evergreen trees, twisted olives, and the roar of an "immemorial waterfall" (ME II, 65–66). That waterfall rewrites the image from paragraph two of the "Conclusion," in which "the water flows down indeed, though in apparent rest" (R, 234). In its context here, the water plunges down, but "with a motion so unchanged from age to age as to count . . . as an image of unalterable rest." The Wordsworthian, emblematic reading of woods decaying never to be decayed has been restored, though it has been marked as an explicitly aesthetic or willed construction. Nature and culture conspire to set an ancient scene. The air in this "time-worn place" is "pure and thin," but it is also "an air of immense age." The natural scene becomes a figure for the extreme gradualism of Marius's vision (and, indeed, of the novel's historical vision in general):

> On this day truly no mysterious light, no irresistibly leading hand from afar, reached him; only, the peculiarly tranquil influence of its first hour increased steadily upon him in a manner with which . . . the place . . . had something to do. . . . It was as if the spirit of life in nature were but withholding any too precipitate revelation of itself, in its slow, wise, maturing work. (ME II, 65–66)

As Marius sits in an olive garden on the Sabine Hills overlooking the city, he begins a conversation with himself. He takes as his model for this "dialogue of the mind with itself" the *Conversations* of Marcus Aurelius.[6] Since Marius has become amanuensis to the emperor, he has transcribed and internalized these *Conversations*. The lesson Marius found "most serviceable" begins his meditation: " 'Tis in thy power to think as thou wilt." Marius begins to meditate on the efficacy of a controlled self-consciousness by first becoming conscious of what it is that he wills, namely, "an eternal friend to man, just hidden behind the veil of a mechanical and material order" (ME II, 63). He asks himself: Is the perception of that "friend" simply "a matter of choice"? "Dependent upon some deliberate act of volition on his part? . . . Might the *will* itself be an organ of knowledge, of vision?" (ME II, 65). The "conclusion" Marius reaches in this chapter represents Pa-

---

6. DeLaura traces the debt to Arnold in Pater's description of Marius's vision (David DeLaura, *Hebrew and Hellene in Victorian England* [Austin: University of Texas Press, 1969], pp. 277–78). See also "Arnold's Version of Transcendence: The *Via Poetica*," in Nathan A. Scott, Jr., *The Poetics of Belief: Studies in Coleridge, Arnold, Pater, Santayana, Stevens, and Heidegger* (Chapel Hill: University of North Carolina Press, 1985), pp. 39–61.

ter's rewriting of the "Conclusion," because Marius decides what in that earlier essay was left undecidable (ME II, 71). There, extreme materialist and idealist systems of thought were represented as canceling one another out; here, Marius wills the priority of mind over matter.

Marius slips from thought, through reverie, toward vision, in a movement similar to the slippage in person at the beginning of "The Child in the House." Perhaps reverie may be defined as that state of mind in which a blurring of interior and exterior takes place or, in terms of narrative figures, a blurring of the first person into the second or third. The figure of specularity signals this state, as Marius projects the past course of his own life into the figurative distance as a visual image. He sees himself journeying toward himself on the road below, literalizing the figure of life's "journey" at the same time that he casts it in specular terms:

> All around him and within . . . turning to reverie, the course of his own life hitherto seemed to withdraw itself into some other world, disparted from the spectacular point where he was now placed to survey it, like that distant road below, along which he had travelled that morning. . . . Through a dreamy land he could see himself moving, as if in another life, and like another person. (ME II, 66)

This prospect of self-reflection produces a feeling that Marius registers as gratitude:

> It was as if he must look round for someone else to share his joy with: for someone to whom he might tell the thing, for his own relief. (ME II, 66–67)

We cannot fail to note, in passing, that "relief" is at issue in the projection of companionship. Thus, to the senses already established for Pater's figure of relief, we should add the sense of relief from solitude. This desire for ideal companionship but thinly disguises the familiar, romantic fear that there is no one "to whom he might tell the thing." "Must not the whole world around have faded away for him altogether, had he been left for one moment really alone in it?" (ME II, 67). But Marius need not fear, for he is never "really" alone: "In his deepest apparent solitude there had been rich company."

The feeling of lively gratitude, which was the result of one self-division, produces another and yet another. Memories of "actual" companions on his life's journey prompt Marius to imagine the possibility of "an unfailing companion, ever at his side." And from this projection of an ideal "other," Marius constructs his vision of transcendence:

> It was as if there were not one only, but two wayfarers, side by side, visible there across the plain, as he indulged his fancy. . . . He passed from that mere fantasy of a self not himself, beside him in his coming and going, to those divinations of a living and companionable spirit at work in all things, of which he had become aware from time to time in his old philosophic readings—in Plato and others, last but not least, in Aurelius. Through one reflection upon another, he passed from such instinctive divinations, to the thoughts which give them logical consistency, formulating at last, as the necessary exponent of our own and the world's life, that reasonable Ideal, to which the Old Testament gives the name of *Creator*, which for the philosophers of Greece is the *Eternal Reason*, and in the New Testament the *Father of Men*—even as one builds up from act and word and expression of the friend actually visible at one's side, an ideal of the spirit within him. (ME II, 67–68)

This process of reasoning from experience is very much like what we saw in "The Child in the House," where Florian passed too from "instincts" to the "thoughts which give them logical consistency." But in *Marius the Epicurean* there is an even more explicit acknowledgment of the constructive "will" involved in this sort of reasoning; the "instinctive divination" comes first, and then Marius looks for support in the history of philosophy. He adduces historical evidence to give his "fantasy" the sense of "actuality." The argument here is that the historical frequency of this will to believe tends to validate Marius's personal speculations. This "necessary exponent" of "the world's life" is explicitly modeled on a personal figure, as the example of the "friend" serves to show, whose "spirit" has been "built up" as an ideal through a mental act of summation and projection.

Finally, Marius's vision is not merely supported by historical evidence; it is a vision of divinity *as* history. For in the last movement of Marius's visionary speculations, the "divine companion" is imagined as a transcendent mind, an idealized projection of individual memory, a resting-place or repository for all the disparate moments of experience:

> Might not this entire material world . . . be . . . but reflections in, or a creation of, that one indefectible mind, wherein he too became conscious, for an hour, a day, for so many years? . . . How had he longed, sometimes, that there were indeed one to whose boundless power of memory he

could commit his own most fortunate moments, ... one strong enough to retain them even though he forgot, in whose more vigorous consciousness they might subsist for ever, beyond that mere quickening of capacity which was all that remained of them in himself! ... To-day at least, in the peculiar clearness of one privileged hour, he seemed to have apprehended that in which the experiences he valued most might find, one by one, an abiding-place. (ME II, 69–71)

The projection of a transcendent power of memory stabilizes the self, but it in turn has been generated "exponentially" on the model of that very self. Of course, we have again the "abiding-place" that Pater often calls the House Beautiful. In this ideal vision the material world does fade and "dissolv[e] away all around him," but Marius experiences that dissolution as hope and joy, not as solipsistic panic. His joy is expressed in a (muted) figure of the Apocalypse; as the "prison-wall" of the material world falls away, "he felt a quiet hope, a quiet joy dawning faintly ... like the break of day over some vast prospect with the 'new city' ... in the midst of it" (ME II, 70).

The specular structure of *Marius the Epicurean* cannot be fully appreciated unless we also see that Pater has thematized its construction as part of Marius's story. Not only does the narrator look back toward Marius as if toward an earlier phase of his own identity, but Marius also projects from himself as his "divine companion" the vision of an ideal and transcendent retrospective capacity, which is figured in this novel by its narrator. In this case, the narrator concludes by calmly stating that this moment of vision passed, that Marius never again felt this degree of concentrated focus, and that he was not essentially changed by this experience. Marius passes on, to experience a realization of his vision in "actual things," and from the point of view of the next chapter, this moment seems chiefly preparatory. But the moment is preserved, even as it is annulled, by a narrator within whose capacious memory all of Marius's moments find rest and continuity, a figure of the "more vigorous consciousness" within which they "subsist for ever."

## 4 · Typology as Narrative Form

At the moment of his death, the central character of Pater's novel remains only passively committed to Christianity, but the novel as a whole is more actively, though ambivalently, engaged. That complex relation, as we have seen in Pater's earlier work, is in no sense a direct embrace of Christianity; but neither is it a full disengagement, for Pater preserves on the level of aesthetic form what he rejects on the level of positive belief. He turns the figures of Christianity toward his own end, using them to structure his representation of historical and aesthetic development as narrative form.

Pater had a clearly developed sense of the "aesthetic" residue left behind when a creed becomes outworn as positive belief and can be regarded in its historical value alone. He explained this in the earliest published version of his essay on Coleridge, an essay that deeply laments Coleridge's inability to change with the times:

> Religious belief, the craving for objects of belief, may be refined out of our hearts, but they must leave their sacred perfume, their spiritual sweetness behind.[1]

In Pater's novel, as in his Renaissance essays, the nostalgia for "objects" is renounced in favor of representations. Pater finds in typological strategies of narration a systematic technique for preserving not the "objects" themselves but the memory of those objects. His narrative could be described in this sense as the ritual repetition of inherited forms whose value is thereby shifted from the "objective" or positive realm of belief to the secondary, "transfigured" realm of the aesthetic. These forms or patterns are one sort of "sacred perfume" that remains as a refined testament to the continuing presence of an attenuated, nostalgic, secularized, and aesthetic form of belief; Pater has an abiding "faith" in the shape of historical time itself and in the aesthetic types that embody its spirit. Typological methods of interpreting history, of interpreting individual experience, and of interpreting texts were prevalent in the mid-nineteenth century, and those methods inform Pater's novel in each of its several dimensions: in its reading of historical development, in Marius's reading of his own experience, and in our reading of *Marius the Epicurean*.

In fact, the general issue of interpretation unites these several levels of the novel's form, and its various narrative strategies as well.[2] As we

---

1. *Westminster Review*, n.s. 29 (January 1866), 126–27. See my discussion of "the historicity of myth," above, Part Two, sec. 3.

2. Crane first advanced this argument when he chose *Marius* to represent one of his three categories of plot formation, the "plot of thought," whose structure is governed by the synthesizing principle of thought, idea, or theme, rather than by action or character. See R. S. Crane, "The Concept of Plot and the Plot of 'Tom Jones,'" in *Critics and Criticism* (Chicago: University of Chicago Press, 1952), pp. 66–67. By using the term "interpretation" for this synthesizing principle, I emphasize the fact that the "thought" which synthesizes any particular "plot of thought" will have its own particular ideological coherence.

have seen, the narrative pointedly establishes the familiar analogy between individual and cultural development. The narrator establishes, and keeps alive in readers' minds through continual reiteration, a pervasive historical analogy between the culture of Victorian England in the 1880s and second-century Rome in the Age of the Antonines. But that is only its most obvious point, for the narrative commentary is obsessed with the principle of historical analogy in general, with relations of similarity and difference among all ages of cultural history. Together, Marius and the nineteenth-century commentary engage in exercises of memory and analogy from their vastly different points of time; together they contribute to a dense layering of temporalities in the narrative.

An important narrative strategy emphasizes these analogies and the resulting shifts between various layers of time: between prospection beyond the tenuous present tense of the represented action, and retrospection, backward in time, sometimes from Marius's point of view and sometimes from the narrator's. Many readers have complained that very little dramatization occurs in present narrative time: very few words are directly spoken; nothing "happens." Each event is first mediated by the consciousness of Marius and then again by the narrating voice; no event appears *sui generis*, isolated in its own present. But perhaps as much is gained by this strategy as is lost. "Foreshadowing" is a suggestive term for what goes on in the opening chapters, where the triumph of Christianity is premised outright in the opening phrase:

> As, in the triumph of Christianity, the old religion lingered latest in the country, and died out at last as but paganism—the religion of the villagers, before the advance of the Christian Church; so, in an earlier century, it was in places remote from town-life that the older and purer forms of paganism itself had survived the longest. (ME I, 3)

Paganism too, it seems, had its own "pastoral" past—before the advent of Christianity—to which we readers of the novel now nostalgically look back. The cultural development of paganism can be seen, in "historic retrospect," to foreshadow the later cultural development of Christianity. Paganism was "secularized," incorporated, and transcended historically to become Christianity. In other words, the very term "foreshadowing" should remind us that even our simplest critical vocabulary acknowledges the debt of secular narrative to typological conventions, but the simpler modern term merely represents a residue of the complex system to which it alludes.

## Typology as Narrative Form · 205 ·

As the first sentence of chapter 1 predicts the outcome of the novel's major cultural development, chapter 2 anticipates the outcome of Marius's personal development and the end of the novel's plot. Marius's temperament

> kept him serious and dignified amid the Epicurean speculations which in after years much engrossed him ... and made him anticipate all his life long as a thing toward which he must carefully train himself, some great occasion of self-devotion, such as really came, that should consecrate his life, and, it might be, its memory with others, as the early Christian looked forward to martyrdom at the end of his course, as a seal of worth upon it. (ME I, 18)

"Suspense" has no place in a novel whose most general and fundamental, as well as local and intimate, narrative strategies are so deeply prefigurative. Overt narrative clues make it clear that these early experiences prepare both Marius and the reader for later experiences. Their very value lies largely in their anticipatory function; we begin to look for later, analogous experiences to unfold. What happens is always less important than how it happens and what it will come to mean later in the narrative, when it is echoed in a later stage of a developmental "series." Events come to the reader already interpreted, in other words, presented as they will *later* be seen—both by Marius and by the nineteenth-century narrator—to be significant.

The density of this interpretive mediation and of the temporal layering related to it must be called to account, and as the term "foreshadowing" suggests, my account will be typological. Pater's literary use of typology is neither orthodox nor consistent throughout the text, but its logic is pervasive, and indications in the text argue that its logic is applicable to a reading of the novel. Most important, some thorny problems and apparent contradictions, which have plagued readers of this great novel, resolve themselves under its light: the division of narrative attention between Marius's development and that of his culture, for example, or the troublesome coexistence of cyclical and conservative with linear and progressive schemes of historical development, both seemingly endorsed by the novel.[3] Finally, understanding Pater's use of typology will help us propose a new solution to the perennial problems raised by the novel's ambiguous, deeply ambivalent, and yet profoundly coherent closure.

---

3. Avrom Fleishman penetratingly articulated these issues in *The Historical Novel: Walter Scott to Virginia Woolf* (Baltimore, Md.: Johns Hopkins University Press, 1971), pp. 169–78.

On all these levels, then, *Marius* bears the "sacred perfume" of Christian narrative, one instance of the way forms of thought may be said to go "underground," where they lead a "buried life," to use Matthew Arnold's phrase, and Pater's: "The spiritual forces of the past, which have prompted and informed the culture of a succeeding age, live, indeed, within that culture, but with an absorbed, underground life" (R, 198).[4] While not assenting to Christianity on the level of doctrine or belief, Pater may be seen still to appropriate and to preserve its principles of organizing human time, on the level of narrative form.

Typology above all asserts a certain interpretation of the shape of time and its ways of unfolding in history, a vision in which earlier events are seen in retrospect to have prefigured later, structurally analogous ones. Similarly, present events, persons, institutions, and texts may be seen prophetically, as prefigurations of greater fulfillments in the future, higher developments of the "type." Most important, the type is realistic, absolutely concrete in the historical sense; and this fundamental feature serves to distinguish typological relations from symbolic or allegorical ones. But before considering the profound appeal of the typological vision of history for the late nineteenth century, perhaps the case for Pater's familiarity with typological methods should be made, and it can be made very briefly.

From the earliest centuries of the Christian era, typology has developed as a "rhetoric of high spiritual authority"[5] a venerable array of techniques designed simultaneously to represent the phenomenal world and to gesture toward the transcendent, designed to mediate the claims of positive, historical knowledge and the belief in a force that is beyond history and capable of ordering or directing it. Auerbach's seminal 1944 essay "Figura" noted that figural interpretations of Scripture were prevalent in most European countries until the eighteenth century, when they markedly faded from view.[6] But a major retrieval of the method took place in the nineteenth century as one expression of the age's widespread interest in various historical methods of exegesis, a retrieval whose full dimensions have been coming

---

4. On the idea of cultural "survivals," see Willian Shuter, "History as Palingenesis in Pater and Hegel," *PMLA* 86 (May 1971), 411–21.
5. The phrase is Steven Zwicker's, from "Politics and Panegyric: The Figural Mode from Marvell to Pope," in Earl Miner, ed., *Literary Uses of Typology from the Middle Ages to the Present* (Princeton, N.J.: Princeton University Press, 1977), p. 115.
6. Erich Auerbach, "Figura," in *Scenes from the Drama of European Literature* (New York: Meridian, 1959), pp. 11–76; see esp. p. 61.

to light in Victorian studies of the past fifteen years or so.[7] Not only renewed attention but also a more fully self-conscious attention seems to have been devoted to the method in the Victorian era: the language of types and figures had been common in English ever since the late medieval period, but it is astonishing that the *Oxford English Dictionary* gives 1845 as the first date for "typology"—that is, the self-consciously systematic "*study* of symbolic representation," the "-ology," the *logos* of the types.

Whether Pater knew it as a systematic method or not, as the modern comprehensive term "typology" suggests, he was surely acquainted with its procedures, as well as its spiritual (and aesthetic, or literary) rationale. Christian typological thinking was practiced at least as early as the Pauline epistles and certainly by the earliest church fathers (Tertullian, Origen, Augustine), all of whom Pater knew well and all of whom he mentions in *Marius the Epicurean*. His deep interest in high church ritual, his readings of ecclesiastical history, and his role in religious and intellectual controversy at Oxford are well-known and well-documented.[8] But he could easily have assimilated the method through his native literary tradition, whose typologically inspired writers include Milton, Herbert, and Bunyan, among many others.

Pater's immediate literary environment, too, provided authoritative models, for figural methods of representation in literature and painting were fashionable as early as the 1840s and 1850s. Several recent studies have demonstrated the role of typology in the works of major figures of the period: the "artistical-scientific-historical" vision of Carlyle, especially in *Past and Present*; the Tractarian doctrines of Analogy and Reserve represented in the poetry of Keble, Williams, and Newman, as well as their concern with the historical development of Christian practice; the moral aesthetic of Ruskin, especially in volume 2 of *Modern Painters*; the figural realism of Pre-Raphaelite painting during the years of the first Brotherhood (1846–53); the temporal shifts of Rossetti's sonnets; the evolutionary vision of transcendence in Tennyson's *In Memoriam*; and the secularized hagiographies of George Eliot's fiction. Such pervasive use of figural techniques by writers and artists who anticipated a large audience argues the currency of the

---

7. The initial study was George P. Landow's *Aesthetic and Critical Theories of John Ruskin* (Princeton, N.J.: Princeton University Press, 1971), followed by Herbert L. Sussman's *Fact into Figure: Typology in Carlyle, Ruskin, and the Pre-Raphaelite Brotherhood* (Columbus: Ohio State University Press, 1979), and George P. Landow's *William Holman Hunt and Typological Symbolism* (New Haven, Conn.: Yale University Press, 1979).

8. See Michael Levey, *The Case of Walter Pater* (London: Thames and Hudson, 1978).

"language of types" in mid-nineteenth-century discourse. Pater might well have expected his figures to be recognized.

In the earlier part of the nineteenth century, before this documented revival in the mid-Victorian period, the literary history of typology is somewhat obscure.[9] But typological thought seems to reemerge first as symbolic, static, and ahistorical—that is, not strictly typological in the Christian sense at all, but in the Neoplatonic sense, as, for example, in Wordsworth's "Types and Symbols of Eternity" from the Simplon Pass episode of *The Prelude*, or Carlyle's *Zeitbild*, or "time-figure," from *Sartor Resartus*. In two senses, the Victorians historicized these universal types: they reclaimed the historically based Christian reference of the types and figures and used them to interpret secular history.

Illuminating as it is, much of the recent study of Victorian typology is needlessly limited. Its focus has remained primarily on the strengths of the method as a poetic or pictorial mode of symbolic figuration and not as a narrative or explicitly temporal representation. Possibly because attention to Victorian typology began with a study of Ruskin (who himself set a strong precedent for using his method as a key to symbolic significance), typological criticism of the period still largely concentrates on the interpretation of visual art or on the type as figurative image, not on the type figurally unfolding in time.

When a Victorian artist uses certain charged images, such as strayed sheep or a young boy in a carpenter's shop, that artist expects the biblical allusion to place his work in a context of scriptural analogues. He may allude to a story or cycle of stories, but his representation translates narrative into image. On the one hand, typological interpretations of images often reduce the complexities of the method to a dictionary of types that can be read by substituting one term for another; this sort of simplification can lead to an allegorization of history in which its linear dimension disappears in easy conflations of one age with another and its concreteness evaporates too, as a result. On the other hand, types seen simply as images can suggest, through their allusion to a biblical story, the basis for interpreting a scene morally or tropologically, but this sort of typological reading also easily succumbs to the pressure of allegory (as in Ruskin's famous interpretations of Tintoretto, for example). Either sort of interpretation tends to be by virtue of the substitution of one term for another

---

9. Paul Korshin has contributed to an understanding of early-nineteenth-century typology. See his *Typologies in England, 1650–1820* (Princeton, N.J.: Princeton University Press, 1982).

"symbolic" but not fully typological. A fully typological interpretation must be grounded in historical actuality, must preserve the integrity of separate historical events, and must not allow the linear, "horizontal" dimension of history to disappear in allegorical, "vertical," spiritualizing or symbolic substitutions.

*Any* use of typology, however "symbolic" or cursory, implies analogies backward and forward in time. But in one sense at least, the typological organization of narrative time can transcend its uses as a mode of visual symbolism. Typology has the further power to represent movement or change in time, to embody the dialectic of anticipation and retrospection, prefiguration and fulfillment. In narrative, the typological progression can be enacted in narrative sequence; analogical relations across time can unfold *in time*, as a series of progressive fulfillments. As narrative form, typology can become not only a lexicon of types and symbols but also a grammar; not only symbolic but also fully historical; not only a rhetoric but also a logic of temporality.

Can it be argued that the text of *Marius* presents us with a legitimate occasion to read typologically? Then, where can we see typological modes of organization in its narrative form? The two questions must be taken up together, beginning with basic guidelines limiting the cases for which a typological reading would be necessary, illuminating, or at least justified. The literary use of typology, writes A. C. Charity, simply expresses a particular view of history and its workings in literature. It need not signal an exclusively Christian orientation, but may form "a basis for conversation between the Christian and the 'humanist' writer or scholar." A legitimate discussion of typology in a work of literature depends simply on "the actual presentation of the idea of prefigurations in biblical and non-biblical literature, rather than the discursive theoretical study of this idea . . . wherever . . . a writer has attributed significance to an apprehended analogy between different events," but "only in so far as the texts themselves can be reasonably viewed as expressing, or involving, or presenting . . . a concept of prefiguration and fulfillment."[10] In other words, we must find relatively explicit signs in the text that such a reading is called for—what Charity calls the "actual presentation" of prefiguration and fulfillment—if we are not to be like overzealous exegetes who

---

10. A. C. Charity, *Events and Their Afterlife: The Dialectics of Christian Typology in the Bible and Dante* (Cambridge: Cambridge University Press, 1966), pp. 2–3. For other discussions of the literary use of typology, see Miner, *Literary Uses of Typology*; Frank Kermode, *The Genesis of Secrecy* (Cambridge, Mass.: Harvard University Press, 1979); and Northrop Frye, *The Great Code* (New York: Harcourt Brace Jovanovich, 1981).

allegorically read preconceived patterns "into" the text, which they then take to refer to a reality "outside" the representations of the text. And that "actual presentation" must take place within an explicitly Christian context of discourse—not necessarily a context of avowed belief or uncomplicated doctrinal orthodoxy, but a Christian context nonetheless—in order for an author's use of typological structures to be distinguished both from the analogical structures of many (if not most) secular histories and also from similar proleptic structures in more strictly secular literature.[11]

The cultural context of *Marius* is certainly Christian: for all Marius's ambivalence about embracing Christianity as belief, the thematic content of the novel is largely devoted to the rise of Christianity as a historical force. Pater's use of a specifically typological form is another of his characteristically ambivalent and ironic secularizations. *Marius* was planned as the first of a trilogy of novels; each novel of the trilogy would be set in a different historical period, but each would deal with "the same problems, under altered historical conditions."[12] We have already seen that *Marius* posited the "same problems" in nineteenth-century England and second-century Rome. The second novel, the unfinished *Gaston de Latour*, began to examine the "same problems" during the religious wars of the late sixteenth century in France, and the third was to have dealt with England in the late eighteenth century. In a letter to Violet Paget ("Vernon Lee"), Pater explained that his trilogy would deal with the development of a "sort of religious phase possible for the modern mind . . . the condition of which phase it is the main object of my design to convey."[13] Thus *Marius* was ultimately to have been merely the first part of a much larger project, which in its entirety would more clearly have illustrated stages in the development of this modern "religious phase."

That trilogy, had it been completed, would have demonstrated (in the familiar three stages) that the church as a historical institution had already changed a great deal over the course of centuries; it would have implied that both the church and the individual consciousness had always faced the "same problems, under altered historical condi-

---

11. Robert Hollander's morphology of secular medieval literary adaptations of typology is helpful here, though Pater's use spans several of his categories. See his "Typology and Secular Literature: Some Medieval Problems and Examples," in Miner, *Literary Uses of Typology*, pp. 3–19. I have derived the criteria invoked here both from Charity and to some extent from the implications of Hollander's categorization. His discussion of "Christian typology" proper takes a modern novel (Dostoevsky's *The Idiot*) as its chief example.

12. *Letters of Walter Pater*, letter 96, p. 65.

13. Ibid., letter 78, p. 52; see also Evans's note 2. Pater is responding to the argument of her essay "The Responsibilities of Unbelief."

tions"; and it would have directly illustrated, in the last novel of the trilogy, the exact nature of a new "religious phase" possible for the modern mind. But *Marius*, even though it is but one term of that projected three-part analogy, offers the same comforts to the reader who, following its internal order, learns to read analogically. Reassurance of this sort was in high demand in the novel's contemporary climate of reception. Pater's contemporary W. H. Mallock, for example, explained the tremendous popularity of Mrs. Ward's *Robert Elsmere* (1888), the story of a doubting Anglican clergyman plagued by conclusions drawn from his reading of Darwin and Renan, as an "expression of the devout idea that the essence of Christianity will somehow survive its doctrines."[14] That remark could apply with equal justice to *Marius*, which proposes a secularized faith in historical process itself.

Pater's projection of this novel as the first of a series not only identifies its thematic interest in Christianity as historical, not doctrinal, but also suggests why a typological form would be particularly significant. The typological analogies established by the trilogy would imply not only that "the modern phase" retained essential features of Christianity, but also that it retained those features as parts of a more highly developed form. Pater's formal motives, in other words, seem ambivalent: both conservative (to represent modern, relativizing thought as incorporate within the larger Christian pattern) and progressive (to show outmoded forms as accommodating *to* the modern system by which they were superseded). The spiritualizing, conservative element of typological thought attends to analogies between historically disparate events, thereby preserving their "sameness," the steadfastness in their deep structure over time; and on the other hand, the historicizing, progressive element attends to their difference, to their change or growth over time.

The chief use of this exegetical system has always been to preserve whole dispensations and whole literatures from receding into the past as outworn and useless when a new order supersedes them, and at the same time to preserve (unlike allegory) the specific historicity of each one. Thus, early Christian typology, developed over centuries of prac-

---

14. From "Amateur Christianity," *Fortnightly Review* 57 (1892), quoted in U. C. Knoepflmacher, *Religious Humanism and the Victorian Novel: George Eliot, Walter Pater, and Samuel Butler* (Princeton, N.J.: Princeton University Press, 1965), pp. 9–10. See also Pater's review of *Robert Elsmere*, collected in *Essays from the "Guardian"* (EG, 55–70). Pater found Elsmere's doubt more dogmatic than orthodox faith; his own more refined relativism could entertain Christianity as a "great possibility" simply by virtue of its historical actuality (EG, 67–68).

tice, preserved the "Old" Testament by redefining its pivotal events and figures as prefigurative of the "New." The bondage in Egypt and the events of the Exodus, for example, were reinterpreted as prefigurations of the Passion and the Resurrection. Late medieval and Renaissance typologists, then, admitted pagan and classical figures to the Christian literary community "retroactively," seeing them as predictive of Christian virtues and as striving unconsciously toward the Christian dispensation. Thus Dante admits Statius to Purgatory, imagining that he had been converted to Christianity by Virgil's Fourth Eclogue (*Purgatorio* 21–22). And seventeenth-century Puritan typologists, saving not only the past but also their own present, read contemporary political heroes as fulfilling both biblical and classical types, as in Marvell's treatment of Cromwell, for example.

These generalizations are meant only to suggest the gradual secularization of typology itself; once secular history becomes the province of typologists, any historical analogy between an earlier event and a later event has the potential to be interpreted typologically. These stages of literary secularization were fulfilled, so to speak, in the nineteenth century, when typology was used simultaneously to preserve Christian modes of thought and signification and at the same time to figure forth modes more "developed" or "evolved" than the Christian modes. In this ambience of comforting ambivalence, Christian forms of figuration were used nostalgically to express the faith that even though Christianity was being superseded through historical process, the essence of Christianity might survive the passage of its doctrines, might be preserved in the shape and structure of historical time. Of course, the system depends on time being seen as shape or structure, and that is a function of retrospection.

In determining the legitimacy of a typological reading, then, context is all-important, a construal of "context" that goes beyond the explicitly Christian *content* of the plot of Pater's novel. But the Christian content of the novel alone would legitimate a typological reading, if one should be suggested by "the actual presentation of the idea of prefiguration and fulfillment" in the text itself. And here we may turn to Pater's explicit uses of both typological concepts and typological techniques, at the level of form where concept and technique inextricably blend and reinforce each other.

## 5 · Typological Ladders

The developmental plot of *Marius the Epicurean* stresses the analogical relationship between Christianity and Marius's childhood "Religion of Numa" in order to show that the essence of paganism survives even after its practices are absorbed and superseded by the early Christian church. In the culture at large, pagan reverence for the earth is transformed into Christian burial of the dead; the pagan sentiment for maternity is fulfilled in devotion to the Holy Mother; the pagan ritual use of the substances of everyday life (bread, wine, oil, and water) becomes the foundation of the Christian sacraments. Christian ritual, so regarded, is simply old wine in new bottles, a more highly developed devotional practice that "gathers" previous forms within its structurally analogous though more spacious, "generous," or "expanded" order (ME II, 125–27).

Marius's recovery of ritual in his later years returns him to his physical and spiritual "home." For Marius, the very essence of religion was this return to origins, self-consciously enacted in ritual. As "The Child in the House" explores the personal and psychological significance of "home," Pater's *Greek Studies* essay the importance of indigenous influence on the growth of mythic story, as we shall see. For Marius, the "spell of his religion" had been, for the first, "a part of the very essence of home"; he yearned, "ever afterward," we are told in chapter 2, for home "which, throughout the rest of his life he seemed, amid many distractions of spirit, to be ever seeking to regain" (ME I, 12, 22). Marius recovers this sense of home and family in the church in Cecilia's house, where the pastoral "usages and sentiments" of pagan family life have been transformed into a self-conscious cultural institution. In other words, Marius's return also marks progress on his life's journey.[1] His recovery also marks the discovery of something new—an ideal as well as historically institutionalized version of the family that is nevertheless fully concrete, visible, actual.

There can be no doubt that we are to regard the scene in Cecilia's house typologically, for Pater describes it explicitly in the language of types. Marius himself interprets it typologically, thinking "of chaste women and their children—of all the various affections of family life under its most natural conditions, yet developed, as if in devout imita-

---

1. In a version of the "circuitous journey" which M. H. Abrams explores in *Natural Supernaturalism: Tradition and Revolution in Romantic Literature* (New York: Norton, 1971), pp. 141–324.

tion of some sublime new type of it, into large controlling passions" (ME II, 97). The most fundamental typological conclusions are very easy to draw: this cultural form preserves the "natural conditions" of its type, achieves a certain new development, and also anticipates yet another, more "sublime new type," possible in the future. Christian family life, already a fulfillment of Marius's own family (and of pagan family life in general), prefigures more perfect forms to come, further fulfillments of "that instinct of family life, which the sanction of the *Holy Family* was, hereafter, more and more to reinforce" (ME II, 98).

The Christian attitude toward the family, then, represents the growth in communal self-consciousness registered in the transition from the "natural" to the institutional, as well as an institutionalized aspiration toward further cultural self-consciousness. Projecting that aspiration as a cultural ideal ("the sanction of the *Holy Family*") will ensure higher and higher developments of the "actual" or historical family "hereafter." (This is a secularized "hereafter," which refers to the historical future, but the apocalyptic and spiritual reference of the "hereafter" hovers nearby.) In Marius's case, Christian ritual not only idealizes home and family as part of its worship, it enables him literally to recover his actual home, as he returns to bury the ashes of his pagan ancestors, thus incorporating his lineage into the community of the new dispensation, personally comprehending his whole family's history in the new cultural order.

Thus Christianity typologically fulfulls Marius's pagan past, but only after he goes through a "worldly" middle phase, representing the entangling complications of historical life that make resolution necessary and possible on a "higher," more developed plane. Before he sees the family of Christians in Cecilia's house, for example, he moves within the cosmopolitan family of the Emperor Marcus Aurelius, whose ideas of communal life mark a certain progress beyond paganism yet remain inadequate in many ways. Marius's feelings of dissatisfaction propel him onward in his search, through several stages that are represented sequentially in the novel as smaller analogical developments within the overarching personal and cultural renewal represented by the rise of Christianity. The progressive arrangement of families links Marius's personal growth inextricably to the growth of his wider culture.

The same sort of serial development proliferates throughout the novel. Pater organizes the stages of Marius's growth and the growth of his culture in narrative sequences that one might call "typological ladders," for they embody a view of historical development in which each stage builds on the previous stages and at the same time prefigures even "higher" developments in the future. These typological ladders illustrate, on the level of narrative form, Pater's characteristic serial figure for historical development. Marius's individual growth is prompted by his yearning toward greater fulfillment in certain constant areas of human life, and Pater's narrative structure conveys this developmental principle almost obsessively. The serial presentation of families in the novel, of mother-figures, of cities he passes through on his life's journey, of companions who accompany him, emphasizes Marius's quest for spiritual fulfillment among the things of *this* world. Each one prepares him to encounter the next; not only does he learn the limitations of each stage, he learns greater skills of apprehension and comprehension with which to grasp the next one. As *Bildungsroman*, the novel employs these ladderlike structures to focus on Marius's "education." As a philosophical "romance," the novel replicates, in the changes represented by each series or ladder, the characteristically romantic three-stage development from a "natural" state, through a sophisticated, "worldly" state of knowledge and experience, to a higher state of nature and innocence regained. When the familiar romantic pattern is crossed with the typological ladder, the middle term need no longer indicate an antithetical or "fallen" state; it may merely indicate an intermediate stage in an ongoing process of development.

For example, the "sentiment of maternity" as the "central type of all love" (ME I, 22) is embodied first in Marius's own mother, then in the sophisticated, complex, enigmatic Empress Faustina, the "mistress and mother of palaces," and finally in Cecilia, who refines maternal love into simplicity once more, while devoutly imitating the Virgin Mother. Even as a boy, Marius "came to think of women's tears, of women's hands to lay one to rest, in death as in the sleep of childhood, as a sort of natural want" (ME I, 21). Flavian's pagan "nuptial hymn" begins with a meditation on "nature as the universal mother" (ME I, 113). But a higher culture unexpectedly rejuvenates even nature in the Antonine Christian church, a figure of maternity who is "in truth no alien from that old mother earth" (ME II, 119). Marius's own death and presumed Christian burial, then, fulfill previous types of maternity. Ministered to by chaste Christian women, he is assumed into the family of the church and into the earth, another type of mother.[2]

---

2. For another view of Marius's nostalgia for home and mother, see Michael Ryan, "Narcissus Autobiographer: *Marius the Epicurean*," *English Literary History* 43 (Summer 1976), 184–208, a psychoanalytic reading of Marius as an "autobiographical allegory." William Shuter offers a view of the mother from the standpoint of comparative

Marius's language is yet another figure of maternity, for he and Flavian were "involved in a kind of sacred service to the mother-tongue" (ME I, 97). They had hoped to serve their mother-tongue, to raise her from her fallen, "divided" state, by reuniting the "learned dialect" with the "colloquial idiom" (ME I, 95). But Flavian's euphuism, though it does manage to unite past and present by blending archaisms with racy neologisms, does not manage to renovate the language, for Flavian dies before the lovely *Pervigilium Vereris* is finished. His "Pagan end," represented by the corruption of the plague, will stand in ironic relation to Marius's own death. Before that ambivalently Christian "end," however, rejuvenated language sings forth from the church in Cecilia's house, where Christian children create a sound "so novel . . . as to bring suddenly to the recollection of Marius, Flavian's early essays towards a new world of poetic sound" (ME II, 96). Pater explicitly places the pagan poem in relation to the Christian service of worship as prefiguration to fulfillment; language too experiences a rebirth in this general cultural renaissance.

Marius searches through the cities of the world for higher forms of communal life, and those cities in the novel form another typological series, each one real in its own right, each one pointing toward further fulfillment in the next city and finally in the next world.[3] His lifelong quest is conveyed from the first in a secularized metaphor of the apocalyptic marriage: he hoped for a vision, "as of a new city coming down 'like a bride out of heaven' " (ME I, 32). From Pisa, Rome beckons him onward. But no actual community fulfills "the great Stoic idea, that we are all fellow-citizens of one city" (ME I, 219). Fronto's Stoic discourse *The Nature of Morals* proposes all of humanity as a commonwealth of the mind, but Marius wants to find an actual community, not an intellectual abstraction (ME II, 11–12). Similarly, Marcus Aurelius, extrapolating the idea of an unseen Celestial City, *urbs beata*, from his own internal spiritual order, is powerless to establish it in the actual world: the emperor "had but divined . . . the void place which other experience than his own must fill" (ME II, 40).

But Marius has learned from the emperor the efficacy of his own, internal quest. Building on the imperial lesson that "it is in thy power

---

mythology in "History as Palingenesis in Pater and Hegel," *PMLA* 86 (May 1971), 411–21. Neither of these approaches contradicts a typological reading; in fact, the tropological level of the fourfold method accords well with a psychoanalytic reading.

3. Sudrann first noted the development of cities in the novel, identifying the "heavenly city" as one of three central "images" of the hero's quest for the vision incarnate, whose cumulative, unifying force lends coherence to the novel. See Jean Sudrann, "Victorian Compromise and Modern Revolution," *ELH* 26 (1959), 425–44.

to think as thou wilt," Marius consolidates his internal order on the Sabine Hills, where he feels "a quiet hope . . . dawning faintly . . . like the break of day over some vast prospect with the 'new city,' as it were some celestial New Rome, in the midst of it" (ME II, 38, 63, 70). In the next chapter he sees the church in Cecilia's house. The Christians are certain that a heavenly city will descend at the end of time, "like a bride out of heaven," but they have faith as well that the celestial city will to some extent be achieved in human time. Marius finds their own community the highest development of earthly citizenship to date. Throughout his works, Pater imagines true culture as a sophisticated union of manners and morals, a "music, or kind of artistic order in life," a "mode of comeliness in things" (ME II, 4). Like the conception of the *Holy Family*, the vision of a City of God provides a "sanction"—both a spiritual model and the commmand to institute that model ever more surely on earth—what Pater called in *The Renaissance* a "law" of development. And here, with exquisite wit, Pater implies that the earthly, Christian community has come close to establishing a real *beata urbs*, when he calls the culture of the early church its "divine urbanity" (ME II, 121).

The same sort of typological progression can be seen in the arrangement of minor characters, especially guide-figures and companions: the young priest of Aesculapius, Flavian, Marcus Aurelius, Cornelius, and of course that "divine companion" whom Marius envisions on the Sabine Hills, Each one defines both Marius's progress in actual friendship and, more important, a stage in the development of his capacity to internalize companionship, to conduct, in other words, instead of an interior monologue, the modern "dialogue of the mind with itself," deplored by Arnold but represented by Pater in this novel as the essential dialogue. Each companion represents the current state of his interior order.

The young priest of Aesculapius, for example, as the "type" of youth, first makes Marius conscious that he should develop his capacity for vision (ME I, 38–39). Flavian personifies the charm of pagan life, "the depth of its corruption, and its perfection of form" (ME I, 53). His horrible death from the plague, though, is the emblem of a "pagan end" in which corruption utterly obliterates perfection of form, preserving nothing beyond an inconsolable alienation. Flavian's death forces Marius onward in his quest. Each death, as Gerald Monsman has observed, signals the end of one stage in Marius's pilgrimage and the beginning of the next.[4]

---

4. Monsman, *Pater's Portraits*, p. 49.

Marcus Aurelius then teaches him to conduct a continuing "conversation" with himself, a discipline through which one learns to communicate with the divine *Logos* internally (ME II, 46–47). Pater interprets such a deepening subjectivity as "progress," while explicitly anticipating the role of Christianity in deepening that subjectivity further:

> Marius, a sympathetic witness of all this, might almost seem to have had a foresight of monasticism itself in the prophetic future. With this mystic companion he had gone a step onward out of the merely objective pagan existence. Here was already a master in that craft of self-direction, which was about to play so large a part in the forming of the human mind, under the sanction of the Christian church. (ME II, 50–51).

As in *The Renaissance*, Pater approves the development beyond the "mere objectivity" of pagan existence and registers that development as an aesthetic acquisition, the "craft of self-direction."

But the emperor's commitment to the actual world falls short: he tolerates evil, despises the body, and his philosophies seem mere intellectual abstractions (ME II, 51–53). Cornelius, the Christian knight, is explicitly compared with Aurelius on these points and deemed superior. Cornelius seems to Marius "a sort of outwardly embodied conscience" (ME I, 233). When searching for the secret of his spiritual power, Marius wonders of what intellectual system Cornelius in the "sensible exponent" (ME I, 234), and when Marius achieves his own willed belief in an external friend, he uses the same word: his "divine companion" seems the "necessary exponent of our own and the world's life" (ME II, 68).

In this scene on the Sabine Hills, Marius does in fact achieve his vision by multiplying his own consciousness exponentially; through a series of projections, as we have seen, he manages to envision, first, companionship on his journey and, finally, a permanent and divine friend. As Marius experiences his visionary projection, the narrative commentary traces the history of belief in this "reasonable ideal" typologically, from the Old Testament idea of the *Creator* and the Greek *Eternal Reason*, to the New Testament *Father of Men* (ME II, 68). Marius's ideal of companionship as brotherhood perhaps represents an even more humanized ideal. All these companions—the young priest, Flavian, the emperor, Cornelius, and finally the "divine companion"—seem, in a sense, epiphenomenal, representative reflections of Marius's consciousness. Pater's narrative strategy here projects Marius's internal "dialogue" outward, externalizes and fictionally imagines it as interchange between characters (though actual dialogue is notoriously absent). In this novel the central character may be known—and learns to know himself—through the "company" he keeps.

## 6 · Christian Historicism

All Marius's "sensations and ideas" are arranged in these narrative sequences, which I have called typological ladders. Marius climbs, step by step, through earthly embodiments ever closer to spiritual fulfillment. Pater emphasizes this serial structure by multiplying it on every level of the plot. Critics have sometimes missed its organization entirely because of the deeply textured surface of the narrative, the associative procedures of Marius's consciousness, and the nineteenth-century narrative commentary.[1] But these mediating layers of texture, though much less schematic than the typological ladders, nevertheless keep the typological dialectic active in other ways.

The nineteenth-century commentary reinforces the novel's serial organization by repeatedly calling attention to the structure of historical analogy. But at the same time the narrator emphasizes the secularized transformations that characterize typology in a specifically nineteenth-century vision. And finally, this narrative commentary complicates the forward motion of the typological ladders through its retrospective stance, shifting rapidly back and forth between memory and prefiguration, nostalgia and anticipation, making the dialectical movement of typological historiography and narration an activity of the text on a more intimate level.

---

1. T. S. Eliot brutally dismissed the possibility that Pater was in control of his structure, and he set the tone for much modern criticism of the novel when he called it an "incoherent . . . hodge-podge." Monsman notes Eliot's remarks (*Pater's Portraits*, pp. 65–66) and the relatively recent willingness of critics to champion the structural coherence of the novel. My argument—that the novel is emphatically structured, though the structure is obscured by a complicated texture of mediating layers—draws not only on Monsman's analysis (ibid., pp. 65–97) but also on Billie Andrew Inman, "The Organic Structure of *Marius the Epicurean*," *Philological Quarterly* 41 (April 1962); Knoepflmacher, *Religious Humanism*; James Hafley, "Walter Pater's 'Marius' and the Technique of Modern Fiction," *Modern Fiction Studies* 3 (1957), 99–109; David DeLaura, "*Marius* and the Necessity of Religion," in *Hebrew and Hellene*, pp. 263–85; and esp. Shuter ("History as Palingenesis," pp. 411–21), who calls *Marius* Pater's "most ambitious treatment of historical palingenesis."

Thus, in Part the Fourth, interpreting the mature ritual of the early church, Pater directly articulates the "law of development" under which earlier, historically specific forms are seen in retrospect as prefiguring later and more highly developed but structurally analogous forms. He figures the Christian church as both the embodiment and the executor of that law:

> The faithful were bent less on the destruction of the old pagan temples than on their conversion to a new and higher use . . . Already, in accordance with . . . maturer wisdom, the church of the "Minor Peace" had adopted many of the graces of pagan feeling and pagan custom; as being indeed a living creature, taking up, transforming, accommodating still more closely to the human heart what of right belonged to it. In this way an obscure synagogue was expanded into the catholic church . . . Ritual, in fact, like all other elements of religion, must grow and cannot be made—grow by the same law of development which prevails everywhere else, in the moral as in the physical world . . . In a generous eclecticism . . . and as by some providential power within her, she gathers and serviceably adopts, as in other matters so in ritual, one thing here, another there, from various sources—Gnostic, Jewish, Pagan—to adorn and beautify the greatest act of worship the world has seen. (ME II, 124–27)

This "law of development" fosters larger, more complex, "eclectic," and humanistic institutions. Indeed, the young church represents an "expanded" order as well as a more human one, "accommodating still more closely to the human heart what of right belonged to it." These are secularizing principles, approving human rather than divine right, conflating the moral and the physical worlds, regarding a cultural institution as a natural, "living creature." And the notion here that religion "must grow and cannot be made" emphatically challenges the orthodox conception of divinity, opposing historical evolution to immediate creation *ex nihilo*.

Pater here attempts nothing less than the synthesis of a providential understanding with an evolutionary understanding of historical change. This powerful and paradoxical attempt is profoundly indicative of the imaginative trials of the late nineteenth century. In Pater's synthesis, cultural forms are simultaneously seen to be the expression of a providential order—to be shaped from without—and to grow organically from within. Pater rejects organicism as a theory of aesthetic creation, as we have seen, because it does not do justice to the supreme self-consciousness of the creative artist. But he finds it more congenial as a theory of historical change, through which even aesthetic objects are continually recreated. Even so, Pater's theory of historical development is not purely organicist, but a complex synthesis that allows him to preserve the divine order without personalizing its "artist"; to reconceive the notion of a transcendent creator who is immanent in history at times of periodic intervention, as a creative power internalized within a shapely, periodic process; and therefore to conceive divinity neither as an external presence nor as an absence, but as an internal force, a spirit no longer beyond but within creation. Thus, in the passage above, the divine function has been internalized by the evolving historical institution of the church, and its paradoxical status is registered in the tension of a metaphor: "*as* by some providential power within her."

That metaphor testifies to the creative power of the narrative artist, who may at first be suspected of usurping the place of the divine "artist." The divinely creative or "aesthetic" function does not necessarily disappear when God "disappears," but its continued visibility depends, in other novels, on the novelist overtly assuming the role of "providence" in his fictional world or, in this novel, on the novelist assuming the role of one who sees divine order still evident in the "actual" world.[2] The voiced commentary of this novel does not represent the "maker" of this fictional "world," only its historian and interpreter. What historical process has internalized, this novelist externalizes again, bringing out of the vast historical continuum one representative age, typical of the times when culture renews itself. The narrator does not presume to replace the divine artist, but to perform an exegetical function. Culture, not Nature, is the great Book of inscribed revelation to be interpreted; or rather, Pater's synthesis of organic and providential models has the added effect or reinterpreting the cultural as the "natural" growth.

The narrative ostensibly presumes to represent history, mimetically to reproduce the shape of something already shaped. Though this presumption is disingenuous (as we shall see), it helps us specify the particular role the nineteenth-century narrative commentator takes toward developments in the second-century world Marius inhabits. Those developments take place in stages describing the progress from a state of nature, through a "worldly" state of culture, to a higher state of communal self-consciousness in which culture becomes "natural" once more. While the narrative structure represents the shape of historical time, the nineteenth-century narrator represents the higher

---

2. On various forms of providentialism in nineteenth-century fiction, see Thomas Vargish, *The Providential Aesthetic in Victorian Fiction* (Charlottesville: University Press of Virginia, 1985).

state of awareness in which historical process becomes conscious of itself. In other words, the narrator of this novel does not adopt the role of providence, external and prior to creation, but again represents the creative function absorbed within history itself.

Accordingly, the narrative commentary reinforces the novel's typological structure with local, more intimate narrative devices that operate on the level of the sentence. The formal dynamic of prefiguration and fulfillment is profoundly a part of this narrative vision. Let us look in detail at one example from the passage we have already been examining. Again, Pater figures the early Christian church as an embodiment of historical process:

> Gathering, from a richer and more varied field of sound than had remained for him, those old Roman harmonies, some notes of which Gregory the Great, centuries later, and after generations of interrupted development, formed into the Gregorian music, she was already . . . the house of song—of a wonderful new music and poesy. As if in anticipation of the sixteenth century, the church was becoming "humanistic," in an earlier, and unimpeachable *Renaissance*. Singing . . . burst forth . . . ; the Jewish psalter, inherited from the synagogue, turning now, gradually, from Greek into Latin—broken Latin, into Italian, as the ritual use of the rich, fresh, expressive vernacular superseded the earlier authorised language of the Church.(ME II, 125)

Pater has placed the outer limits of his narrating perspective far beyond the temporal domain of the novel. This vertiginously "long view" retrospectively encompasses not just the second century A.D., but also the sixteenth and the nineteenth centuries—indeed, all ages of history up until the present time of Pater's writing.

Within this spacious order, the narrative distinguishes between separate ages, stressing differences in their degrees of development while at the same time emphasizing the structural analogies between them. Thus, from the vantage of present fulfillment in the second century ("gathering . . . "), this passage remembers the prefiguring synagogue (as well as pre-Gregorian music) and anticipates ("centuries later . . . ") further fulfillments of a developed, "humanistic" sort. The very structure of these sentences enacts the typological dialectic of prefiguration and fulfillment. Their temporal layers shift against one another, switching back and forth between prediction and retrospection, preserving several levels of past time at once, reviving them in juxtaposition with the second-century present and with various levels of the historical future beyond that present.

The "future" envisioned here in retrospect will be conscious of the secularizing tendency inherent in history's "law of development," for the humanizing principle of that law, when raised to the level of cultural self-consciousness, will be recognized as "humanistic." The quotation marks emphasize that the principle will know itself as such in the period later to be known as "the" Renaissance, though the sixteenth century is only one renaissance in Pater's historical (and typological) series. Already, in fact, the church is becoming "humanistic," though Pater's quotation marks also ironically call attention to his anachronistic use of that term here. The Christian church itself, then, is a type, prefiguring a later "unimpeachable" Renaissance, Pater's own favorite metaphor for historical palingenesis, a process that always blends the absolutely permanent and the absolutely new. The Christian church embodies the very principles that will eventually lead culture beyond Christianity. That shift will occur not through periodic intervention of the divine in history, but through historically periodic renewal on these Christian principles, renewal that is always a survival or a revival of earlier forms.

Typologists read history as the great Book in which divinity reveals itself, and they read with a certain interpretive will. The search for analogous, progressive stages of development is motivated by the desire to adduce evidence of a divine presence in history, and finding such patterns yields a reassured faith in that presence. Typology, like every other hermeneutic method, participates in this peculiar paradox of interpretation—and gains thereby a "creative" power—that what is sought determines what will be discovered. To establish faith in the divinity within history, in other words, is both the motive for and the inevitable result of this particular method's version of the hermeneutic circle. For this reason, both change and stasis reinforce the typologist's predetermined faith—because divine power may be felt both in the gradualized progress marked by successive fulfillments and also in its apparent opposite, the steadfast, unchanging analogous structure replicated by each stage. There is, then, within the method, an incentive to multiply both difference and similarity, thereby creating a pattern whose greater complexity testifies to the greater presence of divinity within history. A typological novelist who presumes only to be interpreting may in all good faith at the same time be exercising a creative function. In typology, historical interpretation, exegesis of texts, analysis, and aesthetic creation of structure and texture intersect, perpetuating a love of design for its own sake, because signs of power reside in the complications of the design itself.

Typology in this sense always potentially verges on a kind of aestheticism at the same time that it ostensibly remains a purely historical method. If this line of argument should suggest that in the nineteenth century the method could be used self-consciously to unite historicism and aestheticism—generating at once a historicist aesthetic and an aesthetic historicism—it will only emphasize the appeal of the method for Pater. The spiritual and the aesthetic dimensions of typology, indeed, are very close. In fact, its self-conscious recognition of an aesthetic dimension is a part of its versatility. The method aspires to be an art, not a science of interpretation, a sophisticated exegetical system in which history may be read aesthetically, as if it were a text; the typological text may be read as a representation of history; and all texts may be read historically, like any other cultural artifacts, in analogical and developmental relation to one another.

## 7 · Literary History as "Appreciation"

Pater's novel explores these textual implications of typology and at the same time calls attention to its own status as literary text. Formal manifestations of typological thought become more frequent, more explicit, and more varied in technique as the novel progresses to its typological denouement, the Christian service in Cecilia's house. That crucial chapter, for example, as well as the one before it, is introduced with biblical epigraphs that themselves interact typologically.

The first, from the Old Testament Book of Joel (2:28), prefigures the second, from the New Testament Acts of the Apostles (2:17). Thus "your old men shall dream dreams" is fulfilled, both literally completed and transcended, by the structurally analogous addition, creating an expanded, later textual order that comprehends both: "your old men shall dream dreams and your young men shall see visions."[1] Epigraphs like these, prompting a typological reading, were common in the period, especially in the visual arts.[2] But a larger point is at

---

1. In their biblical form, both verses contain both clauses; the Old Testament verse, then, is fulfilled by simple repetition within the new context (though the order of clauses is reversed in Acts 2:17). Pater's choice to split the verse and divide it between his two chapters calls attention to its halves as stages in a developmental progression.

2. See Sussman, *Fact into Figure*, pp. 49, 56. A good example is Millais's *Christ in the House of His Parents* ("The Carpenter's Shop"), which shows the boy Jesus with a wound in his hand, prefiguring the stigmata. The painting was originally exhibited with no title but with the words of Zechariah 13:6: "And one shall say unto him, what are these wounds in thine hands? Then he shall answer, Those with which I was wounded in the house of my friends."

stake here, for this is one of many ways the text of *Marius* calls attention to itself as text. In this case the epigraphs set in motion an awareness that whole texts, when viewed in "historical retrospect," can be seen to relate to one another typologically, the later text fulfilling and completing the earlier one. Pater develops, in other words, a typological framework for the novel's dense intertextuality.

This framework demonstrates his view that texts "appreciate"— literally gain in aesthetic value—over the historical course of their reception, their active appreciation by later readers. When a text is appreciated in a later age, it is at once appropriated, preserved, and transcended, as it is gathered up into a more complex order. Pater's novel imitates this historical process of literary "appreciation" through its densely intertextual form.

The historical *pastiche* of *Marius the Epicurean* is neither random nor merely stylized.[3] Instead it is Pater's most articulated literary experiment in the composite form we have come to associate with his aesthetic historicism. In addition, and as usual, Pater casts an aura of generalized value around each concrete work of art he revives from the past. In literary terms, one consequence of this is that each quoted fragment possesses not only a concrete textual value but also a *generic* value. Because the narrative form of *Marius the Epicurean* represents the compendious perspective within which all these earlier texts are gathered, appreciated, and therefore both historically and aesthetically transcended, the novel becomes a veritable encyclopedia of genres, an appreciation of the history of literary change at the moment of its absorption in the modernist anthology, the repository where "fragments are shored" against the ruin of the end of time.[4]

The novel as a whole plays on this concept in several ways. Just before Marius dies, his life is described in a metaphor that compares his hoped-for vision to the recovery of a unified text:

Throughout that elaborate and lifelong education of his receptive powers, he had ever kept in view the purpose of preparing himself towards possi-

---

3. In contrast to mine, see René Wellek's view of "the limitations of 19th-century aestheticism, . . . its Alexandrian eclecticism, which made it impossible for the age to create a style of its own and which encouraged historical masquerade" in *A History of Modern Criticism, 1750–1950*, vol. 4: *The Later Nineteenth Century* (New Haven, Conn.: Yale University Press, 1965), p. 399.

4. For a fuller version of this line of argument, see my "Pater in the 1880s: Experiments in Genre," *Journal of Pre-Raphaelite Studies* 4 (November 1983), 39–51, esp. 47–48. Geoffrey Hartman sketches another view of the coexistence of genres in "impressionist" prose in *The Fate of Reading and Other Essays* (Chicago: University of Chicago Press, 1975), pp. 269–70.

ble further revelation some day—towards some ampler vision, which should take up into itself and explain this world's delightful shows, as the scattered fragments of a poetry, till then but half understood, might be taken up into the text of a lost epic, recovered at last. (ME II, 219–20)

The "ampler vision" hypothesized here would incorporate his partial, earthly experience within a completed, transcendent spiritual order. At his death he has not achieved this "ampler vision," though he dies still hopeful; perhaps death will bring the transcendence he seeks. This remains, at the end of the novel, a crucially open question.[5]

However, transcending both Marius's life, which ends as the novel ends, and the cultural history of Christianity, which continues beyond it, Pater's narrative form supplies that "ampler vision." Like the "lost epic, recovered at last," it takes up into itself and comprehends not "this world's delightful shows" but their literary analogue, "the scattered fragments of a poetry, till then but half understood." The novel's vast inclusiveness may be seen, then, in formal strategies other than the shifting temporal layers that enact the narrator's access to any conceivable past age of history; it may be seen also in this intertextual comprehensiveness. The narrative form encompasses and transcends other literary forms, recontextualizing them as *past* forms. Thus the narrative form of *Marius* imitates the principles of historical development advanced in Pater's description of the growth of ritual, in which the Christian order was seen to absorb and supersede the pagan. By incorporating and transcending the world of second-century literature within its nineteenth-century literary order, this novel makes a similar point about the "growth" and development of literature. The interpolated second-century fragments stand in relation to the novel as a whole as an "old" testament to a "new." The novel gathers up the disparate texts of the second century and "comprehends" them—both incorporates them in a larger, later order and understands them "at last," by subjecting them to its historicizing framework and perspective.

The novel historicizes those second-century texts in part by regarding them as earlier developments in a long, continuous literary history, comparing, for example, Apuleius with Swift and Gautier (ME I, 60–

---

5. The possibility of transcendence is belied by the fact that Marius recreates his original innocence and receptivity through an act of metaphorical self-obliteration, wiping "the tablet of the mind white and smooth" once more. On the other hand, the novel argues forcefully that the very possibility of transcendence depends on presenting such a *tabula rasa* for "whatsoever the divine fingers might choose to write there" (ME II, 220). (Note the inscriptive sense of receptivity here.)

61). Regarding the earlier texts as parts of a larger, later whole reduces their priority, and the greater literary self-consciousness represented by that later capacity for inclusiveness would, of course, represent a positive formal value here. But the novel also historicizes second-century literature by advancing a further judgment regarding the relative value of entire genres of literature. Many of the second-century texts are allegories, and by enclosing and transcending them this novel seems to imply that its own historicizing, typological, "realistic" techniques represent a higher as well as a later development of literature. The novel as a genre typically sanctions historical, mediated access to the spiritual over a more directly spiritualizing mode of access, such as the symbolic, metamorphic, or allegorical, and Pater's novel makes that generic sanction a self-conscious part of its particular narrative form.[6]

If the novel as a whole suggests that allegory has been superseded by more historicizing forms, Marius as protagonist exemplifies the process of "outgrowing" allegory on the individual level. The allegories of the "Golden Book" that stimulated him as a young man to delight in metamorphosis—in those "sudden, unlooked-for changes of dreams"—do not serve, as he grows older, to explain how (or whether) such transformations can actually occur. Other allegories, such as the tale of Cupid and Psyche, prompted a search for the ideal, and that search continues all his life, culminating in his experience on the Sabine Hills, after which Marius decisively commits himself to search "for the equivalent of that Ideal among so-called actual things" (ME II, 72). In this climactic scene, Marius definitively chooses, after a "lifelong education of his receptive powers," an interpretive bias. He decides to believe in the presence of a "divine" companion, and he decides, once and for all, "to hold by what his eyes really saw." In other words, he raises his lifelong temperamental bias to the level of self-conscious theory, and with this newly consolidated self-consciousness he establishes an interpretive will, a principle of reception, "the will as vision."

In the two chapters that directly follow this crucial experience, Marius, explicitly renouncing allegory, sees a typological vision. These twin chapters are linked by a common title, "Two Curious Houses," and by those typologically related epigraphs: "Your old men shall dream dreams and your young men shall see visions." Let us return briefly to these chapters, for they join the problem of interpre-

---

6. See Michael McKeon, *The Origins of the English Novel, 1600–1720* (Baltimore, Md.: Johns Hopkins University Press, 1987), esp. chaps. 2 and 6.

ting history with the consideration of how an individual learns to interpret his own past experience; they link the development of Christian ritual with the development of Marius's identity; and they implicitly relate allegory to novel generically and typologically, as old literary dispensation to new.

In the first curious house, two older men appeal to Marius's imagination with their allegorical discourses. These are none other than Lucian and Apuleius, "the literary ideal of his boyhood" (ME II, 76). Lucian's *Halcyon* examines the divine power of metamorphosis, and in that dialogue Socrates concludes that it is as easy for the gods "to refashion the form of a woman into that of a bird" as for children "to take wax or clay, and mould out of the same material many kinds of form" (ME II, 83). Apuleius's discourse *On the God of Socrates* advances the Neoplatonic notion of "a hierarchy of divine beings, associating themselves with particular things and places, for the purpose of mediating between God and man" (ME II, 88). These "divine powers of a middle nature" are "interpreters" between heaven and earth, coming down to man from above (ME II, 89). At first, Marius is tempted to believe, to receive this mystical theory, but he objects because it is too easy; it "assumed the thing with too much facility, too much of self-complacency" (ME II, 90). He turns away from these "mystic essays after the unseen," for after all, "to indulge but for an hour fantasies, fantastic visions of that sort, only left the actual world more lonely than ever. . . . For himself, it was clear, he must still hold by what his eyes really saw (ME II, 90).

Directly after rejecting the old dream of allegory, Marius sees the "visionary scene" of the church in Cecilia's house, a "vision" of youth and renewal, a visible and historically concrete vision, not a mystical vision (ME II, 105–6). The scene fulfills, in the typological sense, the full extent of his life's progression, "accumulating all the lessons of his experience since those first days at White-Nights" (ME II, 97). In this visionary moment it is as if the whole narrative unfolding of his development were telescoped, conflated, reduced to a single point in time, a single image, in exact accordance with his newly achieved self-consciousness, or will: "translated here," that is, "as if in designed congruity with his favorite precepts of the power of physical vision, into an actual picture" (ME II, 97). This is the single point of imagistic or scenic typology in the novel, appropriate here to emphasize the visual actuality of this particular kind of "visionary" moment. Marius interprets the scene as if he were looking at an early Pre-Raphaelite painting; he reads and interprets its typology. In fact, the "Two Curious Houses" form a sort of diptych, whose epigraphs prompt the expanded typological interpretation that begins in a reading of the actual scene. A crescendo of typological techniques has been building toward the unmistakable explicitness of the chapters' epigraphs, and Pater chooses this place in the narrative, as we have seen, to use his most explicit typological language (ME II, 97).

By renouncing allegory, Marius does not in the least renounce the ideal dimensions of his quest. Typology, too, involves progress toward a spiritual realm, though its access to the spirit is mediated by the physical. It stresses "horizontal" or linear progress in time, not the allegorical, symbolic, metamorphic, or "vertical" translation from one state to another. But the typological method of reading involves a "vertical" motion as well, toward a state of spiritual perfection traditionally conceived as beyond this world and beyond historical time. This way of reading earthly experience, then, accommodates both past and future within historical time, simultaneously points "up" toward a higher, timeless reality and "down" to its foundations in the concrete, time-bound world.

What Marius sees in Cecilia's house also links the human to the divine, but the mediating agents are not Neoplatonic angelic intermediaries but concrete, visible, historically specific forms. This progressive fulfillment in the direction of spirituality does not entail abrupt metamorphic transformations, but gradual historical change:

> It was the old way of true *Renaissance*—being indeed the way of nature with her roses, the divine way with the body of man, perhaps with his soul—conceiving the new organism by no sudden and abrupt creation, but rather by the action of a new principle upon elements, all of which had in truth already lived and died many times. (ME II, 95–96)

The "divine way" is also the historical way. Holding by "what his eyes really saw," Marius's interpretive will binds him to contemplate spiritual realities through the mediation of their most perfect earthly forms.

To circumvent these actual earthly forms in favor of ideal, immediate spiritual solutions might be reserved as "a fine, high, visionary consideration, very remote upon the intellectual ladder, just at the point, indeed, where that ladder seemed to pass into the clouds, but for which there was certainly no time left just now by his eager interest in the real objects so close to him, on the lowlier earthy steps nearest the ground" (ME I, 132). For now, Marius remains on the "lowlier earthy steps nearest the ground," instead of soaring "into the clouds." Mystical vision represents a distinct spiritual possibility, but one that speaks neither to the senses nor to historical experience. In this two-chapter debate on the relation of the human to the divine, Marius abandons hope of immediate access to a transcendent realm and decides to read actual experience for signs of divinity gradually unfolding within historical time. An interpretive language of types in the narrative grows directly from the creative power of this "will as vision," and Marius then discovers what he seeks. Marius self-consciously wills a certain *sort* of vision: visible, concrete, and historical—not "mystical." Apuleius's allegorical dream had suggested "a celestial ladder, a ladder leading from heaven to earth" (ME II, 90), but Marius's vision suggests an earthly ladder, leading from earth to heaven.

We, too, in the course of our reading, must learn to adopt principles of typological interpretation if we are to understand the significance of *Marius the Epicurean*, and especially the implications of its closure. All the narrative features we have examined—the overarching analogies between paganism and Christianity, between second-century Rome and nineteenth-century England; the outright narrative predictions of the future; the juxtaposed and shifting layers of narrative time; and especially the serial dynamics of the plot, through which the cultural milieu surrounding Marius develops in "typological ladders"—all of these features work together to set up a powerful prefigurative momentum. As we gradually begin to perceive this temporal logic, we develop the expectation that patterns of past experience, already repeated and partially fulfilled within the narrative present, will be repeated again and further fulfilled in the future, beyond the time of the narrative frame. That expectation, which amounts to "faith" of a certain aesthetic sort, is simply the result of learning to read the narrative form typologically. Just as we begin to understand that analogical relations progressively unfold throughout the novel, we also understand the implication that these patterns will continue in historical development even after the novel ends. The elaborate multiplication of analogy involved in Pater's typological ladders establishes a horizontal and vertical momentum that carries the reader's imagination, with the force of its logic, into the historical future.

Any expectation that the "typological momentum" of the novel will carry us out of time into eternity is of course thwarted; in its secularized form, typological momentum points only toward further fulfillment in the historical future, not toward apocalypse. To maintain his synthesis of evolutionary and providential orders in human history, Pater's secularized typology must set aside creation *ex nihilo* as well as apocalypse—Christian concepts of the beginning and the end of time—and stay firmly fixed "in the middest," in history.⁷ Thus, the typological ladders point toward heaven but remain on earth, fixed in their concrete foundations. But their teleological force is nonetheless relentless. The notion that the typological momentum continues, once established, is as old as Augustine: "All these things that we read as having been foretold and fulfilled in the past are still being done under our eyes in the present."⁸ Even though the notion of an apocalyptic end of time seems more and more remote, faith can remain in the steadfast progress toward it.

The individual death of the protagonist is one version of the conventional novelistic, secularized apocalypse. But Marius's death is hardly apocalyptic, even in novelistic terms, since like his "vision" it is the perfect fulfillment of his life: tentative, skeptical, receptive, gradual, silent. Pater chooses not even to represent apocalypse as an internal phenomenon, in the form of a full revolutionary conversion of Marius to Christianity. Despite his belief in the "divine companion," despite his "vision" in Cecilia's house, Marius does not in the end convert fully, internally, as an expression of his own will. Essentially passive, he is taken up, without his expressed wish or consent, into the Christian communion. As his ancestors were buried long after their pagan "ends," Marius officially becomes a Christian only after his death, and in the retrospective interpretation of others.

The impetus to make Marius explicitly Christian comes not from within Marius himself, as a feature of his own development, but from without, from the surrounding community. The central focus of the novel, its plot of individual development, seems at the end to have been subsumed by the plot of cultural development. This passivity on Marius's part has caused frequent complaints about the closure of the novel: that no progress has taken place, either in Marius's soul or in the historical culture; that Pater evades the question of Christianity's doctrinal exclusivity; that the conclusion is inconclusive.⁹ Marius

---

7. Frank Kermode, *The Sense of an Ending: Studies in the Theory of Fiction* (Oxford: Oxford University Press, 1966).

8. Quoted in Jean Daniélou, *The Lord of History* (London: Longmans, 1958), p. 10, n. 1.

9. For the most powerful statement of these objections, see Harold Bloom, "The Place of Pater: *Marius the Epicurean*," in *The Ringers in the Tower: Studies in Romantic Tradition* (Chicago: University of Chicago Press, 1971), pp. 185–204. Lawrence Evans offers an anthology of critical views on the ending of the novel in his bibliographical essay on Pater in David Delaura, ed., *Victorian Prose: A Guide to Research* (New York: Modern Language Association of America, 1973), pp. 344–51. But Evans is prejudiced against the idea that the ending might present a coherent synthesis, and he favors only readings that emphasize the irreconcilable nature of its conflicting impulses. Monsman disagrees that the ending is inconclusive. His pregnant use of the word "momentum"

does end where he began, still Marius "the Epicurean," a further development of what he always was, not a changed man. But the closure of the novel comes to seem both organically and historically inevitable the moment we understand its concern to resolve issues of greater scope than the religious commitment of one individual.

The total narrative form of this work encompasses the life story of one illustrative individual in a much larger scheme. Its cultural specificity is not mere "background" against which an individual fate is staged, nor simply realistic detail textured in a certain density to suggest historicity. In this novel the *Zeitgeist* has its own plot. The "time-spirit" comes to life and develops within the individual soul of Marius, but it also has a life and a will of its own. According to the temporal logic of the novel, that life is understood to continue beyond the end of Marius's individual life and beyond the end of the novel. *Telos*, in its secularized version, becomes teleological momentum; the apocalyptic "hereafter," beyond the end of historical time, in its secularized version becomes the time beyond the novel's closure. Even the *telos* of narrative, the aesthetic finality of its closure, is not final, for this closure remains emphatically "open," bursting its fictional boundaries and expanding into the "real" future beyond.

Read in the context of these principles, the ending of the novel is powerful, even though Marius makes only the most ambiguous commitment to Christianity. Pater does beg that particular question, but he does so in order to demonstrate that the question should not be put; the force and coherence of the narrative do not depend on such commitment on the part of the individual. Marius dies, but his culture lives on to express its own powerful commitment to Christianity as a positive, historical fact.

Marius's individual will is subsumed in the will of the rising cultural force: to make of him an expression of its most perfect development at that time. At his death, he is no converted Christian, no Christian martyr—the narrative tells us explicitly that he is not (ME II, 213–14). He is and remains by nature "the Epicurean," but he is also the "last of his [pagan] race" (ME II, 207). His culture assimilates him, converts him externally even though he himself never converts internally, culturally translates him into something he is not by nature, "takes him up" into a new cultural epoch, exactly as he translated his own ancestors into the Christian dispensation without their expressed

---

with regard to the ending of the novel suggested to me the idea of a specifically "typological momentum," though Monsman does not invoke a typological context (see *Pater's Portraits*, p. 97).

wish or consent. And this subsumption of Marius by his culture recapitulates the way that the nineteenth-century narrative form comprehends the texts of the second century and the way that present-day readers, following the logic of Pater's narrative form, try to comprehend—to understand, incorporate, and historicize—the text of *Marius the Epicurean*. The truly apocalyptic or anagogic position in this novel is held by the reader in the present, at the "end" of time.¹⁰

An active conversion on Marius's part would falsify the historical vision of the novel, as a passive conversion by his culture does not. Pater must leave the soul of Marius "open," for he must be both Christian and yet not Christian, in order to represent both the pre-Christian Epicurean and the post-Christian Epicurean, both of whom could also be "essentially" Christian. Pater's "ambivalence" about Christianity and about cultural progress is not indecision but a strong synthetic tactic. He implies that progress has been made in Marius's soul and in the culture around him: typological progress that is also conservative of the essence of the past—in this case of paganism—as future progress in the 1880s would have to be in order to preserve the "essence" of Christianity without its doctrines. To that end, Pater emphasizes essential features of Christianity other than the ones most emphatically cherished by the High Victorians. Instead of its ethical or doctrinal exclusiveness, Pater stresses the cultural self-consciousness of Christianity, its preromantic interiority, and especially its historical sense, its sense of the "sacredness of time" (ME I, 6).

"Marius could not remain Marius and renounce."¹¹ And Marius does in the end remain Marius. He does not embrace Christianity; Christianity embraces him, fulfilling, in the increasing self-consciousness of cultural life around him, his pagan or "natural" instinct for devotion, his love of ritual, his reverence for communal life. But his soul has made progress on its life's journey—internal, spiritual progress that recapitulates external, cultural progress, as the chapter titles testify: just as Hadrian's phrase is superseded by Tertullian's, Marius's "*Animula Vagula*," his little, wandering life, has achieved a higher state of awareness to become "*Anima Naturaliter Christiana*"—his rational soul, by natural instinct Christian.

He is, at his death, still "unclouded and receptive," conscious still

---

10. Frye's description of the "anagogic phase," when literature imitates "the total dream of man . . . inside the mind of an infinite man," is very close to my sense of what Pater's narrative frame accomplishes here. See Northrop Frye, *Anatomy of Criticism* (Princeton, N.J.: Princeton University Press, 1957), p. 119. Anagogic literature is mythopoeic and encyclopedic.
11. Bloom, "The Place of Pater," p. 192.

of "a pledge of something further to come"; and so, as readers, we have been formally trained to be (ME II, 220). The typological momentum promises new cultural forms more various and more beautiful than those of the second century—perhaps in the nineteenth century or even in the twentieth. The logic of this narrative form instills a certain faith that "these things are still being done in the present." Pater's novel is committed to "the devout idea that the essence of Christianity will somehow survive its doctrines," the idea that there is in fact a "religious phase possible for the modern mind." In that modern phase, essential Epicureanism and essential Christianity might survive together in a new, late-nineteenth-century aesthetic form whose temporal logic, now transvalued and secularized, remains nevertheless a testimony to the paradox of its "Anima Naturaliter Christiana."

# P·A·R·T · F·O·U·R

# "Recovery as Reminiscence": The *Greek Studies* and *Plato and Platonism*

• Pater's volume on Plato collects a series of lectures on the place of Plato in the history of philosophy. The lectures were meant to give the subject a "popular" treatment, and the volume was popular indeed. It was very well received by critics, and Pater counted it as the favorite among all his works.[1] Perhaps because they were written as lectures, the essays on Plato display an exceptional crispness and clarity of formulation. In new terms—motion and rest, centrifugal and centripetal, Ionian and Dorian—these essays rehearse the dialectic of aesthetic historicism on the stage of ancient Greece.

In *Plato and Platonism* and the *Greek Studies*, Pater becomes a "student of origins." He begins, as usual, with a strong commitment to absolute historicity, change, and difference—in attention to the specific landscapes, "races," and material practices of Ionians and Dorians, for example. And, as usual, his method works from that point to its dialectical antithesis, the commitment to search out permanence and repetition in the universal "tendencies" of "the human mind itself." Perhaps Pater was thinking of his own work when he compares the forms of ancient Greek art and philosophy to living organisms.

> All things are at once old and new. As, in physical organisms, the actual particles of matter have existed long before in other combinations; and what is really new in a new organism is the new cohering force—the *mode* of life. (GS, 215)

---

1. See William E. Buckler, *Walter Pater: The Critic as Artist of Ideas* (New York: New York University Press, 1987), pp. 287–95.

· 236 · *Greek Studies* and *Plato and Platonism*

All art "grows" in history, constantly exfoliating new developments of the original "matter." But according to Pater, art not only "grows"; it also is aesthetically "made," and therefore it simultaneously yields the sense of immeasurable age and imaginative revival. This intersection of organic and aesthetic models of creation is a distinguishing feature of Pater's aesthetic historicism, as we have seen. In the *Greek Studies*, Pater discusses the figure who coaxes new forms of coherence from "received" practice, the figure of the Interpreter. He intervenes in organic culture to stimulate reflection, self-consciousness, and representation. Thus the Interpreter embodies the force of cultural evolution, through which ritual practice becomes art and literature; and after that crucial transition from archaic to literary and historical culture, the Interpreter facilitates a periodic return to the ground of tradition and the further evolution of cultural types.

What happens when Pater investigates the figurative "ground" of his aesthetic historicism? His "Greek" studies (not only the posthumously titled *Greek Studies* but *Plato and Platonism* as well) do precisely that. Those essays retrospectively arc back over all the intervening ages to return to the origins of the tradition in which they still participate.

> Besides [the] conditions of time and place, and independent of them, there is also an element of permanence, a standard of taste, which genius confesses. This standard is maintained in a purely intellectual tradition. . . . The supreme artistic products of succeeding generations thus form a series of elevated points, taking each from each the reflexion of a strange light, the source of which is not in the atmosphere around and above them, but in a stage of society remote from ours. This standard takes its rise in Greece, at a definite historical period. (R, 199)

Framed by a commitment to historical particularity, this passage from *The Renaissance* describes the "remote" and "strange" origin of a standard of historical repetition. The figure of the "series of elevated points" recalls the relief of periodic return to that "high" standard.

Both the *Greek Studies* and *Plato and Platonism* enact the "relief" of that return. In both volumes Pater attempts to delve beneath the ground, so to speak, in an archaeological exploration of the prehistoric, mythic world of oral tradition. For Pater, mythic story evolves within a primeval, undifferentiated unity prior to the primary division of self-consciousness which makes for representation. Both literature and history come into being through successive "divisions" of this originary, mythic field. Pater formulates a history of myth which traces its evolution in three phases, and it is interesting to note that his own exposition of the history of myth is a recognizable example of his third, or "ethical," phase. In that phase, the persons and events of myth are reinterpreted as "abstract symbols, because intensely characteristic examples, of moral or spiritual conditions" (GS, 91–93). Pater traces this spiritual development through analogical repetitions, and thus his histories of myth become an example of his own myth of history. Like typological exegesis, this mode of interpretation finds greater spirituality in the later phases.

*Plato and Platonism*, too, explores the origination of history and literature, through the figure who forms the "standard of taste" for late-nineteenth-century English historians of philosophy.[2] In this work Pater attends to the history of philosophy as well as to the philosophy of history. He sees the figure of Plato as an embodiment of the moment oral tradition is transformed into literary representation. Thus the figure of Plato marks the end of one line of development and the beginning of another. To articulate the manifold richness of inarticulate prehistory that he comprehends, Pater makes Plato the third term of a dialectical genealogy, and to emphasize that point he repeats it in another figure. The figure of Socrates, too, synthesizes philosophical prehistory, and Plato gives that prior, unwritten synthesis a literary form. In the specular relation between Socrates and Plato, Pater imagines the generation of literary history. The "actual" Socratic dialogue becomes articulate through the aesthetic representation of Platonic dialectic.

Mythic character is fundamental to Pater's theory of literary history, and his figure of Plato is a modern re-creation of the form of mythic characterization. In the Paterian Plato the forces of prehistory and history have been conflated, consolidated, and totalized under the auspices of a mythic name. Like the refined figures of Persephone, or Dionysus *Zagreus*, which had been separated out in time from the mythic manifold of Demeter or Dionysus, the historical differentiations marked by later "Platonism" may be seen as "aspects" of a former, mythic totality. Pater's frequent analogies between Plato and contemporary nineteenth-century figures make it seem as if Pater is "identifying" with Plato. But like the narrator of "The Child in the House" or of *Marius the Epicurean*, the persona created here need not

2. Richard Jenkyns (*The Victorians and Ancient Greece* [Cambridge: Harvard University Press, 1980], pp. 227–61) and Frank M. Turner (*The Greek Heritage in Victorian Britain* [New Haven, Conn.: Yale University Press, 1981], pp. 369–446) have done invaluable work in this area.

be identified simply with the historical Pater. It would be better to insist on the effacement of that individuality, for the lecturer on Plato stages a transparency like that of "Diaphaneitè," transmitting received views with a coherence that gives them aesthetic form.[3] It is always worth insisting on the status of Pater's persona as an aesthetic creation, a figure, for again Pater stages the modern voice as the medium of historical recollection.

## 1 · Histories of Myth: The *Greek Studies*

Pater's analyses of Greek myths are grounded in the historical sense, though they tend finally toward a myth of history. He begins by emphasizing the absolute historicity of myth, interpreting it as the expression of specific, material practices, which he calls "modes of existence" (GS, 10):

> Myth is begotten among a primitive people, as they wondered over the life of the thing their hands helped forward, till it became for them a kind of spirit, and their culture of it a kind of worship. (GS, 29)

In this view, religion reflects the material culture of a people; it is expressed in a story, a "projected expression" composite of themselves and their crop in mutual dependency.

Therefore, Pater argues, we should speak not of the religion but of the *religions* of ancient Greece, each one expressed by its own "sacred representation or interpretation of the whole human experience" (GS, 10).

> As the religion of Demeter carries us back to the cornfields and farmsteads of Greece, and places us, in fancy, among a primitive race, in the furrow and beside the granary; so the religion of Dionysus carries us back to its vineyards, and is a monument of the ways and thoughts of people whose days go by beside the winepress, and under the green and purple shadows, and whose material happiness depends on the crop of grapes. ... That garland of ivy, the aesthetic value of which is so great in the later imagery of Dionysus and his descendents, the leaves of which,

---

3. Shuter calls for an end to treating *Plato and Platonism* simply as a stage in the evolution of Pater's thought, and for an end to treating Pater's view of Plato as a mask for his own ideas (William F. Shuter, "Pater on Plato: 'Subjective' or 'Sound'?" *Prose Studies* 5 [1982], p. 215).

Histories of Myth · 239 ·

floating from his hair, become so noble in the hands of Titian and Tintoret, was actually worn on the head for coolness. (GS, 9–10, 21)

Each "mode of existence" is "peculiar" to a certain race, class, and geographical location, and each myth changes in time as the people's mode of existence changes. "The wilder people have wilder gods, . . . changing ever with the worshippers in whom they live and move and have their being" (R, 203). Of course, this stress on the absolute historicity of cultural products is the familiar starting-place of Pater's "historic method."[1]

In this volume Pater relies on the other principal argument of the "historic method" as well, when he insists that the theory of development is as much the key to "the comparative science of religions" as to any other of the human sciences (GS, 11):

> Here again, . . . the idea of development, of degrees, of a slow and natural growth, impeded here, diverted there, is the illuminating thought which earlier critics lacked. (GS, 121–22)

In the *Greek Studies*, Pater works back through the history of a myth's development toward the original "mode of existence" that the myth expressed. "We feel our way backwards," he explains, and we "must be content to follow faint traces" (GS, 111–12). These "traces" lead the "student of origins" toward an original mythic unity that can never be directly grasped or known. Later literary expressions of the original material lend only mediate access to the time when "use and beauty are still undivided" (GS, 197):

> Their story went back . . . with unbroken continuity . . . to a past, stretching beyond, yet continuous with, actual memory, in which heaven and earth mingled. (GS, 33)

In other words, Pater conceives prehistoric culture as an originary manifold from which mythic "conceptions" (and later, literature) are articulated by degrees. Even though he places quite a pointed emphasis on the material ground from which myth grows, Pater portrays this

---

1. Iser points to Pater's participation here in an anthropological model current in the nineteenth century, which explained myth as a consecration of basic human needs and practices and "reduced all phenomena that claimed to be supernatural or religious to their human origins, as exemplified by Feuerbach's anthropological reduction of Christianity" (Wolfgang Iser, *Walter Pater: The Aesthetic Moment* [Cambridge: Cambridge University Press, 1987], p. 107).

ground as forever inaccessible and inarticulate. History is the record of differences and divisions, of growth away from an original mythic unity.

In the *Greek Studies*, Pater develops a theory of literary history which describes the emergence of literature against this prehistoric background. All Greek myths, he claims, develop through the same three phases: an oral, "half-conscious, instinctive" phase, "living from mouth to mouth," in which concrete features of nature are first seen as symbolic; a written, "conscious, poetical or literary, phase," in which natural symbols are interpreted as the characters and incidents of narrative; and a self-conscious or "ethical" phase, in which character and plot are reinterpreted as "abstract symbols, because intensely characteristic examples, of moral or spiritual conditions" (GS, 91–93). In each phase, then, acts of interpretation generate greater levels of generalization and spirituality than in the former phase. These phases of myth provide yet another formulation of the three-stage romantic dialectic of development. As usual, Pater's analysis equates the "higher" development with the later, more abstract phase.

How then do mythic stories form and transform themselves? As in *Marius*, Pater offers in the *Greek Studies* both evolutionary and aesthetic explanations of the process. On the one hand, he describes the evolution of myth as "a struggle for life," in which some myths "never emerged from that first stage of popular conception, or were absorbed by stronger competitors" (GS, 113). Stories begin "like other things . . . for which no one in particular is responsible." In this stage of archaic collectivity, the division between "nature" and "culture" has not yet taken place.

But on the other hand, the mechanism to which Pater ascribes this "natural selection" is clearly not natural at all. Myths that die do so because "they lacked the sacred poet or prophet, and were never remodelled by literature." In other words, someone in particular *is* responsible for the survival of a story. To become "fit" enough to "survive," popular conception must be seized by a poet, a prophet, or a priest-exegete and "remodelled by literature."[2] This moment of aesthetic responsibility marks the division between nature and culture and the emergence of distinctly divided roles or functions ("poets," "prophets," "interpreters") against the archaic background of communal wholeness. In the *Greek Studies*, Pater manages to balance the claims of both evolutionary and aesthetic explanations by focusing

---

2. Pater plays here both with Social-Darwinian and Hegelian connotations of "survival."

Histories of Myth · 241 ·

toward the mythic moment when "natural" and "cultural" explanations have not fully distinguished themselves from one another. As in *Marius*, Pater wants to have it both ways: literature grows organically, and it is aesthetically made.

Yet myth must evolve into literature or it dies, never to emerge from prehistoric obscurity. Thus, according to this view, the very category "literature" is defined by its consciousness of having revised earlier mythic material. The literary process of "remodelling" myth fundamentally depends upon the development of character, which "fixes" and at the same time "humanises" man's conception of the unseen. A primitive people first "project" away from (and therefore reflect back to) themselves a recognizable image of their total culture. In this stage, to "humanise" means to "condense" the flux of natural conditions into one familiar form.

> The office of the imagination . . . is thus to condense the impressions of natural things into human form; to retain that early mystical sense of water, or wind, or light, in the moulding of eye and brow; to arrest it, or rather, perhaps, to set it free, there, as human expression. The body of man, indeed, was for the Greeks still the genuine work of Prometheus; its connexion with earth and air . . . [was] direct and immediate. (GS, 32–33)

That the human body can serve as such a complex and totalizing image indicates at once the closeness to nature of the mythic imagination and at the same time the beginning of its separation *from* nature, because the "refining" of nature in man's own image has already begun. The history of myth describes further developments in this process of "humanising" nature.

The full process of character formation involves a dialectic of condensation and generalization through which a character is gradually "arrested" and at the same time "set free," both embodied and spiritualized. Beginning in the care of an individual vine, for example, as the vine-grower "stoops over it, coaxing and nursing it, like a pet animal or a little child," the mythic consciousness attributes a spirit first to one vine and then to the whole species (GS, 13). But after being generalized, this spirit must again be "condensed"—fixated and totalized—as a personal spirit. As they dream and brood over the life of their crops, an ancient people "harmonise" those dreams into a human character. Mythic imagination is "a unifying or identifying power, bringing together things naturally asunder . . . welding into something like the identity of a human personality the whole range of man's experiences" (GS, 29). But after disparate material conditions are identified as a person, the process of spiritualization—and even of further embodiment—goes on. The establishment of character enables incident or plot, and the further elaboration of plot brings mythic character closer and closer to human moods, sympathies, and conduct. Both "A Study of Dionysus" and "The Myth of Demeter and Persephone" are essays in the articulation of this process.

For example, early in her development, Demeter represents the chthonic forces of the earth in general. Demeter and Persephone are not at this point clearly differentiated from one another. Later, two personae express the division of earth's cycle into seasons of hot and cold, fertile and barren, summer and winter. With the *"invention"* of Persephone (GS, 122)—that is, her separation from the manifold concept of Demeter—the earth's seasonal changes are definitively interpreted as a mother's grief at separation from her daughter. (The earliest division of self-consciousness, the initial separation of nature and culture, is thus expressed through the separation of two characters from the primeval manifold, which is in turn expressed by their personal separation from one another.) This characterization provides the framework for appropriate incident; Demeter searches for Persephone across the vast earth and over the course of the seasonal year, and "she becomes in her long wanderings, almost wholly humanised" (GS, 118).

Demeter and Persephone, then, embody the contradictions of time and nature in a familial or genealogical relation between two persons.[3] Dionysus, on the other hand, incorporates natural oppositions under the auspices of one persona. Thus he becomes, as Pater entitles his study, the "spiritual form of fire and dew." The alternating harshness and solace of early spring, its erratic chill and warmth (both dangers to the growing vine), are personified in the complex life history of Dionysus, who was "born" twice, first in the fire of Zeus's lightning approach to Semele, and then, after a protective gestation in the cloudy thigh of Zeus, through Hye, the dew (GS, 26–7). These incidents of a life story "explain" the origins of his contradictory and erratic character, and his character, conversely, resolves the contradictions of nature by unifying them as aspects of one person's life history.

Both "literary" and "ethical" phases of myth register an increase in spirit, which is produced through this dialectical process of generalization and "condensation." First the single vine is granted a spirit, then that spirit is generalized to cover all vines. Finally, the general characteristics of all vines are transfigured as one human form, unified

---

3. Patricia Drechsel Tobin, *Time and the Novel: The Genealogical Imperative* (Princeton, N.J.: Princeton University Press, 1978).

Histories of Myth · 243 ·

and "projected" as the character Dionysus. Narrative incidents collect around this center of attention and are then more generally interpreted themselves, so that finally, in the "ethical" phase, the spirit of Dionysus comes to represent the force of life itself.

> He is the soul of the individual vine, first; . . . afterwards, the soul of the whole species, the spirit of fire and dew, alive and leaping in a thousand vines, as the higher intelligence, brooding more deeply over things, pursues, in thought, the generation of sweetness and strength in the veins of the tree, the transformation of water into wine . . . ; and shadowing forth, in each pause of the process, an intervening person. . . . So they passed on to think of Dionysus . . . not merely as the soul of the vine, but of all that life in flowing things of which the vine is the symbol, because its most emphatic example. (GS, 13)

It is interesting to follow Pater's figural maneuvers in this passage. He uses an ostensibly material transformation (of water into wine) to represent a "spiritual" transformation (of a natural symbol into a "higher" potency). The "generation of sweetness and strength in the veins of the tree"—in other words, the transformative power of nature—has been metaphorically equated with the conversion of water into wine, or the transformation of nature into culture. (This figure is also resonant, for anyone reading in Pater's tradition, with the Christian association to the miracle at Cana; thus the "higher intelligence" seems also to hint at the secularization-effect produced by the transformation of Greek myth into Christian story.) In this "higher" phase, the rarefied, cultured product of the vine, the wine, symbolizes the original, natural power hidden within the growing plant. What is "expressed" or squeezed out of the original vine is made to symbolize what was occult, interior, and hidden.[4] Finally the vine, which in the first stage was represented by "Dionysus," becomes itself the representative symbol of "all life." We begin with the vine and we end with the vine, but in the end the exemplary organism has become a symbol of the "spirit" in nature. This circuit of figuration uses personification as an intermediate stage, between nature and pure

---

4. See also the process of figuration in the following passage: "The history of Greek art, then, begins, as some have fancied general history to begin, in a golden age, but in an age, so to speak, of real gold, the period of those first twisters and hammerers of the precious metals. . . . The heroic age of Greek art is the age of the hero as smith" (GS, 192–93). Here again a spiritual or mythic meaning (a "golden age") is grounded in a realistic, historical phenomenon (surviving objects crafted in gold).

spirit. Thus the figure of personification is itself the symbol of a certain figurative agenda here: to grant "spirit" to organic matter.[5]

Representing "spirit" is most commonly a matter of figuratively dividing an interior from an exterior. In this connection, Pater offers a wonderful little myth of aesthetic history to explain the invention of modeling in sculpture. This art form has particular significance in the *Greek Studies* because of its human subject of representation, and here Pater interprets its formal invention as the establishment of insides and outsides:

> The love-sick daughter of the artist . . . outlines on the wall the profile of her lover as he sleeps in the lamplight, to keep by her in absence— . . . The father fills up the outline . . . and hence the art of modelling from the life in clay. (GS, 231)

This tiny "butterfly wing" of incident (as Pater calls it) gathers complicated resonances in its context. As he did explicitly in "Winckelmann," Pater draws on the Hegelian description of art history, in which different art forms successively represent stages in the growth of world-historical self-consciousness.[6] Here the human form is granted interiority as the father "fills up" the empty outline with solid matter. (And incidentally, the paternal figure in this little story is a recognizable secularization of God as artist, endowing the human form with "life.") Thus even Greek sculpture, which in "Winckelmann" stood for the earliest and most purely physical or "objective" stage of aesthetic form, is seen to have resulted from the division of exterior form and interior content. Even within the "repose" of classical origins, the romantic spirit has already begun to brood.

In his essay "Romanticism," written in 1876 between his studies of Demeter and of Dionysus, Pater uses similar terms to describe the two "tendencies" in aesthetic history.[7] Classical art begins by

---

5. See the Hegelian analysis of Anthony Ward in *Walter Pater: The Idea in Nature* (Worchester and London: Macgibbon and Kee, 1966), esp. pp. 67–80. On the figure of personification, see Barbara Johnson, *A World of Difference* (Baltimore, Md.: Johns Hopkins University Press, 1987), pp. 45–46, 96–97, 192–93.

6. R, 209ff. For a comment on Pater's use of Hegel here, see Donald Hill's textual and explanatory notes to Pater's *The Renaissance: Studies in Art and Poetry, The 1893 Text*, ed. Donald L. Hill (Berkeley: University of California Press, 1980), p. 432. See Iser, *Walter Pater*, pp. 24–28, for analysis of this "expressive" aspect of art.

7. For relative dating of the "Romanticism" essay and the early "Greek Studies," see Samuel Wright, *A Bibliography of the Writings of Walter H. Pater* (New York: Garland, 1975), p. xv. The essay was retitled in *Appreciations* (1889) as "Postscript," which, as Bloom points out, suggests that it is being presented as a critical credo. Bloom goes on to argue that the essay is meant as a reply to Arnold's "Study of Poetry," in which Pater opposes his own standard of "energy" to Arnold's moral standard. See Harold Bloom, introduction to *Selected Writings of Walter Pater*, ed. Harold Bloom (New York: Columbia University Press, 1982), p. 220, n. 1.

choosing an outward form and then fills it up with matter. The classicist has been impressed with "the comeliness of the old, immemorial, well-recognised types in art and literature" and "will entertain no matter which will not go easily and flexibly into them" (A, 257). Romantic art, on the other hand, begins with "untried matter, still in fusion." Romantic artists must

> by the very vividness and heat of their conception, purge away . . . all that is not organically appropriate to it, till the whole effect adjusts itself in clear, orderly, proportionate form; which form, after a very little time, becomes classical in its turn. (A, 258)

These two "tendencies" describe movement in opposite directions, romantics burning away excess matter to create form, and classicists filling up an empty (though prior) form with appropriate matter. Each movement figuratively "begins" with a different pole of the formal dialectic: romantic art with matter, classical art with form. Pater himself "begins" with the classical moment of the dialectic, but even so, a prior phase is implied, for how otherwise could the classical form have become so "well-recognised"?

One effect of Pater's chiasmic formulation here is to associate both "form" and "matter" with the novelty of emergent "spirit," the vector force toward future transformation which Pater associates with romantic "energy":

$$\text{romantic: matter} > \text{form (spirit, energy)}$$
$$\text{classical: form} > \text{matter (spirit, energy)}$$

The temporal dimension of this dialectic is signified by the dialectical reversal of the term "form": the significance of romantic "form" is itself transformed through time into its very opposite, the "well-recognised type," the classical form. "Matter" and "form" in this essay are every bit as relative and dialectically dependent terms as are "classical" and "romantic."[8] By emphasizing the dialectical relation, through his repeated definition of these movements as "tendencies," Pater manages to argue both for permanently coexisting ideal structures and for alternating periods of art-historical difference; thus he manages to balance material and formal principles in his own theory.

---

8. For a helpful discussion of the difference between the form/matter distinction and the form/content distinction, see Claudio Guillen, "On the Uses of Literary Genre," in *Literature as System* (Princeton, N.J.: Princeton University Press, 1971), pp. 109–10.

That in itself is his most brilliant accomplishment in this essay, which works throughout to relativize all such critical distinctions.

But for our immediate purposes the importance both of Pater's myth of the sculptor's lovesick daughter and of his essay on romanticism is that they show the language of insides and outsides operating not only to describe the coherence of any particular art form, but also to describe principles of art-historical development. History begins when inarticulate matter is given "spiritual form," and ever afterward the gradual expression (externalization, objectification, "projection") of interiority describes the course of that history.[9] Both literature and history are simultaneously established in this initial division of mythic unity, and this moment is expressed by means of personal figures. Mythic characters incorporate, by representing in one place, the vicissitudes and contradictions of nature, material practice, and temporal process. Divisions in time, which Pater also seeks to convey through dialectical forms of argumentation, are in this mode spatialized as a body. Pater's historicism relies on this form of mythic personification as the paradigm for aesthetic-historical objectification of "spirit."

In the *Greek Studies*, for example, Pater totalizes primitive culture in such a personal figure: a primitive people "can but work outward what is within them," Pater explains simply (GS, 212). Or elsewhere, he explicitly figures the moment of emergence into art and history as the moment an "informing" soul is breathed into matter to create a body:

> A world of material splendour, moulded clay, beaten gold, polished stone;—the informing, reasonable soul entering into that, reclaiming the metal and stone and clay, till they are as full of living breath as the real warm body itself; the presence of those two elements is continuous throughout the fortunes of Greek art after the heroic age, and the constant right estimate of their action and reaction, from period to period, its true philosophy. (GS, 223)

In other words, Pater operates these personal figures on the usual graduating levels of generalization: the level of the artist, expressing individual interiority; the level of the *Zeitgeist* in its particular stage of development; and the level of the transhistorical *Geist*, expressed through periodic "phases" of developing self-consciousness. It is clear

---

9. See Ward on Pater's reading of Hegel's *Phenomenology*, in *The Idea in Nature*, pp. 44, 67, 71.

that a version of mythic personification is fundamental to Pater's Hegelian scheme of spiritual growth in history, but what is most interesting about his transposition of Hegelian development is precisely the degree to which he unintentionally exposes Hegelian historicism as itself a modern mythology, rationalized through personal figures.

## 2 · The House Beautiful and Its Interpreter

Who or what is responsible for the unfolding expressiveness of aesthetic history? One important line of argument in the *Greek Studies* is devoted to answering this question. In another attempt to formulate the inarticulate, prehistoric ground of development, Pater emphasizes the temporal priority of ritual, or religious "usages," over "conceptions" or stories. Myth emerges from its prehistory to enter its "literary" phase at the moment it can be seen as "divided" between "outward imagery" and "inner sense." The various versions of a "literary" myth progressively interpret the religious ritual, which becomes more impressive to worshipers as its "outward imagery" more precisely expresses its "inner sense" (GS, 121). In this reflexive relation between unconceptualized ritual and interpretation or narrative, Pater finds the mechanism through which practice is gradually coaxed into self-consciousness. And the agency of this process is a personal figure.

Before there were storytellers, Pater explains, *exegetae* conveyed the significance of ritual practices to the people (GS, 227). In mythic culture, the office of dividing "outward imagery" from "inner sense" and relating them to each other falls to the priest-exegete, or "interpreter."

> There were religious usages before there were distinct religious conceptions, and these antecedent religious usages shape and determine, at many points, the ultimate religious conception, as the details of the myth interpret or explain the religious custom. The hymn relates the legend of certain holy places, to which various impressive religious rites had attached themselves—the holy well, the old fountain, the stone of sorrow, which it was the office of the "interpreter" of the holy places to show to the people. (GS, 120)

The establishment of mythic character and of the role of *interpreter* are thus dialectically related events, and the interpreter thus becomes a sort of artist of historical development.[1] Character emerges from "the primitive mythical figure" through the ritual dramatization of "mysteries" (GS, 121), and that character is embellished through the exegetical intervention of "interpreters," who "project" expressive incident in more and more elaborate sequences. Because mythic "representation" is already the result of "interpretation," the two terms are consequently used interchangeably in the *Greek Studies* (e.g., GS, 10). In Pater's scheme, then, the literary functions of character, plot, and concept or theme all serve to embody an interpretation of something prior to themselves; narrative is the form of the already-interpreted which demands further interpretation.

Pater's italicized stress on the word "interpreter" suggests an attempt to focus attention on its nuances. The "inter-preter" puts himself between, divides, or intervenes. In the specific case of mythic Greek culture, the interpreter intervenes between a people and themselves, establishing the distance of self-consciousness between unconscious practice and representation. In this sense the interpreter is absolutely the precondition of historical expression, for without interpretation a figurative "inside" has not been divided from a figurative "outside." But in Pater's work the function of the interpreter is of course not limited to the evolution of culture from its prehistoric, archaic state.

Toward the beginning of "Romanticism," Pater places the same italicized stress on the role of the interpreter. He is at pains in this immediate context to argue that the terms "classical" and "romantic" should be understood not as absolute opposites but as relative "tendencies" in the history of art. In the midst of this exposition of his fundamental argument, Pater imagines the "House Beautiful," his spatial representation of all aesthetic history gathered together in one place:

> In that *House Beautiful*, which the creative minds of all generations—the artists and those who have treated life in the spirit of art—are always building together, for the refreshment of the human spirit, these oppositions cease; and the *Interpreter* of the *House Beautiful*, the true aesthetic critic, uses these divisions, only so far as they enable him to enter into the peculiarities of the objects with which he has to do. (A, 241)

---

1. This is the basis, in philosophy of history, for Pater's "modern" belief in the creative potential of criticism.

That "House Beautiful," like a body with an indwelling spirit, houses all the spirits of all the ages. The model of a mythic body, federating disparate natural impressions in one spirit, has here been generalized and transposed; now a "House" federates many spirits of culture under one roof. Pater's modern, mythic conception re-collects all the differences of time in one place. The secularization of Bunyan's House Beautiful is telling, for this is a dwelling for the figures of aesthetic and historical culture, not the place of sacred reward.[2]

This passage makes it clear that dialectical "divisions" alone testify to the specificity of life and development in historical time, but from the perspective of the House Beautiful, those divisions are preserved, annulled, and transcended in a unity that is beyond time. The Interpreter plays a major role in each phase. At the origins of history, as we have seen, he presides over the necessary divisions that create literary myth, and here at the other end of the line, "the true aesthetic critic" imagines the reunion of those divisions that, from this point of view, can now be seen to have been merely provisional.

The very evolution of art and literature are made to seem the results of these fundamental acts of personal intervention. Here again we see Pater's initially firm commitment to particularity: the aesthetic critic "uses these divisions" in order to penetrate the "peculiarities" of each different object. But this "first step," the commitment to historicity, occurs in a context that subverts it with a strong image of transhistorical totality. Assigning such a vast role to the creative powers of interpretation is a powerful gesture of self-aggrandizement, for Pater himself is engaged in externalizing myth's "inwardness." His *Greek Studies* are themselves a contribution to the latest phase of "ethical" mythology.

## 3 · The Philosophy of Mythic Form

In Pater's *Greek Studies* we can clearly see the conceptual struggle within historicism—between historical differentiation and transhistorical unity, stability, and iteration. On the one hand, Pater claims that myth rises out of specific historical conditions, and yet on the

---

2. For other discussions of the Paterian "House Beautiful," see "The House Beautiful and the Cathedral," in Richmond Crinkley, *Walter Pater: Humanist* (Lexington: University Press of Kentucky, 1970), pp. 104–30; and " 'House Beautiful,' " in Iser, *Walter Pater*, pp. 81–83.

other hand, he claims that it "arose naturally out of the spirit of man." He emphasizes the permanence of mythic conceptions, their presence still within us. They are powerful

> because they arose naturally out of the spirit of man, and embodied, in adequate symbols, his deepest thoughts concerning the conditions of his physical and spiritual life, maintained their hold through many changes, and are still not without a solemnising power even for the modern mind, which has once admitted them as recognised and habitual inhabitants. (GS, 151)

Pater's characteristic generalization of "the spirit of man" represents a transhistorical, essentialist, aesthetic figure, as we have repeatedly seen in this study, and it reflects the tendency toward synthesis and totality which forms one pole of his aesthetic historicism. If Pater's assertion of the absolute historicity of each phase of myth—its difference from others, its grounding in the peculiarities of a specific culture—were to be carried through, the resulting emphasis would be on temporal and geographical change. But this is not the case. In the *Greek Studies*, by far the greater emphasis is placed on stability, continuity, and repetition.

The volume emphasizes the similarities between mythic and modern consciousness. Pater approaches Greek mythology through the lens of his own present culture, asking, "What is there in this phase of ancient religion for us, at the present day?" (GS, 151). This approach, on the general cultural level, is analogous to the individual approach announced in the "Preface" to *The Renaissance*: "What is this song or picture . . . to me?" But that search for continuity and similarity crucially begins in a profound recognition of difference. Pater's appreciation of the distance between past and present leads to an attempt to bridge that distance with analogy. This quintessentially Paterian strategy at once tacitly acknowledges the difficulty of penetrating historical otherness and at the same time assumes that "the composite experience of all the ages is a part of each one of us," that awareness "at the present day" *can* adequately reach across the abyss of historical difference. And this binocular strategy, asserting difference while bringing it into analogy with the familiar, will as usual tend both to modernize the past and to traditionalize the present.

Pater's "modern mind" has admitted mythic conceptions as "recognised and habitual inhabitants": "there are traces of the old temper in the man of today," he asserts (GS, 100). The "phases of Greek culture" are "not without their likenesses in the modern mind" (GS, 81). For Pater, nineteenth-century English romanticism is a modern, self-conscious version of an ancient mythic consciousness. In the essay on Demeter he sees the romanticism of Wordsworth and Shelley as a modern revival of the animistic sense in which nature and "personal intelligence" inform and express one another. At the same time, conversely, he is eager to discover the romanticism in Greek myth. As in *The Renaissance*, he is at pains to throw into high relief the "worship of sorrow" (as Goethe called it) within classical Greek culture and religion (GS, 110). This move toward analogy accomplishes more than a reinterpretation of classical Greece, though that in itself remains a formidable mark of Pater's originality in these essays.[1] To discover the "worship of sorrow" within classical culture also implies its analogy with Christianity, and that further analogy in turn implies that both mythic and Christian culture prefigure their secularized, modern form in the romanticism of the nineteenth century. As in *Marius*, Christianity is secularized from both sides when it is seen as the middle term of this three-stage development.

Pater—like Sainte-Beuve, of whom he writes—delighted in

> tracing traditions in [literature], and the way in which various phases of thought and sentiment maintain themselves, through successive modifications, from epoch to epoch. (A, 244)

Pater calls this practice the "philosophy of literature." His strong emphasis on continuity in a myth's history is displayed so frequently that he often seems more interested in how "phases of thought and sentiment maintain themselves" than in their "successive modifications." Distinctions between "phases" as usual depend on the initial assumption of a continuous field, or of an overarching whole; all analogies in the "comparative science of religions" or the "theory of 'comparative mythology'" are made against this background (GS, 11, 112).

As long as Pater concentrates on Greek myth, he can base his assumption of continuity on the common language of the versions. Character names accompanied by epithets indicate fundamental unity behind or beneath apparent diversity. Demeter *Courotrophos*, Demeter *Erinnys*, Demeter *Thesmophoros*—all are "aspects" of the same mythic "person," gathered together and federated by

> the *name*, the instrument of the identification, of the given matter,—of its unity in variety, its outline or definition in mystery, its *spiritual form*. (GS, 37)

---

1. Pater "ranks among the true discoverers of Greek Romanticism" (Iser, *Walter Pater*, p. 114).

This argument should remind us of Pater's use of the "type" in *The Renaissance*, as well as of his understanding of the unifying function of mythic characterization here in the *Greek Studies*. The name is a "centripetal" force, and Pater is clearly sensitive to the aesthetic dimension of this nominalism, in which the name brings about the impression of unity among otherwise disparate features. Epithets can also indicate specific "phases" in the historical unfolding of a manifold conception.

Pater has explored this idea before in his mythic reading of the Mona Lisa, to whom he gave, as if they were her epithets, the aspects of both classical and Christian figures:

> as Leda, [she] was the mother of Helen of Troy, and, as Saint Anne, the Mother of Mary. (R, 125)

Pater's method of interpretation in the *Greek Studies* sheds a retrospective light on his treatment of the Mona Lisa, still his most famous re-creation of mythic character. She represents the "spiritual form" of history grown conscious of itself, the disparate forms unfolding in time here gathered under the auspices of one person, one character, one name. So too the stability of character in the conceptions of Demeter, Persephone, Dionysus, and Apollo is represented by their names, and a residual recognition of the differences and contradictions that have been provisionally or nominally unified is represented by their various epithets.

As long as Pater concentrates on Greek mythology, he can base his assumption of continuity on the name, but when Pater's analogies are no longer underwritten by a common language and cultural tradition, they become at once more striking and at the same time more farfetched. In an essay strictly on Greek subjects, Pater's analogies seem at first designed to illustrate the unavailable past by means of the present, to familiarize his readers with ancient conceptions that might otherwise remain occult, foreign, and inaccessibly different. But that rationale begins to strain when the analogies attempt to bridge great gulfs of historical difference. The relation between Dionysus *Eleutherios* and Dionysus *Zagreus* is asserted in the name, but how can the same "person" be the mother of Helen of Troy and the mother of Mary?

Pater's strategy of familiarization may be seen to operate with striking effect in the violence with which different traditions are yoked:

The Philosophy of Mythic Form · 253 ·

> The libations, at once a watering of the vines and a drink-offering to the dead— . . . must, to almost all minds, have had a certain natural impressiveness; and a parallel has sometimes been drawn between this festival and All Souls Day. (GS, 123)

Or, for example, while Pater is considering the Eleusinian mysteries, arguing that ritual enactment formed the dramatic basis of literary myth, he reminds us of the Christian "mysteries" of the Middle Ages. Both Greek and Christian "mysteries" present

> an artistic spectacle, . . . a dramatic representation of the sacred story . . . and what we really do see . . . are things which have their parallels in a later age, the whole being not altogether unlike a modern pilgrimage. The exposition of the sacred places . . . is not so strange, as it would seem, had it no modern illustration. (GS, 122–23)

Pater's "modern illustrations" are taken from the realm where religious and aesthetic value interpenetrate. When he calls the first historical period of Greek art "the age of graven images," his unmistakable biblical allusion recalls the language of prohibition from the Exodus narrative (GS, 224). He ends his essay "The Bacchanals of Euripides" by alluding to the medieval Christian transformations of Euripides in the *Christus Patiens* of Gregory Nazianzen, and he calls the workman of the marbles of Aegina "the Chaucer of Greek sculpture" (GS, 80, 268).

The cross-cultural analogy represents Pater's most powerful historicizing trope. Like all such tropes, it works always to relativize *both* terms of the analogy, each becoming the background for the other; the secularization-effects of the analogy extend both backward and forward in time. On the one hand, they work to familiarize the past, the culturally different, the inaccessible; on the other hand, they defamiliarize the present, the modern, the habitual. Their particular effect is most interesting and problematic when Greek myth and Christian story are brought into analogy with one another. Greek myth and ritual are vaguely Christianized, with a resultant reduction of the difference, the otherness, of Greek myth. By the same token, the Christian story is mythologized or anthropologized. Christianity is seen as a later development of something already there and an early development of something yet to be.

This strategy breaks down the notion of origins, for as Pater traces back into the obscurity of the prehistoric, there is always something prior to the earliest known recorded form. Even the Olympian gods were "conscious also of the fall of earlier divine dynasties . . . , the weary shadows of an earlier, more formless, divine world" (R, 224). And this strategy also works to generate abstract, "ethical," recurrent analogous forms seen from the point of view of retrospective reflection. Within the logic of these historicizing tropes, both Greek myth and Christian story become merely phases of something *else* that transcends them both: the identity, the continuity of Western culture, retrospectively contructed.

Let us look at some examples from the *Greek Studies* of these "ethical" types in the process of formation. Pater explains the conception of Demeter by comparing her to the Egyptian Isis, the German Hertha, and the later Greek conception of Pan (GS, 97). But his most radical effort to familiarize us with Demeter ends by relativizing his own culture's chief myth as well, for he sees Demeter in her "ethical" phase not only "humanised" as a mourning mother but also as *mater dolorosa*, Our Lady of Sorrows (GS, 114). In "Winckelmann" Pater had claimed that "there is no Greek Madonna; the goddesses are always childless" (R, 217). But in the *Greek Studies* these historical analogies work both ways, paganizing the Christian at the same time that they Christianize the pagan. As Demeter becomes Our Lady of Sorrows, the Virgin Mary implicitly begins to seem more like a fertility goddess.[2]

Finally, interpreted as both, she can be neither. What is left of the history of her transformations is Pater's distillation of an abstract, "ethical" type that federates her periodic manifestations under the auspices of an aesthetically constructed unity. From Pater's long view, Demeter the wanderer may be seen alike in the Greek myth, Michelangelo's *mater dolorosa*, and the peasant women of Corot or Wordsworth. Her conception becomes so extensive that Pater's "Demeter" finally names a transhistorical *ethos*, the "sentiment of maternity."

Pater likewise finds the types of Dionysus everywhere in art and history. As a romantic lover, Dionysus is represented with Ariadne by Titian and Tintoretto; as patron of reed instruments, he phases into Marsyas, the satyrs, and Pan; as "inherent cause of music and poetry" he is assimilable to Apollo (GS, 23, 17–18).[3] But Pater describes

2. On the significance of the Magna Mater in Pater's works, see Gerald Monsman, *Pater's Portraits* (Baltimore, Md.: Johns Hopkins University Press, 1967), pp. 18–20, 27–29, 106–7, 137–38, 166–71.

3. The dialectical relation of Dionysus to Apollo especially highlights the point where separate mythic persons are exfoliated expressions or aspects of a mythic manifold. These transhistorical myths of history seem to be a period phenomenon—see, e.g., Nietzsche's *Birth of Tragedy*. On the relation between Pater and Nietzsche, see Patrick Bridgewater, *Nietzsche in Anglosaxony* (Leicester: Leicester University Press, 1972), pp. 21–36.

him as the young, suffering god in terms that tacitly though patently allude to Christ's passion and resurrection:

> A type of second birth, from first to last, he opens, in his series of annual changes, for minds on the look-out for it, the hope of a possible analogy, between the resurrection of nature, and something else, as yet unrealised, reserved for human souls; and the beautiful, weeping creature, vexed by the wind, suffering, torn to pieces, and rejuvenescent again at last, like a tender shoot of living green out of the hardness and stony darkness of the earth, becomes an emblem or ideal of chastening and purification, and of final victory through suffering. (GS, 49–50)

This describes a "worship of sorrow" indeed, and the masochistic sexuality of the passage recalls a recurrent strain in Pater's own romanticism.[4] "Minds on the look-out" for the "hope" of this analogy must be retrospective and historicist, and Pater's coy tentativeness only emphasizes the potential force of this "something else, as yet unrealised, reserved for the human soul." But if the conception of Dionysus eventually comes to incorporate seasonal change, the seeds of cultural renaissance, the resurrection of Christ, enthusiasm and ecstasy in general, and the rebirth of the individual soul—where, then, is "Dionysus"?

Dionysus as a "person" disappears in the kaleidoscopic array of his "aspects." And as the culturally specific mythic character disappears into an infinite number of "possible" analogical relations, the spiritual value of the conception correspondingly grows. As Pater points out, "the human form is a limiting influence" (GS, 34). But Pater's form of interpretation undoes that limitation. He concentrates (perforce) on the period of time after the personal, mythic character has coalesced as a unity, when reflection paradoxically seems to reverse the concentration of physical form. The same struggle he recognizes in the history of Greek art is also apparent in his own work:

> there is a struggle, a *Streben*, as the Germans say, between the palpable and limited human form, and the floating essence it is to contain. (GS, 34)

This spiritualizing tendency is intimately tied, in Pater's scheme of mythic development, to the passage of time and the distance of retrospection. His own long view stresses the "ethical" phase of myth, "in

---

4. On masochism in romantic literature, see Mario Praz, *The Romantic Agony* (London: Oxford University Press, 1970).

which the persons and the incidents of the poetical narrative are realised as abstract symbols, because intensely characteristic examples, of moral or spiritual conditions" (GS, 91). But Pater's is not only a particularly late development of the ethical phase; it has also been located in a cross-cultural register. That crucial focus causes Pater's scheme of the three phases of myth to be transposed or transfigured. The schematic development Pater offers for Greek myth—oral, literary, and ethical phases—is transposed in the larger conceptual scheme of his own cross-cultural perspective to the Greek, the Christian, and the modern, synthetic, and secularized phases.

The deeper Pater goes beneath the surface of historical change (or the "higher" above it), the more equivalencies he finds, until all phenomenal manifestations seem to be only "aspects" of the same permanent material, shaped anew from time to time. He uses, for example, the history of a symbol to illustrate the flexibility with which it can be adopted to almost any use. The pomegranate,

> because of the multitude of its seeds, was to the Romans a symbol of fecundity, and was sold at the doors of the temple of Ceres, that the women might offer it there, and bear numerous children; and so, to the middle age, became a symbol of the fruitful earth itself; and then of that other seed sown in the dark under-world; and at last of that whole hidden region, so thickly sown, which Dante visited, Michelino painting him, in the *Duomo* of Florence, with this fruit in his hand, and Botticelli putting it into the childish hands of Him, who, if men "go down into hell, is there also." (GS, 150–51)

Finally there are pomegranates everywhere, their dizzying profusion testifying to nothing so much as the fluidity of signification. In a chain of symbolic appropriation over time, Pater's pomegranate represents fertility as well as the barrenness of the underworld, sexual generation as well as the fertility of the earth in general, the mythic underworld as well as Dante's literary inferno, and finally the Renaissance association of the infernal fruit with Christ himself, the penetration of the mythic underworld by Christian poet and its appropriation by Christian painter. Needless to say, the story of Persephone, eating six seeds in the despair of Hades, is quite lost.

Similarly, Pater finds the myth of Persephone everywhere:

> Her story is, indeed, but the story, in an intenser form, of Adonis, of Hyacinth, of Adrastus—the King's blooming son, fated in the story of Herodotus, to be wounded to death with an iron spear—of Linus, a fair

child who is torn to pieces by hounds every spring-time—of the English Sleeping Beauty. (GS, 109)

Here we see the extreme form of literary comparativism at work, with all its gains and attendant losses. All stories for a moment seem to be the story of Persephone, in one "phase" of its development or another.[5] In Orphic poetry she is associated with Dionysus *Zagreus* (GS, 44, 51), so that even the largest most comprehensive and "separate" mythic forms seem finally only shape-shifting "aspects" of one another.

This phenomenon is at the foundation of mythic conception itself, since myth attempts to represent the whole of human experience, in all of its aspects. Neither the characters nor the stories will stay separate; they ramify into one another with more complexity and confusion the closer one looks. The dialectical duality of Persephone's character testifies to its mythic, unifying power; the fact that Persephone and Dionysus can "mean" the most opposite things—can even blend into and "mean" each other—is exactly their point. My crucial point is that Pater conceives his histories of myth in precisely the same way. His cross-cultural analogies finally reveal so many connections and overlappings that every version of every story seems to be part of a vast totality, a deep and stable structure that reiteratively expresses itself throughout history.

Pater considers this problem himself in the *Greek Studies*. He recalls that Plato objects in *The Republic* to all episodes of mythology that represent doubling, disguise, or metamorphosis, because those episodes violate the stability of form and teach a dangerous "Heraclitean philosophy of perpetual change." But Pater defends those episodes of doubling and transformation against Plato's charges; for Pater, characteristically, they signify spiritual "presence":

> Stories in which, the hard material outline breaking up, the gods lay aside their visible form like a garment, yet remain essentially themselves, —[are] not the least spiritual element of Greek religion, an evidence of the sense therein of unseen presences, which might ... be recognised ... by the more delicately trained eye.... Whatever religious elements they lacked, they had at least this sense of subtler and more remote ways of personal presence. (GS, 119–20)

He attributes to these stories a "quite biblical mysticity and solemnity," bringing mythic metamorphosis into a familiarizing analogy

---

5. A similarly extreme, "mythic" literary-historical method is practiced by Frye with some of the same results. See esp. Northrop Frye, *The Secular Scripture* (Cambridge, Mass.: Harvard University Press, 1976).

with Judeo-Christian transfiguration. It is clear that his own historical analogies highlight episodes of just such doubling and transformation in time. As it grows less "personal" and more "remote," religious "presence" is more clearly aestheticized; the dizzying play of secularization-effects generates aesthetic value where a more directly accessible "presence" was once thought to have been. In the "ethical" or abstract phase of myth, Pater attends more to repetition than to difference, more to the characteristic element than to the character. As myth is historicized, and thus released from its culturally specific religious function, its aesthetic value appreciates proportionately, fed by the energy of these transformations.

From one point of view, to secularize is to "demythologize," to empty a cultural form of its religious content and to refill it with aesthetic value. But in Pater's case, to secularize is also to "remythologize," to posit a mythic unity and structure of repetition in history that transcends its different periods or "aspects."

## 4 · The History of Philosophy

Published in 1893, *Plato and Platonism* was based on the series of lectures Pater delivered at Oxford in 1891–92, close to the end of his life.[1] He had been thinking about Plato and the history of Greek philosophy throughout his career,[2] and in many ways the volume stands as a summary statement not only of Pater's views on Plato but also (and more important for our present purposes) of his own most habitual argumentative strategies. In *Plato and Platonism* he is more explicit than ever before about many issues that will seem familiar to us by now.

For example, Pater opens by grappling with the adjustment of the organic model of development to the aesthetic model: "With the world

---

1. A useful compendium of sources on Pater as a lecturer may be found in Wright, *Bibliography of Pater*, pp. 179–83.
2. Pater began lecturing on "the history of philosophy" as early as 1867 (ibid., p. 182). He probably read Grote's *History of Greece* in 1861, Zeller's *Philosophie der Greichen* in 1863, and K. O. Müller's *Die Dorier* in the 1870s (Billie Andrew Inman, *Walter Pater's Reading: A Bibliography of His Library Borrowings and Literary References* [New York: Garland, 1981], pp. 25, 64–65, 98). On the contemporary sources of Pater's argument in *Plato and Platonism*, see William F. Shuter, "Pater on Plato: 'Subjective' or 'Sound'?" in *Prose Studies* 5 (September 1982), 215–28; and Turner, *The Greek Heritage*, pp. 406–14.

of intellectual production, as with that of organic generation, nature makes no sudden starts" (PP, 5). Following out the implications of that opening analogy, he asserts in no uncertain terms that political institutions, laws, arts, and language, "all the products of mind, the very mind itself . . . are 'not made,' cannot be made, but 'grow'" (PP, 20–21). Therefore traces of previous forms of life will be visible in later forms, as if preserved in geological or archaeological strata. Bits of older philosophies reside within Plato's formulations as "minute relics of earlier organic life in the very stone he builds with" (PP, 7). And yet within this very statement is a tacit acknowledgment of the aesthetic, shaping act implicit in historical conception, for Plato "builds" with the "stone" that has been formed from the residue of previously organic life. His work marks the transition from oral to literary culture, prehistoric to historical culture, organic to aesthetic culture.

Pater makes it clear that Plato has always "seemed" to be the "creator of philosophy" only because of his consummate literary form. Close to Pater's claim that "nature makes no sudden starts" is his explicit acknowledgment that to "fix" on this beginning is his own aesthetic choice. Indeed, Pater begins by stressing the "organic" beginnings before this "aesthetic" beginning, the prehistoric oral culture that survives only in fragments, the "unconscious poetry" that precedes philosophy (PP, 5–7). One of the tenets of Pater's particular version of organicism holds that the basic genetic material is present from the first; the "seeds" of all science were "dimly enfolded" in the mind of antiquity, to be "fecundated . . . in after ages" (PP, 18). He proceeds to argue that no matter is new under the sun. But the other side of Pater's synthetic view emphasizes the difference of forms rather than the sameness of matter:

> It is hardly an exaggeration to say that in Plato . . . there is nothing absolutely new: or rather . . . the seemingly new is old also, a palimpsest, a tapestry of which the actual threads have served before, or like the animal frame itself, every particle of which has already lived and died many times over. Nothing but the life-giving principle of cohesion is new. . . . In other words, the *form* is new. But then, in the creation of philosophical literature, as in all other products of art, *form*, in the full signification of that word, is everything, and the mere matter is nothing. (PP, 8)

The juxtaposition of figures in this passage expresses Pater's attraction to both organic and aesthetic models in this ongoing argument, with images of revisionary writing and weaving followed by an image of the generic "animal frame." The very principle Pater here asserts must be reflexively applied to his own text, for all these figures are familiar Paterian material: the metaphor of the palimpsest has figured prominently in *Marius*; the recycled "threads" are familiar from the opening paragraphs of the "Conclusion" and the essay on Coleridge; and the example of the animal frame resonates with the description of the physical basis of life in the "Conclusion" as well as with Pater's many mythical portraits of "spiritual form"—the Mona Lisa, Dionysus, now Plato himself.

In fact, what we find here, as in the *Greek Studies*, is Pater's representation of the pivotal and mythic moment when organic, unconscious life first develops consciousness, when history and literature emerge within and against the primeval manifold. Pater focuses this moment in the history of philosophy by explicitly relying on Hegel's definition of tragedy, which takes the life and death of Socrates as its case in point. Genuine tragedy, Hegel argues, cannot be "merely personal." Instead, it occurs when two "opposed Rights come forth" and "the one breaks itself to pieces against the other." In the case of Socrates, Hegel defines these two opposed Rights as, on the one hand, "the religious claim, the unconscious moral habit," and, on the other hand, "the equally religious claim, the claim of consciousness." This conflict engenders the moment when the claim of consciousness emerges as "the common principle of philosophy for all time to come" (PP, 91–92). In Hegel's example, the historic shift into consciousness—indeed, the shift into history itself—is represented by Socrates and the concretely dialectical response to his life and teachings: the death penalty, which, instead of obliterating them, immortalized the claims of consciousness. Pater refigures this Hegelian example to make Plato the representative of literary self-consciousness retrospectively acknowledging its Socratic, preliterary, "organic" roots.

Pater's treatment of his own "historic method" is much more explicitly linked in *Plato and Platonism* to the contemporary influence both of Hegel and of Darwin than ever before (PP, 8–9, 19). Pater implicitly makes a distinction between two aspects of the method, which we would call the synchronic and the diachronic, but both these aspects of his method have been influenced by Hegel and by Darwin. On the one hand, Pater pursues the uniquely adjusted synchronic "fit" between an organism and its environment, attempting to "replace" the doctrine of Plato within the "conditions" of its production. This argument has affinities with Pater's understanding of natural selection as well as with his belief in the personal character of the " 'Time-Spirit' or *Zeit-geist*":

> That ages have their genius as well as the individual; that in every age there is a peculiar *ensemble* of conditions which determines a common character in every product of that age . . . ; that nothing man has projected from himself is really intelligible except at its own date, and from its proper point of view in the never-resting "secular process"; . . . by force of these convictions many a normal, or at first sight abnormal, phase of speculation has found a reasonable meaning for us. (PP, 9–10)

The weirdly twisted pine tree that is unintelligible on an English lawn becomes intelligible when we imagine the Alpine forces that have "determined" its shape; so too "fantastic doctrines" like Plato's " 'communism' " must be seen amid the conditions that produced them. This synchronic aspect of Pater's historic method might be called "anthropological" in a particularly prestructuralist mode, and in *Plato and Platonism* he frequently reaches toward racial and geographical arguments as ways to make this approach more concrete. Often Pater places the word "environment" in quotation marks, as if to call attention to the neologism of the hour (e.g., PP, 10). He is sharply aware of the contemporary vogue for this line of argument, naming it as one of the most popular questions of his own day (PP, 154).

In *Plato and Platonism*, Pater seems to have theorized the dialectical relation between the synchronic and diachronic aspects of his "historic method," treating them both as parts of the "centripetal" tendency, the unifying force that spatially links organism to environment and temporally links "one period of organic growth to another" (PP, 105). (Pater tellingly describes this "centripetal" force as the organic become conscious of itself.) The relation between synchronic and diachronic is expressed in the form of the volume, which in its largest sense is an attempt to describe the history of philosophy using Plato as the figure of originary wholeness. Antecedent forms of thought that give rise to Plato's philosophy are treated as the synchronic "environment" within which he writes. Not until chapter 6 does Pater turn to the argument that we must judge Plato by his followers as well as by his antecedents. Thus the form of the volume is itself an essay in the "historic method": five chapters "placing" Plato within the "conditions" of his own time and place, then five chapters exfoliating Plato's "genius," his doctrines, and their influence in later ages.

The form of Pater's diachronic argument displays the full finesse of his dialectic (though the diachronic dimension is finally subsumed by the synchronic, as we shall see). Pater first sketches a three-stage dialectical process leading up to Plato, in which the philosophies of Heraclitus, Parmenides, and Pythagoras represent thesis, antithesis, and synthesis—the principles of "motion," "rest," and "number." The Heraclitean flux and the Parmenidean One are evaluated antithetically, from two sides, both for what each doctrine has contributed to Platonism and for what has been most stringently argued against each one. Heraclitus rightly appreciates the radical uniqueness of phenomenal forms, but his "centrifugal" doctrine leads to chaos. On the other hand, Parmenides creates a conception of unity, but at the expense of color and form; his idea of the One seems to many people to be "but zero, and a mere algebraic symbol for nothingness" (PP, 40). In an intensely witty formulation, Pater explains that the reaction against Heraclitus' philosophy of motion was a "fixed idea" with Plato (PP, 12). Likewise, Plato reacted against the Parmenidean "infectious mania . . . for nonentity" with a more mobile *axiomata media* (PP, 40, 42).

Pater's interpretation of the Pre-Socratics calls attention to the dialectical reversal that engenders the doctrine of rest directly out of the doctrine of motion: Zeno, favorite disciple of Parmenides, was an adept in "dialectic art," and Zeno's paradox demonstrates that "perpetual motion is perpetual rest" (PP, 28–30). The Pythagorean theory, however, achieves a reconciliation of motion and rest without conflating the two principles as a paradoxical identity. The theory of number and music formulates *cosmos* as "unity in variety," structure in motion (PP, 52). For Pater, the essence of the Pythagorean doctrine lies not in the infinite but in the finite, and he defines "art as being itself the finite, ever controlling the infinite, the formless" (PP, 60). This emphasis is characteristically Paterian. Though this dialectic of motion, rest, and number is once again the familiar tripartite scheme of romantic history, "music" (the chosen end term of Pater's dialectic) privileges a "higher multiplicity" rather than a "higher unity," motion directed toward rest rather than rest itself, dialectic rather than paradoxical identity or harsh dualism.

Indeed, one dimension of Pater's argument in *Plato and Platonism* treats each of the historically concrete figures (Heraclitus, Parmenides, Pythagoras, Socrates, the Sophists, and Plato) as representatives of permanent "tendencies" or recurring types in "the human mind itself." Pater argues, for example, that the Heraclitean doctrine of perpetual flux has only been fully realized in his own age:

> It is the burden of Hegel on the one hand, to whom nature, and art, and polity, and philosophy, aye, and religion too, each in its long historic series, are but so many conscious movements in the secular process of the eternal mind; and on the other hand of Darwin and Darwinism, for which "type" itself properly *is* not but is only always *becoming*. (PP, 19)

In this view, the theory of development itself has developed from an ancient seed, "fecundated . . . in later ages." Similarly, Pater finds Greek, Indian, and Christian expressions of the Parmenidean One (PP, 40–41), and he asserts that Pythagoreanism represents a permanent instinct "of the human mind itself," which is therefore expressed as a periodically recurring emphasis, a tradition in human history. This amounts to asserting the periodic recurrence of a theory of recurrence, since the Pythagoreans contributed the doctrine of spiritual preexistence to the Platonic synthesis. Pater closes the chapter on Pythagoras with a quotation from Vaughan's "The Retreat" and the invocation of Wordsworth's Intimations Ode, thus bringing the philosophy of preexistence, recurrence, or "re-action" up to date (PP, 73–74). Elsewhere in the volume, Pater names various historically recurrent forms of "animism" ranging from the Homeric conception of an anthropomorphic pantheon, to Plato's theory of ideas, to the "survival"[3] of this spiritual condition in the primitive negro, to the culture of Wordsworth, Shelley, Goethe, and Schelling (PP, 168–69). In each of these cases, historical difference is practically effaced in the service of familiarizing analogies.[4]

So we see that the extremely broad-brush cross-cultural analogies that Pater drew throughout the *Greek Studies* operate in *Plato and Platonism* as well, on the largest level of its argument. In *Plato and Platonism* less emphasis is placed on the specific relation of Greek to

---

3. In nineteenth-century anthropology the word "survival" carried overtones of Tylor, Hegel, and possibly Vico. See William Shuter, "History as Palingenesis in Pater and Hegel," *PMLA* 86 (May 1971), 411–21. On Vico in the English nineteenth century, see Peter Allan Dale, *The Victorian Critic and the Idea of History* (Cambridge, Mass.: Harvard University Press, 1977), pp. 50–51, 106–9; and A. Dwight Culler, *The Victorian Mirror of History* (New Haven, Conn.: Yale University Press, 1985), pp. 80–81, 139. On Vico and Pater, see Inman, *Pater's Reading*, pp. 148–57.

4. See U. C. Knoepflmacher's treatment of these analogies in *Religious Humanism and the Victorian Novel* (Princeton, N.J.: Princeton University Press, 1965), pp. 175–78, and David DeLaura's response in *Hebrew and Hellene in Victorian England* (Austin: University of Texas Press, 1969), pp. 297–99.

Christian religious expression, and more emphasis is put on the general structure of repetition implied by these analogies. This "side" of Pater's historicism has always been present, and it has always tended toward a myth of recurrence which transcends the diverse, ephemeral surface of things in the search for a deeper (or "higher") structure of permanent form. But this dimension of historicism has never before been so explicitly formulated as the framework of a volume's general argument. Pater might say that the form of *Plato and Platonism* truly expresses its matter, for in his discussion of Plato's theory of Ideas, Pater discusses the formation of these general Forms. Nowhere else in his works do we find such a crisp and summary statement of Pater's understanding of the problematic relation between representative terms and particular instances.

Chapters 3 through 5 construct a second level of dialectical argument. Chapter 5 concentrates on the Sophists, the contemporary background against which Pater defines himself, while chapters 3 and 4 focus on Pythagoras and Socrates, precursor figures of synthesis who are each identified with Plato. In other words, after Pater has sketched the three-stage dynamic of Pre-Socratic development, he turns to focus on two figures, each of whom mirrors and prefigures Plato's own dual nature. Both these prefigurative relations mediate the emergence of Plato from the obscurity of the preliterary, the development of self-consciousness from within an "organic" ground. This function is especially clear in Pater's treatment of Socrates, whose relation to Plato he takes as the model of "educated common-sense" transformed into a higher, "mystic intellectualism" (PP, 85). The Platonic dialogue is "the literary transformation ... of what was the intimately home-grown method of Socrates" (PP, 177). Though we have no writings of Socrates, we have in Plato's literary recreation the memory not only of a vivid historical character but also of the prehistoric roots of literature itself.

But Pater's ability to cast Pythagoras as a mythic figure of synthesis is also due in part to the fact that his writings have not survived except in fragments; "nothing remains of his writings: dark statements only ... in later authors" (PP, 52). In other words, the Pythagorean theory has the status of primitive, mythic unity, and Pythagoras' life is also susceptible to such a mythic interpretation, because many stories have been passed down of his descent from Apollo and his legendary reincarnation as "various persons in the course of ages" (PP, 53–54). As usual, Pater bolsters this mythic interpretation with historical evidence, giving it a slightly allegorial twist. Pythagoras was a native of Ionia who later settled in a Dorian city, and Pater makes that geographical movement and habitation symbolic of Pythagoras' philosophy, its self-conscious choice of a "musical discipline" over the fluidity of the phenomenal world. For Pater, Pythagoras embodies the dominance of centripetal forces over centrifugal forces, which he will find so saliently at work in Plato (PP, 56).

The relation between Plato and Pythagoras is abstract. Plato, like Pythagoras, consummates the development of the Pre-Socratics. By identifying him with Pythagoras, Pater suggests that Plato assimilates the synthetic, "musical law" of unity in variety. But Plato's relation with Socrates, on the other hand, is historically concrete. Like Pythagoras, Socrates was a "two-sided being" (according to Alcibiades in the *Symposium*), and Pater plays with this traditional notion in several ways (PP, 76). The ungraceful appearance of Socrates (again as attested by Alcibiades) suggests to Pater the Platonic distinction between phenomenal appearance and a higher reality, as if the source of Plato's theory of ideas might have been his puzzlement at the rude physiognomy of his master. This personal connection with Socrates is at the heart of Pater's interpretation of Plato. In a characteristic transition he passes, after a typographical break, from considering Socrates' vision of an afterlife to imagining its effect on Plato: "Plato was then about twenty-eight years old" (PP, 97). Pater loves to imagine these moments of timely conjunction, when two historical figures may be conceived in personal relation; his fables of historical transmission turn on such pivot-points, which seem to enfold the past and the future in a blaze of imagined presence.[5] These moments are themselves two-sided figures, for they join two historically separate persons in a momentary unity, from which will issue the divided forms of the future.

In Pater's historical dialectic, a "two-sided" figure signifies the momentary synthesis of past influences and the generative force toward further development. Thus Pater also interprets Socrates' synthetic nature in terms of its historical generativity. In his own time, Socrates gave rise to antithetical classes of enemies—both the Sophists and the anti-Sophists opposed him—and in later days his constitutional "twofold power" gave rise to "an influence... of which there emerged on the one hand the Cynic, on the other the Cyrenaic School" (PP, 75, 87, 89). Plato of course is also a two-sided figure, joining in his philosophy the greatest possible demand for certainty in knowledge

---

5. The relation between Pico and Ficino, for example, which is historically documented (though not as Pater reports); or the imaginary relation he constructs between Goethe and Winckelmann; or the momentary image of Raphael, at age nineteen, watching Leonardo and Michelangelo work (R, 36–37, 196–97, 127).

with the utmost possible uncertainty in his method of inquiry (PP, 188). This paradoxical union is the generative seed of two very different traditions in the history of philosophy, both of which Pater attributes to the influence of Plato: an ontological tradition, which develops from his demand for absolute knowledge, and a skeptical tradition, which develops from his dialectical method (PP, 192–96). In Pater's history of philosophy, then, Plato figures as mythic unity, expressed in literary form. He represents a moment of wholeness that will be split afterward into "divergent streams," a synthesis of everything that came before it, which generates everything that came after. Pater's Plato enfolds within him the entire history of philosophy.[6]

## 5 · The Anecdote of the Shell

The nature of the relation between general terms and particular objects of experience, says Pater, is "one of the constant problems of logic," and what Plato's commentators have called his "theory of ideas" is not so much a theory as a way of regarding this relation (PP, 150–51). Pater presents his readers with the three "fixed and formal" answers to this problem—realism, nominalism, and conceptualism. Then, instead of explaining Plato's theory of ideas, he gives the "modern view" of the "nature of logical 'universals' " (PP, 151–52).

Pater's modern view synthesizes elements of all three "fixed" formulations. He tacitly agrees with the realists that the general term is *res*, a real thing. He agrees with the conceptualists that general terms are the product of subjective thought, but he interprets "subjective" not on the individual level but on the level of general culture. This is a crucial move, and it enables him to base his own "theory of ideas" on a collective or "general consciousness, a permanent common sense." Finally, he gives the nominalist his due by explaining that the individual is in touch with this collective consciousness through the medium of language. The language provides general terms as outlines that

---

6. Harvard MS. 3, "History of Philosophy": "successive metaphysical systems have been, in fact, little more than so many recombinations of the pieces which Plato had so long ago placed, once, for all upon the board" (Inman, *Pater's Reading*, 42). Jenkyns recalls Whitehead's remark that European philosophy could safely be characterized as a series of footnotes to Plato and comments: "This is a remark which could only have been made in the later nineteenth or earlier twentieth century" (Richard Jenkyns, "Plato," in *The Victorians and Ancient Greece* [Cambridge, Mass.: Harvard University Press, 1980], pp. 227–63).

the individual then fills up with meaning, "drop by drop," through personal experience in time. On the other hand, the language develops these general terms over the course of historical time as a result of particular experience. Whether a particular experience "survives" to become a general term has everything to do with conscious repetition; the formation of a type, in other words, is a testimony to its perceived recurrence, the residual evidence of a tradition that has formed "in the human mind itself."

Let us look at one telling example. Pater argues that the quarrel between Plato and the Sophists was in part quite characteristic of its age, and in part it was "a mere rivalry of individuals." As such, he goes on to say, the quarrel might have been remembered "only as a matter of historical interest." I would like to focus on that striking word "only." What sort of interest does Pater have in mind that would surpass the merely historical? He goes on to explain:

> It has been otherwise. That innocent word "Sophist" has survived in common language, to indicate some constantly recurring viciousness, in the treatment of one's own and of other minds. (PP, 115)

The sense of repetition generates a value that has its basis in, but tends to transcend, the historical. A term's survival in the "common language" is evidence for the general value of that term, and conversely, the process of survival involves repetition in contexts other than the original, "only" historical, context. The transposition of a term from one particular historical context to another actually generates representative value, which can then be used to "figure" further particularity. In Pater's interpretation, then, the history of language is another vehicle of his aesthetic historicism.

Pater analyzes this same process in the chapter on Plato's theory of ideas, where he discusses the operation of general terms. Well aware that the "type" might seem to violate the claims of each particular instance, he begins by playing devil's advocate for the particular:

> We cannot love or live upon *genus* and *species*, . . . but for our minds, as for our bodies, need an orchard or a garden, with fruit and roses. Take a seed from the garden. What interest it has for us all lies in our sense of potential differentiation to come: the leaves, leaf upon leaf, the flowers, a thousand new seeds in turn. It is so with animal seed; and with humanity, individually, or as a whole, its expansion into a detailed, ever-changing, parti-coloured history of particular facts and persons. Abstraction, the introduction of general ideas, seems to close it up again; to reduce flower

and fruit, odour and savour, back again into the dry and worthless seed.
We might as well be colour-blind at once . . . ! (PP, 155)

The value of particularity here is clearly associated with organic, historical process, whereas "abstraction" obliterates the temporal dimension so necessary to produce difference. Pater then considers the state of things from his own present-day perspective, when everything seems to be classified and "reduced to common types." Into the garden of unfolding difference the philosopher-as-classifier has come.

To that gaudy tangle . . . the systematic, logical gardener put his meddlesome hand, and straightway all ran to seed; to *genus* and *species* and *differentia* . . . with—yes! with written labels fluttering on the stalks, instead of blossoms. (PP, 156)

The "seed" here has been wittily transvalued from its context in the earlier passage. Instead of the organic potential for future growth and differentiation, it now figures the messy and decaying end of a life cycle. Blossoms have been replaced by labels, organic life by writing, and unfolding differentiation by names, categories, *differentia*. The "logical gardener" tends to the generic names of things, not to the unique particularity of living things themselves. He has transformed the profusion of natural process and has made of it a ruined garden. Pater's secularizing wit here turns on the notion that too much naming in the garden has resulted in a fallen language as well as the ruination of the Edenic garden.

And according to the hypothetical case Pater is putting, all this is the result of a "generalising movement" that effectively begins with Socrates and Plato. The Homeric world before this "generalising movement" began now seems to be a golden age, when "experience was intuition, and life a continuous surprise, and every object unique, where all knowledge was still of the concrete and the particular, face to face delightfully" (PP, 156). In this figure the value of particularity is clearly associated *not* with history but with a myth of immediacy. Pater has taken Socrates and Plato as the dividing line between mythic immediacy and historical mediation, the beginning of a process that has culminated in the modern "reduction" of everything to "common types."

But Pater's argument then turns abruptly to defend the modern profusion of general terms. The particular instance gains in value through classification, he argues. What seems at first to be a reduction of concrete experience turns out to be its enhancement. The general term has a power to focus the intense particularity of a concrete form.

To illustrate this epistemological process, Pater tells a little story, which I call "The Anecdote of the Shell."[1] Unlike the trained naturalist, an ordinary person picking up a shell on the seashore will not understand the value of classification, "the subsumption of the individual into the species." That ordinary person with his seashell is like a child with a toy. When the child goes to school, he must put away his toys, and it seems for a very long while as if he studies everything except the thing itself. He studies other shells, the perfect type of each sort of shell, the general laws operating in the life of shells. But when he comes out of school and again on the seashore finds another shell, his "converse with the general" enables him really to see the shell in all its vivid concreteness. Through his knowledge of its difference from other objects, even its difference from its own perfect type, he sees the shell's particularity as if for the first time. Indeed, he has learned "*about* it." It has been enriched by juxtaposition with everything around it, everything that is "*not* it," and now "the whole circumjacent world [is] concentrated upon, or . . . at focus in, it." We should recognize here Pater's figure of concentric definition, which features a point focused within a surrounding field.[2] A long experience in time has engendered this ability to collapse time: to see "in a single moment of vision," to read "by a kind of short-hand," the shell's "legible" alliance with the entire world (PP, 157–58).[3]

Pater's "Anecdote of the Shell" bears a marked relation to Plato's own pedagogical allegories, but it is significant that Pater shifts his emphasis from the individual's process of learning to the general historical process, and in so doing also changes the figure:

> You may draw, by the use of this coinage (it is Hobbes's figure) this coinage of representative words and thoughts, at your pleasure, upon the accumulative capital of the whole experience of humanity. (PP, 159)

Here Pater throws the emphasis on the long course of general history that has produced (or "coined") general terms for individuals to spend in their own experiences of learning. The language is like a communal fund: it provides general terms that individual experience draws upon,

---

1. After Wallace Stevens's "Anecdote of the Jar," which considers the same problem from the other direction, focusing on the power of a concrete form to organize the "slovenly wilderness" around it.
2. See above, Part Two, sec. 5.
3. See McGrath's treatment of this anecdote, which he correctly calls a "parable" (F. C. McGrath, *The Sensible Spirit* [Tampa: University of South Florida Press, 1986], pp. 154–62).

and each generation can contribute to the fund by coining new general terms, new "common types," that accrue value through the accumulated sense of repeated use.

Pater holds fast to the "modern view" in this understanding of the historical construction of general terms. For him, as for Darwin, "the 'type' itself *is* not but is only always *becoming*" (PP, 19). And yet, at any given time, it effectively *is*. As Pater explained in his description of Diaphaneitè, certain general types are recognized by "the world." Such a general category is treated as given, *datum*, its value produced by the accumulated repetitions of past experience. Pater's is a limited, historical idealism.

What is most important for us to see is that this treatment of general ideas differs radically from Plato's. Pater elides the difficult notion—which he, following Aristotle, duly mentions—that Plato makes his Ideas "separable" from their phenomenal, shadowy instantiations (PP, 163). Instead, Pater continues to focus on the Platonic figure of the "ladder" by which we reach the Forms by means of their phenomenal forms. According to Aristotle, Plato's great step beyond Socratic induction was in making the Ideas "separable" from their instances, but according to Pater, Plato's advance over Socrates was instead to make the Ideas real things and then to make them *persons* (PP, 166–67). Thus, even while preserving his "modern" emphasis on the historical construction of general ideas, Pater manages to invest them with a mythic, Platonic value.

Pater follows Plato in claiming the "enthusiasm" for ideas as a true form of possession (PP, 172). But his possession by the ideas, types, or Forms differs significantly from Plato's. Like other "moderns," Pater's greatest affinity is for the other "side" of Plato's doctrine—not its passion for the acquisition of "'eternal and immutable ideas,'" but the practice or method of a tentative, hesitant, never-concluding aspiration toward "ideals" (PP, 195). This modern emphasis is all on the side of becoming, of process, of "tendency." Its philosophical practice is called dialectic.

## 6 · Dialogue and Dialectic

On the one hand, Pater's interpretation of Platonic dialectic assumes the priority of real dialogue, of an actual conversation between two or more different interlocutors. On the other hand, that reality exists in memory or aspiration—in life, but not in art—and Pater is unusually sensitive to the fact that what we actually have before us is a literary form, the written record or imaginary representation of an experience, not the thing itself. For Pater, the memory of the Socratic method, preserved in Plato's literary form, stands as one more mythic representation of a lost archaic past when experience was direct, informal, and took place "face to face." The informal, oral conversations of Socrates figure in Pater as "the first rough, natural growth," the organic ground from which Plato's written, formal Dialogues spring (PP, 79, 177). However, if the Dialogues are but a representation of experience, figures of life and not life itself, still they get closer to the reality of experience than Sophistic argument, which Pater characterizes as "mechanical" by comparison (PP, 100).

For Pater, dialectic is the most lifelike form of philosophical inquiry. Plato himself admits that " 'like ourselves, our discourses . . . have much participation in the temerity of chance' " (PP, 185). In his discussion of Plato's method, Pater focuses on this quality of accident or surprise, of new information or argumentative force suddenly appearing from "without," as if in conversational exchange. For that reason the dialogue form appropriately "figures" and lends its name to the dialectical method of argumentation (PP, 183). In dialogue, the philosophical advantages of subjective relativism take literary form; points of view are represented as separate persons, proper names marking their difference from one another. Both dialogue and dialectic make difference, separation, and distinction graphically visible as a part of their effective method. The search for knowledge is seen as a function of communal experience, and it is developmental in form. Knowledge unfolds in time. A sequence of conversational exchanges represents the necessarily tentative, skeptical approach to knowledge, the repeated adjustments in response to new information, the never-concluding aspiration toward a view more complete than anyone's "separate" human perspective could ever achieve.

Dialectic represents the life of the mind as movement toward that complete perspective. The movement is never-ending, because complete knowledge can never be fully achieved in human time; like "life itself," the dialectical method admits further possible movement until the end (PP, 185). One of Pater's favorite figures for the dialectical process compares it to the ascent of a mountain. On the way up, one perspective succeeds another until finally, at the mountaintop, the climber achieves "what Plato would call the 'synoptic' view of the mountain as a whole" (PP, 180). But as Pater notes, while in the process of climbing, when dealing with other persons, there is room for error up until the very last moment. "Another turn in the endless road may change the whole character of the perspective" (PP, 190). A literary dialogue closes, and thus it provides an equivalent of the synoptic view in its retrospective "sense of an ending." But the dialectical process never ends. For those who pursue it thoroughly, it is "co-extensive with life itself" (PP, 185).

Portraying dialectic as "co-extensive with life itself" is quite a different matter from saying that it is "like" life. On the one hand, Pater assumes that an actual dialogue took place prior to Plato's literary re-creation; his belief in the mythic priority of Socrates to Plato, of oral culture to literary culture, leads Pater to make actual dialogue between persons the model for dialectical method. Yet, on the other hand, he assumes that "the dialogue of the mind with itself" is the original activity, which both actual conversation and literary dialogue simply express (PP, 183). To make "the dialogue of the mind with itself" his fundamental category in a discussion of Plato is a bold and characteristic move on Pater's part, which again reveals much more about his own "modern view" than it does about Platonic dialectic. In *Plato and Platonism* this last Paterian adaptation of Arnold's famous phrase has the effect of equating dialectic with the rise of self-consciousness, interiority, and aesthetic-historical expression.

Pater develops this side of his argument in several ways. For example, he makes a traditional association of Socrates and Plato with the rise of Greek humanism or individualism. Against the "lifeless background of . . . the unconscious social aggregate," the "conscious individual, . . . the Greek had stepped forth, like the young prince in the fable, to set things going" (PP, 21). This romance "fable" casts Socrates as the practitioner of the momentous historical shift inward, the first philosopher to turn from star-gazing to the "cosmical order" within. Thus it is truly said, Pater reports, that "Socrates brought philosophy down from heaven to earth" (PP, 81). Again equating dialectic with an interior process, Pater formulates the difference between sophistry and true dialectic as a matter of insides and outsides. The essential sophistic "vice" derived from the fact that their hold on things was merely external, or "*superficial*," whereas dialectical treatment yields and expresses an internal hold on the subject matter under consideration (PP, 116–18). The essential function of the Socratic method was to create such a self-conscious interiority, "to flash light into the house within."

> Fully occupied there, as with his own essential business in his own home, the young man would become, of course, proportionately less interested . . . in what was superficial, in the mere outsides. (PP, 120)

This domestic fantasy of internal order is more Pater's than Plato's, a variation of the Paterian figure of the "house of thought." Pater goes on to attribute to Socrates a desire, which Pater calls the "central business of education," to teach young men their importance to themselves (PP, 90, 120, 139).[1] The fulfillment of humanism in Paterian terms is found here at its very origins in the sense that self-knowledge is somehow "sacramental" (PP, 91).

Pater manages this remarkable shift inward in part through his treatment of the Platonic doctrine of recollection. He discusses the *Meno* in his chapter on the Pythagorean influence. "Eristic Meno" asks Socrates whether learning can reasonably be possible: How can we reach the utterly unfamiliar? How can we learn what we do not already know? Of course, the famous Platonic answer is that we *do* already know: one can learn because one innately has access to knowledge through reminiscence. Learning is a matter of gradually becoming conscious of this innate potential, fleshing it out in terms of finite experience, through dialectic, in time.

Plato dramatizes this doctrine through the dialogue between Socrates and Meno's slave boy, who discovers within himself a knowledge of geometry as he is guided by the graduated questions of Socrates. The Socratic method "induces" knowledge, or causes it to be expressed, and perhaps at this point we can begin to appreciate Pater's attempt to assimilate Platonic recollection to his own Hegelian scheme of expression in history. With this anecdote of Meno's slave boy, Pater (as well as Plato) purports to show innate knowledge coaxed out and revealed—to prove, in other words, that "recovery is an act of reminiscence" (PP, 65).

In fact, the story shows more forcibly (though also more tacitly) the power of dialectic, of leading questions from without, of the guiding authority of another interlocutor. Pater's figures reveal the essential role of the dialectician: "the reasonable questions of Socrates fall like water on the seed-ground, or like sunlight on the photographer's

---

1. Bloom notes that this emphasis is "highly Paterian, and closer to Pater's Marius than to Plato" (introduction to *Selected Writings*, p. 239, n. 19).

negative" (PP, 63). Dialectical treatment, then, is as necessary as water to organic growth or, with even more intense a wit on Pater's part, as the process of photographic "development" to a "negative." Socrates' own favorite figure—which portrays his questioning as "being after all only a kind of mid-wife's assistance"—admits to less intervention than Pater's (PP, 83). But Pater, too, throws the emphasis on reminiscence and recovery:

> Those notions were *in* the boy. . . . Ancient, half-obliterated inscriptions on the mental walls, the mental tablet, seeds of knowledge to come, shed by some flower of it long ago. . . . (PP, 66)

Everything is inside ("present from the first," as Pater describes Leonardo's prevision of the Mona Lisa), the "seeds" of all knowledge waiting for the appropriate "tendency" or care in order to "develop." Like the Interpreter, the dialectical interlocutor coaxes articulation from within a mythic wholeness.

Through a modern transposition of Platonic recollection, Pater establishes the basis for treating "the dialogue of the mind with itself" as the original dialectical activity. The dialectic that is "co-extensive with life itself" is essentially this "continuous company we keep with ourselves through life" (PP, 185). But in order for that "company" to have any potential for dialogue or conversation, it must be diversified. In this respect, Pater's forceful emphasis on the personal quality of Platonic ideas serves him well, and here again it should be noted that his emphasis is characteristically Paterian rather than Platonic.

For Plato "all knowledge was like knowing a *person*," Pater repeatedly argues, because knowledge is emergent, slowly developing, and plastic or physiognomic (PP, 129). Like Adam naming the animals, Plato gives names to invisible acts, processes, and abstractions; he conceives of the ideas as living things (PP, 141). Pater criticizes the Eleatics' anti-Homeric aversion to polytheism as well as their anti-anthropomorphic conception of deity; their conception of the One was without color and form, without personal presence, a god "neither here nor there, then nor now" (PP, 33). But in Plato, Pater argues, the One becomes "delightfully multiple, as the world of ideas." According to Pater, Plato restores the Homeric pantheon as an allegorical pantheon of Virtues, "like a recrudescence of polytheism in that abstract world; a return of the many gods of Homer, veiled now as abstract notions" (PP, 46, 168–69). As a result of Plato's mode of conceiving the ideas, then, the world within is now a populated place: "he made us freemen of those solitary places . . . he peopled them with intelligible forms" (PP, 143).

Not only does Pater re-allegorize the Platonic ideas as persons, he also imagines the mind populated with the various aspects of its own personal identity. All these internalized characters take part in "the dialogue of the mind with itself": the *advocatus diaboli*, the dog, the child, the youth, each one offering from time to time his characteristic point of view (PP, 183–84). Thus Pater imagines the diverse "company we keep with ourselves." The Paterian "dialogue of the mind with itself," as Part One of this book made clear, is an achievement of conscious self-division which permits both mobility and fixation; here we see the same sort of conscious self-division equipping the mind with all possible points of view. In our discussion of *Marius* we found a historical-fictional world peopled with epiphenomenal projections of the central self, each one representing a stage in the *Bildung* of our protagonist, and here we see all those stages of growth potentially contained in one place. Pater's conception of the "dialogue of the mind with itself," in other words, has been enriched once more within the context of *Plato and Platonism*. What Pater has imagined in this little vignette of the internal company is a figure of the mind itself as mythic manifold, enfolding in its interior all the "aspects" of the complete person, all possible moods and points of view, all moments and stages of a life history which unfolds in time.

In this sense, dialectic operates on the principle of Justice, as it is defined in the fourth book of *The Republic*: "the doing, by every part, in what is essentially a whole consisting of parts, of its own proper business therein" (PP, 111). This proportionate relation of parts to a whole is also expressed in Pater's dominant figure of synthesis in this volume, the figure of music. Musical form is "synthetic" both synchronically and diachronically; it emphasizes proportionate relation both at every moment, as harmony, and also over the course of time, as sequence. Used in *The Renaissance* to stand for the ideal goal of all aesthetic expression because its content is not separable from its formal relations, music is used in *Plato and Platonism* to represent aspiration in general within "the human mind itself." The aesthetic aspiration *toward* musical form has become in this last volume historical aspiration *as* musical form. For Pater, dialectic is that form, in which all life as well as "all art constantly aspires towards the condition of music." Like music, dialectic figures the sense of life as temporality, as the pleasure in relations unfolding in surprising ways at each moment, the sense of total form accumulating as growth over time.

Pater takes account of this aesthetic element in his understanding of dialectic. According to Plato's own figure in *The Republic*, to pursue the dialectic is to enter upon "a voyage of discovery" (PP, 114).

> Socrates says: "I do not yet know, myself; but, we must just go where the argument carries us, as a vessel runs before the wind." (PP, 185)

But Pater questions this figure. He cogently points out that often the dialogue in progress produces a feeling of continuous surprise, as if its movement were random, and yet at times the dialectic seems clearly guided by "a kind of 'Providence' " (PP, 184). With the subtlest of secularization-effects, Pater recognizes in that "kind of 'Providence' " a figure for the "end" of literary form, the moment of closure which lends a retrospective coherence and shape to the work as a whole. After all, as a model for dialectical process the ascent of a mountain does envision the end of the journey at the highest point, the position on the mountaintop where "the 'synoptic' view of the mountain as a whole" is available at last (PP, 180).

In this volume Pater has formulated a theoretical model to accommodate the paradox of an unguided search that is nevertheless in the hands of "a sort of 'Providence.' " Both functions may be figuratively understood as aspects of one mind: the experiencing aspect in the midst of dialogue is supervised by the aspect of the dialectician, who lends direction while effacing his guiding role. Dialogue is a *figure* for dialectical method, and the "dialogue of the mind with itself" is simply another figure for those mobile parts of a divided whole, understood as the self-divisions of an individual consciousness as well as the divisions of history. By internalizing the figure of the dialogue, Pater transfigures it, making the figure metafigural: a general model of the aesthetic function controlling the "organic."

Pater criticizes the Sophists because they have no real goal for their superficial inquiry, whereas the goal of Platonic dialectic is absolute: the complete knowledge of the Beautiful and Good "as in itself it really is." While Pater has, with his "modern view," put more emphasis on the process toward the goal than on the goal itself, there is nevertheless a strong sense of teleology in this volume. "Our pilgrimage is meant indeed to end in nothing less than the *vision* of what we seek" (PP, 192). Until the end of the journey we cannot see, "as if in a single moment of vision," all the stages of ascent and perspective which comprise the "synoptic" view from the mountaintop (PP, 158). But at the closure of a Platonic Dialogue, one has access to the process as a completed form. Pater has faith that aesthetic form can provide a modern "equivalent for" or "sense of" Platonic Form. He approximates in the literary form of his own volume that synoptic view, providing at once a sense of lively exploration and a sense of providential teleology which is one effect of his formal stance of distant retrospection. In the final section of this study we shall see how this late volume appreciates life in time from the perspective of completed form.

> It is a life, a systematised, but comprehensive and far-reaching, intellectual life, in which the reason, nay, the whole nature of man, realises all it was designed to be, by the beatific "vision of all time and all existence." (PP, 183)

## 7 · Paterian Recollection: The Anagogic Mind

The Paterian Plato is constructed as a mythic whole, a figure who synthesizes all philosophies before him and generates all that come afterward. His relation to Socrates serves to emphasize Plato's emergence as a distinct figure against the background of orality or prehistory, and thus Plato/Socrates becomes one of Pater's "two-sided" figures, representing both the mythic manifold and its break into literature and into history. Pater's own relation to Plato, as it is constructed in this volume, is another such "two-sided" figure, a "twofold power, an embodied paradox" (PP, 87).

Like Plato's literary re-creation of Socrates, we might think of Pater's Plato as merely a "stage disguise," were it not for independent evidence (PP, 75). That Pater's interpretation of Plato largely recapitulates contemporary sources only makes this point all the more interesting,[1] for Pater has effectively shaped the perspective of his lectures to synthesize the "received" or "common" views of his contemporary historical moment. With the persona adopted in these lectures, therefore, Pater attunes the "Diaphaneitè" to the music of his own day. In so doing, Pater tacitly casts himself as a modern Ficino, "translating" Plato to his own later age, re-creating a Plato who would be recognized by his contemporaries in the late nineteenth century and who is recognizable now as a particularly late-nineteenth-century Plato. The Paterian Plato is a figure "fitted" to its intellectual environment.

Pater's identification with Plato works both ways, as do all the

---

1. Esp. Grote and Müller (see above, Part Four, sec. 4, n.2).

modernizing tropes we have been examining. As a result of this "two-sided figure," a Platonic Pater comes into being as surely as the Paterian Plato. Pater attributes to Plato the synthesis that (as almost all critics have agreed) he himself worked out in many forms throughout the course of his career. He begins his dialectic with the atomism of the Heraclitean flux. Recognizing the problems with that doctrine, he imagines its opposite—an equally facile, undifferentiated unity—and uses that opposition dialectically to generate the "music" that to Pater represents not only the unity of matter and form but also, and perhaps even more important, change controlled by permanence, the process of consciousness stabilized in the end through historical retrospection. The question raised for Plato by the doctrine of Heraclitus is the question raised in the "Conclusion" to *The Renaissance*, and at the end of Pater's career we find him quoting from the same passage of the *Cratylus* that provided the epigraph to that incendiary early essay (PP, 14).

In *Plato and Platonism*, Pater considers this passage from the *Cratylus* at greater length. The challenge Socrates offers as a response to the Heraclitean doctrine, read in its Paterian context, is the question of historical change: "Now, how could that which is never in the same state be a thing at all?" (PP, 16). How can change be conceived so that its force toward dissipation and fragmentation is controlled at some point? How can change be conceived so that it does not obliterate identity? Pater answers this question on the level of historical as well as phenomenological discourse. The present study has been devoted to an examination of Pater's answering figures. His figures of "development" play one kind of "music" which harmonizes the colorful flux with its deep structure. Pater's "historic method" allows simultaneously for constant transformation on one level and profoundly stable identity on another. Thus Pater re-creates for the nineteenth century the synthetic manifold he has attributed to Plato. He synthesizes the representative thinkers of his time—the figures of Darwin and Hegel prominent among them—in the complex unity of his own "historic method." But he ends by portraying these forces of thought as "permanent tendencies" in the "human mind itself," and in this register he transcends historical change with his own myth and figures of permanence.

Pater describes a Plato who like himself lives at the end of a long tradition. Though Plato, when he is regarded retrospectively from the late nineteenth century, usually represents the beginnings of philosophy, Pater portrays him as already "late," "eclectic," "encyclopaedic," and "weary" of sectarian debate, not "fresh" in the "morning of the mind's history" (PP, 6). Like Heraclitus, Plato "feels already old" (PP, 13). In this assimilation of Plato to his imaginative perspective at the end of the line, Pater achieves renewed energy for his own age: if Plato himself appears as a "late" product of culture, then there is hope that the late nineteenth century too may mark a beginning, when seen from a still later perspective. Pater strikingly associates Plato's dialogue form with the skeptical, dialectical essay, the "characteristic literary type of our own time," and he claims that the essay came into being along with the "relative spirit" in the Renaissance of the sixteenth century (PP, 174–75). Thus Pater characteristically extends "our own time" to include the modernism of the Renaissance and of Plato's age as well. In other words, on one level Pater realizes how forced this analogy might seem, and yet he argues that the Platonic Dialogue is "essentially" an essay, passing now and then back into the "poetry" of the former, primeval era (PP, 176). When in the service of this analogy he identifies Plato with Montaigne or, even more improbably, with Thackeray, all readers must be aware that Pater is assimilating his own modernism to Plato's (PP, 132, 175).[2]

To be "modern" in this sense is precisely to be "late," "eclectic," "encyclopaedic," and even "weary." Taking the long view, assuming the stance of vast retrospection, is one essential aesthetic gesture of this modernism; a pervasive strategy of cross-cultural analogy is the other. The creation of the Paterian Plato simultaneously modernizes Plato and transforms Pater into a very old thing indeed, as he identifies with the origins of his literary and philosophical culture. As usual, this figurative maneuver begins with the prospect of great difference, but in its most extreme form, as here, it ends by collapsing difference into similarity. As Pater demonstrated in "The Anecdote of the Shell," a long experience in time is necessary to develop the ability to read the world "by a kind of short-hand," to see things whole, "in a single moment of vision" (PP, 158). Pater certainly takes this long view in *Plato and Platonism*, and the effect of his gesture in its particular context is to collapse the differences of historical time in a moment of vision, which is represented by the lecturer's perspective in the present.

Pater's long view is an attempt to represent the perspective *sub specie eternitatis* like that of Parmenides, but with a difference (PP, 27). Even in this extreme statement of his historicism, Pater holds to the process of reaching back through difference to unity, rather than

---

2. On the assimilation of Plato to Montaigne, see Turner, *Greek Heritage*, p. 407; on Pater's projective relation to Plato, see DeLaura, *Hebrew and Hellene*, p. 299.

reaching for a direct, unmediated vision of unity. His approach is more like Augustine's in the *Confessions*, with Books 10 through 13 approximating the perspective *sub specie eternitatis* only after Books 1 through 9 retrospectively proceed through the vicissitudes of earthly experience.[3] But unlike the *Confessions*, where the totalizing perspective is relegated to the last few chapters, *Plato and Platonism* displays the effects of this perspective throughout. Thus the emphasis finally rests in the "synoptic view" from the mountaintop, rather than in the process of reaching that summit. Pater writes from the end of the line, after the climb.

Like Plato's, his is an "encyclopaedic view" (PP, 6). Using the analogy of the Platonic dialogue to describe dialectical thought, Pater writes that the "full light of indefectible certitude"

> can only happen by a *summary* act of intuition upon the entire perspective, wherein all those partial apprehensions, which one by one may have seemed inconsistent with each other, find their due place. . . . The mind attains a hold, as if by a single imaginative act, through all the transitions of a long conversation, upon all the seemingly opposite contentions of all the various speakers at once. (PP, 181)

To Pater, historical life, like the dialogue, seems contradictory or fragmentary only if one looks at an isolated part of its development. But from the point of view of the end, all contradictions are at last resolved into perfect form. "Perfection . . . is attainable only through a certain combination of opposites" (PP, 24).[4]

But dialectic is "co-extensive with life itself," as we have seen (PP, 185), and Pater has been at pains to portray the vivid, lifelike quality of "suspended judgment," the doubtful intellect aspiring in the midst of life, rather than resting in "the full light of indefectible certitude" at the end. Until life is over, the place where "all those partial apprehensions . . . find their due place" can only be in the mind of the Interpreter. The "synoptic view" from the mountaintop is an anagogic perspective, figuratively possible only when life itself has come to an

---

3. I am indebted to the analysis of Augustine in William C. Spengemann, *The Forms of Autobiography: Episodes in the History of a Literary Genre* (New Haven, Conn.: Yale University Press, 1980), pp. 1–33.

4. See "For the way to perfection is through a series of disgusts" (R, 103) and "But if he ['man'] was to be saved from the *ennui* which ever attaches itself to realisation, even the realisation of the perfect life, it was necessary that a conflict should come, that some sharper note should grieve the existing harmony, and the spirit chafed by it beat out at last only a larger and profounder music" (R, 222).

end.[5] And this is the perspective Pater adopts in *Plato and Platonism*, where all the "permanent tendencies" of the "human mind itself" are gathered together in one place, each a part of the great "dialogue of the mind with itself" which now is quite literally all-inclusive. The diachronic dimension of the historic method gives way to the synchronic, and the volume is dominated by the anagogic mind that "comprehends" all the divided forms of life in time. In this volume, the end of time is figured by literary closure, specifically the end of a Platonic Dialogue. At the moment of its closure, dialectic—which is movement *toward* this complete perspective—is replaced by the "summary" or "synoptic view." From the point of view at its end, the unguided journey is felt to have been in the hands of "a kind of 'Providence' " after all, and that particular "kind" of secularized Providence has been identified with the Interpreter himself.

This particularly Paterian anagogical perspective must also be seen as a modernization of Platonic recollection. Pater's aesthetic historicism has all along had this "aspect," but never before has it been so pervasively entertained as in this volume, where the point of view at the end of the line returns upon itself to examine the "ground" of its being. If "the composite experience of all the ages is part of each one of us," Pater can "remember" Plato as a part of his own historically spiritual preexistence (B, 196). This view solves the problems of historical skepticism with a certain secularized faith. Because the past in all its variety exists within, a differentiated company of voices engage there in "the dialogue of the mind with itself," and there they may be re-collected through a discipline of introspection that is indistinguishable from historical retrospection. Pater's great vision assumes the power of each individual to imitate "the secular process of the eternal mind," to take the perspective from which individual identity may be lost without regret, subsumed in the wholeness of a secularized eternal life.

> It is humanity itself now—abstract humanity—that figures as the transmigrating soul, accumulating into its "colossal manhood" the experience of ages; making use of, and casting aside in its march, the souls of countless individuals, as Pythagoras supposed the individual soul to cast aside again and again its outworn body. (PP, 72–73).

---

5. My conception of encyclopedic form and of formal anagogy is derived from Northrop Frye, *Anatomy of Criticism* (Princeton, N.J.: Princeton University Press, 1957), esp. pp. 119, 127, 311. See above, Part Three, sec. 7.

# Afterword

And yet, with a kind of inconsistency in one who had taken for his philosophic ideal the μονόχρονος ἡδονή of Aristippus—the pleasure of the ideal present, of the mystic *now*—there would come, together with that precipitate sinking of things into the past, a desire, after all, to retain "what was so transitive." Could he but arrest, for others also, certain clauses of experience, as the imaginative memory presented them to himself! In those grand, hot summers, he would have imprisoned the very perfume of the flowers. (ME I, 154–55)

This particular "kind of inconsistency" has been the object of my attention throughout the preceding pages. In the short passage above, the narrator of *Marius the Epicurean* exposes several characteristically Paterian elaborations of it.[1] For example, the spatial metaphorics of imprisonment and "arrest" stand as usual for the retrospective, metafigural capacity and are ironically opposed to the temporal implications of textuality. (I call this opposition "ironic" simply because the retrospective narrator, who exposes with his wistful humor the futility of Marius's youthful desire to imprison the transient perfume of experience, is engaged in just such a metafigural enterprise.) But the opposition of spatial figuration and textuality is itself "inconsistent," for in this passage the model of textuality alone cuts both ways: it underwrites both the attempt to retain or "arrest . . . certain *clauses* of

---

1. Many thanks to Jonathan Freedman for reminding me of this passage.

experience" as well as the relentless passages of " 'what was so *transitive*' " (emphasis added).

This passage illustrates another dimension of the formal tension between "the ideal present" and "the imaginative memory" as well. For Pater makes it clear that the devotion to an ideal present has its own long history, and Marius's seemingly personal attraction to "the mystic *now*" is also, ironically, a cultural artifact. Here it is historicized by means of a quoted tag from Aristippus (as a similarly conflicted devotion is historicized in Pater's "Conclusion" through the epigraphic figurehead of Heraclitus). Marius's life history may be traced as a temporalized extension of such moments of attachment to the historical culture, and it is not an exaggeration to say that in Pater's work the achieved figure of the "person" may be described as the formal composite (retrospective and totalized) of such " 'transitive' " moments. This is also the case with the Paterian critical persona, which is a composite figure too. In this particular passage, Pater places himself within, and differentiates himself from, a more localized tradition by transvaluing Arnold's "imaginative reason" to generate the characteristically Paterian "imaginative memory." Thus at several levels the "form" of this passage ironically mirrors its "content," for even as it regrets a particular "kind of inconsistency," the passage reenacts it.

From the point of view of my study, this "kind of inconsistency" has been seen, in its various narrative extensions, as a coherent relation. Aesthetic historicism is a complex or, to use a Paterian formula, "many-sided" dialectic. On the aesthetic "side," Pater describes a moment of complete receptivity or identification followed by a moment of critical detachment from the object of attention. My reading depends upon the notion that this act of detachment re-creates the object as a function of the past, and it is this emphasis in my description of aestheticism which highlights its relation to historicism. The ideal present (to use the vocabulary of our passage above) is the moment of absorptive subjectivity, when the object is "impressed" upon the malleable subject and remains indistinguishable from it. The moment of critical discrimination necessary to distinguish the object is equally necessary to stabilize a subject overwhelmed by its impressions. Thus the aesthetically re-created senses of objectivity and of subjective identity are constituted correlatively, and both are produced as effects of the passage of ideal present moments into the past. It is this recognition of temporality—"that precipitate sinking of things into the past"—which turns the dialectical engine of aestheticism, and turns it in the direction of historicism.

On the "side" of historicism, Pater begins by acknowledging epistemological difficulties that are structurally similar to those involved in the procedures of "aesthetic criticism." He begins, in other words, with the moment of identification between subject and object. Projected into the field of historical inquiry, this identification constitutes the epistemological problem we today call "cultural relativism." Pater was acutely sensitive to this problem—as in his aesthetic criticism—yet while he insists that the moment of identification is the necessary "first step," he also insists that it is only the first step (R, viii). In the effort to restore a sense of objectivity, he proposes an aesthetic solution in which the sense of historical difference is recreated from within the present subject as a representation. "We cannot truly conceive the [past] age: we can conceive the element it has contributed to our culture: we can treat the subjects of the age bringing that into relief" (B, 196). The lines of "relief" separating subject and object are drawn provisionally, of course; this operation manages to provide not objectivity but only the "sense of" objectivity, together with the tacit acknowledgment that such a "sense" is an aesthetic reconstruction. An awareness of the skeptical dimension of historicism, in other words, returns us to the aesthetic. Pater's historical representations are all bracketed by this awareness.

This sort of perspectivism concentrates on the present moment not as the ideal "*now*," but as the end point of a long history, the retrospective position from which the past may be totalized, its continuity may be constructed, and its differences may be gathered up into an identity. There is, in other words, a "kind of inconsistency" in Pater's treatment of the ideal present moment, which becomes in his work both the figure of radical discontinuity and the figure of retrospective totalization. If the impulse toward "modernity" may in several senses be considered the opposite of the impulse toward "history,"[2] Pater holds the two together in a radically conservative, dialectical relation. I have argued that it is Pater's strength to have practiced this "kind of inconsistency" as well as to have theoretically examined its consistent practice.

2. As Paul de Man has persuasively argued. See "Literary History and Literary Modernity," in his *Blindness and Insight: Essays in the Rhetoric of Contemporary Criticism* (1971; reprint, Minneapolis: University of Minnesota Press, 1983), pp. 142–65.

# Index

Aesthetic, the, 4–5, 41, 58–59, 63, 67
Aesthetic historicism, 1–4, 7, 48, 68, 80, 82–83, 87, 144, 146, 153, 178, 193, 224, 235–36, 283–84
Aestheticism, 1–4, 12–13, 26–37, 46–49, 55, 59n, 90, 153, 165, 283
Allegory, 61–62, 63, 75, 95, 100–103, 105–8, 115, 117, 119–20, 133, 206, 208, 227–30, 269
Anagogy, 8, 10, 233, 277–81
Analogy, 63, 170–71, 186, 204–5, 209–11, 214, 250–58, 263–64, 279; and production of "spirit," 223–24, 237. *See also* Typology
Anthropology, 123, 239n, 261, 263n
Appleman, Philip, 142
"Appreciation," 2, 152, 162, 172, 224–25
Apuleius, 191, 226–28, 230
Archaeology, 91, 156, 161–64, 166–67
Arnold, Matthew, 32–33, 47, 51, 53, 55n, 89n, 109n, 136, 142, 157n, 178, 199n, 217, 244n, 272, 283
Auerbach, Erich, 2, 139–40, 206
Augustine, Saint, 118, 207, 231, 280
Autobiography, 44–46, 83n, 146–47, 185–93

Background (and foreground). *See* "Relief"
Beer, Gillian, 142
Berkeley, Bishop George, 20–21
*Bildung*, 105, 215, 275
Biology. *See* Science

Bloom, Harold, 3, 115n, 117n, 120n, 121n, 142, 173, 193n, 197n
Brontë, Charlotte: *Jane Eyre*, 192
Browning, Robert, 46, 152n, 154–55, 175–77
Bunyan, John, 10, 37, 207, 249

Carlyle, Thomas, 32, 47, 73, 82n, 92, 93n, 142, 160n, 183, 207–8
Character, 52, 72, 93–94; characterization, 174, 179–81, 183–84, 241–44; mythic, 10, 120, 183, 237, 241–42, 246, 248, 251–52, 257, 260, 264, 266, 277. *See also* Figure, figuration: personal; Figure, figuration: representative
Charity, A. C., 209
Chemistry. *See* Science
Closure, 109n, 123, 205, 216; of *Marius the Epicurean*, 230–34; of Platonic Dialogue, 276–77, 281
Coleridge, Samuel Taylor, 73, 125, 142, 173. *See also* Pater, Walter: "Coleridge"
Composite form, 2, 80, 123, 171, 177, 225; aestheticism as, 43, 45; historicity of, 90–91, 94; Pater's critical voice as, 2, 43–46, 53, 238, 283; personal identity as, 36–37, 71, 75, 193, 195, 275, 281, 283. *See also* Intertextuality
Conservatism (Pater's), 2, 5, 13, 36, 63, 167, 182–83, 205, 211, 233, 284

Content: crisis in conception of, 17, 24–25; Pater's revised notion of, 22, 34–35, 40–42, 63, 179; as spirit or soul, 17, 115, 118–19, 121, 162, 244. See also Form
Culler, Dwight, 142

Dale, Peter Allan, 3, 47, 73
Dante Alighieri, 115, 128, 134–35, 140, 149, 173, 212, 256
Darwin, Charles, 3, 16, 122, 142, 211, 260, 263, 270, 278
de Man, Paul, 36n, 59n, 66n, 102n, 167n, 187–89, 284n
Demeter, 238, 242–43, 251, 254. See also Character: mythic
Dialectic, 159–60, 246, 249, 270–77; dialectical reversal, 158, 164, 172, 245; Platonic, 237. See also Form: dialectical
Dialogue, 46, 115–16, 218–19, 270–71, 276, 279–80; as figure of prehistory, 237, 268, 270–71; "of the mind with itself," 109n, 115, 217, 272, 274–75, 281; Platonic, 264, 271–72, 276–77
Dionysus, 237–38, 242–43, 254–55, 257; in relation to Apollo, 66n, 254n, 260. See also Character: mythic

Ekphrasis, 149–53
Elgin marbles, 149, 162
Eliot, George, 142, 181–82, 207
Eliot, Thomas Stearns, 2, 35, 123, 129n, 198, 219n
Etymological wit: "aesthete," 90n; "analysis," 20; "appreciation," 172, 225; "criticism," 40–41; "data," 48, 82–84; "disgust," 133–34; "ecstasy," 30–32, 35; "experience," 42; "figura," 139–40; "interpreter," 85, 248; "legend," 94–95; "mystic," 116; "style," 92, 139; "urbanity," 217. See also Wordplay
Evolution, 3, 50, 122, 139–40, 151; and aesthetic creation, 164–66, 220–22, 240–41, 249. See also Darwin, Charles; Gradualism
Expression (historical), 6, 8, 116, 125, 149, 177–78, 192, 244, 246–49

Fact, 79–85, 94; vs. historicity, 90. See also Figure, figuration: of factuality
Ficino, Marsilio, 135, 277
Figure, figuration: 5–6, 68, 74, 116, 118, 124, 134, 153, 174, 188–89, 243–44; of factuality, 85, 87, 94; genealogical, 5, 60, 67–68, 132, 136–37, 193, 242; of ground, 9–10, 87, 106, 108, 155, 157, 161–67, 236; of identity, 189–90; personal, 5–6, 10, 66n, 74–75, 91, 104–5, 113–20, 123–24, 127, 147, 187, 190, 200, 201, 241, 243–44, 246–48, 261, 265, 270, 274; representative, 93–94, 129, 141, 156, 172, 189, 262; serial, 105, 111, 124, 126–27, 136, 157, 171, 191–92, 205, 214–15, 230; sexual, 60–62, 96, 112–13, 120; spatial, 5, 10, 22–25, 37, 74, 119, 125, 155–56, 282–83; specular, 187–91, 197–98, 200, 202; temporal, 5, 23–25, 29–30, 74, 119, 138, 282–83; textual: 38, 45, 225–26, 282–83; transparent, 172–84; "two-sided," 10, 265, 277; typological, 208, 212. See also Character; Form; Metafigurality; Organicism; "Relief"; Temporality; Type; Typology
Fixation, 17, 29–30, 36, 49, 95, 97–98, 100, 137, 153–55; through characterization, 241–44; of dates, 83, 85–86; as effect of quotation, 39–40, 44; idée fixe, 124–26, 128
Foreground (and background). See "Relief"
Form, 244–45; and content, 42, 63, 245–46, 283; developmental, 90, 118, 122, 263; dialectical, 60–62, 67, 132–37, 151, 159–60, 262, 265–66, 275; and matter, 245–46, 259; musical, 42, 129, 131, 137–38, 156, 194, 196–97, 217, 222, 262, 265, 275, 278; narrative, 109–10, 203–24, 226–28, 233–34, 248; Platonic: 266, 270, 276; spatial, 69, 71, 143–47; "spiritual," 246, 252; temporal, 42, 45. See also Composite form
Formula (Paterian), 51, 84, 96, 125–26, 130, 135, 140
Frank, Joseph, 145

Gautier, Théophile, 112, 226
Geist, 8, 72–75, 104–5, 116, 246. See also Zeitgeist
Generalization, 7–9, 52, 264; historical process of, 195–97, 266–70; linked levels of, 8–9, 72–74, 92–93, 101, 116, 118, 124, 129–31, 166, 197, 246–47; laws of development, 54, 56, 65, 137–38, 140, 160, 217, 220; the name as, 120, 128–30, 251–52; the school as, 87, 129–31. See also Fixation; Zeitgeist

Genre, 81, 91, 147, 149, 225, 227
Goethe, Johann Wolfgang von, 36, 92, 96–98, 109–10, 143, 145–46, 151, 158–60, 185, 251, 263
Gosse, Edmund, 46
Gradualism, 171, 182, 191, 199, 229, 239

Hardy, Thomas, 142
Hegel, G. W. F., 3, 8–9, 37, 40, 52n, 72–74, 149–51, 153n, 166, 180n–81, 183, 240, 244, 246–47, 260, 263, 273, 278
Heine, Heinrich, 104, 112
Heraclitus, 4, 14–16, 23, 257, 262–63, 278, 283
Herbert, George, 207
Hill, Donald L., 3, 73, 83, 85
Historicism, 1–5, 46–57, 80, 90, 142–43, 153, 157, 165, 284
Historicity, 54–56, 65, 82–94, 101–2, 105, 107–10, 170–71, 195; of myth, 103–10, 122, 232, 238–39; of narrative form, 109–10, 235. *See also* Particularity; Style
Homer, 149, 263, 268, 274
Hopkins, Gerard Manley, 120n, 139n
"House Beautiful" (Pater's figure of), 10, 37, 145, 196–97, 202, 247–49
Hugo, Victor, 44, 109–10
Humanism, 17, 61, 93, 98, 100–101, 115–18, 152, 165, 218, 220, 222–23, 241, 272–73. *See also* Figure, figuration: personal
Hume, David, 20

Impressionism (Pater's), 6, 21, 34–36, 68, 77, 84–85, 92, 116, 125, 127, 130, 132, 139–40, 142–43n, 146–47, 149, 156, 161, 163–64, 166–67, 194–95, 225n, 283. *See also* Expression
Impressions, 20–21, 34, 283
Inman, Billie Andrew, 3, 73, 83
Interpreter, 85, 111, 221, 247–49, 274
Intertextuality, 43–46, 113, 224–30; allusion, 32–33, 40, 51–53, 208, 253; biblical, 75–77, 107n, 119, 136, 224, 253, 256; quotation, 14–15, 38–41, 89–90. *See also* Composite form
Iser, Wolfgang, 3, 73

James, Henry, 6
Johnson, Samuel, 21
Joyce, James, 2, 123

Kant, Immanuel, 20, 24, 36
Keats, John, 4, 46
Kermode, Frank, 139n, 140n, 162n, 231n

Legend, 82–98, 101, 108, 110, 113–14, 133, 264
Levine, George, 142, 181n
Literature, 82; as composite form, 224–28; evolution from myth, 236–37, 239–42, 246–49, 264
Locke, John, 20

McGann, Jerome J., 32n, 34n, 80n
McGrath, F. C., 3, 41n, 72–73, 178n, 181n, 269n
Maternity, 112–13, 120, 215, 254
Memory, 10, 35–37, 119. *See also* Composite form; Retrospection
Meredith, George, 142
Metafigurality, 9, 22–24, 68, 99–100, 121, 154, 158, 175, 193, 276, 282
Mill, John Stuart, 51n, 55n, 73, 141
Milton, John, 207
Modernism, modernity, 2, 31, 140n, 210, 217; Mona Lisa as representation of, 116–20; and myth, 250; recollective, 2, 46, 58, 80, 94, 167n, 172, 284; recurrent, 2, 14–15, 279; "relief" of modern art, 149–56
"Modern thought" (Pater's representations of), 12–15, 18, 27, 29, 43; as "relative spirit," 49–51, 53–56
Moment (aesthetic or epiphanic), 4, 28–30, 35, 115n, 138, 155, 194, 198, 282–84
Mona Lisa (Pater's figure of), 10, 34n, 86–87, 97, 102, 111–24, 151, 166, 252, 260, 274
Monsman, Gerald, 29, 66n, 81n, 91n–92n, 100n, 115n, 119n, 132n, 146, 147n, 170n, 173n–74n, 176n, 183n, 184n, 193n, 217, 231n–32n
Montaigne, Michel, 44, 279
Morris, William, 58–69, 80; *Defence of Guenevere*, 60–64; *Earthly Paradise*, 64–65, 68
Music. *See* Form: musical
Myth, 54, 82, 95, 101–2, 122, 145, 170–71, 238–58; evolution of, 236–37, 239–40; mythopoeia, 82, 122–23. *See also* Character: mythic

Nietzsche, Friedrich, 167n, 254n
Nominalism, 140, 252, 266–70. *See also* Generalization: the name as

### Index

Novalis, Friedrich von Hardenberg, 38–41, 43, 45–46, 89

Objectivity, 16–18, 42, 50–51, 82, 96, 99, 102; aesthetically reconstructed sense of, 3–4, 32–35, 88–89, 110, 203, 283–84; figure of objective (or historical) "distance," 16, 19–20, 31–32, 37, 48, 55, 68, 70, 81, 182. *See also* "Outline"
Ontogeny and phylogeny, 74, 105, 122
Organicism, 9, 50, 74, 104, 108, 145n, 161, 267–68; and aestheticism, 130, 220–22, 235–36, 258–61, 264, 268, 271, 274, 276
"Outline," 17, 20, 49–51, 71, 154

Paget, Violet (pseud. Vernon Lee), 169–70, 210
Parmenides, 262–63, 279
Particularity, 4, 7–8, 82n; as historicity, 52, 54, 56, 90. *See also* Historicity
Pater, Walter. Works: "Aesthetic Poetry," 4–5, 57–77, 69, 94, 106, 117, 162; "The Bacchanals of Euripides," 253; "The Child in the House," 7–8, 190, 193–98, 200–201, 213, 237; "Coleridge," 49–51, 53, 71, 109, 140–41, 172–74, 177, 203, 260; "Conclusion," 1–32, 40, 43–44, 46–47, 49, 51, 55, 57, 65, 69–70, 72, 80, 85, 89, 109, 117, 122, 138, 146–47, 170, 175, 184–85, 199–200, 260, 278, 282; "Diaphaneitè," 7, 166n, 172–84, 194, 238, 270, 277; *Gaston De Latour*, 210; *Greek Studies*, 10, 213, 235–36, 238–58, 263; "Joachim Du Bellay," 86–87, 92; "Leonardo Da Vinci," 83–88, 95–102, 111–23, 125–26, 128, 132–34, 144, 159; "Luca Della Robbia," 143–53; "The Marbles of Aegina," 253; *Marius the Epicurean*, 7, 9–10, 26, 37, 63, 80, 168–34, 237, 240, 260, 282; "The Myth of Demeter and Persephone," 242, 251; "Pico Della Mirandola," 93, 103–9, 119; *Plato and Platonism*, 7–8, 10, 63, 235–37, 258–81; "The Poetry of Michelangelo," 130, 132, 134–37, 147–48, 164–66; "Preface," 33, 42, 48, 50–52, 70, 84, 130–31, 140, 143–44, 147, 179, 250; *The Renaissance*, 7, 9–10, 47, 79–67, 251–52; "Romanticism (Postscript)" 244–46, 248; "Sandro Botticelli," 82, 124–28; "The School of Giorgione," 42, 58n, 83–84, 129–31, 137–38; "A Study of Dionysus," 242–43; "Style," 48n, 140; "Two Early French Stories," 91, 144; "The Will as Vision," 197–202; "Winckelmann," 109, 143–47, 150, 157–67, 173–75, 177, 254
Pattison, Mrs. Mark, 47, 88n
Persephone, 237, 242–43, 256–57. *See also* Character: mythic
Plato, 10, 43, 134–35, 173, 183, 185, 237, 260–62; theory of Ideas, 264–66, 270, 274–75. Works: *Cratylus*, 14–15, 122, 185, 278; *Meno*, 273; *Republic*, 257, 275–76. *See also* Pater, Walter: *Plato and Platonism*
Popper, Karl, 54, 56
Postmodernism, 2, 4, 147, 184n
Pound, Ezra, 2, 123
Pre-Raphaelites, 4, 207, 228
Pre-Socratics, 262–66
Providentialism: and aestheticism, 166, 221, 276–77, 281; and evolution, 220–22
Pythagoras, 262–65

Ranke, Leopold von, 55
Realism, 52, 86n, 101, 106, 125n, 153n, 170, 206, 227; and typicality, 181–82
Reception: aesthetics, 44, 84, 86, 151, 227; receptivity, 123n, 226n, 230, 233–34
"Relief" (Pater's figure of), 6, 9, 35, 66, 68–71, 75, 77, 100, 121, 154–60, 175, 200, 236; ekphrastic use of, 148–53; ground literalized, 108, 161–67; recursive, 147, 158, 164, 171, 184
Repression, 76–77, 154, 156, 158. *See also* Impressionism
Retrospection, 48, 50, 67, 119–21, 124, 138, 145–46, 155–56, 158, 167n, 171–72, 179, 182, 197, 278; as "comprehension," 10, 36, 121, 193, 226–28, 233–34, 281; as rhetorical effect, 38–39, 43, 45, 121–22, 186–89, 277. *See also* "House Beautiful"
Revival, 58, 64–79, 81, 98
Romanticism, 49, 65, 124; vs. classicism, 244–46; consciousness as self-division, 3–4, 21, 25, 31–32, 35, 45–46; expression, 177–78, 200–201; historical narrative as self-divided identity, 59–60, 79–80; and myth, 250–51; three-stage sequence, 79–80, 215, 240, 251, 262
Ronsard, Pierre de, 87, 92, 127–28
Rossetti, Dante Gabriel, 207

Ruskin, John, 31n, 51–53, 62, 79, 82n, 142, 147, 165, 207–8

Science, 32, 49; biology, 49–50, 74–75, 122, 139–41; chemistry, 34, 50, 135, 140–41; history, 54. *See also* Evolution; Ontogeny and phylogeny
Secularization, 7, 36–37, 75, 119, 189–93, 196, 201–2; and the aesthetic, 61–63, 99–100, 203, 206, 221–22, 258, 276; Christianity historicized, 76–77, 202–3, 210–11, 233–34; double effect of, 75–76, 100, 136, 165, 253–58, 268; history as, 93, 129, 201–3, 221–22; humanism, 61, 98, 100–101, 136, 165; internalization, 74, 114, 129, 179, 260, 281; intertextuality, 75–76, 119–20, 227–28; *Last Supper* as emblem of, 98–102; and narrative form, 109–10, 213–23, 230–34, 276–77; of pagan culture, 63, 171–72, 204, 251; of typology, 172, 205, 211–24, 230–34. *See also* Humanism
Shelley, Percy Bysshe, 45, 65, 251, 263
Shuter, William, 73, 183n, 206n, 215n–16n, 238n, 263n
Socrates, 10, 14, 228, 237, 260, 264–65, 270–72, 278
Sophists, 264–65, 267, 271, 276
Spatial form. *See* Figure, figuration: spatial; Form: spatial
"Spirit of the Age." *See* Zeitgeist
Stevens, Wallace, 269n
Style, 91–93, 124–25, 140; historicity of, 87, 89, 93, 107–10, 127, 145n; inscriptive sense of, 92, 110, 116, 139; Pater's, 37–46, 48–49; "personal," 44–46, 147, 188. *See also* Expression; Impressionism; Pater, Walter: "Style"
Subjectivism, 12, 18–26, 33, 44, 49, 51, 83, 146
Swinburne, Algernon Charles, 34n, 112
Symbolism, 95, 101–2, 106, 119, 206, 208, 227

Temporality, 36–37, 138, 167. *See also* Figure, figuration: temporal; Form: musical
Tennyson, Alfred Lord, 121, 142, 207
Thackeray, William Makepeace, 279
Tractarianism, 106, 207

Transmission (historical), 94, 98–99, 112, 180. *See also* Reception
Type, 7–8, 93n, 97–98, 124–43, 252; archetypes, 262–63; Christian, 139, 213–19; diachronic use of, 124, 126, 131–39, 193, 208–9; evolutionary, 49–50, 74, 108, 139–43; "given" vs. modern, 174–77, 182, 245; historical development of, 195–97, 267–70; of personal style, 124–28; as plastic impression, 132, 139–40; and realism, 125n, 181; as standard, 137–38; synchronic use of, 124, 127–31, 139, 180, 208; "transparent," 174–77, 180–84. *See also* Generalization
Typology, 7, 9, 119, 136, 172, 206–9, 211–12, 219, 223–24, 227–30; as aestheticism, 223–24; as narrative form, 203–5, 209, 211, 213–23; secularized, 230–34

Unconscious, 160–61, 179, 183, 198; collective, 76–77, 155, 161–67; Freudian, 163n; prehistory as, 259–60

Vasari, Giorgio, 83, 95, 133, 148
Venus of Melos, 90–91, 151, 162
Verrocchio, Andrea del, 87, 96, 114, 133–34, 148
Vico, Giambattista, 2–3, 263
Virgil, 149, 194, 212

Ward, Anthony, 73
Wilde, Oscar, 27, 33n, 46
Wollheim, Richard, 13
Woolf, Virginia, 2, 123
Wordplay: "burden," 197; "host," 98; "passage," 23, 28, 30, 35, 38; "paternity," 136–37; "quicken," 27, 39; "recovery," 66; "relief," 69; "revival," 69; "secretion," 135; "strain," 197. *See also* Etymological wit
Wordsworth, William, 16, 21–22, 45, 66n, 104–5, 155, 194, 199, 208, 251, 254, 263

Yeats, William Butler, 4, 120, 123

Zeitgeist, 8, 72–75, 87–89, 92, 103–10, 129, 179–80, 184, 189–90, 192–93, 232, 246, 261

Library of Congress Cataloging-in-Publication Data

Williams, Carolyn, 1950–
   Transfigured world: Walter Pater's aesthetic historicism / Carolyn Williams
     p.  cm.
   Includes index.
   ISBN 0-8014-2151-9 (alk. paper)
    1. Pater, Walter, 1839–1894—Aesthetics. 2. Pater, Walter, 1839–1894—
Knowledge—History. 3. Historicism. I. Title.
PR5138.A35W5  1989
824'.8—dc20                                                              89-42883

www.ingramcontent.com/pod-product-compliance
Lightning Source LLC
Chambersburg PA
CBHW031429160426
43195CB00010BB/671